# Dangers of Youth

## *States, People, and the History of Social Change*

SERIES EDITORS ROSALIND CRONE AND STEVEN KING

The States, People, and the History of Social Change series brings together cutting-edge books written by academic historians on criminal justice, welfare, education, health, and other areas of social change and social policy. The ways in which states, governments, and local communities have responded to "social problems" can be seen across many different temporal and geographical contexts. From the early modern period to contemporary times, states have attempted to shape the lives of their inhabitants in important ways. Books in this series explore how groups and individuals have negotiated the use of state power and policy to regulate, change, control, or improve people's lives and the consequences of these processes. The series welcomes international scholars whose research explores social policy (and its earlier equivalents) as well as other responses to social need, in historical perspective.

3 Young Subjects
Children, State-Building, and Social Reform in the Eighteenth-Century French World
*Julia M. Gossard*

4 Indentured Servitude
Unfree Labour and Citizenship in the British Colonies
*Anna Suranyi*

5 Penal Servitude
Convicts and Long-Term Imprisonment, 1853–1948
*Helen Johnston, Barry Godfrey, and David J. Cox*

6 In Their Own Write
Contesting the New Poor Law, 1834–1900
*Steven King, Paul Carter, Natalie Carter, Peter Jones, and Carol Beardmore*

7 Looking After Miss Alexander
Care, Mental Capacity, and the Court of Protection in Mid-Twentieth-Century England
*Janet Weston*

8 Friendless or Forsaken?
Child Emigration from Britain to Canada, 1860–1935
*Ruth Lamont, Eloise Moss, and Charlotte Wildman*

9 Fraudulent Lives
Imagining Welfare Cheats from the Poor Law to the Present
*Steven King*

10 Slow Train to Arcadia
A History of Railway Commuting into London
*Duncan Gager*

11 Prisoners' Bodies
Activism, Health, and the Prisoners' Rights Movement in Ireland, 1972–1985
*Oisín Wall*

12 To Detain or to Punish
Magistrates and the Making of the London Prison System, 1750–1840
*Kiran Mehta*

13 Dangers of Youth
Age, Criminality, and Juvenile Justice Reform in Third Republic France
*Briony Neilson*

# Dangers of Youth

*Age, Criminality,*
*and Juvenile Justice Reform*
*in*
*Third Republic France*

**

BRIONY NEILSON

McGill-Queen's University Press
Montreal & Kingston • London • Chicago

ISBN 978-0-2280-2433-0 (paper)
ISBN 978-0-2280-2434-7 (ePDF)
ISBN 978-0-2280-2435-4 (ePUB)

Legal deposit second quarter 2025
Bibliothèque nationale du Québec

Printed in Canada on acid-free paper that is 100% ancient forest free (100% post-consumer recycled), processed chlorine free

McGill-Queen's University Press in Montreal is on land which long served as a site of meeting and exchange amongst Indigenous Peoples, including the Haudenosaunee and Anishinabeg nations. In Kingston it is situated on the territory of the Haudenosaunee and Anishinaabek. We acknowledge and thank the diverse Indigenous Peoples whose footsteps have marked these territories on which peoples of the world now gather.

Library and Archives Canada Cataloguing in Publication

Title: Dangers of youth : age, criminality, and juvenile justice reform in Third Republic France / Briony Neilson.
Names: Neilson, Briony, author.
Series: States, people, and the history of social change ; 13.
Description: Series statement: States, people, and the history of social change ; 13 | Includes bibliographical references and index.
Identifiers: Canadiana (print) 20240503813 | Canadiana (ebook) 20240503848 | ISBN 9780228024330 (softcover) | ISBN 9780228024347 (PDF) | ISBN 9780228024354 (EPUB)
Subjects: LCSH: Juvenile delinquents—France—History—19th century. | LCSH: Juvenile delinquents—Legal status, laws, etc.—France—History—19th century. | LCSH: Juvenile delinquency—France—History—19th century. | LCSH: Child rearing—France—History—19th century. | LCSH: Criminal justice, Administration of—France—History—19th century.
Classification: LCC HV9154 .N45 2025 | DDC 364.36094409/034—dc23

This book was designed and typeset by studio oneonone in Minion 11/14. Copyediting by Kathryn Simpson.

# Contents

# Tables and Figures

# Acknowledgments

Many people, in countless ways, have inspired and contributed to the formulation of ideas that find expression within these pages. I would especially like to thank Nick Riemer, Christina Neilson, Robert Aldrich, James Findlay, Charlotte Legg, James Keating, Elizabeth Smith, Sophie Loy-Wilson, Marc Renneville (and all the team at the Centre pour les humanités numériques et l'histoire de la justice, CLAMOR), Nina Parish, Michael McDonnell, Frances Clarke, Julie Kalman, David Garrioch, Claire Eldridge, Tom Hamilton, Sara Beam, Robin Walz (and everyone in the online French crime history group), Shaïn Morisse, Isobelle Barrett-Meyering, and Bruce Gardiner.

Original research is inevitably made up of false starts and serendipitous discoveries, all of which demand time, funding, and sustained support – increasingly scarce resources within the neoliberal university sector. For their assistance in facilitating my research in France, I would like to thank the archivists and librarians at the Bibliothèque nationale de France, the Archives départementales de l'Yonne, the Archives nationales de France, the Archives de Paris, and the Musée social. Although, in the end, not all of these collections proved central to this book, they all in different ways helped shape its contours.

I would also like to thank the staff at the University of Sydney's Fisher Library, especially in interlibrary loans, who facilitated the gathering of essential resources from far and wide.

At McGill-Queen's University Press, I'm grateful to Richard Baggaley, Catherine Bienvenu, and especially Kathleen Fraser and Kyla Madden for their expertise and patience in preparing the final manuscript.

Finally I thank my family and friends for their support, belief, and encouragement. I am sincerely grateful.

# Dangers of Youth

# Introduction

In 1889, as France's republicans celebrated one hundred years since the French Revolution and more than a decade in power in the nation's parliament, journalist and social commentator Ali Coffignon sang the praises of the republic's social and political achievements. Significantly, in Coffignon's view, what particularly distinguished the Third Republic regime, in place since 1870, was what it had accomplished for the nation's young. "The First Republic (1789)," he wrote, "proclaimed the rights of man; the Second (1848) consecrated the rights of the citizen; the honour of the Third is having recognized and sanctioned the rights of the child."[1] For Coffignon, as for many of his contemporaries, the Third Republic was defined by its defence of children: creatures who, as a result of their incomplete growth, were considered unable to fully exercise their developing reason or reliably restrain themselves. These assumptions would prove pivotal to the reformulation of ideas about juvenile delinquency, including, and perhaps most importantly, with regard to the conceptualization of young people's criminal responsibility.

Society at the end of the nineteenth and start of the twentieth centuries, in France as in many other parts of the world, was deeply preoccupied with the question of youth. French society was also greatly exercised by the problem of criminality, especially recidivism. Criminality and childrearing were tightly entangled with one another, as reformers were convinced that what lay at the root of most, if not all, habitual criminality was an unstable or disorderly early life. Reformers in this period firmly believed that tackling issues relating to young people was the key to reducing crime. Criminality, these reformers contended, was largely a product of upbringing, and a person's earliest years were critical for the formation of values, behaviours, and habits that they would carry through their lives.

Between the 1880s and the outbreak of the First World War, formative debates and legislative reforms would profoundly reshape the way that young people were conceptualized and treated in French society, including within its criminal justice system. When it came to childrearing, what distinguished the Third Republic was, as Coffignon signalled, its concern about children's welfare. In practice, as this book will reveal, what this amounted to was an intensification of state involvement in family life. In the final decades of the nineteenth century, the "rights" of children were increasingly prioritized by legislators, taking precedence even over the rights of their own parents. The state introduced landmark laws that enabled it to remove children deemed to be in "moral danger" from their parents' custody. New legislation significantly curtailed the authority of parents, especially fathers, and family life in general was subjected to increasing intervention and surveillance by the state, supported and facilitated by private philanthropy.[2] So intense and fundamental was this culture of intervention and protection that the Third Republic has earned the label of "Republic of the weak."[3] This culture of "protective intervention" did not only affect young people; it similarly inflected the treatment of women, who, along with children, were considered naturally vulnerable and therefore in need of special legislation and state-sanctioned measures of protection.[4]

While one might readily dispute the extent to which these interventionist measures, which functioned within highly paternalistic discourses and practices, actually represented a respect for children's rights, as advocates like Ali Coffignon claimed, what is indisputable is that young people were considered of critical importance to the French Third Republic. For republicans, effective childrearing was essential to the solidification and indeed the very survival of the republic itself. Amid a groundswell of activity aimed at shaping the lives of young people, juvenile offenders were a primary preoccupation for reformers, legislators, and administrators. Young people's waywardness was overwhelmingly viewed as a product of neglectful or abusive parenting, and reformers and legislators sought to intervene in order to protect children from exploitation, abuse, and neglect, and also in order to provide greater institutional guidance in the interest of ensuring their transformation into productive, law-abiding, and patriotic French citizens.

## Creating Child and Adolescent Offenders: The Landmark Law of 22 July 1912

As part of this upsurge in reform measures for young people, on 22 July 1912 the French parliament passed legislation "sur les tribunaux pour enfants et adolescents et sur la liberté surveillée" (on courts for children and adolescents and probation). This legislation, which came into effect six months later, marked a fundamental shift in the judicial handling of juvenile offenders in France, instituting a specific judicial process for juveniles, entirely distinct from adults. Among its most important provisions was that henceforth no child aged under thirteen at the time of the offence in question could be criminally prosecuted for breaking the law. Instead, their case would be dealt with by a civil law jurisdiction (*chambre de conseil*) that, rather than imposing a punishment, could, if the circumstances were deemed necessary, subject the child to "measures of supervision, surveillance, of education, reform and assistance."[5]

In setting down that children under thirteen were never to be subjected to punitive measures, the 1912 law systematically set children off from adolescents. Older juveniles, meanwhile, were removed from the regular adult criminal court and, following a thorough investigation into their background and social (especially familial) circumstances, would be brought before a specialized court, overseen by dedicated, specialized judges. These new courts were to be set up across the country, with hearings restricted to only a specified range of people, including the juvenile's immediate family, members of charitable organizations or public welfare, and delegates of the court.[6]

The 1912 law on courts for children and adolescents represented both a major turning point in the conceptualization of the young offender and a confirmation of informal approaches already in place in France's larger jurisdictions by that time. These approaches aimed to protect young people from prosecution and punishment, which were considered harmful and counterproductive for their long-term prospects. What is particularly notable about the 1912 legislation is that, for the first time in French law, it set down an absolute, age-defined threshold for the automatic and irrefutable presumption of irresponsibility in children. Although the word "responsibility" was not explicitly uttered within the terms of the legislation, the law effectively decriminalized the actions of children under thirteen.

This was the first time since the codification of French law in 1791 that a minimum age of criminal responsibility had been laid down. In this way, the 1912 legislation can be considered to mark the official birth of the child offender as a discrete legal category in French criminal law, demarcated not only in opposition to adults, but also in relation to adolescent offenders. For historian Michelle Perrot, the 1912 law's recognition of children under the age of thirteen as entirely distinct from older offenders and their immunity from criminal prosecution and punishment makes the legislation "a veritable Code of childhood."[7] For Robert Badinter, who served as France's minister of justice between 1981 and 1986 under President François Mitterrand, the 1912 legislation was significant in recognizing the juvenile offender as qualitatively different to older offenders, rather than simply as a "little adult" who could be dealt with within the mainstream criminal justice system.[8]

But the importance of the 1912 law extends further: it represents a major shift in the recognition paid to chronological age as a meaningful and incontrovertible criterion in the evaluation and treatment of juvenile delinquency in modern French history. This acknowledgment of chronological age by criminal justice reformers lies at the heart of this book. *Dangers of Youth* examines the concern about young people and criminality that enveloped French society at the end of the nineteenth century and that culminated in the passage of the law of 1912. In particular, this book traces the increasing importance attributed to chronological age in the treatment of juvenile delinquency in the French Third Republic.

## Chronological Age as a Criterion for Criminal Justice

It is important to be clear from the outset that the decades preceding the outbreak of the First World War did not mark the first time that chronological age became important in the assessment of juvenile offenders in French criminal justice. Indeed, as we shall see, some of the essential groundwork for changes implemented at the turn of the twentieth century had been laid many decades earlier. For instance, the penal codes of both 1791 and 1810 had transformed the way that chronological age functioned within France's judicial system, introducing for the first time into French criminal law a single age threshold (sixteen) for the category of juvenile.[9] Codification's recognition of age sixteen as a meaningful marker of maturity in the prosecution of lawbreakers stood in sharp contrast to the system that had previously been in place. Under the Old Regime, multiple stages of immaturity had been recognized; physical development, rather than the more bureaucratic measure of chronological age, was examined in order to determine what – if indeed any – measures of leniency or decisions of irresponsibility might be attached to a juvenile prosecuted for an unlawful act. Codification, by contrast, set down chronological age – an abstract, universal principle – as the factor that determined the available punishment to be meted out to young offenders. Significantly, until 1912, France lacked a minimum age of criminal responsibility.

The revolutionary penal code of 1791 transformed the status of young people within the country's criminal justice system, protecting lawbreakers under the age of sixteen from the harshest penalties. In order for judicial authorities to be able to implement chronological age in the way stipulated by France's codified system of criminal law – and in order to be able to do so with accuracy – the state needed to know with precision the birthdates of its citizens. At the end of the eighteenth century the French Revolution ushered in an important change in the deployment of chronological age as a standard bureaucratic measure and as the proper business of the state. This shift was marked by a new policy in recording children's births. Whereas in the past, the recording of births was the prerogative of the Church, from 1792, it became a legal requirement that all births in France be registered promptly with authorities in the local town hall. This requirement, which would be reaffirmed in the Napoleonic civil code in 1804, contributed to what the sociologist Judith Treas has termed "age exactitude," in reference to similar developments witnessed in the United States around a century later.[10] Over time, there emerged an increasing sense that chronological age carried with it certain meanings. While in earlier centuries, a person's progression through different stages of life had been marked by the celebration of ritualized ceremonies, the sense that a particular chronological age carried with it specific significance with attendant social rights and responsibilities was very much a product of modern times. As several scholars have explored in the context of Europe and North America, the rise of greater age consciousness had significant implications for the management of young people's lives, including within the domains of labour, education, and health.[11]

This consciousness about age intensified as time went on. The late nineteenth and early twentieth centuries in France witnessed a particularly acute interest in age and the distinctions of life stages in human development. This concern, driven by ideological imperatives (particularly republicanism and nationalism), had its roots in transformations to French society emerging out of the Revolution of 1789 and increasing industrialization. As it did elsewhere, the industrial economy had a profound impact in France on experiences and conceptualizations of childhood, as various historians including Colin Heywood and Miranda Sachs have shown.[12] Age, rather than physical development, increasingly came to determine a young person's readiness for entry into the adult world. In traditional rural society, there had been no fixed age at which children were considered ready to take part in farming work; they simply became involved gradually, contributing in incremental ways as they developed in strength. During the Old Regime, for instance, boys would begin to help with farming work from around seven or eight years of age and entered apprenticeships in workshops or domestic service around the age of fourteen.[13] By the early decades of the nineteenth century, with the movement of rural populations to the cities and the development of mechanized labour (which was less dependent on brute strength than traditional farming work had been), the employment of children in industry aroused concern among reformers and resulted in the passage of France's first child labour laws.[14] A moratorium was placed on children's participation in the labour force, with chronological age functioning as the crucial yardstick governing fitness for entry. Child labour laws passed in 1841, 1874, and 1892, combined with Jules Ferry's laws on compulsory primary schooling adopted in the early 1880s, effectively "made puberty the threshold for leaving childhood,"[15] but crucially it was chronological age rather than any physical evidence of maturation that determined that threshold.

According to civil law in late nineteenth-century France, childhood was understood to consist of three perceived stages: *petite enfance*, stretching from birth through to the age of six, during which children were entirely dependent on adults; *enfance*, which encompassed children aged from seven to thirteen, who, from the early 1880s, were obliged to attend primary school;

and *jeunesse*, which began at fourteen and continued through to adulthood, marked either by entry into marriage or by reaching the age of civil majority at twenty-one.[16] The Ferry laws of the early 1880s achieved what one observer at the time referred to as the "radical holy trinity" of free, compulsory, and secular primary education for children between the ages of six and thirteen.[17] As well as redefining the expectations of childhood, these laws also had a transformative effect on age-based categories in French society. The legal requirement that children attend school until the age of thirteen (or at least until the age of eleven if they had obtained their *certificat d'études primaires*, as specified under Article 6)[18] made school-leaving into a universal rite of passage, a central marker of progression in life, especially among children of the working classes who generally did not pursue higher stages of education. It also served as a bureaucratic threshold marking off childhood from adolescence.

If French society around the turn of the twentieth century was fascinated by children and childhood, it was also highly exercised by the nature and experiences of adolescence. Indeed, according to the pioneering historian of youth Philippe Ariès, adolescence became the privileged age of the twentieth century – overtaking childhood, which had predominated in the nineteenth.[19] Research into child psychology and education theory, which flourished from the 1870s, fuelled a greater sensitivity to age.[20] By the turn of the century adolescent psychology had similarly emerged as a prominent area of research, and adolescence became a stage of life of acute concern for governing authorities.[21] It was in the second half of the nineteenth century that adolescence acquired its modern meaning and importance, applied first to boys of the middle classes before then being transformed into a formally age-defined social category. In effect, as historian Agnès Thiercé puts it, what had initially been a class-defined life stage ("un âge de classe") became identified from the 1890s as a universal life stage ("une classe d'âge").[22] Similar patterns were observable in other countries.[23]

When set within the context of these significant shifts in the conceptualization of childhood and adolescence as distinct phases of development, in some ways France's system of criminal law stands out as remarkably slow to formally recognize these life stages. But this is not to say that before 1912 there was no recognition of age as a meaningful factor in the evaluation of criminality and determination of treatment in the French criminal justice system. Indeed, as has been mentioned, codification in the late eighteenth century introduced a single age threshold for the category of juvenile. All offenders under the age of sixteen were afforded inalienable protections, shielded from sustaining the harshest penalties. Chronological age, in other words, was made to serve as a protective cloak. Section 5 of the 1791 code, relating to "the influence of convicted offenders' age on the nature and duration of punishments [*peines*]," set down that under no circumstances could an offender under the age of sixteen be executed; such a penalty would systematically be commuted to twenty years' detention in a *maison de correction* – institutions for juveniles that the revolutionaries intended to be distinct from an adult prison but that, as we will see, would take many years to actually materialize.[24] The penal code's age-based protections were not limited to young people, with agedness (over seventy-five years) similarly a guarantee against the harshest penalties.[25]

France's codified system of criminal law rested on the rationalist idea that individuals should be answerable for their actions and subjected to punishment only if they satisfied two criteria: first, that they were able to understand the law (the cognitive factor), and second, that they were able to control their own actions (the volitional factor).[26] Both the 1791 and 1810 penal codes also specified that when presented with a defendant under the age of sixteen, as well as determining the *actus reus* (that is, that the juvenile was the agent responsible for committing the unlawful act in question), the court was required to make a statement on the young person's *mens rea* (or moral culpability). This all-important moral capacity, known as *discernement*, essentially amounted to the ability to distinguish right from wrong and served as the basis of criminal liability.

In contrast to the system of the Old Regime, neither the revolutionary nor the Napoleonic codes acknowledged a minimum age for the prosecution of juveniles. Instead, these codes centred their treatment of juveniles on this question of "discernement," a capacity that was effectively understood never to be entirely absent in even the youngest child, but presumed to be exercised imperfectly up to the age of sixteen. "Discernement" applied to adult defendants also; an adult demonstrated to be in a (permanent) state of "démence" (insanity) could not be considered responsible for their actions and therefore could not be punished.[27] But whereas for adults, "discernement" was presumed to be present unless contradictory evidence could be provided, in the case of juveniles, France's penal code required that its presence or absence be assessed in each and every case, and in ways that afforded considerable discretionary powers to judicial authorities.

Whether a juvenile was deemed to have committed an offence "avec discernement" or "sans discernement" would have an important bearing on the measures that could be taken against them. Under the terms of Article 2 of Section 5 of the 1791 penal code, and later taken up in Article 66 of the 1810 code, a juvenile charged with an offence who, it was decided, had acted "sans discernement" would be acquitted. But, critically, this acquittal did not necessarily mean simple release. Indeed, as the legislation laid out, "depending on the circumstance," the juvenile could be returned to their parents' care or detained in a "maison de correction" for a length of time left to the decision of the court though not extending beyond their twentieth year. This provision empowered courts to remove many young offenders from their parents' custody for lengthy periods of time. Article 66 of the penal code was a remarkably powerful mechanism placed at magistrates' disposal. As Patricia O'Brien has noted, "Article 66 was the only form that the indeterminate sentence took in nineteenth-century French penal law."[28] According to historians Françoise Tétard and Claire Dumas, 95 per cent of juvenile offenders prosecuted and detained in institutions in France in the nineteenth century were placed there under the article's terms.[29]

Through Article 66, the treatment of juvenile offenders constituted a form of exceptional justice, and as we shall see in chapter 3, the discretionary powers invested in magistrates became a major concern for reformers at the end of the nineteenth century. Reformers expressed grave reservations about the efficacy of a system that allowed juveniles to be acquitted of an offence on the grounds of having acted "sans discernement" yet simultaneously deprived them of their liberty. What particularly troubled them was the fact that the length of detention was usually far greater than for convicted juveniles found to have acted "avec discernement," who were treated as responsible agents (albeit not subjected to the harshest penalties). According to many, acquittal followed by detention under Article 66 was considered a worse fate than conviction and short-term imprisonment. Moreover, since as a result of important legislation passed in 1850, juveniles acquitted under Article 66 were regularly held within the same correctional institutions as their convicted counterparts, young people themselves were led to wonder whether it might not, in fact (and certainly in the short term), be preferable to be found to have acted "avec discernement" and endure a conviction with a shorter period of imprisonment. As the following chapters will explore, these paradoxes were at the top of reformers' minds as they sought to legislate more effectively on juvenile justice at the turn of the twentieth century.

## Histories of Crime, Incarceration, and Juvenile Justice

Criminality and the efficacy of the nation's criminal justice system, especially its prisons, were issues of particular prominence in public discourse in France in the late nineteenth and early twentieth centuries. *Dangers of Youth* contributes to existing scholarship by highlighting the contours and importance of this period in the formation of ideas about age, criminality, punishment, and reform. Existing studies on the history of modern imprisonment in France have often tended to focus on earlier phases of reform and practices of punishment and incarceration. A leading light in this historiography is of course Michel Foucault, who emphasized in his landmark 1975 book *Surveiller et punir: Naissance de la prison* (published in English in 1977 as *Discipline and Punish: The Birth of the Prison*) the importance of reforms introduced in the period between the late eighteenth and the mid-nineteenth centuries. Foucault draws attention to shifts away from physical, spectacular forms of punishment in the early modern era towards more insidious, generalized forms of imprisonment, correction, and regulatory control, which he sees as defining the modern and contemporary periods.

According to Foucault, as we will see in further detail in chapter 4, the modern prison reached its most perfect expression around 1840 with the founding of the Mettray agricultural colony for juvenile delinquent boys. Other historians, including Jacques-Guy Petit and Patricia O'Brien, however, have highlighted slightly different chronologies to that of Foucault. Focusing on the period from just before the French Revolution of 1789 (when Enlightenment ideas and utilitarian philosophy about justice were making themselves felt) through to 1875 (when the French parliament adopted a landmark law on cellular imprisonment),[30] Petit argues that it is this legislative measure that represents the modern prison's apotheosis. O'Brien, meanwhile, lays emphasis on the practices and shifts that took place between the introduction of the Napoleonic penal code in 1810, which saw a "massive commitment of funds by the state to the development of a new national system of punishment," and 1885, by which time, she writes, "alternatives to incarceration in prisons were legally defined and developed."[31] These alternatives included the transportation of convicts and petty offenders to France's overseas *bagnes* (penal colonies) and the introduction of parole and suspended sentences.

*Dangers of Youth* picks up the baton from these earlier studies, revealing the importance of the turn of the twentieth century for ideas about the purpose and efficacy of imprisonment. In France, as in other places, this was a period of considerable flux in the treatment of criminality. As historical sociologist David Garland has written in reference to Britain, the period between 1895 and 1914 marked a major point of rupture in ideas and practices of criminal justice. Most notably in these years a new logic of "penal welfare" emerged, focused on achieving the offender's reform and compliance through various forms of intervention supported by a variety of knowledge systems including criminology, psychiatry, and medicine.[32] France around the turn of the twentieth century similarly witnessed the solidification of this kind of penal-welfare logic. And it was this logic that lay at the heart of the distinct system of justice for juveniles created in 1912.

Before the 1960s and the advent of the new social history, the establishment of juvenile courts in various parts of the world at the turn of the twentieth century tended to be viewed uncritically, with scholars essentially reiterating the attitudes of reformers from the time. Typical of criminologists' views, British scholar Leon Radzinowicz presented the welfare-oriented ethos of these systems as evidence of the progressive evolution of criminal justice procedure away from "barbarity" and towards greater humanitarianism.[33] Foucault issued a major challenge to these interpretations in *Surveiller et punir* by arguing that the humanitarian trappings of criminal justice reforms in the modern era belied the authorities' intentions for social control.[34] Many of Foucault's essential arguments have been repeated by other prominent scholars, including Michael Ignatieff and David Garland.[35] In a similar vein, sociologists Jacques Donzelot and Philippe Meyer cast the reform of criminal justice, including the establishment of juvenile courts in the pre-war years, as a more insidious system of social control. In their view, assessing juvenile offenders within their own judicial space and removing children under the age of thirteen from prisons and correctional facilities simply offered a more effective means for the state and associated stakeholders to assert their power and dominance. In this assessment, the juvenile court functioned as a powerful tool at the disposal of the ruling classes, enabling them to articulate and protect their own values and interests.[36]

Similarly, in the context of the United States, sociologist Anthony Platt challenged historians' uncritical characterization of the reform movements of the Progressive Era, arguing that while "child savers" were usually presented as "fundamentally benevolent, humanitarian and gradualist" reformers, intent on enshrining a humane type of justice for children, in fact, they were more interested in protecting their own social interests and values.[37]

The history of juvenile justice in France around the turn of the twentieth century has also previously been told within the context of medicine and psychiatry. For Jacques Donzelot, the 1912 law, which explicitly laid out a role for medical experts in the assessment of juvenile offenders,[38] marked "the completion of a migration that had brought the psychiatrist from the minor and infrequent role of last resort for difficult cases to that of declared instigator of the lowliest judicial decisions."[39] An impressive and expanding body of work on the history of legal medicine has revealed the growing influence of doctors in the judicial sphere, particularly through the developing fields of psychiatry and forensic medicine,[40] but, as Donzelot himself acknowledges, although the 1912 law carved out a place for medical expertise, since it was left up to the judge's discretion to call on these experts, it cannot accurately be said to constitute the decisive triumph of medicine in the world of law. In the decades following the passage of the 1912 legislation, a climate of mutual wariness prevailed, as judges, Donzelot argues, realized that calling on medical experts as a matter of course would be professional suicide.[41] What is indisputable is that medical science came to occupy an increasingly prominent position in public debate on crime and criminality. In particular, medicine came to be deployed as a vital instrument for dealing with the perceived moral and physical decline of France's population. Anxieties about slow population growth (*dénalité*) plagued the Third Republic, reaching a particular pitch at century's end and continuing for decades to come.[42]

The fin de siècle witnessed the proliferation of what Robert Nye has labelled a "medical model of cultural crisis."[43] Scholars' focus on medicine, however, should not distract from the increasingly important role played by the law and its representatives during the Third Republic in helping to define and shape the response to criminality and the various social issues that were entangled with it. *Dangers of Youth* attempts to refocus our attention on the importance of jurists and the law in the construction of social policy in this period. As such, it issues a corrective to what historian Annie Stora-Lamarre has seen as a tendency among scholars to neglect the law –

its principles, theorists, and practitioners – as an area of inquiry.[44] Indeed, it is clear that in the final decades of the nineteenth century, as Sylvia Schafer has argued, "law emerged as a primary medium for the public regulation of individual and collective moral life … and provided a critical counterweight to the freedoms created by the regime's attempts to loosen inherited restrictions on free expression and association."[45]

## Historicizing Childhood, Criminality, and Chronological Age

In addressing questions of age categories and the treatment of criminality, reformers in France at the turn of the twentieth century grappled with issues of fundamental importance to the functioning of the criminal justice system more generally, especially ones relating to the reform of criminal behaviours and prevention of recidivism. Juveniles – presumed to be at once the most vulnerable and the most malleable members of the population – became the subject of increasingly interventionist methods by the state to prevent anti-social conduct. Part of a movement of child protection (or "child saving") that swept across the Western world from the final decades of the nineteenth century, measures were taken to prevent young people from falling or settling into a life of crime. The scale of this movement is reflected in the substantial and ever-growing scholarly literature that examines this history through both national and imperial lenses.[46]

While historians may have differing interpretations of the nature, experiences, and distinctions of childhood, adolescence, and indeed, adulthood (with its own subcategories, too), and continue to debate the precise moments when turning points and shifts occurred, there is now no question but that the history of life stages constitutes a rich aspect of inquiry. At least since the publication in 1960 of Philippe Ariès's pioneering foray into the history of childhood, *L'Enfant et la vie familiale sous l'ancien régime* (appearing in English in 1962 as *Centuries of Childhood: A Social History of Family Life*), historians have debated the extent to which children in the past were considered qualitatively different to adults and thus segregated from the adult world.[47] In Ariès's contentious thesis, "the child" as a distinct social category only emerged in Europe around the sixteenth century, with no previous conception of childhood as separate from adulthood, nor any notion of adolescence as a distinct life stage. These claims were and continue to be strongly contested, including by influential scholars of French cultural history Natalie Zemon Davis and Robert Darnton.[48] In an important survey article, Adrian Wilson offered a cogent overview of historians' criticisms.[49] In the end, so energetically have Ariès's claims been critiqued that it may be that, as Colin Heywood has remarked, "it was by being wrong more often than right about childhood in the past, but wrong in a very stimulating way, that he made his principal contribution."[50] Ultimately, one point upon which all can certainly agree is that Ariès's most enduring legacy is in having laid out the idea that conceptualizations of children and childhood, far from being timeless and natural, are historically and culturally contingent.[51]

Chronological age has a history, and its construction and valorization warrant attentive historical analysis. This book takes seriously the call by historians of childhood and youth to adopt chronological age as a useful category of analysis, pointing to its cultural contingencies and relevance to interrogations of such crucial questions as identity, agency, and power relations.[52] While childhood, adolescence, and youth (and the populations to which those categories refer) are today generally recognized as significant themes for historical research, there is some disagreement over the extent to which these topics have entered the mainstream of historical concerns. Sarah Maza has recently argued that childhood, unlike other fields that emerged with the rise of social history from the 1960s and which, like gender and race, are held to define a person's identity, remains largely marginalized from historical inquiry.[53] Several scholars, including Stephen Mintz, have rejected Maza's claim.[54] The stakes of this interrogation of chronological age are considerable, not least in a legal context. For instance, Ishita Pande, a historian of post/colonial South Asia and the British Empire, has shown how what she terms the modern "epistemic contract on age," consisting of "an implicit agreement that chronological age is a universal and natural measure of human capacity," functioned within the context of colonial India to legitimize British rule.[55] In this book I seek to demonstrate the value of paying attention to the meanings and values attributed to chronological age in France at the turn of the twentieth century within the context of juvenile justice reform. In so doing, I aim to expose how ideas about age thresholds can reveal much about standards, expectations, and methods of control applied to particular populations at different moments in time.

Existing scholarship on the history of criminality, imprisonment, and correction in modern France has largely neglected the growing importance attributed to chronological age as a tool for the reform and regeneration of the nation's wayward populations. The pages that follow reveal how questions of age were central to thinking about the state's need and right to punish and correct and the efficacy of doing so. In ways that have largely escaped the scrutiny of historians, chronological age became an ever more central tool in the management of juvenile delinquency around the turn of the twentieth century. With the passage of the 1912 law, it became impossible for the criminal justice system to treat a child under the age of thirteen as in any way a responsible agent and subject them to punishment.

By exploring ideas about the significance attached to chronological age for criminal responsibility, correction, and punishment, this book seeks to shed new light on questions of fundamental importance to the history of crime and its management. The treatment of juveniles – that portion of the population considered most receptive to intervention and deserving of non-punitive treatment – offers a window onto understanding the parameters and purpose of the modern system of criminal justice, especially its putative aim to facilitate the reform of lawbreakers. Protected from the harshest penalties and invested with a greater optimism for reform than adults, juveniles were inseparable from the rehabilitative objectives of criminal justice interventions.

## Voices, Sources, and Structure

The focus of this book is on the views and attitudes of social and political elites: individuals who were, without exception, adults. The reader might with good reason question whether adopting such an approach risks perpetuating an "adultist" vision of the young. Indeed, as Harry Hendrick has argued, in much of the research in the area of the history of childhood "children have been denied both a voice and, an essential feature of human identity, a rational standpoint."[56] Clearly, privileging adult perceptions of the young over young people's actual experiences as social actors raises important considerations about agency, as recent work by Stephen Toth and Julia Gossard has perceptively exposed.[57]

The question of the extent to which young people attempted to resist the definitions and prescriptions imposed on them by authorities is one that the sources used in this book do not allow us to address directly. This is a telling absence, for the lack of discussion on these issues within these sources draws attention to the important fact that reformers' attitudes to the management of young offenders' lives were predicated on the classist and ageist assumption that they knew best. Young people – children and, to a slightly lesser extent, adolescents – were seen as powerless victims who, without the interventions of the state and private philanthropy, lacked the capacity to withstand or positively shape the circumstances in which they were placed. A core assumption of this book is not that young people did not have any voice whatsoever, but that in the context of the late nineteenth century their perspectives and needs were considered subservient to the requirements of a wider social good. Adult reformers claimed expertise and special knowledge, systematically undervaluing or outright ignoring the perceptions and perspectives of young people except when they appeared to offer some insight into making the criminal justice system function more effectively.

In choosing to concentrate on the views of adults, my purpose is to shed light on the meanings ascribed to age categories and thresholds at a particularly formative moment in the development of French juvenile justice procedure. The juvenile offender was a major preoccupation for French authorities during the Third Republic, representing an "at once weak and dangerous but indispensable element for the construction of republican society," as historian Martine Kaluszynski has written.[58] By looking at questions of chronological age, criminal responsibility, and reform during the nineteenth century and through to 1912, I historicize concepts of age and reveal the particular motivations that lay behind the construction of age-defined categories in France's criminal justice system, categories that today are largely taken for granted and perhaps even considered "natural."

Prising open a window onto the debates that led to the 1912 legislation, this book offers a contextual analysis of the social and political priorities underpinning the birth of a distinct jurisdiction for juveniles in the French criminal justice system. Age was made to carry greater significance than it ever had before. Ultimately what I seek to demonstrate is that underlying the various reforms to juvenile justice and entangled with a professed concern about the well-being of young people, particularly children, was a desire to produce a criminal justice system that better served the needs of the governing elites of the Third Republic.

Primarily focused on the attitudes of criminal justice reformers and jurists, the following chapters explore the context behind judicial and legislative changes that shifted the conceptualization of juveniles as a distinct category and put in place practices that distinguished between child and adolescent offenders on the basis of their chronological age. Looking closely at debates and concerns that undergirded new understandings about age and the criminal justice system allows us to observe the emergence of chronological age more clearly as a "rational" criterion of classification in the French criminal justice system. This criterion of chronological age served not only to distinguish juveniles from adults (as had been the case since codification more than a century earlier), but also children from adolescents.

*Dangers of Youth* draws together a range of archival and published materials, including case studies, newspaper accounts, scholarly treatises by contemporary penologists, psychologists, philosophers, educational theorists, and social reformers, and printed transcripts of the sometimes heated discussions of reformer organizations. In particular, the book focuses on the opinions and views of criminal justice practitioners and reformers who grouped themselves around an association known as the Société générale des prisons (SGP). Formed in 1877, the SGP would play a critical role in helping to shape and disseminate ideas about criminal justice reform, including the treatment of juveniles, which would culminate in legislative change. These reformers carried a keen interest in the condition of young offenders, seeing this particular issue as the key to breaking the cycle of crime. As we will see in chapter 2, during the Third Republic the SGP sought to bridge civil society and the state. Many of the most prominent statesmen active in the reform of criminal justice were SGP members, including the sponsor of the 1912 law, Senator Ferdinand Dreyfus. Indicative of the centrality of young people to the SGP's concerns, within its first year, the group regularly turned over meetings to discussing the treatment of juveniles, a category of offender whom they considered most deserving of their concern.[59]

The philanthropists, parliamentarians, and jurists adjudicating on questions of criminal responsibility and the treatment of juvenile offending inhabited a world greatly at odds with the lives and experiences of the subjects over whom they deliberated. Their debates about the incarceration of largely working-class young offenders illustrate the tensions and fault lines running through French society in the pre-war decades. These debates had both national and international implications. In France, increases in worker unrest and the activity of violent youth gangs kindled widespread fears of the enemy within. External threats were also salient, as foreign powers (most worryingly among them Germany) continued to flex their military and colonial muscle.

The first chapter provides a survey of the broad sweep of ideas, concerns, and policies regarding young people during the Third Republic, demonstrating how developing discourses and theories concerning childhood and adolescence were central to debates about and approaches to punishment, correction, and republican governance generally in France in this period. Drawing on a range of materials, the chapter highlights the particular anxieties about unregulated male youth – unregulated in the sense both of falling outside the bounds of institutional supervision and of the disorderly behaviour seen to characterize adolescence.

The chapter shows how much of this debate was wrapped up in a concern about the decline of artisan labour and the rise in industrial employment, resulting in greater precariousness for young people and fuelling the formation of gangs of urban youths, the so-called *apaches*. The use of the term "apache," said to have been first applied by Parisian journalists in 1902, suggested a similarity with the perceived wildness and lack of "civilization" of the Indigenous Peoples of North America. While not necessarily themselves young enough to be officially classed as "mineurs" (juveniles), the "apaches" were nonetheless distinguished from wider society by their youth as well as their unruliness.[60] On the other side of the English Channel a similar moral panic raged, further evidence of the international extent of concern about unruly youth in this period.[61]

In chapter 2, the discussion then turns to an analysis of the SGP. This group was a pivotal forum for the articulation of ideas about age, responsibility, and criminality that would contribute to the formulation of numerous pieces of legislation relating to juveniles, including the law of 1912 on juvenile courts. Founded in the wake of the Haussonville Commission, a major parliamentary inquiry into France's prisons, the SGP acted as a lobby group for reform to policy and legislation throughout France. In today's parlance it might be thought of as a think tank. As well as telling the story of the SGP's own reform program, chapter 2 also look backwards in order to demonstrate the extent to which the final decades of the nineteenth century were a continuation of older practices and preoccupations. The chapter situates the SGP within the longer crusade for prison reform over the nineteenth century and in relation to the broader international criminal justice reform movement, analyzing members' backgrounds, attitudes, and their ideas about the relationship between the state and private philanthropy in the regulation of criminality at the turn of the century. In keeping with their gradualist, reformist ethos, SGP members positioned themselves within this longer history of reform, viewing themselves as the heirs to an older line of criminal justice reform organizations founded during the Restoration and July Monarchy of the first half of the nineteenth century. However, although they shared certain core beliefs with their predecessors, they differed from them in asserting the importance of maintaining an independence from the state (while at the same time engaging with it).

Chapters 3, 4, and 5 examine how issues of age functioned within the criminal justice system at the various phases of the prosecution of juveniles. Chapter 3 looks at debates about chronological age in the administration of justice for juveniles throughout the nineteenth century, especially in the decades leading up to the passage of the 1912 law. In particular, this chapter unpacks debates surrounding the introduction of an age threshold for the exercise of "discernement." Such a measure would have seen children under a nominated age protected from any repressive measure. In other words, these debates were about the introduction of a minimum age of criminal responsibility into French criminal law. This proposal, ultimately enshrined by the legislation of 1912, which removed the question of "discernement" for juveniles under the age of thirteen (thereby effectively instituting an automatic presumption of criminal irresponsibility in children), was opposed by some who were concerned about reducing magistrates' discretionary powers over young offenders. Chapter 3 explores jurists' and reformers' debates over the efficacy of "discernement" as a legal mechanism and their varying perspectives on the relevance of chronological age as a measure for responsibility.

Chapter 4 then engages in a close examination of the institutional treatment of juvenile offenders on the basis of age. As the chapter shows, the discrimination of juveniles from older offenders began with their segregation from adult prisoners in the early nineteenth century, continuing through the rise to primacy of *colonies pénitentiaires agricoles* (juvenile colonies for wayward boys located in the countryside) in the middle of the century, and on to the late nineteenth century, which saw an increasing skepticism about the efficacy of incarceration in the treatment of criminality. The chapter examines the emergence of the concept of the *enfant en danger* (the child at risk) and its entanglements with the *enfant dangereux* (the juvenile offender) and explores the increasing emphasis placed on implementing more finely grained distinctions between young detainees on the basis of their chronological age.

Building on these discussions about the efficacy of punishment, chapter 5 shows how questions of juvenile offending, age, and criminal responsibility were implicated in larger debates about the republicanization of the military and the relationship between civil and military authority. Examining debates about military recruitment and methods of discipline, the chapter reveals the tensions aroused by the increasing interconnections of civil society, the military, and correctional institutions as a result of both compulsory military service and republican authorities' deployment of the army as a mechanism for both the formation of republican citizens and the correction of deviance.

Overall this book offers a historical analysis of the conceptualization and treatment of juvenile offenders in modern France, with a particular focus on questions of age and responsibility during the Third Republic, demonstrating the centrality of these issues to debates about punishment and republican citizenship more broadly. Matters of age, criminal responsibility, and punishment were anything but legal abstractions; they were crucial to the conceptualization and realization of expectations and ideals of republican citizenship. Young people were identified as a key component in the construction of a stable, orderly society in which members accepted their place and understood not only their rights but also their responsibilities in order to best conform to the rules of the existing social order. Young people were considered critical to the building and solidification of the French republican nation-state. Correctional institutions for juveniles were viewed as vitally important for the formation of French citizens, working in concert with primary schools and, in the case of boys, with the army to produce responsible citizens loyal to the republic.

# CHAPTER 1

# Raising Children and Adolescents in the Third Republic

In early June 1910, a highly anticipated murder trial began in the criminal court of Auxerre, the Burgundian capital of the Yonne department, southeast of Paris. In the dock were two boys: fourteen-year-old Joseph Vienny and sixteen-year-old Richard Joseph Jacquiard, accused of having murdered five people the previous December. The case was known in the press as the "crime de Jully," in reference to the name of the rural hamlet where the crime had taken place. Vienny and Jacquiard had been born and raised in a rural area of French-speaking Switzerland and had come to France after completing primary school in search of farm work. On the small but prosperous farm at Jully, they had found work as cowherds. The day before the murders, the boys had purchased revolvers and ammunition in order to carry out their attack. Their main motive, it transpired, was financial: the boys had resolved to kill and steal from their employer after accidentally breaking a pitchfork. Bound to replace the broken tool out of their own pockets, the boys saw the expense as a significant setback to their secret plans to save their earnings and travel the world. Inspired by their avid reading of adventure stories, Jacquiard and Vienny dreamed of crossing the seas to Africa, where they would lead thrilling lives of adventure and earn their living by publishing tales of their exciting exploits.[1] In the end, their fates could not have been more different.

On 4 June 1910, the Auxerre jurors handed down their verdict: both Vienny and Jacquiard were found guilty with no extenuating circumstances. Because he had been under the age of sixteen at the time of the events, Vienny had his sentence automatically commuted to twenty years' detention in a *colonie correctionnelle*, the harshest type of institution at the time for juveniles. Jacquiard, meanwhile, although being under eighteen (the age of criminal majority), did not enjoy such dispensation. The age of criminal majority had been raised from sixteen to eighteen in 1906, but lesser penalties for lawbreakers aged between sixteen and eighteen only applied in cases where the young offender was deemed to have acted "sans discernement." Despite this, however, the following month Jacquiard's death sentence was commuted by President Armand Fallières to transportation for life to France's overseas bagne in French Guiana. President Fallières's decision to commute the older boy's death sentence, according to one source, was met with the same "unanimous protestations" as had his commutation of the sentence of child rapist and murderer Albert Soleilland a few years earlier.[2] A committed abolitionist, since assuming the presidency in 1906 Fallières had systematically commuted the sentences of convicts sentenced to death, a pattern of judicial decisions that conservatives alleged was contributing to what they labelled a "crisis of repression" around the turn of the twentieth century.[3]

A sensation in the French press at the time, the "crime de Jully" serves as a good entry point for understanding the nature and stakes of concerns about juvenile waywardness in France around the turn of the twentieth century. The case unfolded within the context of an intense contest over the nation's moral health and values. Even though Jacquiard and Vienny were born and raised in French-speaking Switzerland and not in republican France, their case nonetheless was seized on as an opportunity "to face up to the problem of juvenile criminality [*criminalité de l'enfance*], to study it, not as a polemical argument, but as a lab experiment of interest to humanity as a whole," as a journalist from *Le Matin* newspaper put it.[4]

Invested with a level of education that was not necessarily required in their day-to-day lives or for their employment, the boys belonged to a social type of immense concern to French legislators, reformers, and social commentators in the late nineteenth and early twentieth centuries. Beyond the age of compulsory schooling, but not yet old enough to enlist in the armed forces, youngsters like Jacquiard and Vienny largely escaped the surveillance of the state. Living away from home, they also escaped the surveillance of their families.

The "crime de Jully" and its two young perpetrators were knitted into a hotly contested ideological dispute raging in France in the early twentieth century over the causes and contagiousness of criminality and the challenges of rearing dutiful citizens. The "apache" youth gangs, so-called morally abandoned children (with living but neglectful parents), sex workers, left-wing militants, alcoholics, vagrants, and the "new woman" were similarly identified as problematic in turn-of-the-century France.[5] Individually and collectively, these types were seen to constitute worrying harbingers of a nation in dangerous decline. Occupying an ambiguous position between childish dependency and adult citizenship, Jacquiard and Vienny were seen to embody the dangers of an unregulated society. For supporters of the republican regime, the fact that the two boys were living away from home and earning an independent living was concerning. For critics of republicanism, the boys' ambitious delusions were seen to be the product of republican childrearing that, it was claimed, laid excessive emphasis on rights rather than on responsibilities.

When news had first broken of the Jully farm murders, reports of the carnage saturated the pages of the local, national, and even international press. Headlines drew attention to the brutality of the case and the incongruous setting – a quiet pocket of rural Burgundy was not the typical location for a violent crime of this kind. Indeed, French crime statistics generally suggested a correlation between urban environments and criminality, dovetailing with a longstanding view among French elites that the "classes laborieuses" (working classes) were synonymous with the "classes dangereuses" (dangerous classes).[6] Even though by the 1880s two-thirds of France's population were still living in non-urban areas, over half of all criminals prosecuted lived in towns; this overrepresentation fed a perception that urban living and criminality went hand in hand.[7]

Journalists described Jacquiard and Vienny in the same way they did Parisian "apache" youth gangs, presenting them as yet further evidence of the country's social and moral degeneration.[8] The relationship between the press and criminality was a major area of contention in France around the turn of the century. Stories of these youth gangs peppered the pages of French newspapers to such an extent that tales of their exploits had become readers' daily bread, as one journalist at the time put it disapprovingly.[9]

Among criminal justice reformers, there was a belief that the press, while ostensibly simply reporting on criminal activities, was serving to perpetuate them. Parisian jurist Paul Kahn told delegates at the 1906 International Congress of Criminal Anthropology held in Turin (and presided over by the controversial Italian criminologist Cesare Lombroso) that newspapers' obsession with the "apaches" was inspiring young people to emulate figures they considered "knights of the modern city."[10] In the hands of an opportunistic press, which, as Dominique Kalifa has argued, routinely claimed to be simply reporting the news rather than actively shaping it,[11] the "apaches" were more than a subcultural phenomenon. As the nomenclature of an Indigenous American people suggests, these youth gangs were presented as manifesting a mode of conduct that lay outside the realm of an implicitly European style of "civilization." Newspapers neatly folded Jacquiard and Vienny into this culture, with one journalist from *Le Petit parisien* referring to the boys as "the Swiss 'Mohicans.'"[12]

Every aspect of the case was raked over, often in gruesome detail. The widely read Parisian daily newspaper *Le Petit journal* printed photos of the corpses of four of the victims (their bodies covered with white cloths, with only their heads showing).[13] *L'Illustration* magazine similarly presented graphic images to its readers, justifying its explicit coverage by pointing, in a circular argument, to the exceptional brutality of the events.[14] With an influx of hundreds of visitors to the area, keen to witness first-hand the scene of the bloodshed, local newspaper *L'Yonne* lured them to its office windows by displaying photos of the victims' corpses,[15] while a local photographer produced a series of numbered souvenir postcards with images of Jacquiard and Vienny (see figure 1.1), the surviving victims, and various scenes of the crime.[16]

Vienny and Jacquiard's youthfulness was the factor that attracted greatest media commentary. One journalist for *Le Petit journal* commented that "what adds even further terror to the horror of the crime committed at Jully is the youth of the killers."[17] Reporting on the boys' demeanour in the courtroom, Swiss newspaper *La Gazette de Lausanne* lingered on their childlike appearance, asking how beings so young could commit such a dreadful crime.[18] The boys' petite stature – Vienny was less than four feet tall and Jacquiard just five foot three – made them appear even younger than their age, accentuating the incongruity of their crime.[19] In drawing attention to the boys' youth, journalists sought not to absolve them of responsibility but rather to emphasize the monstrousness of their actions.

Figure 1.1
Postcard of Richard Joseph Jacquiard and Joseph Vienny, 1910

Journalists covering the Jully case laid emphasis on its uniqueness, while at the same time inserting the two young perpetrators into an established chronology of notorious criminal perpetrators. The Jully crime, wrote one reporter for the local newspaper *L'Yonne*, "exceeds in horror all the crimes committed, not only in our region of Burgundy, but even in the most disreputable suburbs … of Paris." The case, the journalist breathlessly went on, "recalls and surpasses in horror the most famous exploits of [Jean-Baptiste] Troppman, [Pierre François] Lacenaire and other bandits whose fame lives on in the legal annals."[20]

In a compendium volume of notable criminal trials for the year 1910, *Le Figaro* journalist Georges Claretie noted the irony that Jacquiard and Vienny should have been tried in Auxerre, the birthplace of republican statesmen Paul Bert, who, along with Jean Macé and Jules Ferry, had spearheaded the campaign three decades earlier to provide free, secular primary schooling in France.[21] For Bert and his fellow republicans, primary education represented the key to forging equality, buttressing political democracy, and building patriotism. Secular education, republicans claimed, would build morally upright, responsible citizens, imbued with a sense of duty and respect for the rule of law. Where traditional Catholic education had served as an arm of conservative authoritarianism, republicans maintained that their own curriculum would, acting in concert with responsible parents, help raise children into good French citizens. Conservative Catholics and monarchists, however, retorted that republican primary schooling, far from guarding against immorality and criminality, in fact fuelled social dislocation. From the 1880s, when the education of the nation's youth was overwhelmingly placed in the hands of republican schoolteachers, juvenile delinquency was said by critics to be providing sharp and disturbing evidence of a society in dangerous decline.

At the heart of this ideological battle was a dispute over the role of republican schooling in sowing the seeds of social dysfunction. While the conservative corners of the press pointed the finger at the secularization of primary education, they also identified another culprit – one to which republicans similarly attributed responsibility: bad parents. It was not so much nature as nurture that was believed to lie behind most criminality, including among juveniles. While ideas of biologically driven degeneration enjoyed some traction in France (influencing, for instance, the novels of writers like Émile Zola), French criminologists and penal reformers tended to emphasize the social environment, especially the family, as the primary factor responsible for fuelling anti-social behaviours.[22] In this way, although French criminologists often employed a vocabulary drawn from medicine to describe the problem of crime, they generally interpreted immoral and criminal behaviours in Lamarckian[23] rather than Lombrosian terms. According to this reading, undesirable behaviours, including criminality, were not fatally cast but rather could be corrected by altering a person's surroundings. The phrase "societies have the criminals they deserve," attributed to the French doctor and criminologist Alexandre Lacassagne, became the mantra for those who advanced this kind of socially embedded explanation of crime.[24]

In 1897, jurist and pioneer sociologist Gabriel Tarde, one of the most outspoken critics in France of Cesare Lombroso and his followers,[25] published an article in which he laid out what he saw as the main source of children's waywardness. "In most cases, if not all," Tarde wrote, "it is in the paternal home that our schools' pupils have sucked the poisonous milk of religious and moral scepticism, of disrespectful and ambitious vanity, precocious greed, vice, even alcoholism."[26] For Tarde, urban life represented the most dangerous context for producing criminality; high-density living and exposure to the many temptations of the street and glittering department stores produced greater anti-social conduct, especially among young people who were naturally impressionable and more easily led astray.[27]

As country boys, Jacquiard and Vienny may have defied Tarde's typical urban criminal type, but in other key ways they embodied a distinctive demographic of "problem youth." Living far from their parents, without any institutional oversight and with a certain degree of financial independence, they were hardly children by middle-class standards, but nor were they yet adults. The boys were seen to embody a certain type of disaffected, rootless, and therefore dangerous young population. Possessed of ambitious delusions of future renown as adventurers and writers, Jacquiard and Vienny had committed brutal acts of violence that were held up by conservative critics as symptomatic of a moral crisis that was the fault of French republicanism. Right-wing politician and novelist Maurice Barrès described in the first volume of his 1897 trilogy *Roman de l'énergie nationale* the devastating effects of republican ideology on French society, particularly its secular education system. Republican schooling, Barrès wrote, was tearing the nation apart, destroying traditional family and social structures, and producing a population of overly educated, ambitious young people who, indoctrinated in their freedoms and rights, were unwilling to submit to authority or respect existing social hierarchies, including generational ones.[28] Young people, in short, were said to no longer know their place.

## Saving Children and Saving France

During the French Revolution at the end of the eighteenth century, Georges Danton is credited with having asserted that "children belong to the Republic before they belong to their parents."[29] While most republicans a century later would not have made quite so strident a claim, they were determined all the same to harness the potential of children as future citizens by more effectively welding the family and the republic together. Good families were seen as the wellspring out of which good citizens would emerge, and interventionist measures adopted to protect children from negligent parents were intended to encourage families to work in concert with the state to raise good (that is, loyal) republican citizens.

As the nineteenth century drew to a close, France could take some comfort from the fact that, on the international stage, youth criminality was not its problem alone, but rather one that was common across industrializing states. As Tarde wrote in 1897, "the ever more common fall of young people into immorality and offending, even crime, is … not exclusively the French malady of our times, it is also the German malady, the English malady, the European malady."[30] A decade later, Georges Morache, a professor of medicine at the University of Bordeaux, made a similar point, arguing that juvenile criminality was not "a social disease specific to the French population alone." On the contrary, he wrote, "it denotes a profound poisoning of modern societies."[31]

Yet although youth criminality was not unique to France in this period, one related factor made its manifestation in the French context particularly alarming: the country's rate of population growth was notably sluggish, especially in comparison to Germany, the now-unified country whose most powerful state, Prussia, had seized the valuable territory of Alsace-Lorraine away from France in 1871. By 1911, 34.9 per cent of the French population was under the age of twenty-one, whereas in Germany the proportion was 43.7 per cent.[32] Fears of depopulation in France, particularly its perceived implications for national defence, would reach fever pitch in the years leading up to the First World War.[33]

Concern about population decline (both qualitatively and quantitatively) along with intensifying international industrial competition and increasing class friction shaped the response of France's governing authorities and social elites to youth-related issues in the final decades of the nineteenth century. During the Third Republic, young people, especially infants and children, were at the heart of state-sanctioned interventions that regulated everything from wet-nursing to physical education and "good" parenting.[34] The imperative for childhood was not that it be enjoyed, but rather properly managed in order to ensure social stability. Indicative of the shift in attitudes was the state's greater willingness to invest financially in childrearing. Whereas officials decades earlier had considered abandoned children to be a drain on the economy, from the 1880s their neglect was taken as a powerful indicator of the nation in decline.[35] Reform undertaken in this context was seen to serve as a form of social medicine; surrounding children with a raft of protective civil laws would ensure their robust development, in both physical and moral terms, for the sake of the *patrie*.

In the face of France's comparatively low natality, a premium was subsequently placed on harnessing all available manpower. What population *did* exist had to be protected and put to the most productive use. To allow young people to succumb to a life of criminality would be to endanger the very survival of French society as a whole. As French jurist Eugène Prévost told the first International Congress on Juvenile Courts held in Paris in 1911, "in the [context of] international competition, increasing by the day, France has too low a birth rate to be able to afford heavy criminality, which produces convicts and prisoners, and not citizens and workers."[36] Strengthening the physical and moral health of the existing population became the priority for French reformers.

From the very birth of the Third Republic in 1870, children were elevated to an esteemed position. In the immediate wake of France's loss to Prussia in the war of 1870–71 and over the decades following, French commentators and statesmen upheld the vital role to be played by children as agents for *revanchisme* and national renewal. Young people born and educated in France in this period were made keenly aware of their patriotic duty to ensure the survival of the nation. Importantly, republicans regularly presented the drive to defend the nation not as something imposed from above, but as an instinctive impulse originating from within young people themselves. Especially in the early decades of the Third Republic, when the French parliament was dominated by conservatives with little if any loyalty to a republican political structure, republicans' concern about young people's well-being was inseparable from a concern about the survival of the republic itself.

The origins of the regime (simply declared in September 1870 rather than birthed through popular struggle or electoral victories, as had been the case with the two previous republics), combined with the dominance in parliament of monarchists hostile to the very idea of a republic (including presidents Adolphe Thiers and Patrice de MacMahon), made the Third Republic in its first years largely a republic in name alone. By the end of the 1870s, republicans had finally risen to a position of power within the national parliament, and once there, they quickly turned their attentions to establishing their ideological influence. This essentially amounted to challenging established structures dominated by the Catholic Church, an institution that republicans viewed as the lieutenant of conservatism. The precarious, shell-like nature of the republic in its first years convinced republicans that the regime's survival depended on instilling popular support. It was here that the education of children came into play, deployed as a primary tool for fostering a sense of loyalty towards and identification with the republic. For republicans, making responsible future citizens was about shoring up the future of the republic itself. Desperate to buttress their power, republicans turned to childrearing, especially primary schooling, to act as shield and sword against their social enemies, especially monarchists but also Bonapartists and, with increasing urgency from the 1890s, socialists.

Republicans' major challenge in the final decades of the nineteenth century was to find a way to encourage France's citizens to embrace political democracy and liberty, while at the same time preventing them from overthrowing the regime. They located their answer in childrearing and education. Being naturally receptive to outside influences and thus easily moulded, children could, through education, be encouraged to become self-regulating and adhere to society's rules and values without even realizing it. The republican primary school aimed to instil in children a respect for and identification with republican ideals of virtue and to voluntarily acquiesce to them.

In themselves and in their relationship to adult figures (especially parents and primary school teachers), children represented many of the essential elements of the republican governing order. They were republicans' primary beacon, serving both as symbols of the forward-looking ethos of the Third Republic regime and as the primary instruments of the republic's construction. By their very nature, children inspired a hopefulness and optimism about the future. At the same time, they were thought to contain within themselves explanations for essential qualities of humankind and carried forward with them the established values of the society into which they were born. In this way, children represented both the past and the future, and provided the bridge between them. In his 1891 work *L'Enfant et la justice répressive*, Bordeaux jurist Emmanuel Lasserre conveyed this sense of the child's simultaneous recapitulation and furthering of human development, commenting that "childhood has throughout time had that rare privilege of inspiring the liveliest interest. This is because it reaches the most intimate fibres of our nature: it surprises us, like a mysterious problem, by the hatching and development of the intelligence; it charms us in reminding us of the past, which is always dear, in showing us the future, which is always cheerful."[37]

## Childhood, Primary Schooling, and Constructing Republican Citizens

The Third Republic witnessed a fundamental shift in the place of children and the experience of childhood in French society. Building on legislation introduced in the 1840s, Ferry's laws of the early 1880s on free, compulsory primary schooling, combined with laws restricting the employment of children, transformed expectations of how a good childhood should be spent, at least up to the age of thirteen when the obligation to attend school ended.[38] The standard childhood was henceforth characterized by dependency and preparation for civic life, as opposed to a time for direct and practical life experience, with all children deserving and requiring protection from premature exposure to the world of adult labour. American historian Viviana Zelizer has described this shift, which was occurring in other parts of the world at the same time, as marking a "sacralization" of children within the family, where their value was henceforth to be measured in terms of feeling, not finances.[39] In universalizing the norms of a healthy childhood and requiring all children to attend school, France's republican regime at the end of the nineteenth century established certain expectations that, as Jacques Donzelot has noted, exposed those who were unwilling or incapable of submitting to its rigours.[40] The so-called "abnormal" child became a focus of concern in this period, with psychologists Alfred Binet and Théodore Simon conducting foundational research.[41]

In the final decades of the nineteenth century, French children's lives became the highest priority and childhood "a political stake,"[42] and it was the primary school that lay at the heart of an ideological reconstruction of the nation. Although from 1889, the army would also play an active role in the formation of male republican citizens, including young offenders (as we shall see in chapter 5), primary schooling played the more foundational role, establishing the forms of belief and habits of moral conduct that were expected to direct the future lives of all children, girls as well as boys. Within republican primary schools new pedagogical practices derived from a new philosophy of education were deployed to satisfy political ends.[43] These practices presented children's own interests and personal fulfilment as being dependent on their adherence to the laws and values of the republic.

"No [government] has pinned greater hopes on the primary school than ours," wrote the prominent republican educational theorist and administrator Félix Pécaut in 1897.[44] In the final decades of the nineteenth century, a time of considerable social conflict in France and tension internationally, children's incremental growth and capacity for improvement provided comforting evidence that things could get better and helped undergird liberal republicanism's emphasis on steady, well-tempered progress. In the decades before the First World War, primary school teachers became the "high priests of nation-worship,"[45] serving as the regime's "ideological cement."[46] According to republican pedagogy, teachers' methods of instruction were as critical as the curriculum they imparted; everything was intended to instil in schoolchildren a sense of attachment to the French republic and a belief that their own self-interest and well-being – even their very identities – were inseparable from its health and survival. This was also a nationalistic project, with the republican primary school serving as a key tool in the transformation of culture from something that was "still fragmented and informal" into something "truly national."[47]

Even more powerfully, advocates touted republican education as a regenerative force capable of reviving a depleted French population. According to republicans themselves, the republican primary school was a school of moralization, and the stage of life to which it attended was seen as vitally important in the formation of responsible individuals who understood their place in the social order. In a course presented to university students at the Sorbonne in 1902, Émile Durkheim described a child's primary school years as a "critical moment for the formation of moral character."[48] Schooling, Durkheim maintained, was an essential instrument for reconciling the competing interests of individual autonomy and social solidarity. "School life," Durkheim wrote, "is but the seed of social life."[49] The "collective life" of the classroom, he remarked, expanded a child's consciousness and "awakens in the child the feeling of solidarity."[50] A similar point about the school as social microcosm had been made by G. Bruno (the pseudonym of Augustine Fouillée, author of the widely read children's text *Le Tour de la France par deux enfants*), in the preface to her 1882 book *Instruction morale et civique pour les petits enfants*. "School," Bruno wrote, "is already, in a nutshell, the image of society and life: there the child finds themselves in contact with classmates, with schoolmasters; it is there that they learn to work, to obey, to respect rules and discipline, to not do unto others that which they would not want done to them."[51]

The republican primary school's ideological purpose was most explicit in its curriculum of secular morality: a program purposed with developing children's emotional and moral intelligence, helping to encourage the release of their latent inclinations, and nurturing them into healthy habits.[52] The secular morality program was consciously crafted to reduce the influence of the Catholic Church, as part of a campaign by republicans that had begun in the early 1880s with the introduction of the Ferry laws, which demoted religion from its longstanding place at the centre of primary schooling. Critical philosopher Charles Renouvier, whom Émile Durkheim would later claim as "his educator,"[53] was among those who proposed the development of a new republican philosophy of education that would help raise "generations capable of judging their governments," in contrast to clerical teaching whose methods of passive learning were better suited, he declared, to "keep[ing] subjects submissive than … form[ing] citizens and men."[54]

Renouvier's contrasting of the republican pedagogical program with clerical styles of instruction was common among republicans. Church-run schools, it was claimed, offered an education that was authoritarian and inert. Several writers, including Durkheim and Jean-Marie Guyau, identified a similarity between hypnotic suggestion and illiberal forms of childrearing.[55] Republican pedagogy, on the other hand, was presented as spontaneous, non-coercive, and appealing to the child's whole being. Behind republican pedagogy's appeal to children's autonomy was a clear ulterior motive: to make children aware and appreciative of their essential condition of dependence within the social order. Dependency – not in the sense of inferiority, but of entanglement – was a condition elevated by republicans in this period and found political expression in the social philosophy of solidarism. With its theory centred on the generative interdependence of social units, solidarism "became the skeleton key to all social problems" in the fin de siècle.[56] Drawing on Louis Pasteur's findings in microbiology, the founder of solidarism, Léon Bourgeois, emphasized the mutual dependence of human beings and thus their duty towards one another.[57]

The primary aim of republican pedagogy, particularly foregrounded by its program of secular morality, was, as Yves Déloye has put it, to "lead human beings to a moral level in which the individual and the universal were combined, in which the human being was at once their own leader and their own servant."[58] Republican pedagogy sought to instil in children an understanding that their own personal fulfilment, on the one hand, and respect for and conformity to the rule of law governing society, on the other, were not only compatible but, in fact, mutually constitutive. Self-discipline and obedience were presented by republican pedagogues not as curtailments to individual liberty, but rather as the very conditions necessary for its fullest enjoyment.

This message was placed front and centre in the *Dictionnaire de pédagogie et d'instruction*, the monumental two-volume reference work edited by Ferdinand Buisson. Director of primary education from 1879 to 1896, before becoming professor of pedagogy at the Sorbonne and then entering politics in 1902, Buisson was one of the most prominent voices on republican education in this period. His dictionary (first published in 1887, with a revised edition appearing in 1911) – a work that Pierre Nora has described as the "cathedral of the primary school"[59] – brought together key voices in republican pedagogy, including Émile Durkheim. In his entry on "éducation" for the revised edition, Durkheim wrote that "liberty and authority have sometimes been opposed as if these two factors of education contradicted and limited one another. But this opposition is false. In reality, these two terms, far from excluding one another, involve one another. Liberty is the daughter of authority certainly. For to be free is not to do what one pleases; it is to be master of oneself, it is to know how to act by reason and do one's duty."[60] Freedom, Durkheim insisted, was synonymous with duty and responsibility.

In a similar vein, in his 1885 book *Manuel de pégagogie psychologique*, Jean Chaumeil, a republican educational theorist, even went so far as to argue that, *pace* Herbert Spencer, it was not liberty but rather discipline that brought greatest fulfilment and was the mark of human progress. "The best governed child," Chaumeil contended, "is the happiest, as the most civilized nation is the happiest, and the most barbarous, the least happy. Civilization is a real discipline."[61]

For republicans at the end of the nineteenth century, the good citizen was an individual who knew how to balance their own personal interests with the rights of others (represented by the republic: its laws and institutions). In effect, responsibility was to the republicans of the Third Republic what liberty had been to the revolutionaries of 1789. In his landmark 1762 text *Émile, ou De l'éducation*, Jean-Jacques Rousseau had argued that liberty and citizenship were resolutely incompatible, asserting that "forced to fight nature or social institutions, you have to choose between making a man or a citizen: because you cannot do both at the same time."[62] A century later, republican pedagogy forged a way through this apparent dichotomy, reconciling the ostensibly antagonistic poles of individual freedom and submission to authority through the concept of duty, which entailed voluntarily directing one's will to the interests of the collective. Breaking with a conception of society as consisting of individuals whose freedom should only be limited to the degree that it ensured the liberty of others, republicans at the end of the nineteenth century reconfigured autonomy in terms of positive, rather than negative freedom. This was part of an intellectual and political movement witnessed in various other parts of Europe and North America in this period, which brought progressivism and social democratic thought to bear on traditional philosophies of liberalism.[63]

In France, philosopher Alfred Fouillée emerged as a particularly key thinker for this transformed idea of freedom. In his 1900 book *La France au point de vue moral*, Fouillée argued that the Revolution of 1789 had precipitated devastating ruptures, with laissez-faire liberalism severing social bonds that led to general instability. Longstanding traditional social arrangements had been upset, Fouillée wrote, such that "instead of each person living in their native sphere, members of diverse classes experienced a sort of sudden 'mixing' ['*brassage*'], raising some, lowering others, making some rich, ruining others."[64] What was needed, he insisted, was a form of liberty that was socially embedded, where healthy social bonds would be nurtured through recognition of individuals' interdependence. Rather than pursuing unfettered rights, individuals needed to be made aware of their responsibilities. Out of this, Fouillée maintained, greater stability would emerge.

No longer viewed as a good in itself, liberty was promoted as a force that, in order to be truly enjoyed, needed to be moderated by morality. True liberty, late nineteenth-century republicans insisted, was not synonymous with licence, but rather with the constant drive to rein oneself in, to exercise self-control. Being free meant acting responsibly, respecting the rule of law and the rights of others. The stability of the republican system and the steady growth of society required that the individual see their own existence and well-being as contingent on the strength of broader social bonds. Republican pedagogy, then, aimed to instil in children the sense that restraining their own desires was, paradoxically, the very articulation of their freedom.

In 1883 philosopher Louis Liard, who would later serve as France's national director of higher education for almost two decades, neatly captured the late nineteenth-century republican theory of liberty in a textbook on morality and civic education written for primary school children. The exercise and enjoyment of liberty, Liard explained to his young audience, was predicated on being moderated by feelings of duty.[65] In a section of text printed in bold in order to drive home its importance, Liard wrote that liberty meant "taking a side [*prendre un parti*] that was not imposed on us, knowing that we could have taken the opposite side."[66] Crucially, Liard's child reader was made to understand that their desire and decision to act morally was an autonomous instinct generated within themselves, not imposed from without: "That rule of behaviour that you follow, no one imposed that on you; you accepted it; you adopted it yourself; you told yourself: I will be hardworking, sincere and obedient [*docile*], and you are [these things] because you willed it."[67]

In seeking to build loyal citizens and transform French society from the inside out, republican pedagogy set a high bar for its practitioners. According to Émile Durkheim, republican pedagogy "creates in man a new man."[68] The means through which education was to achieve this transformation was anchored in liberal ideas of the autonomy of the individual, including children; this "new man" had to emerge as though by nature, springing from within the child rather than being imposed from without. In contrast to the positions of earlier philosophers, including John Locke, who conceived of children as lumps of clay out of which the educator would sculpt the person, republican educational theorists in the late nineteenth century laid a conscious and heavy emphasis on respecting children's agency. Children were presented not as lumps of clay that needed to be impressed or as little animals that needed to be brought to heel, but rather as individuals who lacked experience and required gentle, though decisive guidance.

Republican pedagogy's emphasis on children's autonomy contrasted markedly with the thinking of one particularly influential social theorist in France, Frédéric Le Play. For Le Play, whose patriarchal ideas about strict discipline enjoyed support from Napoleon III during the Second Empire, children were by their nature anti-social beings who needed reining in by assertive teachers and fathers. "The most perfect societies remain constantly subjected to an internal invasion by little barbarians who bring back relentlessly all the bad instincts of human nature," he wrote. "Decadence becomes close at hand," Le Play continued, "as soon as societies neglect for a moment to counter this natural scourge with the discipline of upbringing [*éducation*]."[69] As Alan Pitt has noted of Le Play, "his political creed was never one of simple repressiveness," and "his thought represents one of the more subtle attempts to come to terms with modernity from a conservative viewpoint."[70] Although Le Play continued to exercise particularly important influence on conservatives in the second half of the nineteenth century, his ideas would also provide an important bridging force for liberals, including members of the SGP, as we shall see in the next chapter.

The teacher's purpose, Ferdinand Buisson explained in a lecture to students at the Sorbonne in 1899, was not "to extinguish the human being and … in one fell swoop [*en une fois*], transform him at our will [*à notre gré*]." Rather the teacher was "to take hold of the child, a mobile and plastic being," and shape the "thousand little fleeting acts" that made up their evolving behaviour.[71] This patient, sustained, almost invisible work replaced authoritarian methods of control and physical discipline with calm, reasoned persuasion. Over time, Buisson declared, the teacher's subtle interventions would win over the child, arousing responses in them that, through regular repetition, would gradually settle and solidify into spontaneous habits. Just as "dust which time will turn into hard granite," these actions would eventually become unthinking and inseparable from the child's very essence.[72] In short, actions would become internalized, automatic, and apparently spontaneous.

According to republican pedagogy, children were to develop a respect for order and self-discipline not out of obligation but out of desire. Teachers were called on to forge children's commitment to and investment in republican ideals and values without any apparent appeal to outside forces, especially physical forms of discipline. It was through an appeal to a child's emotions rather than simply their intellect, and by activating their will rather than repressing it, that this allegiance was to be secured. As one primary school teacher explained, rather than seeking to extract the child's obedience at any cost, allegiance aroused by "a mutual love between master and pupils" would make the child desire the rule and develop a love of order.[73] "If the discipline [that the teacher] obtains is only the result of fear," the teacher wrote, "if it provokes in the children terror of the master, hatred for the rule, for the law, however good the results obtained might appear … that discipline is bad."[74] The role of teachers was not to force compliance, but to inspire children's will to voluntarily conform through means that strongly appealed to their feelings. The abolition of corporal punishment in schools in 1882 was just one aspect of what was an overarching ethos of non-physical disciplinary measures intrinsic to republicanism's liberal foundations.[75]

In a famous directive issued to republican primary school teachers in 1883, Jules Ferry invited them to think of themselves as "the auxiliary and, in certain respects, the substitute for the father."[76] Affect served as a central tool of governance for republicans, enabling the extraction of responses and behaviours without any outward signs of pressure. By encouraging children to learn *through* the heart rather than *by* heart, and by appealing to their intuition, republican educators claimed to be *enhancing* children's natures rather than repressing them. According to Buisson, primary schooling should appeal to "sensual intuition," which was "the simplest, easiest form of intuition," "inherent to the human spirit itself."[77] Instead of rote learning or mechanical, repetitive exercises that "stiffen up" the intelligence,[78] in order to get the children to willingly submit to the desired conduct, teachers in republican primary schools were called on to stimulate and appeal to children's affections as would a loving parent. The teacher's role was compared to that of an attentive gardener, not seeking to torture or deform nature's growth, but rather to prepare the ground well, adjusting the conditions of heat and light, to allow the plant or child to fully flourish. In short, the good republican educator "lets nature act."[79]

Republicans' intense focus on childrearing was driven by a belief that childhood constituted a critical stage of life for the formation of the individual. A corollary of this was a perception that undesirable behaviours formed in these years and allowed to develop could only with difficulty later be corrected. At birth, as Émile Durkheim explained, republican developmental theory presumed every child to be born "an almost blank slate," naturally endowed with a particular personality, innate qualities, and abilities that made up their individual being (*être individuel*), but it was the use to which these were put that truly realized their potential as a social being (*être social*).[80] This made the education and upbringing of children socially critical; children were the hinge on which the general progress or collapse of society depended. At the same time that children inspired hope, they also aroused apprehension. Those that deviated from the path of virtue were a constant reminder of the precariousness of moral development and the urgency of timely intervention.[81] The very same qualities of malleability that made children so receptive to positive moral guidance also made them acutely vulnerable to immoral influences, the effects of which would, it was thought, be socially devastating. As veteran criminal justice reformer Félix Voisin told colleagues at an SGP meeting in 1903, "in the field of child protection, there are no mistakes to be made, because they can be irreparable."[82]

## Preventing the Decline into Criminality

Republicans' interest in understanding and harnessing children's development was inseparable from their concern about fighting anti-social tendencies and reducing recidivism in adults. Louis Puibaraud, a high-ranking official within the Paris police with a doctorate in law, spoke for many of his fellow criminal justice reformers when in 1893 he remarked to SGP members that the main priority when it came to young offenders was to "prevent the bad child from continuing to be bad, so that, growing up, he does not become a dangerous man for [society]."[83] Juvenile offenders, considered the least morally corrupted, were taken as representing the easiest point of entry for treatment. The effective management and containment of criminality rested on nipping it in the bud. This required intervention.

When it came to correcting criminality, although young people were seen to offer the greatest hope of redemption, they were also capable of arousing intense horror in adult observers, especially in violent crimes, as we saw in the case of Jacquiard and Vienny. In a lengthy report delivered in April 1904,[84] Jules Jolly, a Parisian lawyer, reminded his fellow reformers in the SGP that criminality could begin at any age, even among very young children. Indeed, he said, "one is sometimes shocked at [children's] precocity for evil."[85] "In earlier times," Jolly remarked, "one spoke readily of the innocence of the child; it was said that the child 'was born good.' Today, instead, it is said that he 'is born bad.'"[86] But Jolly found currency in neither Rousseauist idealism nor Lombrosian pessimism. Instead, he invoked Blaise Pascal's observation that "Man is neither angel nor beast" and declared that "the truth is that the child is born neither good nor bad."[87] The causes of juvenile delinquency, he said, were various: inattentive parents,[88] truancy,[89] and urban life.[90] But far and away the overriding cause, Jolly insisted, was a general lowering of moral standards.[91]

Rather than being governed by inherent characteristics or inherited propensities, Jolly insisted, children were adults in the making, socially embedded and ultimately responsive to the influences of those around them. The child, Jolly observed, "is a little impulsive being … a soft putty which no established and resistant form defends against the hand of the potter."[92] Children's vulnerability to negative manipulation was the very same condition that made their correction so necessary and so worthwhile. Most children, Jolly observed, were eminently salvageable on the important condition that "one gets to them in time."[93] While some small proportion of criminals might be of unsound mind ("en état de démence," as the penal codes of 1791 and 1810 would term it) and therefore could neither be held responsible for nor be prevented from committing further unlawful acts, most individuals who broke the law, it was generally believed, could exercise self-control.

Adolphe Guillot, one of France's most prominent advocates for child protection, was regularly confronted with young offenders through his role as a *juge d'instruction* (examining magistrate) in Paris. A guiding principle for him, and one that was generally shared by his fellow reformers, was that the younger the offender, the greater the chances of redeeming them. As Guillot observed in 1890, "every fallen man carries within him the power to lift himself up," but, he went on, "the chances of conversion decline with age."[94] Guillot also noted, however, that it was not just a matter of the offender's own desire to reform, but also society's greater willingness to invest in supporting that process in the case of younger offenders that was determinant. Contrasting the tasks of reforming the adult and the child, Guillot remarked that "to regenerate the adult, one must struggle against the weakening of the will, the strength of habits, the degradation of the personality, and the legitimate distrust of [public] opinion." When it came to regenerating the child, on the other hand, he pointed to "the pity which he arouses, the vital forces of his nature, the noble ambitions to motivate his efforts."[95] The key to effectively fighting crime, Guillot wrote, was "to act before the evil is too entrenched; hence the obvious need to take care of childhood above all."[96] In an article published a few years later, Guillot reiterated the argument; it was noble and right, he said, to believe in human freedom, in the power of repentance and the "resurrection of good in a fallen soul." However, one also had to recognize, he said, that "in the natural order of things, these transformations are only possible up to a certain point."[97]

Guillot offered the following snapshot of a juvenile's typical descent into a life of crime: Their first encounter with the forces of order usually began around the age of ten, when they were arraigned for vagrancy. These children, Guillot said, typically came from broken homes – often their widowed, alcoholic fathers had taken up with new partners who exercised no maternal care.[98] With no parent at home to supervise them during the day or ensure that they attended school, these children were left to their own devices. Even if they did make it to the schoolroom door, the teacher would often turn them away on account of their being sick, unwashed, or disruptive.[99] Refused entry to the "little palace" of the republican primary school, these children instead would fall prey to the diversions and spectacle of the street – the hawkers, musicians, drunks, and pickpockets.[100] Fellow jurist, philanthropist, and SGP member Georges Bonjean sketched a similar portrait of a child's initiation into criminality in his 1895 book *Enfants révoltés et parents coupables*. It all began with truancy, from which the child would progress to telling lies, aimlessly wandering the streets, consuming unsavoury entertainments, sleeping rough, begging, and inevitably stealing.[101]

Conservatives were quick to point the finger at republican pedagogy for causing a weakening of society's morals, which they argued was reflected in rising rates of juvenile offending. In their view, the removal of religious teaching from primary schools was responsible for opening French society up to rampant immorality. According to Lille lawyer Paul Drillon, society had become reliant on police officers to enforce moral behaviour. In his 1905 book *La Jeunesse criminelle*, Drillon argued that whereas people in the past had been directed by moral values instilled through Catholic teachings, under the force of republican ideology, they had become incapable of exercising self-restraint. This arrangement, Drillon insisted, was less effective than one in which God-fearing individuals constantly felt the all-seeing gaze of the Almighty on them; for, he wrote, "when the policeman is not present ... [and] there is no danger of being seen, when the cat is gone ... the mice dance."[102]

## Republican Primary Schooling and Juvenile Delinquency

The increase in juvenile delinquency rates despite the provision of universal primary education posed something of a conundrum. Indeed, it pushed against the popular aphorism commonly associated with Victor Hugo that to open a school was to close a prison. While the notion that education constituted a magic wand solution to criminality may have never been unanimously subscribed to,[103] by the turn of the century, increasing rates of juvenile offending despite compulsory primary education were placing even greater strain on its validity. For Ferdinand Buisson, however, the allegations regularly levelled at the republican primary school for fuelling juvenile criminality were among "the most serious [pieces of] nonsense and the silliest [pieces of] slander that the blind hatred of school in general and of the secular school in particular could have inspired."[104]

While republicans and conservatives tussled over the alleged connection between republican schooling and juvenile criminality, what both sides could agree on was that education alone was no certain defence against criminality. As Gabriel Tarde pointed out, skills in literacy and numeracy did not provide automatic insurance against anti-social behaviours. "Primary education," Tarde argued, "is only a tool, good or bad depending on the nature of its employment."[105] Jules Jolly, who was among those who agitated against republican pedagogy and the role it was playing in undermining solid moral conduct, told the SGP in 1904 that "it must be recognized that, as soon as the child of the people has learned to read, his little knowledge often only serves to expose him further. It expands his needs, his desires, his passions, without providing him with the means to satisfy them honestly. It invites him to read, and what he prefers to read are immoral books, low-level *feuilletons* or news stories about crimes, which dull his mind [*abêtissent*] and poison him."[106] An ability to read gave children access to new forms of corrupt influences, Jolly argued. And being naturally drawn to improper works, young people's morals were not strengthened by republican pedagogy, but rather were provided with "new weapons for doing harm."[107]

The idea that improved literacy might act as a bulwark against immorality was significantly complicated by the greater press freedoms that the republican government had introduced in July 1881. The literacy rate increased massively in the second half of the nineteenth century, from 60 per cent in the 1850s to just under 98 per cent by the outbreak of the First World War,[108] and produced an unprecedented number of readers hungry for reading materials, the quality of which was highly questionable. Newspapers, which exploded in number and readership around the turn of the century, were seen to pose an especially great danger to public morals. By 1880, Paris alone had sixty-seven daily newspapers, catering to around two million readers.[109] To censor the press would have aligned republicans with the authoritarian methods of Napoleon III, from whose system of governance they sought to distance themselves. So instead of restricting the freedom of writers and publishers, republicans insisted on the responsibility of the reader, leading to a concern about the vulnerabilities of "impressionable" audiences, especially women and children.[110] In his widely read 1895 work *La Psychologie des foules*, Gustave Le Bon expressed concern about the impressionability and moral contagion of the masses, which, he argued, carried dangerous implications for social and political life.[111]

The connection between culture and criminality arose during the investigation and trial in 1910 of Jacquiard and Vienny, the two teenage perpetrators of the "crime de Jully," but the debate about connections between culture and criminality stretched back many years. "Where do children who have learned to read complete their schooling and education?" asked Fouillée rhetorically in an article published in the *Revue des deux mondes* in 1897. "In the press," he responded, which he labelled "the big 'primary school.'"[112] Adventure stories, including the works of Jules Verne, wildly popular among young readers at the turn of the century, including Jacquiard and Vienny, and juveniles detained in Paris's Petite Roquette prison,[113] could have planted (unintentionally, on the part of the author) a seed of desire for a life of adventure in young readers' minds.[114] Guillot had similarly observed in his 1888 book *Paris qui souffre* that he had yet to encounter a murderer who had not received a solid primary education and not developed a preference for "bad literature."[115]

In 1908 Cesare Lombroso came up with a novel solution to the problem of education and immorality, suggesting to delegates at the inaugural International Congress of Moral Education held at the University of London that since education offered no protection against immorality and crime, all schools within prisons should be closed.[116] In his 1912 book on juvenile criminality, a French medical doctor observed that universal primary education was a double-edged sword, improving social standards, while at the same time sowing the seeds of discontent among the socially disenfranchised. The doctor claimed that education had produced a disgust for manual labour among many young people: "we have thrown … into young brains not prepared to receive and ripen them, many ideas that they could not understand, and they imagined, because they had some academic qualification, because they had been to school, because they knew how to read and write, that they knew everything, and that physical work was no longer for them."[117]

Overall, it was the problem of moral contagion posed by the free press and a secular state structure that most preoccupied French criminal justice reformers. From the 1890s, newspapers were competing for readers with eye-catching colour supplements and sensational headlines.[118] By the turn of the century, newspapers were so ubiquitous that they had become "the leitmotif of the street."[119] For Paul Drillon, newspapers were "the mother of all vices,"[120] while for Gabriel Tarde, "the little newspaper … alcoholizes the heart [of the schoolchild]."[121] Veteran prison reformer Charles Lucas told the SGP at the group's first meeting in 1877 that the press was obsessed with crime, dedicating so much column space to it that it was producing a "contagious imitation."[122] According to medical doctor and criminologist Paul Aubry, the press functioned as "an indirect mode of contagion, remote contagion by an intermediary."[123]

While reformers were divided over the extent to which, if at all, republican pedagogy was responsible for fuelling juvenile delinquency, one point on which they could all find common ground was that primary schooling alone was not the only cause. In fact, a more fundamental cause than the school, they believed, was the family. In an article published in 1897, Alfred Fouillée cautioned against drawing direct lines of causation between schooling and immorality. Responding to data indicating that young offenders overwhelmingly emanated from the public school sector, Fouillée argued that the fact that only two out of one hundred children prosecuted in Paris had attended a religious school was a result of the ability of such schools to be selective in the sort of pupils they admitted (a luxury not shared by public schools), and the tendency of families who chose to send their children to religious schools to raise them in a stricter home environment.[124]

The real cause of juvenile delinquency, Fouillée argued, was not the *école sans dieu* (the godless school), but rather the *école sans enfant* (the childless school). Figures published in the Parisian daily newspaper *Le Temps* indicated that more than twenty thousand children in the capital were not regularly attending primary school.[125] Children who did not go to school, he said, were the ones being brought before the criminal courts, reflecting a failure not on the part of teachers, but rather on the part of parents.[126] "The criminality of children," Fouillée concluded, "is in inverse ratio to their assiduousness at school."[127] This argument was subsequently defended by Gabriel Tarde.[128] However, although republican education did not cause the growing rates of criminality among young people, Fouillée believed that it had not done enough to prevent it.[129] In his view, increased incidents of juvenile offending were the sign of a general moral crisis whose main cause was the collapse of stable, attentive family life.[130]

## Challenges to Paternal Authority during the Third Republic

Along with the primary school, family life became a key focal area for legislators and policymakers in the Third Republic. Indeed, it is no exaggeration to say that the late nineteenth century represented a watershed moment in the history of relations between the French state and the family. For republicans, the nuclear family was the primary unit of social organization, the foundation upon which all other forms would be built. As republican legislator Émile Rey observed in 1900, the family was considered the "essential bedrock of civilized societies, the source of all fertile energies and all virtues."[131] Within republican pedagogy, children were to be encouraged to develop first an affection for their own families, and from there a similar affection for their teachers and classmates, which would prepare them later for feelings of patriotism and a deep-rooted sense of *esprit de corps*.[132] Republican ideology tolerated single-parent families but certainly did not encourage them. Although divorce was legalized in 1884, there were only limited grounds for obtaining it. In 1900, over a third of households had single parents (the majority of them headed by women).[133] Single-parent households, it was thought, contributed to juvenile delinquency. For instance, statistics gathered in 1909 revealed that of the 11,553 juveniles under sixteen charged with an offence, 2,722 of them had lost either one or both parents.[134]

Even if a child did have both parents present, depending on the style of parenting their healthy upbringing could nonetheless be compromised. For example, families in which an authoritarian *père de famille* ruled with an iron fist were considered morally unhealthy and socially dangerous. Similar to the reconfiguration of liberty in this period, the role of the state underwent a significant shift, transformed into an instrument of beneficence, which intervened not in order to restrict freedoms but, on the contrary, to realize them. The image of the ideal family structure also underwent considerable transformation during the Third Republic, away from a patriarchal Napoleonic model and towards a conjugal one in which responsibility for childrearing was shared between a stay-at-home mother and a paternalistic father. In concert, the mother and father, joined together in what Émile Durkheim termed the "organic solidarity" of a loving marriage, would exercise an affective authority and perform complementary gender roles that ultimately would produce a well-balanced, well-regulated child – the republic's ideal citizen.[135]

For Durkheim, the state and conjugal family were intimately entwined. Indeed, in his view, not only did the state act to regulate the conjugal family; it was also responsible for having produced it in the first place. "The conjugal family," Durkheim wrote, "would not have been born from the patriarchal family [or the paternal family or any mix of the two without the intervention of a new factor: the State]."[136] According to Durkheim, far from undermining the family, the state enhanced it, by serving as a mediator for the protection of those commonly considered its weakest members: women and children. In Durkheim's view, the state was warranted to intervene in family life by taking care of orphans who had not yet reached twenty-one (the age threshold for civil majority) and who had no guardian allocated to them, as well as being entitled to take action against a father who abused his power by disciplining his child too harshly and to divest of custody parents who neglected their children or allowed them to fall into juvenile delinquency. Rather than being an affront to the rights of the individual, the state acted to help realize those very rights, Durkheim argued. In this way, he maintained, "individualism increases with statism."[137] It was important, however, that the state not overstep the mark; it should intervene in family life only when necessary. Otherwise, the tyranny of husbands and fathers that republicans were attempting to fight would simply be transferred to the hands of the state.

In their ambition to raise devoted citizens and to stabilize the social and political order, republicans at the end of the nineteenth century introduced a raft of new laws aimed at protecting children from parental abuse or neglect. While some longstanding legislation empowered the state to take care of needy or at-risk children, this tended to apply only to orphans or children with unknown parents. These new laws on what was called "abandon moral" (moral abandonment) that were put in place in 1889 and 1898, as we shall see in further detail in chapter 4, effectively breached the magic circle that had long protected families – and most especially paternal authority – from regulation and intervention by the state.

The Napoleonic civil and penal codes of 1804 and 1810 respectively provided some basic groundwork for the emergence of the state's authority over children. However, the scope of the state's powers in those codes was limited and ultimately tended to reinforce rather than undermine the importance of the nuclear family and parental, especially paternal, influence. The most blatant manifestation of the state's traditional deference to paternal rights was the provision of *correction paternelle*, covered by articles 375–78 of the civil code. A relic of private justice reminiscent of the infamous *lettres de cachet* of the Old Regime,[138] correction paternelle entitled fathers (or, in their absence, mothers or legal guardians) to have their child under the age of twenty-one imprisoned. Detention, renewable on parental request, could extend to a period of up to one month for children aged under sixteen, and six months for those aged between sixteen and twenty-one. Although evidence indicates that it was not often practised, this remarkable provision was nonetheless a powerful illustration of the powers invested in parents, especially fathers, in the nineteenth century, with the support of the state. Ultimately, as Stephen Toth has argued, the importance of correction paternelle lies not so much in the frequency with which it was applied, but rather its symbolism, representing the all-powerful father, the *patria potestas*.[139]

Correction paternelle, legally sanctioned in France until 1935, was derived from a conception of the sovereignty of the family, within which the father played the role of law enforcer, adjudicator, and disciplinarian. During the Old Regime and throughout the nineteenth century until the Third Republic, fathers in France wielded an almost unlimited power over their offspring. This power was only temporarily interrupted in the 1790s when the killing of King Louis XVI (the father of the body politic) challenged the dynamics of power. As Honoré de Balzac put it, "In cutting off the head of Louis XVI, the Republic cut off the head of all family men [*pères de famille*]."[140] Ultimately, however, the violence of the Terror discredited the fraternal model of social organization prized by the revolutionaries and was followed by the restoration of paternal power. In the wake of the Terror, the father figure, rather than being seen as a symbol of hierarchy and an obstacle to personal fulfilment and social progress, enjoyed a rehabilitation, held up as a reassuring and steadying influence against revolutionary excess and authoritarian statism.[141]

This longstanding deference by the state towards paternal power derived from the belief that discipline within the family acted in step with the interests of the state and that therefore the absolute authority of fathers over their children worked to produce social peace. It was an idea neatly conveyed by Montesquieu in his 1721 work *Lettres persanes*, where he wrote that "nothing relieves magistrates more or disarms the courts more, nothing in short spreads more tranquility in a State, where customs [*mœurs*] always do better than laws, than to give fathers great authority over their children."[142] Even though, as we shall see, the rights of fathers were increasingly chipped away from the end of the nineteenth century onwards, a notion persisted that within the family, it was fathers who held greater authority over their offspring than mothers. Only in 1970 would French law be reformed such that mothers and fathers were invested with equal powers within the family unit.[143]

By the turn of the twentieth century, the defiance against state tyranny and deprivations of liberty that had so exercised revolutionaries a century earlier had metamorphosed into a concern about protecting children of weak, immoral, or even simply absent fathers.[144] Concerns about child protection came to the fore and fathers' powers over their children were increasingly questioned. In the final decade of the nineteenth century, the idea took hold that the state might dictate the terms of fathers' disciplining of their own children and that it might intervene and deprive parents of custody of their own children in cases where evidence pointed to abuse or neglect. This represented a major shift in established policy and thinking. Instead of turning a blind eye to the actions of parents, particularly fathers, towards their children, legislators came to see that in order "to save the children, it becomes necessary to treat the parents as enemies," as Adolphe Guillot put it in a report for the 1895 International Prison Congress (sometimes also referred to as the International Penitentiary Congress) held in Paris.[145] Child-saving required a fundamental recalibrating of the authority of parents, especially fathers.

The final decades of the nineteenth century witnessed a transformation in the ideal father figure. As Pierre Rosanvallon has written, a paternal model replaced the patriarchal one, and "the sovereign-father gave way to the teacher-father."[146] This shift was supported by a concurrent transformation in women's roles within the family. Republicans laid great emphasis on the role of women as mothers and wives. Mothers were attributed unique and natural abilities to speak to the sensory experiences of their biological children and nurture their early development.[147] In children's earliest years, mothers were to be their principal carers and teachers, before then ceding ground and taking on collaborative responsibility alongside the republican primary school teacher. Women's presumed innate gentleness made them ideally suited to initiating the child into a style of rearing that the primary school teacher would then develop further: guided learning, in which the exertion of force was to be avoided.[148] In the years preceding the passage of the 1912 law on juvenile courts, some reformers, including the legislation's sponsor Ferdinand Dreyfus, similarly advocated for a prominent role for women in children's courts, pointing to their superior capacity to understand children's inner workings.[149] This emphasis on women's central role in childrearing reinforced the notion that the ideal family was held together through bonds of affection and complementary influence.

In 1901 Jules Jolly observed that "the reformatory [*maison de correction*] is better than the street. But the family is better still ... on the condition that it is well guided in its task and controlled if needed."[150] While standard republican discourse suggested that sound morals were within the gift of every well-organized family, the standards of what constituted "good parenting" were characterized by conditions more readily satisfied by a single-income, middle-class family structure with a père de famille breadwinner and stay-at-home *femme au foyer* able to keep an eye on children and ensure their school attendance. This left children from working-class families especially vulnerable, and most at risk of state intervention, as we shall see in chapter 4.

The fact that on reaching adolescence, working-class children, in the absence of schooling provisions beyond primary school level, routinely entered the workforce – a space that was increasingly precarious, as a result of the disappearance of apprenticeships – further exacerbated the dangers. To even secure an apprenticeship was increasingly uncommon by this time, with precarious work increasingly the norm. The apprenticeship system had begun its decline with the revolution at the end of the eighteenth century, when legislators had suppressed guilds and made apprenticeships optional rather than compulsory. By the start of the twentieth century, they had become almost totally obsolete.[151] The collapse of apprenticeships, according to the prominent criminologist Henri Joly writing in 1889, forced young workers to wander from job to job, eventually leading them to a life of vagrancy, pimping, and petty crime.[152]

## Filling the Perilous Void of Adolescence

In his 1909 book *La Criminalité dans l'adolescence*, one of the first dedicated studies of adolescent criminality to appear in French, sociologist Guillaume Duprat argued that adolescence, the start of which he located at puberty, was matched by a particular type of criminality. This criminality, he wrote, was "characterized by violent passions or cruelty, audacity, cynicism, moral callousness, brutal aggression, sudden [*prompte*] action."[153] While younger children typically committed offences like begging, vagrancy, and petty theft, Duprat argued, adolescents tended to perpetrate more serious crimes, and did so with a disturbing nonchalance. Like most commentators in this period, Duprat gendered adolescents as male and pointed to their liminal quality, "frequently oscillat[ing] between early manliness [*virilité*] and late childishness."[154] What was particularly disturbing, according to Duprat, was that while children were not considered active and capable members of society, as a result of labour and education laws that controlled their entry into the adult world of work, adolescents had a more ambiguous status, gradually making their way into the adult world and becoming full-fledged social actors.[155]

Official statistics gathered by the French ministry of justice in the final decades of the nineteenth century and at the dawning of the twentieth painted a worrying portrait of the nation's youth, particularly in urban centres. Between 1880 and the 1900s, for instance, young people under the age of twenty-one accounted for more than half of those arrested in Paris each year.[156] In light of such figures, Albert Giuliani, a doctoral student in law at the University of Dijon, declared in 1908 that "adolescents are an army … the active army of crime."[157] If children represented the most optimistic face of the republic, adolescents embodied its darker side. Adolescence was recognized by reformers in this period as a dangerously unregulated stage of life, a period when passions clouded a person's capacity to reason and when young people began to live more independent lives. Wracked by sudden impulses and exercising greater independence than children, adolescents represented the perils of human development. In order to emerge safely out of adolescence, a naturally turbulent stage, young people required a solid upbringing and social guidance, especially from parents. Unpredictable, noncompliant, and liable to violent outbursts, adolescents embodied much of what provoked anxiety in authorities at the end of the nineteenth century and were particularly prominent figures in French culture and society in the fin de siècle.[158]

The dangers of adolescence, it was thought, were particularly acute for working-class youth who usually entered the workforce at this stage of life. Middle-class boys and girls, by contrast, would either continue on to further schooling or, at least, remain under the watchful eye of their attentive, stay-at-home mothers. Although reformers regularly spoke of an age-bounded category of troublesome youth – that is, one that was ostensibly universal – they had a particular class and gender in mind: the problematic young delinquent was working-class, male, and, especially from the 1890s onwards, adolescent. Michelle Perrot has argued that "childhood is more of a neutral term. Youth is thought of in the masculine sense."[159] As neither children nor adults, adolescents were attributed a status by republican educators, medical doctors, academics, and political reformers that was suspended perilously between private and public life, dependence and independence.[160] What was especially worrying about adolescents was that, unlike children who were required to attend school, they escaped the net of institutional oversight provided by the state and its representatives, especially teachers. In a 1908 article printed in *Le Matin* newspaper, Théodore Steeg, a radical socialist deputy in the French parliament, observed that "we must have the courage to admit it, adolescence, in our society, is morally abandoned."[161]

In the fin de siècle, there was an increasing concern among republicans that the institutional support provided by the primary school evaporated into nothingness on children's graduation, leaving young people vulnerable to anti-social (that is, anti-republican) influences. Adolphe Guillot lamented the condition of contemporary youth, describing the dangers encountered by adolescents who left primary school to enter the workforce and who became prey to myriad immoral temptations (especially alcohol and literature). Guillot described these youths as "birds whose cage doors are opened on a stormy day; they do not have time to take their direction, hardly have they spread their wings when the most violent currents drag them into irresistible whirlwinds and throw them all broken on the ground."[162]

For working-class children, especially boys, age thirteen became recognized as a transition point into a dangerous period marked not only by the biological instabilities of puberty, but also by a lack of supervision and guidance. As Jules Jolly remarked to the SGP, adolescence was the phase when, let loose from the republican primary school that had taken charge of their education and, even more importantly, their moral development, these youngsters would enter the workforce. In these years, Jolly observed, "they escape from the direction of the schoolmaster, without falling under the effective authority of the father, and all this at the time when passions are starting to awaken in them; they thus become easy prey for the temptations of the street."[163] For boys, with the introduction of universal military service in 1889, this period of institutional neglect would be brought to an end with their enlistment in the military. For girls, meanwhile, it would persist for the rest of their lives.

In a series of meetings held in 1904, the SGP dedicated their discussions to the issue of juvenile delinquency. Predictably enough, various members with conservative leanings took to the floor to condemn state-run primary schools for fuelling the problem. Republican schooling, they argued, was raising young people with false expectations and unrealizable ambitions, sowing a sense of contempt for manual labour, and preparing them inadequately for entry into the workforce.[164] François-Charles Merveilleux du Vignaux, a devout Catholic, jurist, and former deputy in the National Assembly, asserted that children educated on the benches of republican primary schools had been overly familiarized with their rights at the expense of their sense of duty and responsibility. The republican curriculum's emphasis on intellectual matters, he argued, had left French children unaccustomed to and indeed contemptuous of manual labour.[165]

In a similar vein, Georges Bonjean told the SGP that the certificat d'études primaires (the qualification presented to children on satisfactory completion of primary school and which was required to be presented to prospective employers) was not a proof of achievement but rather "a certificate of incapacity" that only inflated youngsters' false sense of entitlement.[166] Prominent jurist Henri Robert asserted that "children are given every desire and not the means to realize them, every wish and not the means to content themselves, every passion and not the means to satisfy them."[167] On graduating from primary school, Robert went on, these young people were unwilling to take their place in the workforce and instead became idle and frustrated with damaging consequences: "lazy and useless [*raté*], he is ripe for delinquency, then for crime."[168] Henri Lévy-Alvarès, an eminent Parisian lawyer, warned that the republican education system was giving children an overinflated sense of their rights that, in the case of boys, once they reached voting age, would result in them casting a vote in favour of the most radical candidates.[169]

While conservatives regularly held the republican school curriculum responsible for sowing the seeds of social dysfunction, they also expressed concern about the period that came *after* young people had completed primary school. It was a concern shared by republicans themselves. In an article published in the *Revue pédagogique* in 1895, Paul Beurdeley, mayor of Paris's well-to-do eighth arrondissement, wrote that "almost everything has been done for children while they are at primary school." After that, however, young people entered a "dangerous zone" that, in the case of boys, lasted until they enlisted in the army. "After school!" Beurdeley lamented. "What becomes of the child, what sort of young man, what sort of [adult] man does he become? Are all the sacrifices and efforts gone to waste?"[170] Beurdeley's silence on the absence of structural supports for adolescent girls, which was typical of commentators, is telling: boys were the problem.

For republicans, part of the solution was seen to reside in military service. With the introduction of universal military service in 1889, all boys would enter the army, which was effectively transformed into a "school of moralization," as we shall see in chapter 5. But this "school of moralization," because it did not immediately follow on from primary school, did not entirely address the problem of institutional neglect. Indeed, for several years after departure from the republican primary school and enlistment in the army, the state's supervision of youth evaporated. In an attempt to counter the institutional neglect of adolescents, in the 1890s republicans introduced a program of higher primary education (*enseignement primaire supérieur*), and a flurry of other organizations and events also sprang up, including the Boy Scouts, *colonies de vacances*, Catholic youth groups, *fêtes de l'adolescence* (run by Freemasons and providing a secular substitute for First Communion), and various sporting associations.[171] The purpose of these groups was not to help facilitate social advancement,[172] but rather to prolong adults' supervision of young people's lives outside of the family unit. This was elucidated particularly clearly in a short intervention by Léon

Bourgeois, the radical statesman generally considered the founder of the philosophy of solidarism, on the subject of expanding adolescent workers' access to education beyond primary school level. These were not courses for adults, Bourgeois wrote. "The age we are presently concerned with is not the age of maturity," he observed. "It's the age of formation, that is to say the age of danger." The aim of higher learning beyond the primary school, he remarked, was not simply to provide professional or general instructional courses that might increase knowledge, but rather "to form the mind and character and prepare [the young person] for life."[173]

According to Jean Grosmolard, director of the Colonie correctionnelle d'Eysses, an institution for particularly turbulent delinquent boys, criminality among adolescents was partly attributable to the state's neglect of young people once they had left primary school.[174] Journalist Henry Bérenger contended that the state's abandonment of young people from the moment they left primary school was "the most serious danger threatening the secular State."[175] While republicans concentrated their attention on the primary school, they "were abandoning adolescents to nothingness."[176] Bérenger also pointed to the dangers of discharging children from the highly regulated environment of the primary school right at the onset of puberty.[177] In 1913, Henri Robert described the stage of life that began after leaving primary school as "the dangerous age" – a period when, "imbued with rudimentary knowledge, the adolescent believes himself capable of anything. He cannot yet earn a living. He will easily get into the habit of idleness and bad company."[178] From there, it was believed, a decline into criminality would be almost inevitable. Indeed, as Louis Albanel observed in his 1900 book *Le Crime dans la famille*, although a child, if riddled with vice and inadequately supervised by their family, could become a criminal from an early age, the most dangerous point in a young person's development in terms of their proclivity to crime was considered to be the moment when they left primary school and entered the workforce.[179]

## Conclusion

When it came to responding effectively to criminality, the imperative to ensure healthy child development and the urgent need for intervention dovetailed with a significant shift in thinking about the importance of individual responsibility. While earlier in the nineteenth century the proverb "il faut que jeunesse se passe" had suggested that youth was a stage of life that could – and indeed *should* – be simply waited out, by the fin de siècle this laissez-faire approach was replaced with one in which the state claimed for itself the role of active intermediary. In this way, as we shall see in later chapters, from the final decade of the century, the state in France was invested with increasing powers to intervene in young people's lives in order to break the cycle of not only demonstrably criminal behaviours but also *potentially* disturbing tendencies: what Italian criminologist Raffaele Garofalo referred to in 1878 as "témibilité,"[180] and Michel Foucault a century later would term "dangerosité."[181] For authorities and reformers, it was not the offence committed that was seen as significant so much as the social conditions that lay behind it, for it was these that were believed to set a person down the pathway to crime. For this reason, an "offence" like vagrancy was considered as socially dangerous as murder, as it indicated certain tendencies that, if left untreated, would take root and worsen into serious and intractable criminal behaviours.[182]

Alongside the great optimism about young people acting as instruments for France's moral regeneration was an intense sense of urgency about the need to intervene in children's upbringing in order to secure this happy future. There was an acute sense that children were the product of social conditioning and needed to be protected from bad influences and unwholesome conditions in order to grow into good, healthy adult citizens. French jurist and republican statesman Pierre de Casabianca expressed a commonly held idea when he told the International Prison Congress in Washington, DC, in 1910 that "just as man is whole in the child, so too does the moral health of a nation depend on its youthful generations."[183]

Human perfectibility was believed to be negatively correlated with age; without timely and determined intervention, the juvenile offender would all too easily evolve into the adult recidivist. For French psychiatrists, the child was seen to share basic characteristics with the most intractable antisocial figure of the time: the vagabond, who, as Jacques Donzelot has written, "displayed to the maximum all the pathological effects of the weaknesses of childhood when these were not corrected or checked in time."[184] Young people, especially children, were understood to be acutely vulnerable to bad influences. Yet it was also this very same quality that was thought to make them most receptive to reformative measures. In order to effectively deal with criminality, especially recidivism, reformers believed, one had to concentrate attention and efforts on the young.

CHAPTER 2

# The Société générale des prisons and Reforming Criminal Justice

One day in March 1877, a group of well-to-do men assembled in a spacious apartment not far from the Madeleine in Paris's elegant eighth arrondissement. Their host, René Bérenger, was a man who commanded considerable respect. Labelled by historian Robert Nye "the greatest late-century penal reformer,"[1] Bérenger was a jurist by training and senator in France's parliament. He was also the son of the late Alphonse Bérenger (commonly referred to as Bérenger de la Drôme), one of the country's most esteemed prison reform advocates of the nineteenth century.[2] Within the walls of Bérenger's apartment, high above the pungent smells and general hubbub of the city streets below, this large group of around fifty "enlightened and generous" men, as veteran reformer Charles Lucas would describe them, set to work on laying the contours for a new association focused on improving conditions in the nation's prisons.[3] Two months later, in the town hall of the first arrondissement, just across the road from the Louvre museum, the group celebrated their official inauguration.[4] The Société générale des prisons (SGP) was born.

Initially, the SGP was squarely focused on encouraging investment in prison construction and implementation of cellular confinement, following the passage of an important law in 1875 that, as we shall see, had come out of a parliamentary inquiry in the early 1870s. Over the years, this initial focus on prisons would expand to encompass almost all aspects of criminal justice. Although the treatment of juvenile offenders was just one aspect of the group's concerns, it was a highly prominent one, whose importance only increased with time.

Within the history of juvenile justice reform, the SGP played a vital role in the formulation of key policies and pieces of legislation relating to the treatment of child and adolescent offenders, including, importantly, the 1912 law on courts for children and adolescents. A central forum for debate and dissemination of ideas, the SGP served as a testing ground for new practices of responding to criminality, including among young people. In one way or another, concerns about juveniles – the future citizens of the nation – were closely entangled with all of these practices. From the start, the treatment of juveniles was a core preoccupation for the SGP as the group sought to make France's prison system (and its system of criminal justice, more generally) more effective and socially useful.

In the final decades of the nineteenth century, the SGP acted as a central hub for the expression and testing of ideas about age, responsibility, and criminality – themes that will be further developed in later chapters. This chapter examines the SGP itself, exploring the constitution of its membership, and situating the group within the longer history of nineteenth-century prison reform. The years between the SGP's founding in 1877 and the First World War represent the period of greatest influence for the group. These years were also vitally important in the reconfiguring of the conceptualization of criminal justice, punishment, and the treatment of young offenders. Young people, as we saw in the previous chapter, were a major preoccupation for French society at this time, and they similarly lay at the heart of the SGP's reform program, which, from the start, was dedicated to addressing the problem of repeat offending.

Within the SGP's range of concerns, juvenile offenders represented the lowest-hanging fruit: least set in their ways, it was believed that their immoral and criminal behaviours could most readily be corrected or, even better, prevented from manifesting in the first place. When it came to the pace and extent of their desired social change, SGP reformers were, at best, moderates. What they sought to achieve in reforming criminal justice was to make the law and methods of punishment function more effectively in order to produce greater social stability. Breaking the cycle of crime was one of their primary goals, and in this the treatment of juvenile offenders was a critical part of their mission.

Of the SGP's illustrious membership, the most active participants included various prominent senators, including Bérenger, Théophile Roussel, and Ferdinand Dreyfus, who would take many of the concerns explored within the group into the hallowed halls of the French parliament for formulation into law. Among the most important pieces of legislation to have been significantly shaped by the SGP were the 1885 law on preventing recidivism (sponsored by Bérenger), the 1889 child protection law (sponsored by Roussel),[5] the 1891 suspended sentences law (also sponsored by Bérenger), and the 1893 law on short prison terms.[6] The SGP was also crucial for the passage of the 1912 law on juvenile courts (sponsored by Dreyfus). Grounded in a belief in their own superiority as upstanding members of civil society, SGP members considered it their overarching duty to help guide and support government policy on all aspects of criminal justice. Young offenders were at the heart of the growing emphasis on prevention that came to dominate the agenda of many reform initiatives by the end of the century.

The SGP's members – and Bérenger chief among them – embodied the ethos of the group, which aimed to function as a bridge between the state and philanthropy, between government and civil society. Consciousness-raising was one of the group's central aims from the start; members sought to awaken public awareness for the need for prison reform and lobby government for necessary but costly improvements and investment. As a group, the SGP had something of a hybrid status. It was many things at once: a space in which elites could exchange and debate reformist ideas on criminal justice, a vehicle for the wider dissemination of those ideas, and a lobby group for pressuring government to enact their desired reforms. It was simultaneously, as historian Martine Kaluszynski has observed, a "laboratory of criminal justice legislation" and a "private extra-parliamentary commission forever in session" that served as "both a place for conceptualizing juridical norms through the development or application of knowledge about crime and a political lobby group guiding official and non-official action."[7]

While SGP members shared many fundamental beliefs and objectives, there was always a diversity of views about the best means of achieving them. For instance, as we will see in further detail in later chapters, some members, following Bérenger's lead, urged the deployment of alternatives to the penitentiary for first-time lawbreakers. Others, meanwhile, warned of the dangers of engaging in what they saw as excessive indulgence. Over the years, these two poles would regularly confront each other, with their battle lines particularly well drawn during discussions about the relative virtues of physical forms of punishment. This included the use of corporal punishment to discipline children and the application of the death penalty for perpetrators of serious crimes. While the more liberal-leaning members, including Bérenger, urged restraint when applying corporal punishment to children, those in the more conservative camp, including Henri Joly, considered such measures not only necessary but, moreover, positively edifying.[8] Similarly, during debates over capital punishment, while Bérenger asserted the superiority of the prison as a deterrent against further criminality,[9] Joly argued instead that only the death penalty was capable of offering certain defence.[10]

The SGP was far from being the first prison reform group organized in France, and these Third Republic reformers very much saw themselves as part of a longer tradition. They connected their system of criminal justice to the theories of Enlightenment *philosophes* and revolutionary legislators for whom rehabilitating the criminal was part of the wider project of national regeneration.[11] Even more particularly, they conceived of themselves as the heirs to the reformist movement of liberals of the Restoration and July Monarchy periods. Yet although these late nineteenth-century reformers saw themselves as continuing a campaign for criminal justice reform begun decades earlier, the experiences of their predecessors served more as cautionary tales than inspiring models to be emulated. In the end, the program of SGP reformers was even more ambitious and, ultimately, more successful than that of their predecessors. Among their most lasting legacies would be the reshaping of juvenile justice.

The SGP's founding in 1877 coincided with a dramatic moment in French political history and a turning of the tide in the fortunes of republicans as a governing force. Less than a week before the group's formal establishment in June, the national government was thrown into disarray by the events of the so-called *crise du seize mai* (16 May crisis). This constitutional crisis had seen the nation's monarchist leader, Patrice de MacMahon, avail himself of the significant powers invested in the office of president to dismiss the prime minister, Jules Simon, a moderate republican, and install his own government. The parliament, however, refused to accept MacMahon's new government, prompting new elections in which republicans – for the first time – won the majority. MacMahon's failure to dictate the contours of the government not only signalled the victory of the authority of the parliament over that of the president but also marked a crucial turning point in both France's governing structure and the political fortunes of republicans. Out of the crisis came the retraction of the president's extensive powers and the empowerment of the parliament. In effect, "the republic and parliamentarianism became synonymous."[12] In the years following, as republicans finally became a governing force within the parliament, the Third Republic, which until this point had been essentially led by politicians at best not fully invested in a republican political structure (and in some cases, including MacMahon, actively hostile to it), actually became republican in more than name alone. This transformation of the parliament would have a profound effect on all aspects of French society, including criminal justice.

## Improving Imprisonment: The Haussonville Commission and the Origins of the SGP

The immediate impetus for the SGP's creation was the Haussonville Commission, a major parliamentary inquiry into imprisonment undertaken in the early 1870s. The commission was spearheaded by Gabriel Paul Othenin de Cléron d'Haussonville (Count Haussonville), a twenty-eight-year-old deputy of aristocratic origins and with centre-right political leanings.[13] Loosely reminiscent of the investigation into the state of prisons in the United States carried out by Alexis de Tocqueville and Gustave de Beaumont in the 1830s (a project in which Haussonville's own father had been involved), the Haussonville Commission was tasked with preparing first-hand reports on the current state of prisons within France and internationally. These reports, which were subsequently collated and ultimately filled eight printed volumes, constitute what historian Bernard Schnapper calls "the first political manifestation of a group of men who sought ... to promote social lawmaking."[14]

The commission's findings were not encouraging: France's prisons were chronically overcrowded, with little or no effort made to sort and separate detainees by age or gender. The negative effects of this were both moral and physical; in one prison in the Midi-Pyrénées, syphilis was spread between male and female prisoners who were detained in the same quarters.[15] All delegates agreed that the only solution was the implementation of cellular detention of all prisoners. Although isolation was acknowledged to carry risks of mental disturbance, this was said to be less concerning than the very real damage caused by incarceration in shared spaces[16] and would be offset by regular work and a daily exercise regimen undertaken out of doors.[17]

The detention of juveniles was a major area of concern for the Haussonville Commission. The issue's importance and distinction was reflected in the fact that one of the inquiry's weighty volumes was dedicated solely to the subject. Overseeing the report on juveniles was Félix Voisin, member of the National Assembly from the centre-left. Later, Voisin would go on to become prefect of police and a founding member of the SGP. In 1878 he created the Société de protection des engagés volontaires élevés sous la tutelle administrative, an important group for juvenile offenders, as we shall see in chapter 5. Voisin's summary report on juvenile detention for the Haussonville Commission reflects the general mindset of reformers like himself who would go on to form the SGP a few years later. In his report, Voisin wrote that no matter the offence in question, young people were always deserving of a degree of indulgence because of their incomplete state of moral development, and that those who were held in detention (whether as a convicted offender or acquitted but detained under Article 66 of the penal code) always required an educative, reformative response in order to ensure their healthy re-entry into society.[18]

Such a view was hardly controversial; after all, the idea that juvenile offenders should be treated to a form of detention that improved their morals and readied them for release had long been enshrined in legislation in France. The law "sur l'éducation et le patronage des jeunes détenus" (on the upbringing [and education] and patronage of young inmates), brought into being by the French parliament on 5 August 1850, required that all juvenile detainees be provided with a moral, professional, and religious upbringing (*éducation*). This piece of legislation, known as the Corne law (named after its sponsor, Hyacinthe Corne), stands as a landmark in the history of juvenile justice, and indeed criminal justice in France more broadly.[19] It defined the contours of juvenile corrections for almost a century, until it was finally rendered obsolete in 1945. What Félix Voisin and others concerned about the detention of juveniles observed in the early years of the Third Republic, however, was that although the 1850 law officially stipulated a particular treatment for young people, the reality was very different.

The plight of juvenile detainees was an issue that inspired particular compassion among delegates of the Haussonville Commission. For his part, Haussonville declared young people to be at once the saddest and the most deserving category of prisoner: "the saddest because nothing is more distressing than the spectacle of precocious corruption; the most rewarding [*intéressant*] because nowhere are efforts crowned with such immediate success and do rewards so quickly follow the good works [*l'œuvre*]."[20] The Haussonville Commission's investigation into the detention of juveniles revealed a system in crisis, and not as a result of ignorance or an absence of legislative structure, but rather as a result of inadequate means. For instance, Haussonville reported that although the Corne law of 1850 required that juveniles always be held separately from adult detainees, a lack of adequate infrastructure meant that, in practice, this stipulation was only respected in Paris. "The number of [regional prisons] where there is a permanent section solely turned over to young prisoners," Haussonville observed, "is infinitely small."[21]

The commission's exposure of deplorable conditions of detention and a failure to implement existing legislation were key motivators driving the formation of the SGP a few short years later. The links between the Haussonville Commission and the SGP are obvious; over three-quarters of the national inquiry's fifteen delegates went on to become members of the SGP in the group's first year. Haussonville himself was one of the SGP's founding members, as were Félix Voisin and of course René Bérenger.[22]

In his obituary for Bérenger, published in the *Revue des deux mondes* in 1915, Henri Joly described his fellow reformer as being "not moderately energetic, but energetically moderate."[23] No supporter of revolutionary politics, on his election to the National Assembly in 1871, Bérenger had openly declared his support for the conservative government of Adolphe Thiers and his opposition to the revolutionary Paris Commune. He asserted his commitment to "fighting with all my energy the elements of disorder, violence and hatred for ideas of property, work and religion, which too often in our country have compromised liberty."[24] As a senator (appointed for life in 1875), Bérenger was a self-professed amalgam of disparate political and religious doctrines; in 1899 he described himself to his fellow senators as "a firm republican though conservative, and I intend to be and remain a very firm Catholic."[25]

As a reformer and politician, Bérenger embodied the conciliatory stance between Catholicism and republicanism that was in fact characteristic of the Third Republic, despite frequent assertions that Catholics and republicans were antipathetic. Aligned on many key issues, including family morality, paternal authority, child obedience, opposition to extramarital relations, sanctity of private property, and the importance of temperance, Catholics and republicans, Theodore Zeldin writes, were "occupied by the problems of death, guilt, conscience, the distinction of the valuable from the trivial and the place of the individual in the universe."[26] While other historians have disputed Zeldin's assessment,[27] it does resonate in the case of Bérenger. Bérenger was the quintessential moderate republican. As such, the rise of radical republicanism around the turn of the century pushed him into an increasingly conservative position, and his active campaigning for public morality (especially prostitution) earned him the pejorative label "père le pudeur" (father modesty).[28] What can be said is that in his support for political democracy and individual freedom, especially of conscience, Bérenger's ideas were generally in keeping with those promoted by moderate republicans in the final decades of the nineteenth century. Bérenger and like-minded reformers, such as the legal scholar Raymond Saleilles and high-ranking statesman Jules Simon, believed that social harmony and stability were forged through the protection of people's right to freedom of belief, including a form of secularism that defended a person's freedom of conscience rather than repressing it.

What perhaps defined Bérenger most of all was his unwavering championing of regulation – both by society and within the individual. This commitment had no doubt been instilled very early in his development. Born and raised within a household steeped in the political vision of his father and the *juste milieu* philosophy of the July Monarchy, Bérenger was, according to Henri Joly, driven by a determination to "alleviate recklessness and … prevent excess."[29] As an instrument of social regulation, the law, Bérenger believed, should serve as a counterweight to liberty, preventing it from spilling over into licence. Bérenger was also actively involved in parliamentary debates on the right to association, particularly for industrial unions. Here, too, his vision was one of balancing antagonistic forces in the interests of liberty. According to Joly, Bérenger was scrupulous in his dedication to this issue, seeking to ensure that the interests of workers were protected but only to the extent that this would help preserve "the national equilibrium" and not in such a way that would create a state within the state.[30] Bérenger's vision of liberty, as Joly described it, was one that "supported, assisted, moralized, ensured the provision of justice and protection for all legitimate interests."[31]

For Bérenger, prison reform was part and parcel of his general campaign for regulation and stability. In 1903, looking back on the SGP's creation a quarter of a century earlier, Bérenger painted a picture of a nation that had been in crisis, torn apart by conflict and war. He admitted to fellow SGP members how initially the suggestion for a parliamentary inquiry into the state of prisons had left him dumbfounded. The early 1870s, he said, when France was trammelled by "the most terrible anxieties [*angoisses*]" and "the weight of disasters overwhelmed every heart," had hardly seemed a propitious time for embarking on a costly and distracting investigation, which would surely serve only to further weaken an already enfeebled country. However, Bérenger went on, members of the National Assembly had shown great wisdom in recognizing that the key to rebuilding the nation was to reconstruct it thoroughly, "to make a new France through the renovation of its institutions and through liberty."[32]

One of the inquiry's major practical outcomes was parliament's passage of the law of 5 June 1875, which generalized the implementation of cellular imprisonment throughout France's departmental prisons (*maisons d'arrêt*) – that is, the institutions where convicted offenders serving shorter sentences were held. These were the institutions where the majority of prisoners were detained. The bill, introduced by Bérenger, addressed many of the core shortcomings identified by the Haussonville Commission. In response to the moral and physical contagion found to be running rife in prisons, the 1875 legislation enshrined the principle of separate detention, especially for detainees awaiting trial and those sentenced to short prison terms. It also stipulated the separation of prisoners on the basis of gender and the creation of special institutions for men and women prisoners. Furthermore, the 1875 law set down that all prisoners under the age of forty sentenced to more than three months in prison were to be provided with basic education and moral (that is, religious) guidance – finally realizing the ambitions of reformers from decades earlier.[33] The purpose of isolation was to protect prisoners from immoral behaviours and influences, while the provision of basic education and moral guidance was intended to produce their redemption.[34] In this way, the prison cell, as one SGP member would later put it, would serve as "a sort of bath of conscience."[35]

The 1875 law on cellular confinement represented a major turning point in the official conceptualization of incarceration in France.[36] It was also crucially important in prompting the formation of the SGP two years later. Indeed, according to Gordon Wright, the group's "central purpose (though undeclared) was to use the society as a pressure group for the cellular idea" of imprisonment.[37] The need for such a pressure group was considerable, with both the general population and the government hostile to these measures. Opposition to the idea of detaining prisoners in individual cells rested primarily on one overriding consideration: cost. The expense of constructing and maintaining cellular prisons was a major and longstanding obstruction for French authorities throughout the nineteenth century. While in the 1840s some cellular prisons had been built, these were on a modest scale, and from the mid-1850s, under Napoleon III, prisons were generally put second to territorial exile and transportation of convicts to France's colonial holdings in French Guiana and New Caledonia.[38] Even during the Third Republic, the transportation of convicts continued to enjoy an appeal, with the introduction in 1885 of legislation that relegated repeat petty offenders to France's distant overseas territories. By contrast, the delegates of the Haussonville Commission and, later, members of the SGP held fast to what they considered the moral superiority and efficacies of the well-organized penitentiary. The short-term cost of construction and maintenance, they argued, would be significantly offset by the long-term social advantages of reducing crime.

In 1903, reflecting back on the parliamentary inquiry he had led a quarter of a century earlier, Haussonville remembered the lack of general appetite at the time for improving France's prisons. On first proposing undertaking such an investigation in 1871, he recalled, his suggestion had been met with a general attitude of "scepticism and indifference."[39] Admittedly, France's statesmen did have much to preoccupy them at that time. Still reeling from the Prussian defeat and the turmoil of the Paris Commune, there were major competing demands on the public purse. On top of this, from the middle of the 1870s, the country was badly affected by a worldwide economic downturn, made worse by a series of natural disasters, which pushed more people off the land and into the cities. A fall in demand for French exports put downward pressure on wages and fuelled worker discontent. On a practical level, these difficult economic conditions, combined with political tensions as monarchists and republicans vied for political dominance, made prioritizing prison reform appear "singular, even inopportune," as Robert Badinter has observed.[40] But at the same time, these very same conditions helped justify reformers' demands for change. In the wake of the loss to the Prussian army and the confrontations of the Paris Commune, the prison system was considered an essential component for ensuring the regulation of the general social order. There was nothing especially new in this; in attempting prison reform, advocates in the second half of the nineteenth century were adhering to a pattern of action that had followed every major social upheaval since 1789.[41]

But the challenges in the 1870s for attempting to introduce widespread prison reform were particularly great, with the French parliament at that time at best indifferent to the cause. If Bérenger had harboured any illusions on this score, he was left in no doubt on 5 June 1875, the day that his bill on cellular prisons was to be voted on. On arriving at the National Assembly, Bérenger had found the chamber largely empty and in order to secure the necessary numbers to see his legislation passed, he had had to dash across town to fetch various deputies who were enjoying some light musical entertainment and escort them back to the chamber.[42] Even after successfully shepherding the bill through parliament, Bérenger and like-minded reformers were keenly aware that passing the legislation was just the first of their challenges, and that it was implementing the law that would pose the greatest difficulty.

At that time, France had very few prisons immediately equipped with the necessary infrastructure that would enable ready application of the law. In most cases, implementation demanded significant reconstruction. While the national government set to work converting *maisons centrales* to a cellular configuration, maisons d'arrêt posed a particular challenge. Unlike the maisons centrales, responsibility for the maintenance and operation of maisons d'arrêt was not in the hands of national authorities, but rather local ones who baulked at the high cost demanded for reconstruction and conversion of existing facilities. Despite the provision of national subsidies to help with implementation of the 1875 law,[43] the heavy financial expenditure resulted in significant resistance among local authorities and, in the end, progress was slow. By 1881, only 10 of France's 437 maisons d'arrêt had been transformed into cellular prisons.[44] This slowness of implementation was all the more troubling to reformers like Bérenger who saw cellular confinement as key for reducing recidivism. Maisons d'arrêt, which held defendants awaiting trial and convicted offenders on short-term prison sentences, were precisely the institutions of greatest concern to reformers in the fight against repeat offending.

In his address to the SGP at their first official meeting in June 1877, stalwart prison reformer Charles Lucas drew attention to the inadequate implementation of the 1875 law. He painted a worrying picture of prisons that served essentially as dumping grounds, with little if any consideration given to detainees' age, gender, or type of sentence.[45] Ultimately, the failure of departmental prisons to properly implement the law on cellular imprisonment, despite the SGP's efforts, would be a significant contributing factor to the formulating of the hard-line relegation law ten years later, which saw repeat petty offenders deported for life to France's distant overseas bagnes in French Guiana and New Caledonia.[46] But for René Bérenger, the relegation legislation failed to address the root cause of repeat offending. Two years before its passage, Bérenger told SGP colleagues that "it is not the recidivist who must be expelled from the territory, it is recidivism."[47] Eventually, in an effort to compel local authorities to put the stipulations on cellular imprisonment into effect, parliament passed new legislation in 1893 empowering the national government to assume control of non-compliant maisons d'arrêt.[48]

Ensuring the strict and effective implementation of the 1875 law on cellular imprisonment was the SGP's primary raison d'être from the beginning.[49] Working in concert with the Conseil supérieur des prisons, an advisory body attached to the interior ministry, SGP members took it as their mission to widen popular support for the improvement of prisons throughout France. Taxpayers, they believed, needed to be made to understand that such an expensive policy – and one that, on the surface, might appear to be rewarding offenders for their criminality by providing greater material comforts – was not about privileging offenders, but rather about better serving their own interests and those of society as a whole. In 1879, SGP member Fernand Desportes, a prominent Parisian lawyer and the SGP's founding general secretary, summed up the purpose of the Haussonville Commission as having been to question whether it might be better "to prevent than to punish, to restrain from bad rather than lead back to good, to depopulate prisons rather than improve them."[50] These would serve as guiding questions for the SGP for decades to come, informing the emphasis on prevention that increasingly characterized approaches to managing criminality around the turn of the twentieth century, and most particularly the treatment of juveniles.

## An Apolitical Association of Moderation

From the SGP's initial assembly of 50 members in 1877, within a few short months the number had significantly expanded to 300,[51] and by the end of its first year the group boasted a membership of almost 500. As the years went by, the SGP's membership continued to grow, as did its geographical reach. By 1900 the group had around 1,500 members, the vast majority men; only around 20 of them at that time were women.[52] Women had been involved in associational life in France, including prison reform, from the early nineteenth century, though always in smaller proportion than men. In the late 1880s, two women, Caroline de Barrau de Muratel and Pauline Kergomard, founded the Union française pour le sauvetage de l'enfance, dedicated to the protection of morally abandoned and mistreated children. Within the SGP, women's perspectives tended to be respected insofar as they related to the experience and treatment of women and juvenile prisoners. The treatment and experiences of adult male prisoners, meanwhile, were – implicitly, at least – understood to be the preserve of men.

Although the SGP's most active members were always based in Paris, where the group's meetings were held, by 1914 subscribing members were dotted across Europe and further afield, including in North and South America, Japan, and even South Australia.[53] Described by social commentator Ali Coffignon as "senior officials, judges, economists, politicians,"[54] members were drawn from a range of elite professions: from politicians like Bérenger, Dreyfus, and Roussel through to bankers, engineers, military officers, journalists, writers, publishers, and architects, as well as high-ranking functionaries.[55] Prominent among its military members was Admiral Martin Fourichon, minister of the navy and former governor of Cayenne, who had become interested in penal reform after overseeing the transportation of convicts to French Guiana in the 1850s.[56] Writers Maxime du Camp and Ivan Turgenev were both members, primarily through their interest in the reform of capital punishment.[57]

The men who gravitated to the SGP came from a variety of professions and subscribed to different religious beliefs. Most, however, had had some legal training. In this respect, the group's composition coheres with a pattern identified in French political, social, and cultural life in this period. The Third Republic, especially in the years between the 1877 constitutional crisis and the First World War, has been labelled "the Republic of lawyers"[58] on account of the major influence exercised by jurists.[59] Between 1875 and 1920, one in four deputies in the French parliament was a lawyer; and between 1873 and 1920, more than half of all government ministers and all but three of the nation's presidents (namely Patrice de MacMahon, Sadi Carnot, and Félix Faure) had been trained in the law.[60] Within the national parliament, politicians with a legal background tended to be oriented towards the centre and centre-left. They were determined to ensure the protection of liberties that had been denied under Napoleon III's authoritarian Second Empire, but were also just as determined to protect their own status and uphold a system of social and moral values based on the rule of law.[61] It was a similar state of affairs within the SGP. As table 2.1 illustrates, most of the group's office-bearers through to 1914 were jurists. And although SGP members were by no means all committed republicans, they did nonetheless adhere to a broadly similar program of a respect for moderate republican values. Tellingly, the group nominated as their first president Jules Dufaure. A moderate republican, Dufaure was a defiant opponent of Napoleon III,[62] and a lawyer by training.

While foreign guests did occasionally attend meetings in person, most subscribing members' engagement revolved around the group's published journal, the *Bulletin de la Société générale des prisons* (becoming the *Revue pénitentiaire* from 1892). The SGP's journal, France's first regular periodical dedicated to prison and criminal justice issues, distributed eight times a year, is still in print to this day.[63] Running to several thousand pages each year, the journal was considered "a veritable encyclopedia on French criminal law" that enabled members and subscribers to keep abreast of current institutional practices of imprisonment and the implementation of the criminal law.[64] A vital artery for the shaping of public opinion, the journal was described by Fernand Desportes as "the most powerful tool of advocacy [*propagande*]."[65]

From a historical perspective, the SGP's journal is an invaluable source that brings together a variety of documents relating to criminal justice within France and internationally. In addition to transcripts of the group's own meetings, the journal also offers summaries of gatherings of other reformist and philanthropic organizations, special reports on international conferences and other major gatherings, reviews of recently published books in French and other languages, and shorter accounts of noteworthy criminal cases. It provides vital insights into the attitudes and perspectives of reformers who, although entirely literate, often did not leave published records of their own. In his obituary for fellow reformer René Bérenger, Henri Joly claimed that Bérenger never published a single book or article.[66] This was not entirely accurate; as part of Bérenger's dogged moral crusade, in which Joly was similarly involved and which reached a crescendo around

Table 2.1
Officeholders of the Société générale des prisons (1877–1914)

| Year | President | Vice-presidents | General secretary |
|---|---|---|---|
| 1877 | Jules Dufaure | René Bérenger | Fernand Desportes |
| | *jurist, senator* | Célestin Bétolaud | |
| | *moderate republican* | Martin Fourichon | |
| | | Georges-Louis Mercier | |
| 1878 | Jules Dufaure | François Aubépin | Fernand Desportes |
| | | René Bérenger | |
| | | Célestin Bétolaud | |
| | | Martin Fourichon | |
| 1884 | Jules Dufaure | Henri Barboux | Fernand Desportes |
| | | Eugène Greffier | |
| | | René Marjolin | |
| | | Théophile Roussel | |
| 1885 | Jules Dufaure | Henri Barboux | Fernand Desportes |
| | | Frédéric Cuvier | |
| | | Eugène Greffier | |
| | | René Marjolin | |
| 1886 | René Bérenger | Frédéric Cuvier | Fernand Desportes |
| | *jurist, senator* | Eugène Greffier | |
| | *republican – centre left* | René Marjolin | |
| | | Charles Martini | |
| 1887 | René Bérenger | Frédéric Cuvier | Fernand Desportes |
| | | René Marjolin | |
| | | Charles Martini | |
| | | Théophile Roussel | |
| 1888 | Alexandre Ribot | Frédéric Cuvier | Fernand Desportes |
| | *jurist* | Charles Petit | |
| | *moderate republican* | Charles Martini | |
| | | Théophile Roussel | |
| 1891 | Charles Petit | François Aubépin | Fernand Desportes |
| | *jurist* | A.-J. Duverger | |
| | | Ernest Cresson | |
| | | Georges Dubois | |
| 1892 | Ernest Cresson | François Aubépin | Fernand Desportes |
| | *chief of police* | Georges Dubois | |
| | | Jules Leveillé | |
| | | Félix Voisin | |

Table 2.1 (continued)
Officeholders of the Société générale des prisons (1877–1914)

| Year | President | Vice-presidents | General secretary |
|---|---|---|---|
| 1895 | Félix Voisin<br>*jurist* | Jean-Charles Babinet<br>Gabriel Joret-Desclosières<br>Jules Leveillé<br>Théophile Roussel | Albert Rivière |
| 1897 | Émile Cheysson<br>*engineer* | Jean-Charles Babinet<br>Gabriel Joret-Desclosières<br>Georges Picot<br>Eugène Pouillet | Albert Rivière |
| 1899 | Georges Picot<br>*jurist* | Léon Devin<br>Gabriel Paul Othenin de Cléron d'Haussonville<br>Henri Joly<br>Eugène Pouillet | Albert Rivière |
| 1900 | Eugène Pouillet<br>*jurist* | Arthur de Boislile<br>Léon Devin<br>Gabriel Paul Othenin de Cléron d'Haussonville<br>Henri Joly | Albert Rivière |
| 1901 | Eugène Pouillet | Arthur de Boislile<br>Léon Devin<br>Gabriel Paul Othenin de Cléron d'Haussonville<br>Alfred Le Poittevin | Albert Rivière |
| 1902 | Eugène Pouillet | Arthur de Boislile<br>Albert Danet<br>Gabriel Paul Othenin de Cléron d'Haussonville<br>Alfred Le Poittevin | Albert Rivière |
| 1903 | Alexandre Ribot<br>*jurist*<br>*moderate republican* | Arthur de Boislile<br>Albert Danet<br>Gabriel Paul Othenin de Cléron d'Haussonville<br>Alfred Le Poittevin | Albert Rivière |
| 1904 | Henri Joly<br>*criminologist* | Albert Gigot<br>Paul Jolly<br>Alfred Le Poittevin | Albert Rivière |

Table 2.1 (continued)
Officeholders of the Société générale des prisons (1877–1914)

| Year | President | Vice-presidents | General secretary |
|---|---|---|---|
| 1905 | Henri Joly | Albert Danet | Albert Rivière |
| | | Albert Gigot | |
| | | Paul Jolly | |
| | | Félix Lacoin | |
| 1906 | Albert Gigot | Loys Brueyre | Henri Prudhomme |
| | *jurist* | Émile Garçon | |
| | *chief of police* | Paul Jolly | |
| | | Félix Lacoin | |
| 1907 | Albert Gigot | Loys Brueyre | Henri Prudhomme |
| | | Guillaume Feuilloley | |
| | | Paul Jolly | |
| | | Ernest Passez | |
| 1908 | Henri Barboux | Loys Brueyre | Henri Prudhomme |
| | *jurist* | Guillaume Feuilloley | |
| | | Émile Garçon | |
| | | Ernest Passez | |
| 1909 | Henri Barboux | Guillaume Feuilloley | Émile Garçon |
| | | Étienne Flandin | Henri Prudhomme |
| 1910 | Alfred Le Poittevin | Ernest Cartier | Henri Prudhomme |
| | *jurist* | Guillaume Feuilloley | |
| | | Étienne Flandin | |
| | | Émile Garçon | |
| 1911 | Alfred Le Poittevin | Ernest Cartier | Henri Prudhomme |
| | | Georges Demartial | |
| | | Étienne Flandin | |
| | | Émile Garçon | |
| 1912 | Guillaume Feuilloley | Henri Berthélemy | Henri Prudhomme |
| | *jurist* | Ernest Cartier | |
| | | Georges Demartial | |
| | | Étienne Flandin | |
| 1913 | Guillaume Feuilloley | Henri Berthélemy | Henri Prudhomme |
| | | Ernest Cartier | |
| | | Ferdinand Dreyfus | |
| | | Louis Rivière | |
| 1914 | Albert Rivière | Henri Berthélemy | Henri Prudhomme |
| | *jurist* | Ferdinand Dreyfus | |
| | | Louis Rivière | |
| | | Henri Robert | |

the turn of the century, Bérenger authored a *Manuel pratique pour la lutte contre la pornographie* for the Fédération des sociétés contre la pornographie.[67] It was true, however, that on the whole in his capacity both as a senator and reformer Bérenger did tend to convey his ideas orally. In this way, the transcripts of SGP meetings published in the group's journal offer considerable insight into the mindset and attitude of Bérenger and others like him.

Founding member Léon Lefébure, a politician and journalist, described the group's intention to act as "a massive centre of study, action and information, to which all those interested in the improvement of our prison system can turn."[68] The SGP served as an important forum for the articulation of ideas about criminal justice legislation and policy, seeking to shape public opinion through its journal and influence the formulation of legislation.[69] Its strategy, in short, consisted of "consultation, communication [and] information."[70] SGP members were bound together by the shared goals of enforcing the improvement of prisons and enhancing citizens' sense of their individual and social responsibilities, which would together serve the purpose of producing greater social and political stability.

Members consistently maintained a focus on preserving internal peace, which was pursued through appeal to general principles that it was thought would help insulate the group from turbulence, as well as ensuring an appropriately moderate program and pace of proposed change. As Charles Lucas told the group, their purpose was to rise above politics in order to focus on matters of principle guided by what he termed "science." This entailed, Lucas remarked, fostering "a neutral terrain on which [men] can unite and work together towards solving these great problems which have such attraction for all elevated souls, because they affect the development of civilization, humanitarian progress and human perfectibility."[71] Within what Lucas referred to as "this serene region of science," SGP members would find "the calm of meditative study, where provoking issues [*questions irritantes*] have no access."[72] Lucas's comments were echoed almost twenty years later by politician and jurist Jules Leveillé, who praised the SGP for offering a forum "where the most experienced criminal lawyers in France" could gather, "discuss[ing] freely, with a cool head [*à tête reposée*], without wishing to reach new theories too quickly."[73]

Equally important to the SGP's aim of maintaining internal social peace was its apolitical ethos. While the group most certainly aimed to influence policy and legislation, it did not itself aim to be a political organization.

Shortly after its formation, American prison reformer Reverend Frederick Wines drew special attention to the SGP's non-partisan composition, noting that both monarchists and republicans featured among its members. The SGP, Wines declared, "is free of any religious and political connection: Catholics, Protestants and Jews, imperialists, monarchists and republicans, sit side by side in its meeting rooms."[74]

Speaking at a meeting celebrating the group's twenty-fifth anniversary in 1903, Haussonville described the SGP as "our little parliament" and remarked that on entering the meeting room in a building just behind the law courts in central Paris, all dissidence was left at the door and a culture of mutual respect reigned.[75] Haussonville's sentiments were echoed by Albert Rivière, who observed that "there is a justice that has never been refused at these monthly meetings: it is the generous breath of liberalism and impartiality towards all opinions that animates them, it is courtesy that presides over the discussions, it is the eager welcome ... the wide appeal addressed to all theories, to all systems, to all experiences."[76] On his election as the SGP's president a decade later, Rivière paid homage to members' tolerance for their professional, religious, political, and philosophical differences, and their general civility for one another, even when debating contentious issues. It was, Rivière remarked, "this courtesy, this good humour, this deference for all opinions, no matter the clothing [*habit*], the religion, the politics or philosophy of the practitioner, which makes our little federation [*syndicat*] a circle of friends, where they always have the pleasure of meeting and benefit from exchanging their ideas, whether they come from the bar or descend from a seat on the bench, from a chair at the university [*Faculté*] or from the *Institut*."[77]

This conciliatory atmosphere was further cultivated by the practice, written into the SGP's constitution, of never casting votes on any issue. Although a member might make their position clear by intervening in a meeting (with their comments transcribed and printed in the journal), because issues were never voted on, it is not possible for us to know how widely supported any one issue was. This was equally unclear to the members themselves.[78] Not only did this act as a guard against potential divisiveness, but it was also consistent with the liberal ethos undergirding the group: an association of individuals.

A decade after the group's founding, Bérenger described the SGP as driven by a "spirit of initiative and progress" tempered by "caution without which nothing lasting can be founded." The group, Bérenger declared proudly, was always seeking to position itself "equally distant from utopia, that worst enemy of progress, and immobility which, labelled as social defence or respect for traditions, puts up a systematic barrier to all reform."[79] There was a clear sense among SGP members that individuals on their own were incapable of persuading the public of the need for prison reform; only a group of individuals acting together as an association would be capable of exercising the necessary influence.[80]

In addition to a fundamental respect for the rights and responsibilities of the individual, SGP members also believed in the essential role played by religion in producing a prisoner's reform. In his special address to the group in June 1877, Charles Lucas expressed admiration for the assembled members' distinguished professional positions and for the diversity of their religious faiths.[81] While most members identified as Catholic, the SGP welcomed followers of other Judeo-Christian faiths, and religious tolerance was a core value. The group not only welcomed the faithful, but also clerics. For instance, the period between 1877 and 1900 counted twenty-three rabbis, including the well-known reformer chief rabbi Zadoc Kahn; fifteen Protestant ministers, including Parisian prison chaplain Pasteur Arboux; and twenty-four Catholic clerics among its members.[82] Members were also Freemasons, including Victor Schœlcher, celebrated for his role as a slavery abolitionist.[83] Notable was the absence of any Muslim members. Despite the diversity of its members' faiths, religion informed all aspects of the SGP's work and thinking. Cesare Lombroso once commented disparagingly that so strong was the SGP's attachment to religion that the pages of its journal "sometimes smell[ed] of the sacristy."[84] Religion was also to be found at the heart of the group's philosophy on the moral reform of prisoners. In the early 1870s, Haussonville declared in his report to the parliamentary inquiry into prisons that "the two direct agents of moralization in prisons are first religion and then education. And it will not be surprising that we say religion first." Christianity, in particular, was held to offer a powerful tonic against immorality, according to Haussonville. When it comes "to rais[ing] degraded hearts and bring[ing] them back to the good through repentance and hope," he declared, "no doctrine has arguments as powerful and as touching as Christian doctrine."[85]

Haussonville was not alone among SGP members to be sympathetic to the reformist thinking of Frédéric Le Play, which similarly laid emphasis on religion as a regulating force. Other followers of Le Play among SGP members were engineer and director of the Creusot steelworks Émile Cheysson, jurist Georges Picot, prefect of the Paris police Albert Gigot,[86] and criminologist Henri Joly. All four of these men would serve as the group's president (see table 2.1). Le Play's emphasis on the importance of religion, along with respect for class-based hierarchy and, most importantly, the nuclear family as a bedrock for social stability, found a natural home within the SGP.[87] These followers of Le Play and other reformers and philanthropists in the late nineteenth century were active in the general movement of *ligues*, serving as "veritable moral entrepreneurs" with the aim of ensuring that what they considered to be essential moral standards were maintained.[88]

Although prominent SGP members adhered to Le Play's thinking, as a whole the group deviated from his philosophy in relation to at least one key respect: the role of public welfare.[89] Whereas Le Play had warned of the dangers of following Britain's lead in legislating public assistance, arguing that it destroyed individual responsibility through state intervention in charitable works and in childrearing, members of the SGP tended to hold a more moderate, pragmatic view. Although they viewed the family unit as sacrosanct, they were not averse to breaching that sacred space in the interests of child welfare and broader social well-being. For SGP members, the effective, long-lasting reform of prisons and the criminal justice system more generally was considered to depend on co-operation between private philanthropy and state institutions, working together in concert. The importance of effective co-operation between philanthropy and the state would be one of various lessons SGP members would draw from the protracted and largely unsuccessful struggle for prison reform waged by their predecessors, particularly the Société royale pour l'amélioration des prisons (or simply the Société royale des prisons, the SRP).

## The Longer History of Private Philanthropy and Juvenile Corrections

On their group's formation in 1877, SGP members consciously positioned themselves within the longer movement for prison reform, identifying in particular with efforts undertaken in the first half of the nineteenth century, during the periods of the Bourbon Restoration and July Monarchy. This sense of continuity was reflected in their appointment of long-term prison reformer Charles Lucas as their *doyen*. By then over seventy years old and afflicted by blindness, Lucas was a longstanding advocate for a criminal justice system that ensured public safety by not only removing lawbreakers from society but also working on improving them in order to prepare them for eventual social re-entry. Such a system was in perfect alignment with the SGP's foundational objectives.[90] Lucas's hands-on experience and instrumental role in juvenile justice reform reinforces the centrality of young people to the concerns of the SGP reformers. In the 1840s Lucas helped create dozens of agricultural colonies for juveniles, including the Colonie agricole pénitentiaire du Val d'Yèvre, founded in 1847 near the town of Bourges.

For Lucas, the segregation of juveniles from older prisoners was of primary importance in the interest of preventing the spread of criminal tendencies between incarcerated subjects. Significantly, in Lucas's special address at the SGP's inaugural meeting in 1877 in which he described the current state of French prisons and the need for reform, the veteran reformer remarked that when it came to separating prisoners into difference sections, "the first question posed is that of age."[91] Lucas was generally viewed as essential in the wider development of the agricultural colony as an instrument of moral reform for juveniles. Described by Henri Gaillac as "at once the prophet, the champion and the leader of the agricultural solution,"[92] Lucas was said to have coined the phrase "improving the child by the soil and the soil by the child."[93] Paying tribute to France's pioneering work in establishing agricultural colonies for juveniles, Lucas told SGP members that "if [France] has rivals among other nations, it has no betters in this regard."[94]

In seeking to reform France's prison system, members of the SGP consistently identified with the philosophy and action of reformers like Lucas or Bérenger de la Drôme.[95] Lucas himself likened the SGP to England's Howard Association, which had been formed just over a decade earlier with similar aims of influencing public opinion on the need for and utility of prison reform.[96] SGP members also took inspiration from international organizations, especially the National Prison Association formed in the United States in 1870.[97] But more profoundly still, members of the SGP considered themselves the heirs to France's own prison reform association, the SRP. With a body of members that included judges, ministers, and prominent figures from Paris's charitable sphere, the SRP's composition had certain points in common with the SGP formed decades later.[98] These early nineteenth-century reformers and SGP members shared a concern about the lack of attention paid by the prison administration to the moral improvement of inmates and the absence of post-release support to assist prisoners with their transition to life on the outside. The SRP had aimed to improve the everyday provisions for prisoners, supplying them with better bread, clothing, and religious instruction, in order to encourage their moral regeneration and facilitate their social reintegration on release.[99]

While the revolutionary and Napoleonic regimes had made the penitentiary the centrepiece of their penal systems, laying emphasis on imprisonment as a mechanism for expiation and redemption by means of segregation and edifying labour, in practice, due to a lack of investment, implementation, and adequate infrastructure, France's prisons in the early nineteenth century fell far short of providing the conditions necessary for realizing their primary goal. While revolutionaries lauded the prison as a primary tool of punishment and reform, no penitentiaries were actually constructed under their watch. Under Napoleon I's rule, this total inaction came to an end, with the creation of the first maisons centrales in 1808. But even still, beyond constructing dominating buildings, little if any attempt was made to implement a coherent program of moralization within their thick walls. As for the treatment of juveniles, although Napoleon's penal code of 1810 did set down the important guarantee that all offenders under the age of sixteen were to be spared the harshest sanctions on account of their age and incomplete development, it made no mention of distinct facilities for them. As a result, while a juvenile could never mount the scaffold or suffer the excruciating punishments of an adult offender, until the 1820s there were no sustained efforts made to segregate juvenile inmates from adults within prisons.

Prison reform was a major concern for the restored Bourbon king, Louis XVIII. Just a few months after assuming power in 1814, he identified several priorities, including the importance of separating young prisoners from older ones and the need to provide for prisoners' education, professional skills, and moral improvement. He issued an *ordonnance* declaring prisoners under the age of twenty-five deserving of particular solicitude given that they were "more susceptible than others of recognising their error" and that on their release they were more likely to become upstanding members of society.[100] The following month he announced the creation of separate prison quarters for young prisoners, charging the Duc de La Rochefoucauld-Liancourt with the task of coordinating a building program.[101] His forward-looking plans were interrupted, however, by Napoleon – who escaped from exile in Elba and reclaimed the throne in early 1815, only to be toppled again one hundred days later. Although these events delayed the implementation of reform to France's prisons, a groundswell of support among elite reformers was mounting. Finally in 1819, on the advice of his chief minister Élie Decazes, King Louis created the SRP to make use of this reformist wave and promised financial support for the upgrade of the most dilapidated departmental prisons in the country.[102]

It was under the July Monarchy that some progress was achieved with regard to the detention of juveniles, with the establishment of distinct sections for boys under sixteen in prisons in Lyon in 1833, Toulouse in 1835, and Carcassonne in 1836.[103] The year 1836 also witnessed the opening of France's first dedicated penitentiary for juveniles – the panopticon prison of Petite Roquette in Paris. Constructed at vast expense based on plans by Hippolyte Lebas (best known as the designer of the obelisk at the Place de la Concorde), and opened by King Louis-Philippe himself, Petite Roquette was made up of individual cells radiating out from a central observation tower. Its design was intended to facilitate constant surveillance, though within three years it was noted that the observation tower was, in fact, being used by kitchen staff.[104]

Rather than Petite Roquette prison, the crowning achievement of reformers during the July Monarchy was the creation of "colonies agricoles," institutions dedicated to the incarceration and reform of juvenile delinquent boys (girls would continue to be incarcerated alongside adult women).[105] In contrast to the system of individual isolation at the heart of the Petite Roquette cellular prison, these agricultural establishments sought to regenerate boys by placing them in a rural setting where they would undertake work that was at once socially (and economically) productive and morally edifying. The most famous of these rural institutions was Mettray near Tours, founded by Frédéric-Auguste Demetz in 1839, but it was not France's first. That distinction belongs to the colony established by Joseph Rey, a Catholic priest, at Oullins near Lyon in 1835.[106] Private initiative was vitally important for the creation and maintenance of these juvenile colonies, relieving the state of a considerable financial burden, as will be further discussed in chapter 4. Only at the end of the century did the state begin to take over the management of these institutions,[107] prompting criticism from some reformers including Henri Joly, who railed against the state's "centralizing system … [and] its contempt for liberty."[108]

Even before the creation of private agricultural colonies, philanthropists played a crucial role in the support of juvenile offenders, guiding their transition from detention and into work through charitable organizations known as *sociétés de patronage.* From the 1820s, the first of these organizations emerged, providing support to juveniles on their release from prison and focused on instilling core values of hard work, thrift, and self-discipline, undergirded by religion.[109] In 1823 a patronage society called the Société pour l'amélioration morale et pour le patronage des jeunes libérés des prisons civiles was established in Strasbourg for supervising released juvenile offenders, most of them Protestant.[110] One of the most active of these private organizations was the Société de patronage pour les jeunes détenus et les jeunes libérés du département de la Seine, founded in 1833 by a group that included Charles Lucas, Bérenger de la Drôme, and Frédéric-Auguste Demetz.

In offering charitable support to those in need, sociétés de patronage satisfied a belief that was widely and firmly held by elites that providing relief should be a voluntary impulse rather than a compulsory obligation dictated by the state.[111] Decades later, the reformers of the SGP continued to uphold this core belief in the importance of philanthropic action in the reform of prisoners. By the 1870s, various patronage societies were offering support to juveniles, and into the final decades of the century their number continued to grow. Among the initiatives created in this later period were the Société générale de protection pour l'enfance abandonnée ou coupable, established by SGP member Georges Bonjean in 1879, and the Patronage de l'enfance et de l'adolescence, set up in 1890 by Henri Rollet, also an SGP member, which offered support to abandoned and mistreated children, along with juvenile offenders. Two years earlier, Rollet, a young, up-and-coming lawyer, had also established the Union française pour le sauvetage de l'enfance. This was the beginning of a long association with juvenile justice affairs for Rollet; he would go on to serve as Paris's first juvenile court judge and was described admiringly by fellow jurist Henri Robert as "the secular Saint Vincent de Paul."[112] By the start of the twentieth century, by far the most celebrated of these philanthropic groups for juvenile offenders was the Société de protection des engagés volontaires élevés sous la tutelle administrative. SGP member Félix Voisin would serve as that group's inaugural president and maintained the role through to his death, thirty-six years later. The group focused on assisting boys who had been acquitted but detained in a juvenile colony under Article 66 with enlistment in the military. This trajectory, as we will see in chapter 5, became increasingly recommended by legislators and policymakers at the turn of the century.[113]

As a whole, SGP members envisaged their group as a crucial component in the effective implementation and regulation of criminal justice, an auxiliary support to the actions of the state. The group's first president, Jules Dufaure, gestured to this aim in his inaugural address in 1877, declaring that together they believed that "a free society could add something to that which a regular, well-organized [public] administration was doing."[114] Their objective, Dufaure went on, was not to be "a rival, but [rather] an independent auxiliary of the public administration."[115]

While SGP members viewed themselves as heirs to the SRP, they considered their group different to it in at least one key respect: its political independence. Gordon Wright has described the SRP as a "curious bureaucratic-philanthropic hybrid,"[116] but this does not capture the extent to which the group was intimately attached to, if not inseparable from, the Crown. In 1830, this would prove fatal for the SRP, as it was swept away along with the Bourbon Restoration, replaced by the July Monarchy. The coordination of sustained and generalized prison reform was severely compromised as a result of this political connection. SGP members were acutely aware of this and consciously sought to avoid succumbing to a similar fate. This, they understood, required the group to be more firmly rooted in civil society. In a speech delivered to the Académie des sciences morales et politiques in the 1870s, Charles Lucas observed that while he did "not wish to downplay the services rendered by [the SRP]," it was ultimately – and fatally – "an emanation of royal authority and not social initiative."[117] Prison reform, Lucas declared, "needs to unite with scientific and administrative initiative, parliamentary initiative,"[118] and the best way to ensure broad-based popular support was through association and the wide dissemination of their reform program.[119]

The SRP's demise provided a cautionary tale for members of the SGP. They drew from its example crucial lessons about the importance of maintaining a certain distance from government, while at the same time having the ear of parliament. It was precisely by transcending politics that the SGP hoped to weather any storms, as a result of either government instability or internal divisions within the group itself. In so doing, the group aspired to exercise long-lasting influence, maintain a critical eye on the functioning of the criminal justice system and its institutions, and make appropriate recommendations. Rising above politics required two things: that the group cooperate with but maintain a separation from the government, and that it foster an atmosphere within its membership of social peace. The SGP's intention to retain political independence was made explicit from the start. As the inaugural president, Jules Dufaure, put it, the group was "an auxiliary independent of the public administration."[120]

## Focusing on the Juvenile Offender: Fighting Recidivism

In a presidential address to the SGP in 1887, on the occasion of the group's tenth anniversary, René Bérenger neatly summed up his position on criminal justice reform: "A great wave of opinion carries people to reform their aged criminal laws," he declared. "Liberty calls for new guarantees for the security of citizens at the same time as for the defence of the convicted. Justice demands a repression better proportionate to the moral state of the guilty and sentences which repress without demeaning and which correct while striking down. Humanity rejects pointlessly barbarous sentences and demands to the point of extreme rigorousness, indulgence for the sincerity of remorse and aid after expiation."[121] Punishment, Bérenger insisted, needed to serve a positive purpose, improving the lawbreaker's morals and preventing further crime. "If society has the right to inflict punishments," he observed in 1883 in the context of debates on the territorial exile of repeat offenders (a policy to which the senator was resolutely opposed), "does it not indeed have the duty to liberate [*affranchir*] from these effects those who have manifestly [*notoirement*] raised themselves back up?"[122] For Bérenger, it was the penitentiary, not deportation, that could best serve the rehabilitative ends of punishment for adult offenders.

The idea that prisons should serve a rehabilitative purpose was hardly new; the principle had been enshrined in France's first penal code of 1791. But by the end of the nineteenth century, high rates of repeat offending were straining many observers' belief in the penitentiary's capacity to protect society and improve the prisoner. From around 1880 there began what Bernard Schnapper has termed "a sort of psychosis about recidivism."[123] Hubert Michaux, a high-ranking official in the French colonial ministry, told delegates at the 1878 International Prison Congress in Stockholm that "the difficult thing is not to imprison a man, it is to release him."[124] For Michaux, the most effective solution to the problem of criminality, especially

Figure 2.1
Senator René Bérenger, 1910

repeat offending, was convict transportation. His position would be vindicated in 1885 when the French parliament passed the relegation law.

The passage of the relegation law of 27 May 1885 (sponsored by Pierre Waldeck-Rousseau) coincided with a "noticeable hardening of criminological rhetoric, which increasingly stressed social defence," as Ruth Harris has noted.[125] But for the majority of France's prison reformers, this kind of exile was not viewed favourably.[126] For René Bérenger, the more effective (and cheaper) answer to France's recidivist problem was preventing prisoners from entering prison in the first place. In this spirit, Bérenger sponsored further laws, the first of which was passed just months later, instituting probation, patronage, and rehabilitation outside of a custodial context. Although, as Robert Nye has observed, Bérenger's legislation on probation for first-time offenders, on the one hand, and Waldeck-Rousseau's hard-lined relegation law, on the other, were "apparently contradictory … [they] were in fact intimately dependent on one another,"[127] in the sense that they had the same long-term objective in mind: "to eradicate recidivism."[128] The essential relationship between indulgence for first-time offenders and severity for repeat offenders was summed up by SGP member René Garraud in a comment to delegates at the Brussels International Prison Congress in 1900: the growing leniency shown towards first-time offenders, he said, would not serve the interests of society "if it was not compensated by an increasingly greater severity for recurrences."[129]

Back in 1873, Bérenger had told the National Assembly that recidivism was a symptom of a deficient prison system. Repeat offenders were swelling the rates of crime, he acknowledged, but recidivism itself was the product of the prison system.[130] Too often, Bérenger lamented, far from preventing reoffending, imprisonment actually exacerbated the offender's demoralization.[131] Post-release bureaucratic practices and inadequate supports extended the offender's social dishonour, thereby perpetuating the cycle of crime. Bérenger was concerned, for instance, that individuals' criminal record (*casier judiciaire*), introduced during the revolutionary tumult of 1848, was used by employers to screen prospective employees, thereby transforming what was supposed to be simply a legal document into a social stigma, a new form of (non-physical) branding.[132] Bérenger carried a vision of a criminal justice system that focused on the future of the lawbreaker, rather than their past, and which helped to restore social bonds rather than causing further alienation. He also upheld the idea that keeping a lawbreaker out of prison – particularly first-time and young offenders – by means of suspended sentences or placement in a correctional institution could be more effective in preventing future crime than convicting and incarcerating them.

In addition, Bérenger considered intervention in family life to be key to preventing a juvenile from succumbing to a life of crime. From the SGP's earliest years, Bérenger, along with fellow senator Théophile Roussel, was the group's most vocal advocate for increasing the state's powers to intervene in family life, regulating "healthy" parenting and enabling the removal of children from environments deemed harmful to their well-being and moral development. In his view, morality and criminality were inextricable. "Bad morals," Bérenger told the Senate in 1908, "debase characters, degrade the mind, lower the moral and intellectual level of a people. They are the direst solvent of the family, the most active agent of irregular situations, illegitimate births, lives without work and without rule, the main fuel of criminality."[133]

Over the decades, SGP members would grapple with how to make the generalities of the law best fit to the particularities of the offender, often disagreeing on which priorities mattered most. For some, it was the deterrent function of the law that most needed to be upheld in the interest of reducing criminality. For others, however, the efficacy of the law was seen to rest in its capacity to adapt as much as possible to the particular conditions of the offender and to affect that person's behaviour. One area on which SGP members remained broadly united, however, was the need to protect young people from harmful influences (particularly from within their own families) in the interest of reducing criminality. Like their reformist predecessors of the July Monarchy, whose vision they largely shared, these late nineteenth-century reformers focused particular attention on juvenile offenders, whom they considered to be both more receptive to and more deserving of programs of re-education.

In 1900 Parisian juge d'instruction Louis Albanel wrote that there were only two ways of fighting crime: protecting those not yet lost to a life of crime, and punishing "the incorrigibles, the rebels, in open struggle against society."[134] Juvenile offenders, by virtue of their youth, were positioned at the edge of greater indulgence. Within this context of seeking to break the cycle of crime, the question of the treatment of juvenile offenders made its way to centre stage at the end of the nineteenth century. With criminality conceived as a pathway at the end of which lurked the recalcitrant recidivist, juveniles were identified as the most readily redeemed category of offender.

By the turn of the twentieth century, an international movement was urging greater recognition of the particular needs and conditions of young people, children, and adolescents, in the interest of better combatting the problem of crime. As Sylvia Schafer has noted, French reformers were abundantly represented at these gatherings; the government, for instance, sent twice as many delegates to the International Congress on the Protection of Children held in Belgium in 1890 than any other country.[135] The most effective treatment for young offenders, it was believed, was prevention. As Louis Puibaraud observed in 1893, the main priority was to identify measures that would "prevent the bad child from continuing to be bad, so that, growing up, he does not become a dangerous man."[136]

## Conclusion

In his 1901 book *Misères sociales et études historiques*, SGP member Ferdinand Dreyfus, who in 1912, as senator for the Seine-et-Oise, would sponsor the law instituting a distinct branch of justice for juveniles, remarked that there was no more pathetic spectacle than the one that regularly played out in the nation's courtrooms. "The legal system," Dreyfus wrote, "so solemn and weighty, seems disproportionate when it applies to this particular species of 'defendants.'"[137] Paying tribute to the Ferry laws on education introduced in the early 1880s, which had secured free primary schooling for all children, Dreyfus called for similar efforts to be directed towards juvenile offenders "in order to protect them, straighten them out and bring them back to the right path."[138] With official statistics revealing ever-increasing rates of juvenile offending, the key to fighting "the scourge," Dreyfus declared, was to "fight it in its germ and in its origin." For, he went on, "the little fifteen-year-old tramp you leave unprotected will tomorrow be a thief, and in six years a leader of a gang."[139]

The criminal justice reformers who gravitated to the SGP around the turn of the century resisted determinist conceptualizations of criminality, laying emphasis instead on the importance of personal conduct and social duties. Although these reformers were by no means card-carrying republicans in their political orientation, their general emphasis on the importance of individual responsibility as fundamental social building block did align with the general priorities of the republican regime that aimed to forge citizens aware of their duties as much as their rights. One issue that bound all criminal justice reformers together in this period was a belief that juvenile offenders represented the thin end of the wedge in the fight against criminality and recidivism. Although criminality was not held to be biologically determined, a person's capacity to change their unsound habits was nonetheless considered to be largely a factor of age: the younger the offender, the greater the likelihood of their reform.

Protecting juveniles – or "child saving" – became a means through which the entire problem of crime could be treated, and the cultivation of criminality short-circuited. It was this thinking that lay behind the increasing tendency by the end of the century to intervene, to break the cycle of either disturbing or *potentially* disturbing behaviour. For it was not just the *actual* demonstration of disturbing behaviour that was of concern, but even its potential. "The child of today will be the adult of tomorrow," wrote Georges Bonjean in his 1895 book *Enfants révoltés et parents coupables*. "What future are we threatened with by this most certainly perverted youth," Bonjean asked, "if we don't decide to bring a hot iron to the gangrenous wounds?"[140] Effectively treating young offenders was considered critical for the long-term fight against crime more generally. In the same vein, Lyon criminologist Alexandre Lacassagne and medical doctor Étienne Martin wrote that "it is on childhood and youth that we must act. Any penal measure that does not begin first with the betterment of the child is useless. The moral well-being of societies is in direct proportion to the sacrifices, protection and care given to children."[141] In the face of increasing rates of juvenile criminality and an unimpressive rate of population growth, the stakes could not have been higher.

CHAPTER 3

# Presuming Innocence? Age and Discretionary Justice

The child is a little being whose intelligence charms us through its nascent witticisms [*saillies naissantes*], through the daily progress we witness it make: but when will moral reasoning, the notion of the just and the unjust be in place? When will it exist in its entirety? For the criminal jurist [*criminaliste*], that is the question.

Joseph Ortolan, 1855[1]

In his 1879 book *L'Enfance à Paris*, Count Haussonville presented a detailed portrait of a courtroom episode depicted in a drawing by the celebrated nineteenth-century French caricaturist Honoré Daumier. Haussonville described Daumier's drawing as follows: three magistrates, resplendent in their judicial robes and crowned with *bonnets carrés*, are in the process of questioning a young girl dressed in rags. As one of the judges turns the pages of a hefty legal tome, another takes notes, while the third leans forward attentively, as if to better hear the girl's replies to the questions posed to her. In posture, the girl appears diffident; she stands with her head lowered shyly and plays absent-mindedly with the edge of her tattered apron. To the bench, the diminutive creature seems out of place in a serious court of law. But through Daumier's careful composition of the scene, the girl gives an entirely different impression to the viewer: with her face turned slightly away from the bench and back towards the viewer, the girl, Haussonville wrote, bears an unambiguously "sneaky and insincere facial expression." Daumier's artful composition brings the viewer into a relationship of complicity with the girl, revealing the youngster to be calculating and duplicitous and offering a trenchant social commentary on the foibles of the legal system. The courtroom is in the process of being hoodwinked by a girl of precocious knowingness and devious intent. Far from naïve, the girl is, in reality, a crafty creature who plays up to the magistrates' expectations of childish innocence in order to bend the three men to her will.

This scene of deception, Haussonville claimed, "represents … a sad reality" regularly observed in criminal courtrooms of the French capital.[2] Indeed, visitors to Parisian criminal courtrooms, Haussonville wrote, would be "not only saddened, but sometimes terrified by the precocious perversity of these barely formed characters."[3] The expression "perversité précoce" was commonly used in reference to young criminals throughout the nineteenth century. Its currency reflected the widespread acceptance of the idea of children as naturally innocent and was sustained by the notion that deviance was a force that invaded children rather than springing from within them. As Rousseauist ideas of innate child innocence set down firmer roots, instances when children committed crimes, especially serious ones, caused adult observers to respond with disbelief at their preternatural perversity. In her research on representations of child criminals during the July Monarchy, Cat Nilan has argued that such scenes of premature criminality problematized the narrow nineteenth-century moral conception of the "normal child" as innocent and innately good. She argues that the tension contained within the concept of the child criminal was resolved in the courtrooms of the 1830s and 1840s through a disentangling of "child" and "criminal" so that "either the child is proven not a criminal or the criminal child is proven not a child."[4] In 1840, French psychiatrist Charles Marc described at length a case from fifteen years earlier in which an eight-year-old girl, with a propensity for masturbation, had attempted to kill her parents and had later shocked investigators with her cool demeanour and rational explanations of her motivations.[5] Although commentators held that perversity could manifest itself at any age, the earlier it appeared, the more alarming it was.

Curiously, the Daumier drawing that Haussonville described with such precision does not correlate with any of the works listed in the artist's catalogue raisonné. The closest match is to two preliminary drawings and one watercolour.[6] All three works are of similar dimensions, and all bear the title "*Déposition de mineure (Huis clos – Le flagrant délit)*," but none of them feature the duplicitous facial expression Haussonville details with such evocative attention. Perhaps Haussonville himself was duping his own readers in claiming to have seen a drawing that never existed, or, more likely, he misremembered the particulars. Or maybe the work has simply not survived.

Authenticity to one side, Daumier's drawing of the duplicitous young girl would have readily served the agendas of those in favour of imposing a harsher system of punishment on juveniles, or at least adopting greater circumspection in the assessment of their moral conscience. But Haussonville invoked the drawing for a quite different purpose. Although in general his book, *L'Enfance à Paris*, was dedicated to championing the cause of children who were the "irresponsible victims of sickness, infirmities and poverty,"[7] it was not just young children who were in need, Haussonville pointed out. "In that hot and unhealthy atmosphere of Paris," he wrote, "moral gangrene conquers these young beings quickly and easily" and "guilty passions or criminal attacks can smoulder within the heart and brain of a sixteen-year-old."

As the codified age of criminal majority, sixteen was the point at which the criminal law in France considered a person to be an adult, "having full responsibility for their acts and having the right to no indulgence, nor any longer any attenuation of punishment."[8] According to the penal code, offenders aged under sixteen were protected from the harshest penalties. (In 1906 the threshold would be raised to eighteen, for reasons that will be outlined later.) Most critically, juveniles prosecuted for a criminal offence were even protected from sustaining any punishment at all if the court decided that they had acted "sans discernement." Upon this decision hinged not only the state's need to punish a juvenile offender but also its capacity to detain a juvenile for an indeterminate period of time.

From the final decades of the nineteenth century, criminal justice reformers debated the relationship between a young person's chronological age and their criminal responsibility. Together with their foreign counterparts at international congresses, French reformers and legal theorists deliberated on how society should respond to the growing numbers of young people apparently ripe before their time, who were displaying behaviours and attitudes in advance of their years. They weighed up the extent to which "discernement" acted as a reliable indicator of responsibility and, more generally still, what this all-important yet opaque concept specifically referred to. Should France, these reformers wondered, follow the approach used by all other developed foreign systems and automatically assume young children to be criminally irresponsible on account of their age? Could age alone ever be a guarantee of a lack of "discernement"? If so, at what ages should the lines be drawn between the absolutely irresponsible, the partially responsible, and the fully responsible individual? What about those children who, despite their tender age, committed heinous crimes with an apparently cold and rational intent; should they, too, be exempt from any punishment? And if an absence of "discernement" were to be automatically assumed, did this not suggest a Darwinian philosophy of humankind's natural brutishness, which might bleed into Lombrosian ideas of the "born criminal"?

With these debates as the background, this chapter outlines the court procedure applied to juveniles in French criminal law in the nineteenth century, before the passage of the major innovations ushered in by the 1912 legislation on juvenile courts, which decriminalized offences committed by juveniles under the age of thirteen. In addition, this chapter homes in on the arguments of jurors and reformers over the significance of age categories, centring on two basic and related topics of debate. First, could all children be assumed to be absolutely lacking in moral conscience up to a certain age threshold, and, if so, at what age should that threshold be set? Second, up to what age might the ability to discern right from wrong be considered if not absolutely lacking, then at least in doubt? As we shall see, debate on the relationship between age and criminal responsibility exposed both the fragility of the concept of "discernement" and the significant power invested in the hands of magistrates adjudicating on the matter. This chapter is thus concerned with two types of judgment: the discretion of juveniles accused of breaking the law and the discretionary power of magistrates assessing them.

## *Discernement*: A Powerful and Imprecise Tool of Justice

"Discernement" was the crucial hinge on which the sentencing of juveniles turned in nineteenth-century France. As a legal concept, it essentially referred to a person's ability to distinguish right from wrong. Being aware of wrongdoing and intentionally committing a harmful act were two of the preconditions of criminal responsibility. Broadly equivalent to the principle of *doli incapax* used in English law, according to which culpability depended on a child's awareness of being guilty rather than on the unlawfulness of the act itself,[9] "discernement" was the critical factor in determining whether a juvenile could be held responsible and punished for their actions.

Etymologically in French, the nouns *discernement* and *discrétion* derive from a common Latin root: *discernere.* "Discernement," first recorded in the sixteenth century, deviated from its original meaning of "the action of separating, pulling apart" to refer to the operation by which one distinguishes intellectually between several objects of thought and the capacity to judge something clearly and rationally. "Discrétion" referred to the exercise of "discernement," reason, caution.[10]

In nineteenth-century Christian doctrine, meanwhile, the concept of "discernement" generally referred to the capacity to distinguish good from evil, but also had a more particular meaning, controlling believers' licence to participate in the sacraments of the Church, specifically their right to receive communion. These ideas governing religious practice went back centuries.[11] According to the thirteenth-century theologian Thomas Aquinas, to be eligible to receive the Eucharist, a person had to be capable of bringing to the sacrament an appropriate and sincere feeling of devotion. Because they were not fully in control of themselves, and thus did not act with free will, neither children nor the mentally incapacitated were deemed capable of participating in the sacrament. Up until the thirteenth century, the sacraments of baptism and communion occurred simultaneously, so that at baptism a child was immediately recognized as a full member of the Church, regardless of their age. In 1215, the Fourth Lateran Council transformed this practice, decreeing that only children who had reached the age of discernment were allowed to receive the consecrated host and required to confess their sins.[12] For Aquinas, partaking in communion symbolized that a child had reached that age and understood the difference both between right and wrong, and between ordinary bread and the consecrated host.[13] Without this sense, children were understood to be quite capable of *doing* wrong, but their behaviour could not be considered sinful because it was performed without knowledge.

In the context of France's criminal justice system, the word *discernement* signified more than being able to distinguish right from wrong, but just how much more was not clear. Was it an intellectual faculty, the ability to reason, or a distinct moral intuition, in principle separate from an individual's cognitive capacity? Or was it simply awareness of society's laws and an understanding that certain acts were forbidden? Was it, alternatively, a sort of emotional empathy, the awareness that an act would cause harm to another person? Juridically, the principle of "discernement" essentially rested on a central distinction made in the criminal law between criminal and moral responsibility. As such, it was bound up with the fundamental principle of *libre arbitre* (free will), which assumed that only actions controlled by rational volition were punishable.[14] As pointed out by Louis Proal, a senior jurist, SGP member, and brother-in-law of Henri Joly, the concept of free will was present in Aristotelian ethical theory and in the work of Saint Augustine.[15]

The doctrine of free will was the lynchpin of France's whole penal edifice, for society's right to punish was restricted to those people who could control their own actions. A person could only be punished if the unlawful action was "within their gift" – that is, if they were capable of restraining themselves but had chosen not to. In nineteenth-century French legal doctrine, it was thought that laws should not limit individuals' freedom unfairly and were only legitimate and socially useful if they restrained behaviour over which individuals had control. As the philosopher and educational reformer Victor Cousin explained in his most famous work *Du vrai, du beau et du bien*, published in 1855 and drawn from a course he gave at the Sorbonne: "If man has duties he must possess the faculty to fulfil them, to resist desire, passion, [self-]interest in order to obey the law. He must be free, therefore he is, otherwise human nature is in contradiction with itself. The direct certainty of obligation carries with it the corresponding certainty of liberty."[16] Free will was crucial to moral responsibility, for, as the Swiss jurist Charles Brocher put it, in order to be bound by society's laws, one needed to "feel oneself at once free and required to conform spontaneously to the demands of a superior rule."[17]

Republican reformers at the end of the nineteenth century contrasted the codified legal system, which required its citizens to be conscious of their actions, aware of their freedom, and able to recognize and avoid transgressions, with an Old Regime penal system which, they claimed, had been driven by fear and overt intimidation. A belief in self-control as a precondition for active citizenship lay at the core of the political philosophy of the Third Republic and manifested throughout republican ideology, including in primary schooling, as we saw in chapter 1. Responsibility became inseparable from an individual's degree of liberty and the development of their moral conscience.[18] To have acted "sans discernement" rendered a punitive sanction invalid, as only individuals who acted freely and in full knowledge of doing wrong could be held responsible for their actions. As Fernand Desportes, a Parisian lawyer and SGP member, explained to Haussonville's parliamentary commission into prisons in the 1870s: "the rational man who commits a crime decides to enact his own freedom [*fait acte de liberté*]. He deserves to be punished not for having committed the crime, but for having done it of his own free will."[19] The decision that a juvenile had acted "avec discernement" therefore signified that they had acted in full knowledge of doing wrong, had been able to control their actions, and had nonetheless chosen to commit an unlawful and harmful act.

In its application in French codified criminal law, the stakes in assessing a juvenile's "discernement" were considerable. Depending on how these matters were resolved, the fates of young people could be significantly altered and popular respect for the rule of law potentially confirmed or undermined. Throughout the nineteenth century, most juveniles were prosecuted for a *délit* (offence) rather than a *crime* (felony) and therefore had their cases heard in a *tribunal correctionnel* before a bench of judges rather than a *cour d'assises*, where jurors served. Establishing material responsibility for an offence (that is, whether the person accused was the agent of the offence) was a comparatively straightforward enterprise as it depended on objective evidence, but determining moral responsibility was far more delicate. In his 1878 study of moral conscience and the criminal law, Charles Brocher, a law professor at the University of Geneva, remarked on how difficult it was to assess a person's moral character, which was, he observed, "most often, hidden in the depths of the interior world," only revealing itself on the surface in ways that were easy to misinterpret, leading to inappropriate decisions being handed down.[20]

In the final decades of the nineteenth century, criminal justice practitioners, theoreticians, and reformers engaged in a debate over the basis of expertise that magistrates could lay claim to in determining whether a person had wittingly broken the law. There was an awareness among legal experts in France that the all-important mechanism of "discernement" could be a very imperfect gauge of a young person's morality. As Haussonville's description of the Daumier drawing suggested, it seemed that young people were only too capable of deceiving adults, including learned jurists. Any person who successfully duped legal authorities was a danger to the criminal justice system, effectively exposing its flaws and undermining any claims to be upholding the truth. In a reference book on medical sciences published in 1864, Gabriel Tourdes, a professor of forensic medicine at the University of Strasbourg, wrote of young people's capacity for deliberate subterfuge that "the lightness of infancy does not preclude cunning and dissimulation."[21]

Several decades later, jurists had still not developed an unerring procedure for uncovering courtroom deception. In Paris in 1911, a lawyer told a session of the first International Congress on Juvenile Courts that children had a natural inclination for play-acting and that "with absolute perfection" they would assume a particular character that was not their own but that, "in the eyes of the most perceptive and most attentive observer," would appear real.[22] Mendaciousness in the young was a considerable source of anxiety in fin-de-siècle France, not least for those within the justice system.[23] Paradoxically, a young person with the most innocent of appearances could, in fact, be the most knowing, as the drawing attributed to Daumier seemed to imply. But even if detected, how relevant was a disguised knowingness in determining the appropriate treatment for young offenders? What was of greater relevance: their "discernement" or chronological age?

## Chronological Age and Criminal Responsibility

The juvenile offender as a distinct legal category was no invention of the Third Republic. The idea that individuals who broke society's laws might be deserving of a different treatment on account of their youth and immaturity had deep roots in French legal traditions going back centuries. When it came to the prosecution of criminals, the criminal justice system of the Old Regime, building on Roman law, recognized three stages of human development. Young children under the age of seven were considered entirely irresponsible and therefore not able to be punished. Children between the ages of seven through to around fourteen (though, importantly, an age limit was not explicitly stated) were subject to criminal prosecution, but owing to their inexperience and incomplete development, penalties were to be, in theory at least, less harsh.[24] And finally there were adults, whose maturity was not strictly age-defined but was understood to coincide with the arrival of puberty. Adults were understood to be fully answerable to the law and subject to its full range of punishments.

Codification of the law in France at the end of the eighteenth and start of the nineteenth centuries marked a crucial shift in the functioning of the French criminal justice system, including in respect to juveniles. These new legal codes did not, however, impose a minimum age for prosecution, leaving unspecified when criminal responsibility could be presumed absolutely absent in a child. Without a minimum age for prosecution, even very young children could potentially be held accountable and punished for an offence. For reformers a century later, this became a significant issue of contention. As Félix Drelon told the Chamber of Deputies during discussions on the bill that would become the 1912 law on juvenile courts: "Current legislation does not provide for any criminal irresponsibility; one could bring before the courts, it has been said somewhat humorously but accurately, a child at the breast."[25] In the case of slightly older children, this was more than just a theoretical possibility; in the nineteenth century some toddlers were indeed prosecuted for criminal acts.[26]

In formulating a codified system of justice at the end of the eighteenth century, members of France's revolutionary Constituent Assembly had aimed to put in place uniform and rational processes of administration across the country. They engaged in the overhaul of a system that for centuries had functioned according to an inquisitorial (or romano-canonical) procedure.[27] To the revolutionaries, this system, which routinely drew on physical torture as a source of evidence, embodied the authoritarianism and opacity of the Old Regime that they sought to overcome.[28] In its place, they installed an accusatory system of justice in which jurors, as "citizen judges" expressing the will of the people, would adjudicate. A backlash soon followed, with magistrates defending their professionalism and arguing, amongst other things, that jurors were easily manipulated in political cases. Under Napoleon I's regime, stricter limits were imposed, and over the ensuing decades tensions persisted over the capacity of jurors to fairly impart justice.[29] When it came to the adjudication of justice for juveniles, as we shall see, rather than a concern about impartial jurors, it was the discretionary powers of magistrates that aroused criticism from reformers in the fin de siècle.

Throughout the nineteenth century, French criminal justice procedure recognized only one age-based threshold for prosecution: sixteen. Once beyond that threshold (the age of criminal majority), a young person was immediately considered an adult and accordingly became subject to the full brunt of the criminal law, including its harshest penalties. Upon reaching the age of criminal majority, individuals were believed to possess entire control of their faculties and thus could be held fully responsible for their actions and punished as adults. For juveniles under the age of sixteen, meanwhile, their development was considered to be incomplete and necessitated that a question on their level of responsibility be systematically posed. A juvenile's capacity to discern right from wrong could not be guaranteed and needed to be resolved by the court in each and every case. According to longstanding jurisprudence, a lack of "discernement" could never be assumed, no matter how young the offender. This meant, in effect, that the French criminal justice system did not acknowledge any distinction between childhood and adolescence. It would continue to formally ignore any such distinction until 1912 – far later than most comparable foreign jurisdictions.

Faint precedents for why sixteen served as the all-important age threshold in criminal law – though not necessarily specifically for punishment – can be found at various points in French legal history. It was present, for instance, in the work of the Roman jurist Ulpian and the fourteenth-century legal theorist Jean Bouteiller, and in 1690 King Louis XIII had issued a declaration stipulating sixteen as the minimum age at which a person could become a jurist.[30] Prior to codification at the end of the eighteenth century, French criminal law did not set down that offenders under a certain age threshold were automatically and systematically deserving of treatment distinct from that applied to older offenders. In 1791, some parliamentarians expressed a preference for setting a lower age threshold than sixteen for full punishment. During debates on the draft of France's penal code, one deputy, Dominique Garat, who later became minister of justice, pointed to what he saw as "improper" use of the term "child [*enfant*]" by other members of the National Constituent Assembly. "The individual who has not reached the age of sixteen," Garat observed, "is constantly being described as a child. An individual who is between the ages of thirteen and fourteen is not a child, he is a young man; he is a citizen who can write a will."[31] Ultimately, legislators rejected the suggestion that the age threshold be lowered and settled on sixteen. In so doing, they were apparently simply following existing practices employed in France, or at least in the nation's largest city. For although the Old Regime system did not stipulate a formal age for adulthood in the eyes of the criminal law, in practice, sixteen appears to have been informally taken as a significant threshold point for the application of adult punishments. In eighteenth-century Parisian courts, offenders aged sixteen and below were more commonly given non-adult punishments, even though there was no official need for magistrates to do this at that time. In effect, they made the very distinction that would later be transformed into law in the 1791 penal code.[32]

Under the Old Regime, an offender's age was not always a guarantee of protection against the most draconian sanctions of criminal law. Although the pre-revolutionary system did recognize different age thresholds, which were derived from Roman law, courts had nevertheless employed the principle of *malitia supplet aetatem* – malice makes up for age. The effect of this was that a defendant's youth could be considered irrelevant if the case at hand was particularly serious. This principle persisted in other European legal systems after its disappearance from the French. For instance, various Germanic codes (including those of Austria, Bavaria, and Saxony) had conditions under which a sentence was not alleviated for young criminals whose crime was judged to have been committed in full knowledge of the consequences. English law, too, assumed that children aged from seven to fourteen were in principle doli incapaces, but in serious cases their immorality would override their age.[33] In keeping with the culture of the Old Regime, which relied on exemplary punishment, this system had assumed that when a heinous crime was committed it was appropriate to punish the perpetrator harshly, even a very young one, because it was believed that "the immorality of these crimes must strike the intelligence even of a child."[34]

In contrast, at the turn of the nineteenth century, revolutionary and Napoleonic legislators were careful to specify that *all* young people up to a certain age – even those who had committed serious crimes – were, without exception, always to be protected from the most severe penalties laid out in the penal code. This was one aspect of their emphasis on reducing the arbitrariness of judicial decisions. Accordingly, offenders up to the age of sixteen were to be subjected to less harsh sentences than adults found guilty of the same offence. In a departure from what had gone before, the 1791 penal code drawn up by Michel Le Peletier de Saint-Fargeau made explicit the range of sentences that could be handed down for juveniles under sixteen, thereby establishing some limits to what had been magistrates' almost total discretionary powers. Part of the rationale for codifying the law in the late eighteenth century was to restrain the arbitrary potential of justice. As Robert Nye puts it: "As a reaction against the judicial despotism that had prevailed under the absolute monarchy, judges under the new system [of the 1790s] were allowed virtually no discretion whatsoever."[35]

Yet at the same time, in the case of juveniles, the mechanism of "discernement" invested magistrates with basically unlimited discretionary powers in determining whether to acquit or convict a lawbreaker aged under sixteen. In this way, despite the general curtailment of judicial power of the post-revolutionary criminal justice system, judges managed to retain considerable influence. The provision of "discernement" remained notably detached from any medicalized definition until the establishment of juvenile courts in 1912; by contrast, Article 64 of the 1810 penal code, which governed the judgement of criminal irresponsibility for offenders of any age found to have committed an unlawful act in a "state of insanity" (*état de démence*), supplemented by the 1832 introduction of the general measure of "extenuating circumstances," diluted the autonomy of magistrates by ascribing greater authority to medical experts.

Codification of the criminal law in both the penal codes of 1791 and 1810, along with the Code d'instruction criminelle (code of criminal procedure) of 1808, set down that whenever presented with an offender under the age of sixteen, in addition to resolving the matter of material guilt, courts were required to pose and answer the question of whether the juvenile defendant had committed the unlawful act "avec ou sans discernement." If judged to have acted "sans discernement," juveniles were to be acquitted but could nonetheless be kept in detention if the court decided that their parents or guardians were not capable of providing adequate assurances against further offences. The length of detention was left to the discretion of the magistrate but could not extend beyond the juvenile's twentieth year. This mechanism granting magistrates the authority to remove children from their parents' custody was in effect a precursor to the more generalized practice of state intervention in family matters introduced by reformers at the end of the nineteenth century, including the divestiture of parental authority in cases of neglect or abuse.[36] A judgment of "sans discernement" would result in an acquittal and a clean criminal record. In an effort to render these decisions distinct, it became customary to record them on a red sheet of paper.[37] In practice, however, these distinctions were often ignored or undermined.

## Article 66 and the Incarceration of Juveniles

Acquittal through Article 66 was by far the most common decision extended to juveniles facing criminal charges in France throughout the nineteenth century. Patricia O'Brien writes that only a tiny percentage of all young people detained in correctional institutions had been found guilty. The overwhelming majority – about 96 per cent – were acquitted under Article

66. Despite this, the distinction between a conviction and an acquittal was slippery. For instance, while juveniles who were acquitted as having acted "sans discernement" but incarcerated may not have incurred a criminal record, their offence was formally noted down all the same upon their admission to an institution. In addition, official statistics included acquitted juvenile cases as well as convicted ones, thereby collapsing the ostensibly all-important distinction. Together these practices meant that "acquittal was virtually meaningless in the treatment of designation of juveniles."[38] The dangerous effects of this "meaningless" designation became a major concern for reformers at the end of the nineteenth century, as we will see in the next chapter.

Acquitting juveniles but nonetheless refusing them their freedom by detaining them in an institution constituted a decidedly strange anomaly in penal practice. It also produced a rather paradoxical status for the young detainee who was in effect "virtually acquitted and in fact incarcerated."[39] As Jean-Jacques Yvorel has pointed out, over the course of the nineteenth century, Article 66 was made to serve quite different political ends – from the repressive policies of the Second Empire and the Moral Order of the early years of the Third Republic, through to the more "educational" policies of the opportunist republicans and radicals.[40] Article 66 was, as Dominique Messineo has written, "a flexible instrument dedicated to adapting to the contingency of situations," which was characterized by "an essential uncertainty as to its duration and form."[41] This was, in fact, one of its major appeals for governing authorities; it allowed for a period of institutionalization that was considerably more lengthy than the detention that would result from a conviction. In the case of boys, as we shall see in later chapters, this "institutional protection" was considered vital not only for the successful reform of juveniles but also for their formation as republican citizens, primarily because it affected their progression into the armed forces.

The fact that a juvenile deemed to have acted "sans discernement" could nonetheless be incarcerated shows the extent to which the system, rather than responding to the actual danger posed by the youth, was instead focused on treating the future potential threat – what Garofalo called "témibilité," and Foucault would refer to as "dangerosité."[42] At the time, the mechanism for what was effectively preventive detention was justified by the fact that while incarcerated, the youth was only to be subjected to educative measures, not punitive ones. Detention was not in itself considered a punishment but rather "a prophylactic [that acted] simultaneously in the interests of the juvenile himself and of society."[43] In theory, all juveniles, whether convicted or acquitted, were always to be detained separately from adult offenders. This requirement, however, remained a dead letter well into the nineteenth century. Similarly, the existence in practice of a distinction between the conditions of detention for acquitted and convicted juveniles was not always apparent. One commentator at the end of the century remarked that legislators in the first half of the century appeared only to have "a vague idea of the character to give to the detention of acquitted juveniles."[44]

During the Second Republic (1848–52), this situation was addressed somewhat, yet also further confused. In 1850, as we shall see in greater detail in chapter 4, legislation was introduced specifying that all juvenile boys who had been found to have acted "sans discernement" and thereby acquitted, but who were not to be returned to their parents, were to be placed in a "colonie pénitentiaire." These were effectively prisons without walls in the countryside where the boys would receive a religious and moral education, and be taught a trade, all with the aim of aiding their reform.

The most famous of these juvenile colonies was Mettray, founded by Frédéric-Auguste Demetz. For Michel Foucault, Mettray represented the most perfect example of the modern disciplinary system in operation: its rigid system of timetables and constant monitoring emblematic of the non-physical system of correction that typified the post-revolutionary approach to managing criminality and deviance.[45] The educative program and rural surroundings were expected to regenerate wayward youths and prepare them for a productive, law-abiding life on release.[46] This policy emerged out of the golden age of penology, which, as we saw in the previous chapter, started in the final decade of the Restoration and reached a peak during the July Monarchy.[47] Driven by a combination of liberalism and Christian compassion, reformers of this period such as Demetz and Charles Lucas attempted to offer an alternative to incarceration in prisons by establishing these juvenile colonies. Detention of juveniles found to have acted "sans discernement" was synonymous with reform and rehabilitation, in contrast to juvenile offenders deemed to have acted "avec discernement," who would be faced with a criminal conviction and punishment. However, as we shall see in the next chapter, in practice the actual distinction between acquitted and convicted juveniles within correctional institutions was reduced as a result of the 1850 law, which, in fact, folded acquitted juveniles and ones convicted and sentenced to less than two years' prison into the very same institutions.

The French penal code stipulated that all juveniles, whether convicted or acquitted, were afforded protections from certain punitive responses on account of their youth. Throughout the nineteenth century, the codified system guaranteed that juveniles would never be subjected to the harshest penalties. For instance, juveniles could never be sentenced to execution or hard labour, nor be made to wear the ball and chain, nor be tortured during interrogation. According to the 1791 penal code, they could still be placed on display in the pillory, but only if they had been convicted of a crime that carried the death penalty when committed by an adult. This provision, however, was removed from the 1810 code. Both the 1791 and 1810 codes prohibited the death penalty for juveniles. Juveniles responsible for crimes that when committed by adults carried the death penalty, hard labour for life, or deportation were to receive a penalty of between ten and twenty years' detention in a "maison de correction." If convicted of a délit, juveniles could only be handed down prison sentences that were less than half those that would be given to adults convicted of the same offence.[48] Revolutionary and Napoleonic legislators were concerned to give juveniles penalties that reformed them and prepared them for release, rather than ones that simply punished them.

Protecting juveniles from the most severe punishments was motivated by the hope that they would one day become useful and productive citizens.[49] By the end of the nineteenth century, however, jurists, reformers, and social commentators were drawing attention to an apparently unexpected result of this practice: young people preferred receiving a conviction to an acquittal because it meant that they would, in general, serve a shorter sentence. Acquittal under Article 66 of the penal code empowered the magistrate to have the young person detained in a juvenile colony through to the age of twenty. For young people, this was a significant penalty – lengthy incarceration loomed larger than the taint of a conviction and a short stint in detention.

This system of acquitting young offenders but placing them in detention in juvenile colonies for a substantial period of time had the ready potential to be misinterpreted by young people. Whereas the young girl in Daumier's drawing had played up her innocence in order to win an acquittal, reformers cited evidence of courtroom performances with exactly the opposite intent: juveniles who exaggerated their perversity and emphasized their degree of "discernement" in order to avoid an acquittal and a lengthy period of detention. In a case from the mid-1820s reported in the *Gazette des tribunaux* at the time, a young boy, despite his childlike appearance, insisted to the court that he was over sixteen and was thus given a six-month prison term while his friend, who made no attempt to lie about his age, was acquitted on account of having acted "sans discernement" and incarcerated for four years.[50]

In the 1890s it was alleged that juveniles often deliberately lied about their age expressly in order that the question of "discernement" not be posed, while some boys took on their older brothers' identities for the same purpose.[51] In the 1840s, Gustave de Beaumont and Alexis de Tocqueville had pointed out the anomaly that to be found to have acted "sans discernement" was, from the point of view of the juvenile, harsher than a conviction, writing that "it can be said with reason that, for children under sixteen, it is better to be convicted than acquitted."[52] Half a century later, Louis Puibaraud made the same point at a session of the Paris International Prison Congress in 1895. Acquittal and detention in a juvenile colony, Puibaraud said, seemed to a young person, "not unreasonably, an infinitely more painful punishment, because it is freedom lost for at least four years."[53] When juveniles were brought before the criminal courts, Puibaraud asserted, many had only one idea in their heads: "to establish through their cockiness [*forfanterie*], their cynicism, whatever circumstance of premeditation invented by them, that they had awareness of the wrongdoing committed."[54] Young people, Puibaraud went on, "are not jurists" and were more concerned with purchasing their freedom than with maintaining an unblemished criminal record. Indeed, a criminal conviction could be brandished as a badge of pride and a sure ticket for entry into a gang.[55] With these objectives in view, juveniles had every reason to "act cynically, to simulate that hypocrisy in the inverse direction that could be called hypocrisy of wrongdoing instead of hypocrisy of innocence."[56]

In the fin de siècle, there were considerable long-term social and economic consequences to juveniles acquiring a criminal record early. Of particular concern to reformers, legislators, and policymakers, as we shall see in chapter 5, were the implications for young men's military service. Juveniles' apparent preference for a criminal conviction and short-term imprisonment over an acquittal and lengthy detention was just one aspect of the criminal justice system's functioning towards young people that aroused the concern of reformers and jurists at the end of the century. On an even more fundamental level, many legal theorists and practitioners began to point to the shaky foundations of "discernement" as a legal precept and questioned its relevance and, indeed, its meaning.

## Discretionary Powers of Magistrates

The nebulous grounds on which judges based their decisions of juveniles' "discernement" arose in discussions at meetings of the SGP from the group's earliest years. One member remarked at a meeting in 1879 that most of the time judges did not have any information from which to derive their evaluation and were compelled to make the best assessment they could, based on the circumstances of the offence, the juvenile's performance in court, and their responses during questioning.[57] Confronted with the term's inadequacies and imprecision, some French reformers called for the outright removal of the concept from the pages of the penal code and the code of criminal procedure.[58]

In his 1898 doctoral thesis on "discernement" and the law, Gustave Mabille, a Parisian lawyer, remarked that the penal code offered no definition of the word.[59] This was not entirely unusual. After all, the penal code offered no explicit definition of mental insanity ("démence") either. However, whereas magistrates routinely assessed juveniles without calling on outside expertise, for decisions on mental insanity (covered by Article 64 of the penal code), they were far more inclined to defer to medical experts. As Robert Nye puts it, "in the absence of more precise criteria for deciding questions on penal irresponsibility, judges readily asked specialists in mental illness, though the code made no specific provision for their doing so."[60] When it came to juveniles, by contrast, the process appeared more haphazard. Magistrates would decide that one juvenile had acted "avec discernement," another "sans," but, Mabille asked, "where is the distinguishing criterion to be found?"[61] If "discernement" was understood to mean the awareness that a particular act was illicit and carried with it certain consequences, Mabille argued, one would have to accept that *all* children in urban areas had acted "avec discernement" since they were necessarily exposed to the corrupting influences of the metropolis each and every day.[62] Within the context of increasing protections being extended to children in the interests of their long-term growth and respect for the existing social order, such a suggestion could not be countenanced. Some other solution needed to be found.

Prominent legal theorists remarked that the only means of recognizing the development of a child's reason was by induction and by comparing it to that of an adult. In this vein, Pellegrino Rossi, jurist and, for a brief period, minister of justice in the government of the Papal States under Pope Pius IX, observed that "it is by comparing the speech and actions of the child with our speech and our actions in comparable circumstances that we can conclude through analogy that [the child] understands, reasons, that they distinguish good from bad, utility from harm."[63] Nineteenth-century legal theorists Adolphe Chauveau and Faustin Hélie similarly argued that the only way to determine whether a young person had understood that certain actions were wrong was "through comparing the ideas and actions of the child with our [own] actions and our [own] ideas."[64]

The final decade of the nineteenth century saw a considerable shift in approach as reformers in France demanded that greater efforts be made to attentively examine the circumstances and background of juveniles' cases in the interests of making a more accurate determination of "discernement." Despite the inevitable shortcomings of the existing system, it was hoped that by giving closer attention to the investigation process, magistrates would be able to tailor their response better to the needs of the child and would also run less risk of handing down an incorrect or inappropriate decision.

This wave of concern to modify judicial practice in regard to juvenile offenders represented the first time that jurists had preoccupied themselves with adapting the courtroom process to the particular condition of young people. For the first few decades of the nineteenth century, court hearings for juveniles had been managed according to the same divisions that applied to adult offenders: *contraventions* (minor offences) were judged by a simple police court with a single judge (*juge de la paix*) presiding, délits were heard in a tribunal correctionnel before a panel of three magistrates, while more serious crimes were heard before a jury of active citizens in a cour d'assises. Set up in 1808, these cours d'assises, one of which was established in every jurisdiction, were symbols of the sovereignty of the people. However, as time passed, doubt was expressed over the reliability and competence of jurors to hand down appropriate decisions.[65]

Given that most juveniles committed délits rather than crimes, their cases were more regularly heard in a tribunal correctionnel before a panel of judges rather than in a cour d'assises in front of a jury. In addition, from the 1820s onwards, partly as a way of cutting costs, there was an increasing tendency for prosecutors to refer to lower courts those cases in which juvenile defendants were accused of crimes (which strictly should have been heard in a cour d'assises, as for anyone else). A law passed on 25 June 1824 stipulated that cases involving minors under sixteen years who had no older accomplices and who were accused of crimes not punishable by death, hard labour, or deportation were to be heard in tribunaux correctionnels rather than cours d'assises.[66] This "correctionalization" appealed to parliamentarians across the political spectrum on account of the fact that it promised to expedite the prosecution of juveniles and alleviate the expense of detaining prisoners before trial. Article 250 of the Code d'instruction criminelle laid down that the cours d'assises were to sit only every three months, unlike the tribunaux correctionnels, which sat permanently, meaning that pretrial detention was lengthier for those whose cases were to be heard in the higher court.[67]

As a result of this correctionalization, over time the number of juveniles brought before the cours d'assises grew smaller. Whereas in 1831, 127 juveniles were heard before a cour d'assises, by 1901 that figure had fallen to just 24 (out of a total of 2,103 defendants). Over the same period, the number of juveniles brought before a tribunal correctionnel had greatly increased – in 1831 these courts had tried 2,852 juveniles (2,403 boys and 449 girls). Seventy years later, the number had grown significantly, reaching a total of 5,006 (4,357 boys, 649 girls).[68] From the late 1830s, correctional courts acquitting juveniles under Article 66 became increasingly common. Between 1838 and 1839 alone the proportion of juveniles brought before the court judged to have acted "sans discernement" grew from 13 to 23 per cent in the space of a year. By the 1860s the rate had grown to over 50 per cent, and by the turn of the century 70 per cent of juveniles brought before the court were being acquitted.[69] This shift can be partly explained, as Dominique Messineo points out, by a reform to the penal code in 1832 that decriminalized vagrancy among juveniles, reflecting a desire to decriminalize juvenile offending more generally.[70] In terms of disciplinary control, there was a clear advantage to acquitting juveniles under Article 66: this mechanism enabled magistrates to extend supervisory control for periods much longer than a conviction and prison term would have allowed.[71]

Transferring the majority of juvenile cases to a lower court had broader consequences, including in terms of public perception. It meant that only the most serious cases (for instance, murder or manslaughter) were heard in the cours d'assises. This had the effect of drawing attention to and emphasizing the monstrousness of the most heinous crimes committed by juveniles. Because most juvenile offenders were charged with offences that required a hearing in the tribunal correctionnel, they were effectively grouped into a single class, which, as Kathleen Nilan has noted, "[emphasized] the correctional nature of judicial proceedings against juveniles and … [underscored] the difference between adult and juvenile penalties."[72] By the same token, the fact that it was now only the most serious crimes that would bring a juvenile defendant before the cours d'assises "served to further emphasize the anomalous nature of children who had committed serious crime … [For] no longer mixed in with other juveniles, accused of minor felonies, the child parricides, poisoners, and arsonists would stand alone in the Assizes, appearing to both the court and the general public more aberrant and more dangerous than 'normal' children."[73]

Transferring a juvenile's trial to a lower court had the benefit of enabling judges to exercise greater control over the evaluation of young people, since in the juryless tribunal correctionnel it was their duty to respond to both the question of guilt and that of responsibility ("discernement") and to hand down an appropriate sentence. Jean-Jacques Yvorel has shown that between 1826 and 1904 only a small number of juveniles appeared before a cour d'assises (from a high of 143 in 1829 to a low of just 18 in 1904), of whom the overwhelming majority were male (120 in 1829, 16 in 1904). The number of juveniles heard in correctional courts in this same period reached a peak in the mid-1850s of over 10,000 (8,000 of them male), a circumstance that Yvorel has attributed to the particularly repressive culture of the Second Empire.[74] Even on the rare occasions when a juvenile's case was heard in a cour d'assises, it was still the judge who posed the question of "discernement" to the jury, and it has been suggested that the magistrate's framing of the question had a considerable impact on juries' decisions.[75] On a more general level, Ruth Harris has noted that jurors in nineteenth-century French courts were required to answer "yes" or "no" to a long list of often complicated questions, given no guidance on the governing law by the judge and not offered any formal definition of the crimes they were being asked to assess. They were asked not only whether a criminal act had been committed, but whether it had been done with criminal intent. Without being fully versed in the underlying legal theories, jurors would often return verdicts that excused offenders on the sorts of grounds covered by biologically determinist theories of crime.[76]

For republican legislators, an overarching consideration when it came to the decisions of magistrates generally was that they should not undermine the values or structures of republican authority, a particular priority in the context of anticlerical laws.[77] From February 1879 onwards, successive justice ministers purged the magistrature, emptying the *parquets* of any judges thought to pose a threat to the realization of republican ideals.[78] To this end, in August 1883 a statute was passed investing France's highest court (the Cour de cassation) with the power to remove from the ranks any magistrate who displayed antipathy to the republic.

## The Beginnings of a Specialized System of Justice for Juveniles

In 1890, members of the SGP, including Adolphe Guillot, lawyer Henri Rollet (who collaborated with senator Théophile Roussel on the development of legislation passed in 1889 that deprived unfit parents of custody of their children), and legal scholar Paul Flandin, attempted to tackle the problems with juvenile justice procedure in a more direct manner. They established the Comité de défense des enfants traduits en justice, which would meet once a month in central Paris. This and other similar groups created in other cities throughout the country, including Lyon, Marseille, Montpellier, and Le Havre, would play a pivotal role in shaping legislation on juvenile justice reform at the turn of the twentieth century.

The Comité de défense focused on campaigning for and experimenting with protective measures for juvenile offenders before the establishment of juvenile courts in 1912. Described by sociologist Philippe Meyer as a "holy alliance" of Parisian jurists,[79] the group was crucially important for the development of new approaches to the judicial treatment of juveniles. Consisting of practising jurists, the Comité de défense aimed to be at once "a committee of legislative study, a law school, an organ of reform and a supervisory council [*conseil de contrôle*]."[80] The Parisian group described its mission and aim as "the study, discussion and recommendation of improvements to introduce into the legal regime applied to abandoned, unfortunate, vicious or criminal [*coupable*] children" so as to "detail, codify if possible, the rules indispensable to the investigation of offences for which children are reproached as well as the defence of their moral and material interests."[81] As a result of the efforts of the Comité de défense, Parisian court procedure gradually began to bend and adapt – inasmuch as was possible without legislative change – to the particular needs of juveniles brought before the criminal courts in the French capital. The group was later praised by senator Ferdinand Dreyfus, the main sponsor of the 1912 law on juvenile courts, for having developed "a science founded on experimentation."[82]

One of these reformers' concerns was the perfunctory manner in which juveniles' cases could be dealt with by the criminal justice system, especially those who were caught *en flagrant délit*. During the Second Empire, in an effort to reduce overcrowding in institutions for offenders awaiting trial, legislators had introduced a law that expedited the processing of offenders whose guilt, because they were caught in the act, did not need to be established. This law, passed on 20 May 1863, was an example of what the high-ranking jurist (and later government minister) Jean Cruppi would describe in 1898 as "full steam ahead justice [*la justice à toute vapeur*]."[83]

This expedited approach was recognized by child protection advocates as particularly badly suited to the conditions of juvenile offenders, which required patient investigation not in order to establish material guilt, but rather to understand the social conditions (especially familial ones) that had contributed to their misdeeds. Louis Albanel told the International Institute of Statistics meeting in Saint Petersburg in 1897 that the 1863 law, which was "so humanitarian for adults, became an abuse applied to juveniles" and would, in all likelihood, eventually lead to habitual criminality and forced exile to a bagne.[84] The shortcomings associated with this law motivated Henri Lefuel, a deputy public prosecutor, to set down new procedures in a circular dated 31 October 1891 for processing juveniles. The circular stated that in cases when public prosecutors believed an arrested juvenile could not simply be returned to their parents, an investigation was to be opened and a defence lawyer immediately appointed. Within twenty-four hours of arrest, the juvenile was to be questioned by the examining magistrate, who was supplied with the youth's criminal record and birth certificate.[85]

In 1894, another important shift in juvenile justice procedure took place when Albanel and fellow juge d'instruction Guillot were put in charge of processing and leading the inquiries into all cases involving juveniles within the jurisdiction of Paris. This effectively made Guillot and Albanel specialist juvenile justice magistrates at the investigative level. Historically, the juge d'instruction had a very important role in the French justice system, invested with practically unlimited powers granting access to almost every area of a defendant's life for the sake of assembling material for the trial. Considered a throwback to a shady, inquisitorial system of discretionary justice, the juge d'instruction became a figure of major concern to radical republicans in the fin de siècle.[86] As the preliminary gatekeeper for the prosecution of crimes, the juge d'instruction had the power to throw out a case if he determined that there was insufficient evidence to incriminate a suspect.

In a short pamphlet published in 1890, Guillot wrote of the difficulties of assessing juvenile offenders, especially the question of determining their level of "discernement." It was the most delicate matter, he observed, and required great skill and attention, particularly given that "certain children, with rosy faces and innocent eyes, practise lying with a consummate art."[87] A devout Catholic, Guillot, it seems, had shown sufficient caution to withstand the republicans' purge of the magistracy following their rise to dominance in the late 1870s. Guillot's faith apparently shaped his perception of his judicial role as, according to Pascale Quincy-Lefebvre, he saw himself as a confessor and arbiter of children's moral conscience.[88] In 1906 the anticlerical newspaper *La Lanterne* accused Louis Albanel of being a "clerical magistrate," criticizing him for having demonstrated a partiality inappropriate to his profession by having told a rival newspaper that the rise of juvenile criminality was due to the spread of secular education.[89] A few days later the newspaper issued a retraction of the allegation and reported that far from being an enemy of secular education, Albanel was, in fact, dedicated to the cause of moral regeneration, as was clear from his philanthropic efforts offering support to children from underprivileged backgrounds.[90]

The intention behind this specialization of the two Parisian juges d'instruction, Albanel and Guillot, was to develop a fuller picture of juveniles' social circumstances, thereby enabling the courts to nominate the most appropriate treatment. For reasons that are not entirely clear, the experiment in specialization in Paris was brought to an end in 1899.[91] Ironically, this coincided with the establishment in Chicago of what were generally recognized to be the world's first juvenile courts.[92] The specialization of the juge d'instruction in juvenile justice did resurface in late 1906, however, and in early 1907 the Paris public prosecutor declared that all juveniles' cases would be heard in a single chamber,[93] thus establishing what reformer Marcel Kleine described in 1911 as "a veritable embryo of [a] children's court."[94]

Despite these early experiments implemented in France's larger jurisdictions from the 1890s, the establishment of juvenile courts in the United States was often presented to French reformers as constituting a revolution in justice procedure for young people. The re-appearance in 1906 of a specialized court procedure for juveniles in France was partly due to a revival of interest following a conference held on the subject at the Musée social, an important Parisian centre of research for social issues, in February of that year.[95] Organized by Edouard Julhiet, an engineer by profession, who had been exposed to the existence and operation of juvenile courts in the United States during a recent visit, the 1906 conference marked the beginning of what turned out to be a five-year campaign of concentrated agitation for reform.[96] Impressed by what he had witnessed in the United States, Julhiet had become determined to establish a comparable system in France. Everything about the process employed in the American system emphasized the paternalistic concern for the young person's well-being: the judge, specialized in juvenile cases, sat alongside the juvenile, rather than towering above, so as to underscore his role as confessor and confidant, rather than adjudicator. In a report to the SGP delivered in 1906, Georges Frèrejouan Du Saint, a former magistrate, declared that what defined the American juvenile courts was their concentration on the offender rather than on the offence. Their purpose, he declared, was not to condemn young offenders, nor to judge them, but to save them.[97]

Although admiring the apparent success of the juvenile court system on the other side of the Atlantic, reformers debated whether it could serve as a direct model for France. The American system's use of a single judge, for instance, ran counter to the French revolutionary tradition of a three-judge bench. During discussions in the Senate in 1911, René Bérenger explained the utility of a single judge over a panel of three judges, arguing that such a structure conveyed to young defendants that the law was working in their best interests and they would not be unnecessarily intimidated by the process.[98] Ultimately, however, in the interest of maintaining a check on magistrates' powers, it was decided that a panel would be retained. Another aspect of debate was the nomination of a minimum age for criminal responsibility, something that the codified French system had not admitted.

## Specifying a Minimum Age for Criminal Responsibility?

With regard to its treatment of young offenders, France had an ambiguous status on the world stage of juvenile justice reform, which became increasingly internationalized in the second half of the nineteenth century.[99] Earlier in the century, the penal code's simplified, non-tiered system had provided inspiration for many countries in Europe and the Americas, and its juvenile colonies (most notably Mettray) were considered the template for reformatories across the globe.[100] By century's end, however, France appeared something of a pariah internationally, most notably perhaps on account of the fact that French criminal law did not set a minimum age limit for criminal responsibility.[101] One jurist told a meeting of the Parisian Comité de défense des enfants traduits en justice in 1894 that while their international colleagues had devoted great attention to the "primordial issue" of decriminalizing children's offences, and had moreover formulated practical measures, French discussions had been "as fruitless as they were token."[102] Having previously been a guiding light for the rest of the world by establishing a modern system of criminal justice, France now found itself in a state of clear inferiority "with regard to those whom it had served, as it were, as a generating mould."[103] Juvenile justice was not the only area of the criminal law in which the French system was lagging behind in comparison to other countries – its transportation of convicts to far-flung bagnes was another, even more contentious point of difference.[104]

Unless French legislators were willing to concede that their country's youth were more perverted than those in comparable countries, reformers believed that there was an urgent need to bring the treatment of juvenile offenders into alignment with international standards. This entailed adopting a standardized minimum age of criminal responsibility. In advocating for a distinct system of courts for juveniles and the decriminalization of offences committed under a particular age threshold, reformers saw themselves as helping to restore French honour on the international stage. It was something of an affront to French national pride that many of the various European and American systems that had copied France's codified criminal justice system would introduce a minimum age of criminal responsibility decades earlier than France.[105]

Eventually, in 1912, French legislators adopted a minimum age of criminal responsibility: thirteen. Various reasons were given for France's delay in legislating a minimum age. According to the president of the Paris bar, Henri Robert, it had taken until 1912 because legislators had simply taken it for granted that very young children would not be prosecuted.[106] Whatever the legislators' motives, however, by not setting an age of immunity from prosecution the French criminal justice system acknowledged that "criminal responsibility, *in theory*, exists at any age," to use the words of Louis Puibaraud.[107] Moreover the system assumed that evil, like genius, could manifest itself at any age, no matter how young.

Loys Brueyre, writer, folklorist, and senior functionary in the Assistance publique, described precociously evil children as "Picos de la Mirandole of evil" – a reference to the Italian Renaissance child prodigy Giovanni Pico della Mirandola.[108] Examples of cruel children could be found throughout history, and even in the highest social echelons. For instance, as a child, Louis XIII was said to have enjoyed slowly crushing the heads of sparrows between two stones, while one of the Spanish kings had, as a boy, taken great pleasure in torturing young rabbits and observing their pain.[109] Victor Hugo described children's innate capacity for cruelty in his poem "Le Crapaud" about the callous torture of a toad by a group of boys:

> I was a child, I was small, I was cruel,
> Every man on the earth, where the soul wanders enslaved,
> Can begin thus the story of his life.[110]

For Hugo, the display of wanton cruelty was a universal feature of the human condition and children had as much innate badness contained within themselves as good.

In the late 1890s, Hugo's poem was taken up by the Swiss-born philosopher Albert Schinz in an article on children's morality. Schinz argued that children were natural-born liars and thieves and that they were closer to adults than contemporary culture, blinkered as it was by the Rousseauist myth of the pure and innocent child, often allowed.[111] In fact, Rousseau himself recognized children's propensity for cruelty, but pointed out that children acted without full understanding of the consequences of their actions. In *Émile* Rousseau wrote that "a child wants to disturb everything he sees, he breaks, he smashes everything he can reach, he grabs a bird like he would grab a stone, and suffocates it without knowing what he is doing."[112] Schinz asserted that children, being instinctively malicious, required a system of education that restrained their undesirable tendencies rather than developing their good ones.[113] These ideas pushed against international standards that assumed an automatic lack of responsibility among children and instead validated existing and longstanding practices in the French system.

Finally, on 22 July 1912, after several decades of experimentation and debate, France's parliament officially recognized two new categories in the criminal law: the child offender under thirteen and the adolescent offender aged over thirteen and under sixteen (a further category of young offender had been introduced into French law six years earlier: those between sixteen and eighteen). The 1912 legislation inaugurated an entirely distinct branch of criminal justice for juveniles; not only was the procedure distinct from that of adults, but it also introduced a distinction between juvenile offenders of different ages, effectively acknowledging a fundamental difference between children and adolescents. In a 1914 circular issued by Jean-Baptiste Bienvenu Martin, the justice minister, all of the nation's public prosecutors were reminded that these age distinctions, which formed "the very basis of the new legislation," were to be strictly respected at all stages of an investigation and prosecution.[114]

The introduction of these categories was a major turning point in the formulation of criminal law with regard to young people. For the first time since codification, the law of 1912 introduced an intermediary period "between absolute irresponsibility and criminal responsibility."[115] Henceforth all offenders under the age of thirteen were systematically to be assumed to have acted "sans discernement," regardless of how serious the offence, and could never be given a criminal conviction. All offenders aged between thirteen and eighteen, meanwhile, would be evaluated by magistrates, drawing on detailed information gathered by the juge d'instruction, in order to determine whether a conviction was appropriate. Offenders aged between thirteen and sixteen who were found to have acted "sans discernement" would be acquitted. If they were deemed to have acted "avec discernement," however, they would be convicted but always given attenuated sentences on account of their youth, in keeping with longstanding practice. Finally, for offenders aged between sixteen and eighteen, if they were found to have acted "sans discernement" they would be acquitted, but if not they would be convicted and punished as adults. (The justifications for these age boundaries are explored in the next chapter.)

Ever since codification at the dawning of the nineteenth century, France's modern criminal justice system had operated on the rather extraordinary basis that there was no age at which an individual could not be prosecuted. This meant that, at least in theory, "the child who has just been born could be prosecuted," as juvenile justice advocate and lawyer Marcel Kleine pointed out in 1911.[116] Similarly, in civil law there was no minimum age for correction paternelle – the practice that allowed parents to have their children imprisoned – meaning that, in principle, even tiny infants could be detained on parental request. Thus, as we have seen, although practitioners in the criminal justice system had been devoting greater attention to juveniles' cases from the final decades of the nineteenth century, they had nonetheless been operating within a framework that made no explicit distinction between offenders of different age groups. In only recognizing one category of youth, with no recognition of incremental responsibility, the French criminal justice system assumed that it was impossible to state in advance with absolute certainty when moral conscience was awakened in all individuals. Although age was important in determining whether the question of "discernement" needed to be posed and resolved, age was never to be understood as a priori evidence of a lack of morality or an absence of free will.

Throughout the nineteenth century, the most salient aspect of chronological age for France's criminal justice system was whether a person accused of an offence was older or younger than sixteen. An offender's age was usually proven by a birth certificate; however, in cases when one could not be produced, courts were allowed to employ any means available to establish it. This might include witnesses, written testimonies, or just simple presumption.[117] As time went on, with the differences between these age categories becoming more pronounced outside the domain of criminal justice as a result of legislation on education and labour, jurists questioned the sustainability and utility of the existing structure. Widespread concerns at the end of the century over the number of young criminals who formed part of a so-called "armée du crime" and what appeared to be their increasingly precocious initiation into unlawful behaviour compelled jurists to cast doubt on the legitimacy of the fundamental principles of juvenile judicial procedure that had been in place since codification.

At the same time, republican education and labour laws established universal age thresholds that solidified expectations of how a "good childhood" was to be spent and moreover cultivated a sharper distinction between the life stages of childhood and adolescence, the boundaries of which were defined by their institutional associations. As part of the preliminary debates that preceded the adoption of the bill on juvenile courts, a report was presented to the Chamber of Deputies recommending that the distinction between children and adolescents in the criminal law be set at age twelve, but a Senate commission led by René Bérenger in 1911 suggested it be age thirteen so as to bring it into line with the existing laws governing compulsory education and sexual offences.[118] The age of sexual consent for both males and females was set at thirteen (raised from eleven following reform to Article 331 of the penal code in 1863).[119] It was systematically assumed that any sexual act between an adult and a child under that age had been carried out violently and against the child's will.[120] It is important to note, however, that Article 332 of the penal code specified that a girl was judged responsible and adult in cases of "séduction" from the age of fifteen.[121]

As we saw in chapter 1, reformers at the end of the nineteenth century were increasingly concerned about young people who were beyond the age of compulsory schooling. Changes to the social status of children prompted legal theorists at the end of the century to question the appropriateness of a criminal justice system that, while guaranteeing immunity from the harshest penalties to all juveniles up to the age of sixteen, nevertheless failed to recognize any formal distinction between offenders of different ages and left open the possibility for even the youngest of children to be prosecuted and convicted. Haussonville had told the parliamentary inquiry in the early 1870s that the penal code assumed a relationship between age and responsibility that was "very simple."[122] Similarly Charles Vigneron d'Heucqueville, a jurist, philanthropist, and art collector, observed in his doctoral thesis in law published in 1899 that the system "from the point of view of criminal justice only divides human life into two periods."[123] But beneath this apparently "simple" structure lay a highly complex and ultimately arbitrary procedure of assessment.

The structure of minimal aged-based partition in the criminal justice system appears to have been in keeping with theories of development endorsed by the pedagogy disseminated to public school teachers during the Third Republic, which emphasized the interconnected relationship between stages of development rather than presenting them as disunited and entirely distinct. For instance, Dr Élie Pécaut, who contributed the entry on "human life (ages)" for Ferdinand Buisson's *Dictionnaire de pédagogie*, observed that "any division of ages is fatally artificial; for there are no stops, nor any interruptions in the development of life, and periods succeed one another in imperceptible transitions. In addition, divisions adopted differ from one author to another."[124]

The notion of life stages as being interlocked was reiterated several decades later by Gabriel Compayré, a prominent republican pedagogue and psychologist. In a review article on the pioneering work of American psychologist Granville Stanley Hall into adolescence, Compayré disputed Hall's claim that adolescence marked a decisive break in human development and argued instead that stages of individual development overlapped one another. He compared life stages to the changing of the seasons, and argued that just as "springtime does not always end on 21 June and there can be springlike days in the summer, so childhood is prolonged into adolescence and adolescence into youth."[125] Although both Compayré and Hall agreed that the stages of childhood and adolescence had their own defining characteristics, they described their connection in quite distinct ways. Whereas in Hall's conceptualization, these phases of development were quite separate from one another like the different floors of a house, for Compayré these stages blended into each other like links in a chain and could not be easily detached.[126]

It was a sign of the preeminent position of juvenile justice in learned legal circles by the end of the nineteenth century that in 1890 the International Prison Congress decided to devote an entire section of the congress specifically to the issue from that point forward. At the next congress, held in Paris five years later, organizers anticipated a large audience for the juvenile justice section, reserving the largest room in the Collège de France for its meetings.[127] At these international gatherings, French delegates were made aware of the fact that their country was almost unique in the Western world in not having set a minimum age for criminal responsibility. The only other country not to have recognized a minimum age threshold was Turkey, a country with which France would hardly have wished to be compared. Rather than remain isolated among the "backward," French jurists declared that it was time for France to emerge from its state of torpor and take a stand alongside other "civilized" countries.[128]

In an 1896 book Jacques Bonzon, a Parisian lawyer, issued a scathing attack on the outdatedness of the nation's justice system for children. Referring to unsuccessful attempts made in the early 1880s by Roussel and others to decriminalize offences committed by young children, Bonzon lamented that these noble efforts "lie sleeping in parliamentary archives in a somnolence that nothing can disturb."[129] France's stature on criminal justice issues within the international community at the end of the nineteenth century was uneven, Bonzon remarked. Viewed historically as a pioneer of enlightened, modern methods of justice, in recent times it had fallen well behind other countries. While the penal code of 1810 had been considered avant-garde at that time in its standardized, equitable system of justice, it was now appearing "backward, not only in regard to other peoples, but also to ideas long accepted in France."[130]

The comparative tardiness in formally legislating on juvenile justice was by no means the product of a lack of interest or awareness in France about the needs of young people in trouble with the law. As we have seen, from the early 1890s there had been considerable experimentation in specialized juvenile justice in the nation's larger jurisdictions. In addition, as is explored elsewhere in this book, the prison administration had anticipated the courts in recognizing a distinction between youths over and under twelve and encouraging the creation of special institutions solely for the detention of juveniles under twelve who had been acquitted under Article 66.

To a certain extent, the sluggishness of legislative reform was the result of a tendency for ideas to be discussed, researched in detail, and even sometimes subjected to experimentation before they would be legislated on. As one jurist observed in 1907, "unfortunately, in France, bills are discussed at length before being voted on, if they are not left to sleep forgotten in the boxes of commissions."[131] It was not an unfair assessment. The articulation of ideas frequently preceded their formal recognition in legislation by a substantial margin. As Périclès Grimanelli, a *préfet* and later director of France's prison administration, commented in a speech on juvenile crime to the Paris International Prison Congress in 1895, it was important to make the distinction between the legal system and the force that lay within it. Grimanelli argued that an energy of reform was driving forward a legal framework that itself had become outdated.[132]

The guidance that other countries might offer French legislators when it came to setting an age of criminal irresponsibility could only have been general since the age thresholds chosen for an automatic assumption of irresponsibility varied from country to country. In 1890, for example, English law considered children wholly irresponsible up to the age of seven, and conditionally responsible up to the age of fourteen. In Italian and Russian law, the relative age limits were nine and fourteen.[133] Ugo Conti, an Italian delegate at the 1895 International Prison Congress in Paris, explained that these age divisions had been deliberately selected as they corresponded to childhood and adolescence. Although childhood ended physiologically at age seven, with the occurrence of secondary dentition, Italian legislators had considered it prudent to extend the age limit to nine.[134] In German law, the limits were set at twelve and eighteen.[135]

The lack of agreement among foreign legislators on these age thresholds was interpreted by French jurists as demonstrating their arbitrariness. Emmanuel Lasserre, a civil court judge from Bordeaux, saw the variability of ages as evidence of the impossibility of identifying beyond a shadow of a doubt "the exact time when intellectual light is produced, such that reason is able to weigh the consequences of our acts and conscience to judge the morality of them."[136] Similarly René Garraud, Parisian lawyer and professor of criminal law at the University of Lyon, asserted that the age at which all children could universally be assumed to possess "discernement" was "so difficult to map out, so variable, that [foreign legislations] have not adopted the same rules."[137]

Debate over the matter of whether children under a certain age should be extended an assumption of absolute criminal irresponsibility did not arise for the first time during the Third Republic. In 1832 Pierre Teulon, a deputy in the upper house of the French parliament, had proposed that all offenders under a certain age be assumed criminally irresponsible, or at least that all offenders under the age of twelve be judged in closed hearings so as to protect them, their families, and members of the public from the scandal of an open courtroom trial. Furthermore, in a suggestion that anticipated reforms finally introduced in 1906, Teulon also called for the age of criminal majority to be raised to eighteen, arguing that to assume that a sixteen-year-old had "intelligence ... sufficiently developed to judge the full morality of an action, to appreciate the full criminality of a deed" was "a hundred times more barbaric than the death penalty itself."[138] These suggestions, however, were rejected and the French penal code through the nineteenth century continued to treat sixteen-year-olds as adults.[139]

In 1855 Joseph Ortolan, a professor of law at the Sorbonne and author of important works on constitutional and comparative criminal law, condemned this system and argued that to prosecute a child of six years seemed entirely unjust and anomalous.[140] Ortolan advocated that a minimum age for prosecution be specified – "no matter what one for the moment, make it three, four, five or six years old if you want" – so as to spare young children from an experience that served no rational purpose.[141] In the same year that Ortolan's demands were published, confronted with a growing problem of overcrowding in juvenile colonies, with particularly high numbers of acquitted juveniles, the interior minister reported that *procureurs* were being directed to limit legal proceedings being taken against juveniles, and to only prosecute children under the ages of seven or eight in "absolutely exceptional cases."[142] Prosecutors were therefore encouraged – though not obliged – to take an offender's young age into account when considering opening legal proceedings.

A proposal for the setting of an age of irresponsibility and immunity from criminal prosecution was again raised in 1879 when Théophile Roussel suggested to the SGP that, as was the practice in foreign jurisdictions, young children be exempt from any form of penal prosecution and punishment because they were not sufficiently developed to be considered responsible for their actions.[143] His proposal was heartily endorsed by criminal justice reform veteran Charles Lucas, who suggested that all offenders aged under twelve be protected from prosecution and be sent to educational reformatories.[144] Jurist and republican statesman Charles Houyvet made a different suggestion, proposing that all juveniles under the age sixteen who had only committed a délit be assumed to have acted "sans discernement" and that they be returned to their parents or be sent to a "maison de correction" or a "maison de réforme" where they would be raised for a period not beyond their twenty-first birthday.[145]

In effect, Houyvet was proposing the decriminalization of certain offences when committed by juveniles. In his view, it was the seriousness of the offence rather than the age of the juvenile that was most salient when determining the appropriateness of punishment. Responding to Houyvet's suggestions, Fernand Desportes, a Parisian lawyer and member of the Conseil supérieur des prisons, endorsed the proposal that all juveniles under sixteen who had committed minor offences be automatically assumed to have acted "sans discernement." In addition, Desportes asserted, all offenders under twelve, no matter the nature of the act they committed, should be considered to have acted "sans discernement." Before a child had reached the age of twelve, he maintained, it was not possible to say that they had the "maturity, experience, rational will [*la volonté réfléchie*]" – the necessary components of criminal intent and, thus, responsibility.[146]

Several meetings of the SGP in 1879 discussed the matter of criminal irresponsibility. Ultimately members recommended the penal code be revised such that all offenders under twelve be assumed to have acted "sans discernement."[147] In 1881, Roussel and other senators, including René Bérenger and Jules Simon, lodged a proposal to this effect in the Senate, but it failed to pass, as legislators preferred to leave a system in place that deferred to the expertise of magistrates on evaluating responsibility rather than introducing universal thresholds that assumed irresponsibility under a certain age.[148]

But the issue refused to go away. In the final meeting of the SGP for 1891 Loys Brueyre led a discussion on establishing an age limit for the automatic assumption of a lack of "discernement." Brueyre proposed that all children under the age of ten be considered wholly irresponsible and that those aged between ten and sixteen be evaluated on a case-by-case basis, as under the existing system. He was careful to clarify that his argument was not that a child under ten was incapable of causing harm – "that age," he commented, "shows no mercy, I am aware of that." Nevertheless, he argued, one needed to recognize that from a "philosophical" point of view young children could not be considered criminally responsible for their actions.[149] Even in cases of serious crimes, such as murder or arson, because children lacked the requisite intellectual development they could not be expected to fully understand the consequences of their actions.[150] It was "neither disputed, nor disputable," Brueyre maintained, that children in their earliest years did not have a full awareness of their actions or complete understanding of their responsibilities.[151] Children were guided by spontaneous impulses that made it inappropriate to ever give them a criminal conviction.[152] However, while he suggested that children under ten be considered lacking in responsibility, Brueyre nevertheless maintained that they should be dealt with by the prison administration. While they would always be acquitted, he argued, the child, although irresponsible, should remain eligible to be prosecuted by a criminal court.[153] This would allow the courts to decide on the fate of the child depending on the circumstances of the case. A child under ten, then, might be returned to their parents and given a warning, or placed in the care of another individual or with the Assistance publique. Or in particularly serious cases they might be turned over to the prison administration, where they would receive a correctional education to ensure their reform, and where they would be incapable of causing further harm to society.[154] Behind Brueyre's apparent indulgence, then, lay a keen sense of the need for the law to act in the defence of society.

Despite this, however, Brueyre's SGP colleagues expressed strong reservations about introducing an assumption of irresponsibility into the criminal justice system for children under the age of ten. One opponent was Adolphe Guillot, who began his critique of Brueyre's proposal by arguing that to set a universal age limit was impossible as it was ultimately arbitrary and one would always be "over or below the truth."[155] To illustrate his point, Guillot told of a recent encounter with a child aged under ten who was being held at Paris's Petite Roquette prison awaiting trial. The boy, Guillot remarked, was "quite intelligent, but with a very odd mind, very focused," and would easily fly into uncontrollable rages and carry out acts of excessive cruelty. He had been sentenced to imprisonment after having been convicted of murdering his three-year-old playmate. He had tried to suffocate the little girl and then locked her in a wardrobe after she had refused to let him play with her doll. When the girl's parents had come looking for her, the boy had calmly announced where she was. She was found in the wardrobe desperately struggling for life and died a short time later. There was no doubt, Guillot observed, that the young boy in question was dangerous and had a clear capacity for evil, but the question was: "had he weighed up sufficiently the import [*portée*] of his act?"[156] During his investigation, Guillot had asked the boy why he had committed such a heinous act, to which the boy had coolly replied, "When I get revenge, I'm happy."[157] Examined by a psychiatric expert, the boy was found to be "neither an idiot, nor a madman," not to be subject to delirium, and to have the same thoughts and ideas as ordinary children of his age and condition.[158] If the boy's parents were capable of keeping a close eye on him and guiding him with a firm hand, the examining psychiatrist considered it reasonable to acquit him and return him to their care. The course of action to be taken was left to the presiding magistrate to decide.

In Guillot's view, this system had no disadvantages as it allowed the courts to decide on a case-by-case basis the appropriate response that should be taken. He declared that it would be vastly imprudent to "set in an absolute way, *a priori*, by virtue of a very questionable philosophical assertion, that responsibility only begins at a set date, at such and such an age."[159] Magistrates, Guillot observed, were quite aware of the significant powers invested in them by the penal code to acquit juvenile offenders on the grounds that they acted "sans discernement," indeed "they do it every day."[160] Rather than nominating an age limit, Guillot asserted, courts were quite capable of deciding "humanely, to a large extent, justly, depending on the circumstances, whether there is a need to protect society from a very young child or on the contrary to return him to his family, to give him complete freedom."[161] To introduce a category of irresponsibility for children, Guillot warned, would establish "a very unfortunate [*fâcheux*] precedent" by opening the way to further categories of irresponsibility "whether it be because of gender, [or] because of some kind of abnormality [*déformation*]."[162]

Pasteur Arboux, Protestant chaplain at Petite Roquette prison and fellow SGP member, agreed. He declared that contemporary society was only too ready to find an excuse for human behaviour, which undermined morality: "sometimes it is illness, sometimes it is age, sometimes it is atavism or some circumstance."[163] To suggest that children constituted a special caste, he insisted, would provoke a breakdown of the fundamental principles of criminal justice. Another SGP member declared that to nominate an age under which a child was assumed to lack a moral conscience was "to decree on an unknown" and that it was entirely fitting that France's legislators had not made an explicit declaration in this regard.[164] Several other members pointed to the inability of foreign jurisdictions to reach any consensus on the appropriate threshold. One of them remarked that internationally there was "a veritable cacophony" on the subject and expressed a preference for maintaining the existing system, which acknowledged the "infinite variety, from an intellectual and moral point of view, that children of the same age offered, not only in the same country, but even in the same social milieu, sometimes in the same family."[165] Another member pointed to the difficulty that would likely be posed in even trying to establish a single age threshold appropriate for all children throughout the various regions of France: "The cacophony that is noted in Europe would have to be reproduced in our France. Does a person from Picardy resemble a person from Provence, a person from Normandy a person from Béarn; and, even on the same latitude, is a person from Brittany like a person from Lorraine and above all from Paris?"[166]

For Georges Bonjean, any age limit set for the automatic assumption of a lack of "discernement" would be too high and would introduce a dangerous Darwinian inflection to the due process of the law. Bonjean told delegates at the International Prison Congress in Paris in 1895 that attempting to divide people up "according to specified brackets, in an inflexible way" was pointless, as once it was done all it would take would be three or four people to show its inadequacy.[167] In addition, Bonjean argued, absolving all children under a particular age threshold of any responsibility whatsoever, regardless of the particular circumstances or nature of the crime, smacked of an evolutionist mentality that put human beings on an equal footing with animals. His two decades in the magistracy, he declared, had demonstrated clearly to him that it was an absolute fallacy to believe that all children were inherently irresponsible, and nothing would ever convince him that a human being was "a sophisticated [*perfectionné*] monkey, who has no more of a soul than a beast who drags itself around on four paws."[168] Bonjean supported the retention of the existing system as it recognized that moral conscience was an innate and universal feature of all human beings, no matter their age.

For his part, Pasteur Arboux similarly expressed his support for a system that did not assign a particular age to the appearance of responsibility in juveniles. In his view, the system rightly recognized that evil, like genius, could appear at any stage of life. He reminded his SGP colleagues of Victor Hugo's precocious genius, which, as Chateaubriand had revealed, had first manifested itself before Hugo had even reached the tender age of seven. Similarly, Blaise Pascal had been able to understand the work of Euclid before the age of twelve, while Racine was able to translate the *Iliad* at the age of eleven, having learnt Greek from his Jansenist teachers at the Petites écoles de Port-Royal. From this, Arboux concluded that "everything that was possible for goodness among these geniuses is also possible for evil."[169] The existing legal system was correct, he said, in allowing for the possibility for a child to be held responsible for their actions, even at a very young age. Since there was no clear age boundary between those children who possessed "discernement" and those who did not, Arboux praised the French system for resisting the false claim made by foreign jurisdictions that moral conscience was effectively absent in young children.[170] For Arboux, age was not in itself a reliable index of moral development and, as such, an assessment should always be left to legal authorities to decide.

Arboux's confidence in the ability of magistrates to make an appropriate assessment on a juvenile's "discernement" was shared by Parisian jurist Adolphe Hatzfeld. Hatzfeld remarked to a gathering of the Comité de défense des enfants traduits en justice that while there was a perception in legal circles that the French criminal justice system was backward in only recognizing two periods in human development, he considered it "an act of wisdom and justice" not to trace "a fanciful [*capricieuse*] and illusory demarcation."[171] Hatzfeld argued that legislators had known full well that "childhood comes before adolescence," but had not taken it upon themselves to decide precisely "at what moment one succeeds the other."[172]

Members of the Comité de défense likewise agreed that age alone was an unreliable measure of moral development and that courts were far more capable of making an appropriate assessment without any need to legislate on an age of impunity.[173] Henri Prudhomme, a deputy public prosecutor from Lille, also expressed support for maintaining the existing system, telling delegates at the International Prison Congress in 1895 that he knew of no instances when judges had misused their authority in assessing juveniles' "discernement" and that they uniformly acted with common sense and decency when evaluating the youngsters who appeared before them. He therefore saw no reason to introduce an automatic assumption of irresponsibility for children.[174]

During discussions in the Senate in early 1911 over the bill on juvenile courts, which included the proposal for the decriminalization of offences by children up to the age of thirteen, senator Louis Lemarié, a lawyer by training, expressed his opposition to the idea that age should constitute a reason for the automatic assumption of a lack of responsibility and challenged the proposal that there should not be any punishment for very young children. Lemarié told his fellow senators that such a proposal to set a universal age threshold was "a substantial innovation" that challenged the courts' existing "sovereign power of evaluation" over determining responsibility. He considered it a very serious error to decide in a perfunctory manner that all children under a particular age were not to be criminally prosecuted.[175]

But where reformers like Arboux, jurists like Prudhomme, and politicians like Lemarié saw a danger in setting an age of absolute impunity, others saw an equal risk in leaving the assessment up to the evaluation of individual magistrates. In a presentation to the Comité de défense des enfants traduits en justice in Paris in February 1906, subsequently transcribed and published in the widely read legal journal the *Gazette des tribunaux*, Pierre Mercier, a Parisian lawyer, asked whether "the inflexibility of the law" might be preferable to the "arbitrariness of the judge" and maintained that while it was rare for very young children to be prosecuted and imprisoned, all the same "these dictates do not have the imperativeness of a law."[176] By 1910 it had become rare in Paris for children under the age of twelve to be criminally prosecuted, but this practice was not widespread throughout France and relied instead on the particular mentality of judges in different areas.[177] This geographical variability in the application of the law is one explanatory factor for why the largely Paris-focused reformers of the SGP were eager to see generalized legislative reform that would take discretionary power on whether to punish young children out of the hands of magistrates.

It seems plausible that the very vagueness of the concept of "discernement" was at least part of the reason for its endurance in France's criminal justice system. The legitimacy and meaning of the term was still the subject of interrogation in the 1920s. Under legislation passed by the Vichy regime, the question would be removed.[178] What is certain is that as a legal mechanism, "discernement" – described by one jurist in 1906 as "a practical and sovereign formula" – possessed an elasticity that made it a powerful tool for the magistracy in determining the fates of young offenders.[179] Loys Brueyre declared that it was quite simply "a tool of leniency placed at the disposal of the judge."[180] Dimitri Drill,[181] a Russian delegate at the 1890 International Prison Congress held in Saint Petersburg and the most prominent proponent of the Russian school of criminal anthropology (responsible for introducing Lombroso's theories to Russian readers),[182] asserted that there was no criterion for it and that as a result a judge could proceed "at random, according to his own good pleasure."[183]

In 1903 Paul Drillon, a lawyer and SGP member, conducted a study of judges' rulings on "discernement" across France. His conclusion was that decisions were highly subjective and often motivated by judges' personal attitudes. Many decisions, he found, were based not on judges' assessments of whether the juvenile had knowingly and wilfully broken the law, but instead on their particular opinion about the type of institutions into which the young offender would be sent.[184] Magistrates who were skeptical about the rehabilitative potential of colonies could decide that a juvenile had acted "avec discernement" in order to protect the young person from what they considered to be an unnecessarily lengthy and harmful period of detention. As we shall see in later chapters, reformers became increasingly exercised by the question of how magistrates' decisions affected young people's prospects. In particular, they were concerned about how a criminal conviction and a stint in prison could spark a spiral of criminality that would compromise young men's eligibility to serve in the military.

Reformers also worried about the effects on very young children of being hauled before the criminal courts and incarcerated. In his report to the parliamentary inquiry of the 1870s, Haussonville had argued that there was evidence of "instances of bizarre convictions handed down in certain provincial courtrooms against children almost in infancy," but these were so uncommon that "there does not seem to be a major reason to change the law in this respect."[185] In 1876 the interior ministry reissued a request for prosecutors to refrain from taking legal action against very young children, thereby suggesting that the practice was still alive.[186] Between 1881 and 1888 seven children aged under ten were tried before a cour d'assises, and in 1887 alone scores of children under the age of eight and more than 600 aged between eight and ten had been brought before a correctional court.[187] In 1892 it was alleged that children as young as four were being acquitted and sent to juvenile colonies.[188]

In 1895 an official from the interior ministry reported to the International Prison Congress that it was rare for children under eight to be prosecuted by French courts.[189] However, a decade later there were still juveniles as young as seven being held in prisons.[190] Juge d'instruction Louis Albanel reported that he had seen children as young as four pass through his office in Paris.[191] Whether such incidents were common or not, the point still stood that age was no absolute guarantee against prosecution. It was the view of one SGP member that it was necessary to legislate an age of irresponsibility to send magistrates the strong and unambiguous message that the youngest offenders should never be placed in prison. Otherwise, there would always be some who "will refuse to send these young children into correction and who will sentence them to short terms of imprisonment because there will be nothing in the law to restrain them."[192]

In 1892, the discussion on this subject in the SGP, introduced by Brueyre, reached a rather tense level, with a standoff between those who supported magistrates' autonomy and others who wished to systematically protect children from any prosecution regardless of the circumstances or seriousness of their offence. In an attempt to defuse the quarrel, Henri Joly pointed out that the concerns being expressed over measures that were perceived to signal a weakening of magistrates' authority were ill-founded. The intention, he said, was not to curtail the authority of magistrates but rather to protect children from unnecessary and inappropriate exposure to the corrupting influences of members of the criminal underworld lurking in the corridors of justice as well as in prisons. If a child could be sent directly before magistrates, without passing through the regular channels of pre-trial detention, Joly had no doubt but that they would be "in excellent hands."[193] But well before a child reached the courtroom, an entire "carceral apparatus [*appareil pénitentiaire*]" had to be set in motion, and it was this that caused Joly concern. The issue was not with magistrates, Joly insisted, but rather with "this process [that is] dire for the child, which plunges him into a dangerous promiscuity and which weighs down on him all his life."[194]

## Conclusion

Discussions about age, "discernement," and criminal responsibility in the fin de siècle tipped over into a parallel debate about the power of magistrates in adjudicating on the fates of young people in the criminal justice system and beyond. In 1912, the discretionary authority invested in magistrates would ultimately be at least partially reined in by the decriminalization of offences committed by juveniles under the age of thirteen. This principle, as we have seen, was not universally endorsed by reformers. The suggestion voiced at the end of the century that the criminal law systematically presume that young offenders under thirteen had acted "sans discernement" conflicted with many reformers' ideas about human nature and the foundations of morality. And yet, at the same time, in a context in which correctional institutions for juveniles were often viewed with suspicion by magistrates and juveniles themselves, the absence of a stipulated age below which children could not be prosecuted left the door open to abuse and manipulation.

In never having stipulated an age at which "discernement" could be assumed to be absolutely absent, France's codified criminal justice system presupposed that the basis of moral conscience was innate: a universal feature distinguishing humans from animals. But a concern about the contagion of criminality and a desire to break the cycle of crime eventually trumped these metaphysical disagreements. Reformers anticipated that by removing children from the repressive criminal justice system they would prevent a child's tendency to criminality from worsening. A prison sentence, they argued, ran the risk of perpetuating the very criminality that punishment was intended to prevent by allowing petty offenders to mix with morally bankrupt prisoners in the penitentiary. Their overriding concern was to prevent young people from declining into habitual criminality from which, as we will see in the next chapter, they believed a person would almost never recover.

By specifying an age under which offences would never carry any criminal penalty whatsoever, the law effectively protected young people from the stigma of a conviction. Although, as we have seen, young people themselves were observed to be often only too pleased to be convicted and sentenced to a prison term, reformers had a more long-range view, regarding a criminal record as tantamount to "a death sentence."[195] They argued not only that a conviction would severely limit young people's future opportunities, especially in employment, but, more significantly still, that it also complicated boys' capacity to serve in the regular armed forces, as we will see in later chapters.

In an era of fierce international competition, an automatic assumption of a lack of "discernement" ensured the acquittal of boys under the age of thirteen and their retention of a pristine criminal record, which would in turn subsequently allow them a smooth passage to enlistment in the regular armed forces. That young males were apparently deliberately seeking a conviction, which could disqualify them from military service, demonstrated the significant social implications of a system whose ostensible rehabilitative purposes were misunderstood or rejected by young people. This preference among young people for a conviction and a shorter period of detention would become a prominent issue in the context of military recruitment laws in France in the decades leading up to the First World War. In these years, reformers and legislators actively debated whether or not convicted offenders should be allowed and indeed even required to serve in the French military. Within these debates, questions about age and appropriate disciplinary intervention in the lives of the young, especially boys, came to the fore, as the next chapter will explore.

CHAPTER 4

# Protective Incarceration? Institutionalizing Juveniles

Never let us write on the walls of a children's home
*lasciate ogni speranza* [abandon all hope].
Ferdinand Dreyfus, 1905[1]

Early one morning on a bitterly cold day in late December 1889, nineteen-year-old Georges-Henri Kaps was led out of Grande Roquette prison and into the public square directly in front, where he was to meet his fate beneath the sharp blade of the guillotine. There, at the site at the eastern edge of Paris (not far from Père Lachaise cemetery), a group of curious observers had assembled before sunrise in order to observe the gruesome proceedings that would soon unfold. The early morning light made visibility poor, as did the rain, complicating the assembled group's ability to serve as witnesses to the enactment of state-sanctioned killing. Further obscuring their view was the positioning of the guillotine, which had been placed at ground level, rather than mounted on a scaffold. This was a standard practice introduced in 1870 in an effort to reduce the impression of executions as entertaining spectacle.[2] The onlookers who braved the inclement conditions that morning were relatively few in number. The crowds were far smaller, for example, than those that had flocked to the same spot in January 1870 to observe the

Figure 4.1
Georges Kaps, 1889

execution of mass murderer Jean-Baptiste Troppmann, among them the writers (and, later, SGP members) Maxime du Camp and Ivan Turgenev.[3] Noting the small turnout, *Le Petit journal* attributed this to the bad weather.[4]

Among those present to witness the execution of Kaps was Abbé Faure, chaplain at Grande Roquette prison. Faure had already had a one-on-one meeting with the prisoner. Summoned to assist the young man in preparing for his final moments, Faure would later recount his encounter with Kaps in his 1896 memoir *Souvenirs de la Roquette*.[5] Alone with Kaps in his cell, Faure offered him a cup of rum, which the young man gladly accepted. Kaps spoke of his mother and brother, and asked Faure to hug them for him. The chaplain then invited the condemned man to ask for God's forgiveness for his crime. But this Kaps refused, declaring: "Why would I ask for forgiveness? I killed, I'm being killed; we're even."[6] Faure did not press him further.

Georges Kaps's execution would be the penultimate of a total of six carried out in France that year, half of those in Paris.[7] What may have been running through the young man's head as he laid his head beneath the guillotine's raised blade is anyone's guess, but his cool and calm demeanour was much remarked on at the time.[8] But even more remarked on was the string of events that had led Kaps to his dire fate; for although he was aged only nineteen, the condemned boy was already a veteran of crime. Less than three weeks earlier, a jury had found Georges Kaps guilty of murder with no extenuating circumstances. The death penalty was applied. Kaps's victim was his twenty-year-old mistress, Léontine Drieu. The investigation and trial had found that Kaps's motive for shooting and killing Drieu was that he wanted to prevent her from revealing to others a confession he had made to her privately concerning an earlier crime he had committed in his youth. Back in 1884, at the age of fourteen and a half, Kaps had stood accused of murdering seventy-year-old Vinçard, a lithographer from the neighbourhood of Père Lachaise with a shady reputation as a pedophile.[9] Kaps had vehemently denied having murdered the old man. Through lack of evidence, the charges were eventually dropped and the case remained unsolved. Kaps's private confession to Drieu threatened to bring this earlier crime back to the surface.

At the trial for Drieu's murder five years later, Kaps was defended by Henri Robert, a dynamic young lawyer at the start of what would be a stellar career.[10] Robert was also a member of the SGP, as was the case's examining magistrate, Adolphe Guillot. The investigation revealed that Léontine Drieu had made a living through sex work, and that Kaps had been her procurer. During the trial, Kaps denied having killed his mistress, but did admit to having been her procurer, even presenting this as a point in his favour as, he told the court, "I prefer to live off the prostitution of a woman than off theft!"[11] Kaps also now admitted to the previous murder of Vinçard, but presented it as an act of immaturity – "I was fourteen years old at the time, and I acted *sans discernement*!"[12]

These two murders were not Kaps's only run-ins with the law, however. As he was led out from the Grande Roquette prison and to the guillotine, the youth's gaze would likely have taken in the institution located directly opposite: Petite Roquette. There, within the walls of the panopticon prison for juveniles, Kaps had also been incarcerated for a short period as a thirteen-year-old after being convicted for stealing fruit.[13] Kaps's observations about the effect of this short period of imprisonment would provoke considerable controversy about effective methods of reducing recidivism, especially in young offenders.

In keeping with classical penal theory, Petite Roquette, with its architecture of individual cells radiating from a central observation tower, was intended to offer the greatest opportunities for self-reflection and protection against the further corruption of detainees' morals through their complete isolation. Kaps's experience, however, appeared to demonstrate the very opposite: according to what he told the court, his detention had actually *encouraged* his decline into criminality. "That stay at Petite-Roquette," Kaps declared, "was not beneficial for me." For one thing, the isolation was never absolute – "although you're in your cell," he said, "you see one another on the way to class, on walks, and we communicate a lot of things between ourselves."[14] Far from being redemptive and reformative, the net effect of imprisonment at Petite Roquette, according to Kaps, had exacerbated his anti-social tendencies. He presented the model prison of Petite Roquette as nothing other than a revolving door of immorality: "Everyone knows that when you've been there once, you go back there ... You leave worse than when you enter. The same is true in all prisons."[15] Among the lessons Kaps failed to learn during his months of detention at Petite Roquette was thrift. Henri Joly noted that within a day of Kaps's release, the young teenager had spent the entirety of the nest egg accumulated over the course of his detention, using some of it to purchase the revolver that he would later use to kill Vinçard.[16]

Kaps's case came at a time of considerable debate concerning the efficacy of the penitentiary as a tool of rehabilitation and about the need to protect juveniles from harmful exposure to immoral influences. As we have seen, in the final decades of the nineteenth century, criminal justice reformers increasingly subscribed to the idea that the misconduct of many young offenders was the product of negligent parenting. As a result, many reformers argued that young offenders should be thought of more as victims than as perpetrators and deserved a response that was more welfare-oriented than punitive. Kaps himself had come from a working-class family, and his widowed mother, although honest, had failed to keep an adequate eye on him to prevent his falling into crime. Also to blame for the boy's moral decline, reformers believed, was the magistrate who, instead of acquitting the thirteen-year-old Kaps under Article 66 and sending him into detention in a juvenile colony for an extended period, had chosen to convict and sentence him to a short period of imprisonment in Petite Roquette, after which he had gone on to commit further, worse crimes. How different might Kaps's trajectory have been and how many victims might have been spared if the boy had been taken in hand at the earliest indications of delinquency and placed in a reformatory?

The Kaps case raised serious questions about the handling of juvenile justice and served as a lightning rod for broader debates about the most effective means of responding to youth criminality. For members of the SGP, his case unambiguously encapsulated the advantages of and indeed necessity for decisive early intervention and lengthy detention in order to prevent juvenile delinquents from developing into dangerous and habitual criminals. In January 1889, responding to magistrates' apparent tendency to convict juvenile offenders of minor offences and sentence them to short prison terms in order to be able to spare them from what they considered a damagingly long period of detention in a juvenile colony, justice minister Jean-Baptiste Ferrouillat issued a circular to public prosecutors in which he stated, "I cannot insist enough on the dangers and the drawbacks [*inconvénients*] of such a practice."[17] Ferrouillat insisted on the importance and desirability of imposing lengthy detention on all juveniles, whether convicted or acquitted under Article 66. A brief prison sentence, he maintained, was not conducive to producing "any appreciable change in a child inclined to vice," while a conviction would leave a permanent mark on a young person's criminal record and prevented a patronage society from providing support post-release. Instead, Ferrouillat recommended that convicted juveniles be placed in a correctional institution ("colonie pénitentiaire") and that juveniles found to have acted "sans discernement" and acquitted be similarly detained for a period sufficiently lengthy – several years rather than a few weeks or months – for it to have an impact on their habits and characters.

At a meeting held on 18 December 1889, just hours before Kaps's execution the following morning, SGP members discussed the issue of the negative impacts of short prison terms on juveniles. Albert Rivière invoked Kaps's case explicitly as an example of how short-term imprisonment fuelled criminality by transforming juvenile delinquents into habitual offenders. "There has been much talk in recent times of Kaps," Rivière observed, "who was sent into correction for six months at age thirteen." By contrast, Rivière noted, "nothing is said of the thousands of others who never reappeared before the courts when, having been sent into correction for six or ten years, they stayed there until the age of twenty." Had the thirteen-year-old Kaps been acquitted under Article 66 and sent into a juvenile colony for such a length of time, Rivière contended, "he would not have murdered at eighteen years old and ... no doubt he would have become an excellent soldier, [and] then a good family man like so many others from his milieu and in his condition."[18] While conceding that juvenile colonies were not perfect institutions, Rivière observed that the same could also sometimes be said of high schools, which served a quite different class of youth.[19] The pivotal difference, however, between a high school and a juvenile colony, he insisted, was that the families of boys held in the latter were more often responsible for their children's misconduct through negative role modelling or simple negligence.[20]

For Rivière, as for all criminal justice reformers at this time, the juvenile offenders who posed greatest concern were boys. The virtue of detention in a juvenile colony was that it provided a useful bridge linking the dangerous void between release from primary school and entry into the military. Lengthy detention in a juvenile colony, Rivière argued, maintained all the way "through to the day when he will be taken up by military discipline ... [would] form a happy transition between his two lives: one very rigorous, the other overly free."[21] Echoing Rivière's remarks, lawyer Victor Bournat declared that "these young people must be sent into correction for the longest time possible" and ideally until they turned twenty. Such prolonged detention, Bournat asserted, "is a measure of *protection* for the juvenile and of *security* for society."[22]

Had Kaps been acquitted under Article 66 and sent to a juvenile colony at the age of thirteen rather than being convicted and detained in Petite Roquette, he would more likely have avoided a life of crime. Another point of controversy was the fact that Kaps's stint in Petite Roquette had been only brief. In comparison to the length of detention that would have followed from a decision of acquittal under Article 66 followed by detention in a juvenile colony, which was left up to the discretion of the judge, the length of detention for convicted juveniles was notably short. Various reformers observed that not only would an acquittal followed by lengthy detention in a juvenile colony have better protected public security by removing Kaps from society for longer, it would also have better prepared him for a transition to adult life than detention in Petite Roquette manifestly had. In addition, lengthy detention would have enhanced France's military defence by preventing an otherwise able young man from falling into a life of crime that might complicate his capacity to serve in the army – considerations that were particularly germane after the introduction of universal military service in 1889. As Guy Tomel and Henri Rollet noted in their 1891 book *Les Enfants en prison*, had Georges Kaps been sent to a juvenile colony, he would have emerged with an untainted criminal record, received a basic education, been taught a trade, and, of particular importance at the turn of the century (as will be further explored in the next chapter), transitioned into the Third Republic's other great school – the army.[23] Instead, the boy had been found to have acted "avec discernement," was handed a criminal conviction, and was subjected to a very brief period of incarceration in a prison. None of this had done anything to improve his morals, prepare him for life on the outside, or guard against his committing further crimes as he grew older.

From the time of Kaps's first appearance before a court of law, the boy's fate had rested on judges' simple decision on his "discernement." This concept, as we saw in the previous chapter, was at once all-important yet nebulous. Not only was the criterion for measuring it left unspecified, but magistrates were understood to routinely abuse it, declaring a juvenile to have acted "avec discernement" in order to spare the young person what they considered to be an inappropriately lengthy period of incarceration. Even juveniles themselves were said to be flouting the system, feigning a knowingness in order to be given a conviction that they felt to be less difficult to sustain than an acquittal and protracted period of detention in a reformatory.

To confuse matters further, the distinctions between "avec discernement" and "sans discernement," criminally responsible and irresponsible, and punishment and correction were in many ways meaningless. This chapter explores reformers' concerns about ambiguities in the incarceration of juvenile offenders, illuminating the ways in which chronological age came to play a more important role in the detention of young people in the decades before the passage of the 1912 law on juvenile courts. At least part of the confusion was caused by the 1850 Corne law. This law, which stipulated that all juveniles in detention were to receive a moral, professional, and religious education, elevated juvenile colonies like Mettray to prime position for the treatment of delinquent boys. The Corne law changed the landscape of juvenile corrections by specifying that, unlike in the past, colonies would now receive not only juvenile boys acquitted under Article 66 but also ones who had been convicted and sentenced to periods of detention of between six months and two years. Within the juvenile colony, convicted and acquitted juveniles would be held side by side. This situation of indiscriminate mixing was even more pronounced for juvenile girls. All girls, regardless of whether they were convicted or acquitted but detained under Article 66, were placed in "maisons pénitentiaires." By the time of the Haussonville Commission in the 1870s, all but one of these institutions for juvenile girls were run by religious communities.[24] These unsteady distinctions in the management of young offenders would be further undermined decades later by legislation passed in 1898, on the initiative of René Bérenger, which folded juvenile victims of crime and juvenile perpetrators of crime in together.

## The Origins of Correctional Institutions for Juveniles

Under the terms of France's penal code, there were three categories of juveniles who could be deprived of their freedom by the criminal courts:

1. juveniles convicted by a cour d'assises for a crime committed "avec discernement" (Article 67);
2. juveniles convicted by a tribunal correctionnel for offences or crimes committed "avec discernement" but considered less "serious" and generally carrying a carceral sentence of short duration;
3. juveniles acquitted as having acted "sans discernement" but not returned to their parents (Article 66) and whose length of detention was up to the discretion of the magistrate but could not extend beyond the age of twenty.

According to both the penal codes of 1791 and 1810, juveniles of both genders acquitted but detained under Article 66 were to be detained in "maisons de correction." At their origin, these institutions were intended not only for juveniles, but also for people sentenced by correctional courts to short periods of imprisonment. In the end, such institutions were never actually created, meaning that juveniles were instead regularly detained in adult prisons. In the Restoration period, the dangerous effects of indiscriminate detention of juvenile prisoners became a prominent subject of concern for authorities and philanthropists, who recognized that these conditions served to ingrain and worsen young prisoners' immoral inclinations.

In 1814 François de La Rochefoucauld-Liancourt developed plans for a new type of institution for juvenile offenders, a "maison d'amendement," aimed at achieving their moral reform.[25] In the end, however, the unexpected reappearance of Napoleon I disrupted these plans. Following his definitive exile to Saint Helena, the baton for reform passed to the Société royale des prisons (SRP), the group that members of the SGP considered their forebears, as we saw in chapter 2. The SRP recognized that juveniles required a treatment distinct to that of older offenders and urged their segregated detention. They also made similar arguments on the need to segregate prisoners on the basis of gender, type of offence, and length of sentence.[26] In 1819, the interior ministry issued a decree stipulating that detainees under the age of sixteen and children imprisoned at their parents' request under correction paternelle should always be held separately from adult prisoners.

This same decree also set down that prisoners under the age of nine were to be provided with a special diet in recognition of their developmental needs.[27] From the 1820s the first distinct sections for juveniles within adult prisons were created, beginning with Gaillon (northwest of Paris), followed by Strasbourg, Rouen, and others. These sections, however, did not have the desired effect, as prison administrators failed to shepherd young offenders uniquely into them.[28]

A major turning point in the processing of juvenile offenders occurred in the early years of the July Monarchy. In 1832 Count d'Argout, minister of trade and public works, issued a circular on the "placement into apprenticeship of children judged by virtue of Article 66 of the penal code." This opened the way for certain juveniles who were not returned to their parents to be placed under *tutelle administrative* (administrative guardianship) with a charitable individual or association that would supervise their appointment into an apprenticeship for the duration of their period of detention. This circular introduced probation (*liberté surveillée*) for the first time into French criminal justice practice, prompting the mushrooming of patronage societies for young prisoners in the following years.

What Argout's circular attempted to achieve was the reification of the distinction, enshrined in articles 66 and 67 of the penal code, between the absence and presence of "discernement," and between acquittal and conviction. For Argout, juveniles deemed to have acted "sans discernement" simply did not belong in a prison, which was primarily a place of punishment. Drawing a clear line, Argout asserted firmly that "a prison will never be a reformatory [*maison de correction*]."[29] In asserting the non-punitive purpose of Article 66, Argout was reiterating a clarification issued by the Cour de cassation shortly after the promulgation of the Napoleonic penal code. In 1811, France's highest court had issued a decree specifying that "when defendants aged under sixteen are acquitted for having acted *sans discernement* … it follows that the detention to which they can be sentenced … is in no way a punishment [*peine*], but rather a public order measure [*mesure de police*] suitable for rectifying their upbringing [*éducation*]."[30]

The detention of a juvenile acquitted under Article 66, in other words, was to be understood as a measure of reform, not of punishment. Yet, in the early nineteenth century, in the absence of a distinct institutional framework, the detention of juveniles acquitted under Article 66 was not always devoid of repressive tendencies. And even with the introduction from the 1830s onwards of alternatives to incarceration in penitentiaries (that is, juvenile colonies), the detention of acquitted juveniles continued to carry some punitive connotation, or at least some ambiguity. A Belgian delegate at the 1847 International Prison Congress held in Brussels gestured to this ambiguity when he remarked that "to correct [*corriger*] is to punish in order to educate [*éduquer*]; the word 'to correct' contains within itself the thought expressed by these words."[31]

Argout's 1832 circular provided a third alternative for juveniles acquitted under Article 66 other than detention in a prison or simple return to parental custody: probation. This constitutes, as historian Henri Gaillac writes, "a crucial event in the history of re-education."[32] In enabling juveniles acquitted under Article 66 to serve their period of detention outside the walls of a prison but under the watchful eye of people other than their own parents or guardians, Argout's instruction effectively laid the groundwork for what would become the centrepiece of juvenile correctional facilities for decades to come: the "colonie agricole."

## Juvenile Prisons and Colonies: Petite Roquette and Mettray

The first juvenile colonies, as we saw in chapter 2, were created in the countryside in the 1830s by philanthropists like Charles Lucas, Bérenger de la Drôme, and Frédéric-Auguste Demetz, who observed the absence of provisions for juveniles found to have acted "sans discernement" but whose parents were deemed not to offer a sufficient guarantee against a relapse. Between 1838 and 1850, twelve colonies – all of them privately run – were established, uniquely serving a select portion of young offenders detained under Article 66.[33] In 1847, the Colonie pénitentiaire des Douaires was established near the adult prison at Gaillon. In existence through to 1925, the Douaires juvenile colony developed out of a program introduced in the 1820s that saw select young detainees held in the juvenile section of Gaillon prison sent out during the day to carry out agricultural labour in nearby fields.

At the pinnacle of this plethora of juvenile colonies was Mettray, which during its lifetime was regularly lauded as the jewel in France's penal crown and enjoyed an almost mythical status both within France and internationally. When first established, Mettray, like all other private agricultural colonies in operation prior to the 1850 Corne law, was specifically and solely intended to accommodate juvenile delinquent boys who had been acquitted under Article 66, but not released back to their parents. At its origin, like all cognate establishments, Mettray served as an institution of preventive and strictly non-punitive detention, deliberately created in order to provide an alternative to prison for acquitted juveniles who, precisely because of their incapacity to distinguish between right and wrong, were thought by philanthropists to be the least morally corrupted and therefore the most deserving of their support. Where immediate return to the parents' custody was considered inadvisable, detention in a juvenile colony was also believed to be a better option than incarceration in a prison.

Mettray's founding purpose to take care exclusively of juveniles acquitted under Article 66 was made clear in its statutes. As Mettray's founder Frédéric-Auguste Demetz specified, the institution's purpose was to provide "a benevolent tutelage over children acquitted as having acted *sans discernement*" and "to provide these children, placed in a state of probation [*liberté provisoire*] and gathered in an agricultural colony, with a moral and religious upbringing, as well as primary education; to have them instructed in a trade; and to then place them in the countryside, with craftsmen or farmers."[34] Mettray offered an alternative form of detention to the penitentiary and some form of institutionalization instead of simple release back to the family (considered all too often to be the very source of the juvenile's delinquency).

Although the creation of agricultural colonies like Mettray signalled a significant shift in the response to youths acquitted under Article 66, there were also some developments in the institutional treatment of convicted juveniles, most notably the creation in 1836 of Petite Roquette prison in eastern Paris. While the "colonie agricole" occupied one end of a spectrum of institutions tailored for juvenile detainees, Petite Roquette prison represented the other. Built on a panopticon design, with individual cells radiating out from a central tower, the prison anticipated by almost a decade legislation that made individual imprisonment the prescribed norm throughout France. Petite Roquette held juvenile boys awaiting trial, as well as those acquitted but detained under Article 66 and ones convicted. It also held boys under twenty-one detained at their parents' request (correction paternelle). The conditions for all were the same: isolation.[35]

Initially, Petite Roquette prison functioned on the so-called Auburn model, with detainees separated at night, but brought together for silent work during the day. But after a few years, the regime shifted to the Philadelphia model of total isolation, which was believed to be more effective in helping to protect and reform the young prisoners than mixing with their peers, even in silence.[36] For the following quarter of a century, Petite Roquette would maintain this severe system of total isolation, despite strong criticism from prominent reformers including Charles Lucas. A visit by Empress Eugénie in 1865, which exposed terrible conditions, brought about a turning point.[37] Henceforth the prison would be used only for juveniles awaiting trial and those convicted and sentenced to terms of less than six months, along with youths detained under correction paternelle.[38]

More select in its composition, Petite Roquette continued to apply its hardline method of segregation, with medical doctors arguing into the 1870s for the system's greater efficacy and general superiority over communal detention, and downplaying the negative effects on young people's mental health and development. Dr René Marjolin told the SGP in May 1879 that a cellular regime had no harmful effects on a child's intelligence and general health and that, by contrast, to leave a child "[even] for only a few hours in contact with dreadful good for nothings, the child who is not guilty of any misdeed or who has committed a first-time peccadillo … is to desire his ruin [*perte*], as a few moments of this promiscuity is enough for him to learn how to lie and to make up a story."[39]

Agricultural colonies, on the other hand, were premised on an entirely different model, with an absence of high walls and an embracing of fraternization between the detainees. The original agricultural colonies created by philanthropists during the July Monarchy were founded as sites of rehabilitation and correction, intended to overcome the confusion implicit in the penal code relating to the detention of juveniles acquitted under Article 66. From 1850, however, this distinction was contravened with the parliament's passage of the Corne law.

## The Corne Law of 1850 and the Detention of Convicted and Acquitted Juveniles

As has been mentioned, the Corne law specified that all juveniles – whether convicted or acquitted but detained – were to be provided with an education. This formalized and solidified the assumption that all young offenders needed and deserved a treatment that was directed as much if not more at preparing them for their future lives back in society as at responding to their past faults. While Argout's 1832 circular had opened the way for some juveniles acquitted under Article 66 to be placed outside prison walls, the 1850 law generalized the idea that on account of their age, all juvenile offenders, whether acquitted or convicted, warranted a treatment distinct from the one extended to adult prisoners.[40]

For juvenile offenders, the Corne law introduced a hierarchy of three basic types of institutions of detention for boys and two for girls. For boys, there were maisons d'arrêt, colonies pénitentiaires, and colonies correctionnelles, while for girls there were maisons d'arrêt and maisons pénitentiaires (see table 4.1). Maisons d'arrêt were essentially conventional adult prisons. Boys and girls aged under sixteen who were awaiting trial would be held in these. Juvenile boys convicted and sentenced to periods of imprisonment of less than six months would also be held in maisons d'arrêt, as would boys between the ages of sixteen and twenty-one incarcerated under correction paternelle. While in Paris, Petite Roquette served this category of young offender, in smaller jurisdictions a distinct prison for juveniles rarely existed, meaning that, at best, young offenders were simply held in separate quarters of a regular adult prison. All juvenile girls who had faced court and received their sentence (whether acquitted under Article 66 or convicted) would be sent to a maison pénitentiaire, along with girls under sixteen detained under correction paternelle.

For girls, there was no differentiation made between those who had been sentenced to short and long periods of detention; articles 16 and 17 of the Corne law specified that all were to be sent to a maison pénitentiaire where they would be raised in strict discipline and set to the sort of work deemed appropriate to their gender: sewing, laundering, and housekeeping.[41] "Colonies pénitentiaires," meanwhile, appeared to some extent as just a new name for "colonies agricoles" like Mettray. But in fact these institutions were marked by significant differences. Most importantly, under the terms of Article 4 of the Corne law these "colonies pénitentiaires" would receive not only acquitted juvenile boys but also ones convicted and sentenced to prison terms of between six months and two years. Whereas previously a boy acquitted by a court under Article 66 but not returned to his parents would first serve a period of time in prison, during which he might be exposed to a certain degree of penal deprivation and rigour and observed for suitability for placement in a juvenile colony, the Corne law empowered a court to send the youngster directly to these institutions. In addition, convicted minors would be similarly entrusted to them.

The only difference in treatment for a convicted boy and an acquitted one in a "colonie pénitentiaire" was that on arrival the convicted juvenile was to be held in a separate section for a trial period of three months before being absorbed into the general body of the institution. If after those three months, or indeed at any later point, the boy proved unruly, he could be transferred to a "colonie correctionnelle" – a category of institution intended to be the most severe facility for juveniles. These colonies were supposed to detain convicted juveniles sentenced to more than two years' imprisonment along with any insubordinate detainees transferred from the colonies pénitentiaires. Colonies correctionnelles, earmarked for creation in France and Algeria (a department of France), were to be state-run institutions only, reflecting their underlying purpose as primarily punitive institutions; unlike colonies pénitentiaires, they would not be delegated to private initiative. Until the 1890s, however, no colonies of this kind were established – primarily, no doubt, because of the expense. In 1895, the Colonie correctionnelle of Eysses was created in the Lot-et-Garonne department in southwestern France, taking in disorderly boys transferred from colonies pénitentiaires, as well as convicted juvenile criminals sentenced to maximum penalties. In 1908 Eysses was joined by a further colonie correctionnelle established at Gaillon (on the site of the defunct adult prison that had been decommissioned eight years earlier).

As well as problematically enabling the mixed detention of acquitted and convicted offenders within the same institution, another innovation of the Corne law was its provisions concerning the duration of guardianship for juveniles prosecuted by the courts. Previously, under the Argout circular, administrative guardianship had extended only as far as the term set down at the time of sentencing, which specified the duration of the obligation to detain and raise the minor. Articles 19–21 of the 1850 legislation, however, set down a standard program of post-release support, conducted by the Assistance publique and running for a period of at least three years after the juvenile left the institution. For some, this prolonged monitoring of juveniles after their release may have seemed like surveillance. But in an 1853 circular to prefects, the interior minister, Victor de Persigny, presented the lengthy monitoring as a highly positive development, describing it as "inspired by a healthy and intelligent appreciation of the interest of the child and of the obligation imposed on the administration to raise and reform him."[42]

By cementing patronage as a core feature of treatment for juveniles, the Corne law significantly lengthened both the reach and duration of non-familial control. The only restriction to the length of detention was that it could not extend beyond the age of twenty. Since a young person did not reach full (civil) adulthood until they turned twenty-one, this provision was a

Figure 4.2
A group of boys on arrival at the Colonie pénitentiaire des Douaires, 1895

Figure 4.3
Two young detainees at the Maison d'éducation surveillée d'Eysses, 1929–30

small but significant concession by the state to the authority of families – the thinking was that because they were not yet fully of age, the released juvenile would have to return to their family's care before striking out on their own.[43] In 1906, this provision was modified (by the same law that raised the age of majority from sixteen to eighteen) so that juveniles acquitted under Article 66 but not returned to their parents' custody could be held until they came of age. During the Third Republic these legal arrangements raised considerable debate among reformers who were concerned less than mid-century legislators had been about respecting the rights of parents (especially fathers) and more about protecting the rights of children.

Overall, the effect of Article 66 of the penal code was that youngsters absolved of responsibility for their criminal actions but not returned to their parents' care could be subjected to a more protracted period of detention than their convicted counterparts. And since younger offenders were, because of their age, more likely to be found to have acted "sans discernement" and acquitted, they were the ones who risked being held for the longest periods. Anatole Corne, son of the rapporteur of the 1850 law, summed up the paradox in 1864 when he said: "the younger the child sent for correction,

Table 4.1
Categories of juvenile institutions (1850–1912)

| Maisons d'arrêt | Colonies pénitentiaires | Maisons pénitentiaires* | Colonies correctionnelles |
|---|---|---|---|
| Law of 5 August 1850 | | | |
| Boys and girls under sixteen awaiting trial or sentencing | Acquitted boys under sixteen detained under Article 66 of the penal code | Acquitted girls under sixteen detained under Article 66 of the penal code | Convicted boys under sixteen sentenced to imprisonment for a period of more than two years |
| Boys over sixteen and under twenty-one detained under correction paternelle | Convicted boys under sixteen sentenced to imprisonment for a period of more than six months and less than two years | Convicted girls under sixteen sentenced to a period of imprisonment of any duration | Insubordinate boys transferred from a colonie pénitentiaire |
| Convicted boys under sixteen sentenced to less than six months' detention | Boys under sixteen detained under correction paternelle | Girls under sixteen detained under correction paternelle | Boys aged over twenty-one at the end of their sentence |
| Law of 27 May 1885 | | | |
| | | | Convicted boys under sixteen sentenced to transportation |

| | | |
|---|---|---|
| Law of 28 June 1904 (Article 2) | | |
| | Unruly boys transferred from Assistance publique | Unruly girls transferred from Assistance publique |
| Law of 12 April 1906 | | |
| Girls and boys aged sixteen to eighteen awaiting trial or sentencing. | Acquitted juveniles aged sixteen to eighteen** | |
| Law of 22 July 1912 (Article 21) | | |
| | Offenders aged thirteen to eighteen acquitted under Article 66**<br>Convicted offenders aged thirteen to sixteen** | |

* From 1895, some maisons pénitentiaires were renamed "écoles de préservation," starting at Doullens (Somme), followed by Cadillac (Gironde) in 1905, and then Clermont (Oise) in 1908.

** These laws expressed no distinction between girls and boys, and referred only to "colonies pénitentiaires."

the less ... he is guilty … [while] the more serious the penalty becomes."[44] This anomaly provoked considerable concern among SGP members. Charles Lucas told a meeting of the group in 1879 that while the architects of the 1810 penal code had rightly sought to protect juveniles from the harshest penalties meted out to their adult counterparts, legislators had gone "far too far in the scale of proportional reduction of the length of imprisonment, to the point of reaching reductions incompatible with a penal regime."[45] Théophile Roussel similarly noted the irony that "of two children unequally guilty, the most guilty, who has greatest need for reform, is precisely the one given less time to reform themselves."[46]

## Prison or School? The Ambiguities of Juvenile Institutions

The central purpose of the Corne law was to prevent the spread of immorality and curtail the risk of recidivism by segregating juveniles from adult prisoners and to prepare the young detainees for their release by providing a distinct program focused on their upbringing and education. But in mixing convicted and acquitted juvenile delinquents, the 1850 law undermined a central criterion that had underpinned the creation of juvenile colonies for boys during the July Monarchy.

From the state's point of view, a major benefit of juvenile colonies was that (under Article 6 of the 1850 law) they were all to be run, at least for the first five years after the law's promulgation, by private initiative (with some subsidy from the state). This made them significantly lighter on the public purse than regular imprisonment. While the interior ministry was responsible for the maisons centrales, departments were in charge of maintaining their own maisons de justice and maisons d'arrêt. Although colonies pénitentiaires could have been attached to maisons centrales, which would have enabled the central state to oversee them, this proximity would have risked undermining the non-punitive, humanitarian impulse that was supposed to lie at the heart of these juvenile institutions, as Dominique Messineo has pointed out.[47]

For Hyacinthe Corne, the superiority of private philanthropy in attending to juvenile corrections was not simply a question of simple economics. In line with the dominant views of the French ruling classes in the mid-nineteenth century, Corne considered that the voluntarist impulse of philanthropy and the ostensible intimacy it cultivated between giver and receiver made it superior to anything the state might offer.[48] Explaining the purpose of colonies pénitentiaires, Corne asserted that "the main goal, the one that society has the greatest interest in attaining, is to return to honest and hard-working life the children whom laziness and a bad family upbringing have put on a deplorable slope." The way to achieve this, he continued, was "through the heart … through devotion drawn from the most noble feelings." In this quest, Corne maintained, private institutions were better equipped; for although state institutions might deploy "regular order, an exact discipline," their functionaries lacked "the warmth of soul, the religious zeal that make all the success of moral works."[49]

The intermingled detention of convicted and acquitted juveniles in colonies and maisons pénitentiaires under the terms of the Corne law produced a confusion of categories that reformers would spend the ensuing decades grappling with. The 1850 legislation, as Messineo has astutely noted, "paradoxically … reintroduce[d] the very defect that the founders of agricultural colonies had originally sought to combat."[50] Not only did this risk perpetuating the dangerous contagion that had motivated earlier philanthropists to remove the least corrupted juveniles from prison detention, it also inevitably led to a confusion in public consciousness regarding these institutions' function. As long as colonies like Mettray had only held acquitted juveniles, it was possible to think of them as a sort of school. With the incorporation of convicted juveniles, however, colonies tended to take on a greater association with prisons.

The functional haziness of these juvenile colonies is essential to Michel Foucault's analysis in *Surveiller et punir*. For Foucault, the common detention of acquitted and convicted juveniles in the flagship Mettray juvenile colony made these institutions into a confused mixture of foundling home, prison (albeit one that did not entirely sit within the penal sphere), and training barracks for military recruits. Mettray and all agricultural colonies like it corresponded to what sociologist Erving Goffman would classify as "total institutions" in the sense that each was "a place of residence and work where a large number of like-situated individuals cut off from the wider society for an appreciable period of time together lead an enclosed formally administered round of life."[51] Mettray's first report, dated 23 January 1842, pointed out that the institution's system of rules was "not that of the cloister, the high school [*collège*], the prison or the regiment" although it was reminiscent of all of them in that it "holds all of these disciplines through its rigour and exactitude."[52]

Mettray had a nebulous identity as a site of both punitive and disciplinary detention, where boys were separated from wider society not by high walls but by open fields. "Mettray," Foucault writes, "was a prison, but not entirely; a prison in that it contained young delinquents condemned by the courts; and yet something else, too, because it also contained minors who had been charged, but acquitted under Article 66 of the [penal] code, and boarders held, as in the eighteenth century, as an alternative to paternal correction. Mettray, a punitive model, is at the limit of strict penality."[53] With its detention of various categories of juveniles within a single institution and the absence of any obvious trappings of a prison, Mettray is for Foucault emblematic of what he calls "the carceral archipelago": the most perfect expression of a continuum of control in which the disciplinary and behavioural norms of the prison are internalized and applied to or practised within society at large.[54]

The functional ambiguity of colonies like Mettray that the Corne law produced was further reinforced by the fact that under the terms of the 1850 legislation these institutions were also nominated to serve as sites of incarceration for juveniles held for the purposes of correction paternelle. These issues would erupt into a national scandal in 1910 following the suicide of fifteen-year-old Gaston Contard five days after having been admitted to the Maison paternelle (Mettray's section for youths detained under correction paternelle) on the request of his father, a textile factory manager in Marseilles. The "Contard Affair," as Stephen Toth has outlined, shone light on the ambiguous status of correctional institutions; for advocates they were "schools," while detractors branded them "prisons."[55] Contard's death, the first and only suicide case experienced at the Maison paternelle, prompted a detailed investigation by public prosecutors. On finding that the institution's director, Emmanuel Lorenzo, had not obtained the requisite court order from a local magistrate before accepting the boy into its care, prosecutors charged him with illegal imprisonment, a serious allegation that carried a heavy penalty. Lorenzo's defence countered by arguing that Mettray's Maison paternelle was not a prison but rather an educative establishment equivalent to a boarding school, which made state authorization for detention unnecessary. The fact that boys detained under correction paternelle were held under the civil and not the penal code would seem to support such an argument.

Yet at the same time other factors pushed against the argument that Mettray's Maison paternelle was akin to a school, not least its appearance. Indeed, as Toth has noted, the Maison paternelle was "a facility that bore many similarities to a traditional prison" with its barred windows, its locked doors and iron gates, and its regime of isolated detention and limited physical exercise.[56] In contrast, the Mettray juvenile colony, within which the Maison paternelle sat and which held juvenile offenders who had been prosecuted by the criminal courts and subsequently acquitted under Article 66 or convicted, was notable for the absence of such trappings.

As well as highlighting the ambiguities of institutions like the Maison paternelle – was it a prison or was it a school? – the Contard Affair also raised questions about the extent of parental powers, especially those of fathers. From this, further implications flowed, including questions about whose authority was in fact engaged in the exercise of correction paternelle – was it an expression of state power or paternal control? If the Maison paternelle was to be considered a prison, then it was up to the state, as the only legitimate moderator of punishment, to determine who should be detained within its walls. If, on the other hand, it was equivalent to a school, then a father was entitled to determine how his child was to be raised. At a meeting of the SGP in 1893, Loys Brueyre expressed outrage that correction paternelle enabled the imprisonment of young people under civil law. Imprisonment, he argued, was a punishment and therefore rightly belonged within the provisions of the criminal law.[57] In the case of the Contard Affair, Mettray's director was ultimately exonerated, but the Maison paternelle's reputation was permanently sullied by the scandal. The institution (though not the Mettray colony as a whole) closed its doors definitively in 1910.

The Corne law, which fundamentally altered the composition of colonies like Mettray, dramatically transformed the pattern of juvenile corrections. Indeed, so great was the enthusiasm for colonies among magistrates that within a few years these institutions were becoming seriously overcrowded. A report from the prison inspection service released in 1853 noted that "the number of children subjected to correctional detention has increased in the last few years in a considerable way." It attributed this to magistrates' perception that acquitting juveniles and sending them to a colony for an extended period of time represented a better option than simply releasing them back to their parents or convicting and sentencing them to a short period of imprisonment.[58] Interior minister Victor de Persigny cautioned prefects to be on their guard against opportunistic parents abusing legislators' good intentions by "push[ing] their children to commit offences, in the aim of discharging onto the State the care and duty to raise them, or …

abandoning them to vagrancy and begging."[59] In 1855, de Persigny's successor, Adolphe Billault, noted magistrates' enthusiasm for colonies pénitentiaires; their proclivity for removing juveniles acquitted under Article 66 from their parents' custody and sending them to colonies was leading to a saturation of these institutions. Unable to meet the demand, colonies were refusing admission to youngsters (which, as private institutions, was their right) with the result that many acquitted juveniles were instead being held in departmental prisons, undermining the whole purpose of the Corne law. In light of this, Billault issued instructions recommending that only the most serious cases involving juveniles be prosecuted and that authorities refrain from arresting young vagrants and beggars unless they demonstrated a clear threat to public order.[60]

The idea that for reasons of economy parents would deliberately contrive to have their children charged with an offence in order for them to be found to have acted "sans discernement" and transferred to a juvenile colony found purchase among legislators and reformers throughout the nineteenth century. In 1879 Théophile Roussel claimed to the SGP that colonies appealed to impoverished parents who pushed their children into lawbreaking in order to trigger state intervention and support.[61] Until the advent of the concept of "moral abandonment" in the late 1880s, such assistance was otherwise unavailable. Similar concerns were expressed by members of the SGP in the 1890s in relation to impoverished parents making use of correction paternelle as a cost-effective form of childcare.[62] Henri Joly described how on demonstrating financial incapacity, parents were absolved of the responsibility to pay for the detention of their child that they themselves requested.[63]

## Endangered and Dangerous: The Morally Abandoned Child

In 1855, Arthus Vingtrinier, chief doctor for prisons around the city of Rouen, published a study of the treatment of incarcerated juveniles in France. Official statistics gathered from 1837 to 1854 indicated that juveniles made up one-sixth of the total prisoner population – a proportion unmatched internationally.[64] Noting that many of these youngsters were held in juvenile colonies, Vingtrinier asked whether such institutions were best suited to their needs and expressed particular concern about detainees under thirteen, who, he said, issued for the most part from poor families and were therefore "obviously more unfortunate than guilty."[65] What worried Vingtrinier was the fact that due to limitations on the state's powers to intervene in the raising of children, it was only when a neglected or impoverished child with living parents committed a criminal act that they could be removed from their parents' custody and placed either in a juvenile colony or a prison. For those youngsters who were found to have acted "sans discernement," Vingtrinier asked, "could direct and honest means not be found of arriving at welfare without employing these detours of which morality cannot approve?"[66] It was only during the Third Republic that alternate means were adopted, enabling the state to intervene *before* a juvenile had broken the law. This shift rested on a transformed notion of the role of parents and their fundamental responsibility for the moral conduct of their children.

In his 1879 book *L'Enfance à Paris*, Count Haussonville drew attention to parents' responsibility for the delinquency of their progeny, pointing out the large number of young people who wandered the streets of the capital not because they lacked parents but because the ones they had were inattentive to their needs and their moral development.[67] All too often, Haussonville observed, a juvenile's initiation into immorality and crime began within the family itself. Until the final decades of the nineteenth century, however, Article 66 of the penal code represented a very rare instance in which the state was empowered to intervene in family arrangements and remove a child (temporarily) from their parent's care. (The only other section of the penal code that challenged parental authority was Article 335, which empowered magistrates to divest parents of custody if they were implicated in prostituting their children.)[68] Article 66 thus represented a significant chink in the otherwise impenetrable armour of parental power. For although, as Sylvia Schafer rightly notes, it "did not strip parents of all former legal authority over their children, it transferred the ultimate determination of the child's best interest from parent to magistrate and positioned the parent as the direct object of legal regulation."[69] Under the Third Republic, a groundswell of support developed among criminal justice reformers for greater recognition of the danger parents posed to their children's welfare – moral as much as material – and of the need to protect juveniles acquitted under Article 66 from exposure to the company of other juveniles more depraved than themselves.

The problem of dangerous mixing of juveniles in colonies described in the previous section was compounded by the limited provisions for child welfare that strictly curtailed the state's capacity to remove juveniles from "bad" families. These provisions were put in place in the early nineteenth century. In 1811 Napoleon had created the Service des enfants assistés, a public welfare office that extended support exclusively to impoverished orphans and abandoned children born out of wedlock or to unknown parents. The support, moreover, came with strings attached, at least in the case of boys and at least in theory; in return for their upkeep and care, all male foundlings or orphans were required to enter the navy once they turned twelve. In practice, however, this rarely if ever happened, due to military administrators' concerns about managing wayward boys.[70] During the Second Empire, under the terms of a law passed on 5 May 1869, the Assistance publique was further empowered to take guardianship of children whose parents were in prison or hospital and children of single mothers.[71] The state made no provisions for the care of children who were neglected or abused by their parents. In addition, it restricted its support to younger children. On its establishment, the service did not set any limitations on the age of the child at the time of admission, but from 1823 a ministerial decree set down that only orphans and abandoned children under the age of twelve would be taken in and provided with administrative guardianship.[72] This put young people who lost their parents during adolescence in a condition of particular vulnerability. They were effectively expected to find their own way. Under the terms of the Napoleonic civil code, children with parents who were neglectful or to all intents and purposes absent were ineligible for welfare support. By default, then, it was the criminal justice system that was made to attend to their needs.

In 1881, Loys Brueyre, head of the Service des enfants assistés and SGP member, acted to extend available welfare support beyond orphans, foundlings, and abandoned children to also encompass children who had been accused of petty crime. In so doing, Brueyre spearheaded the creation of a care service for a type of child whom senator Jules Simon referred to as "orphans with living parents."[73] The official label for children in this category was "morally abandoned," and the service ran on an experimental basis for eight years.[74] Significant as Brueyre's measures were, they still only applied to children up to the age of twelve, which jarred with the earliest working definitions of the morally abandoned, set between the ages of twelve and sixteen.[75] When from their earliest meetings members of the SGP turned their attention to morally abandoned children, it was young people in the age bracket between twelve and sixteen – the boundaries for eligibility for public assistance and full criminal responsibility at the time – that these reformers had front of mind. A recurrent subject of discussion by statesmen and reformers for at least a decade, the concept of moral abandonment did not come to its full legislative fruition until 1889.

The law on moral abandonment of 24 July 1889, introduced to the Senate by Théophile Roussel, the senator responsible for a landmark law regulating wet-nursing passed fifteen years earlier, represented a watershed moment in the relationship between the state and the family.[76] It was also a highly significant turning point in the history of children's rights in France, in that it assumed that morally abandoned children required protection from their own parents. Under the terms of the legislation, parents convicted of crimes against the person of their children or of prostituting them would automatically lose custody. Moreover, parents sentenced to hard labour for life or to solitary confinement could be deprived of parental custody, as could those repeatedly convicted of sequestering a child, infanticide, exposing or abandoning a child, vagrancy, or public drunkenness. Parents who repeatedly broke an 1874 law on the employment of minors as travelling performers or "professional" beggars also risked losing custody, as could adults convicted of prostituting minors (not necessarily their own children) and those who abused their right to have their own children detained under correction paternelle – by, for example, using it for economic or other reasons.

The 1889 Roussel law's curtailment of correction paternelle – the father's prerogative to have his child imprisoned as he saw fit – represented a major shift in power dynamics between the state and the family. What had been essentially a father's inalienable right became a mechanism more tightly regulated by the state and one that could backfire on him. For, as a result of these changes, as sociologist Philippe Meyer has observed, "every father requesting correction could, following an investigation of his family, find his right of correction being used against him."[77] In addition, the 1889 legislation laid down that parents whose behaviour was considered unhealthy though not strictly speaking criminal (for instance, habitual drunkenness) could be deprived of custody.[78] Most importantly, the legislation empowered a civil court to remove a child from a family environment deemed to be unsound without that child first having broken any law themselves. In this way, as Sylvia Schafer puts it, the state now took "family order [away] from the realm of nature consecrated by law, as the authors of the Napoleonic Civil Code had understood it, and relocated it in the realm of the social, a realm now both essentially defined and regulated by law."[79] The ostensible purpose of this law and all other measures on childrearing introduced by republicans in this period was not to weaken families but, on the contrary, to strengthen them.

The 1889 Roussel law introduced the idea of parents' moral responsibility for their children's upbringing and was focused squarely on the issue of parental neglect rather than juvenile delinquency. The definitions of moral abandonment enshrined in the 1889 law, first hammered out within the SGP, were predicated on a core distinction between the neglected child – enfant en danger – and the juvenile delinquent – enfant dangereux. While the first could all too easily turn into the second, the law on moral abandonment nonetheless treated them as distinct. Less than ten years later, this distinction between the enfant dangereux and enfant en danger was swept away with the passage of the law of 19 April 1898 "sur la répression des violences, voies de faits, actes de cruauté et attentats commis envers les enfants" (on the repression of violence, assault, acts of cruelty, and attacks committed against children).

The 1898 law was passed in the wake of a horrific, high-profile case known as the "affaire Grégoire," which raised public awareness about the state's powerlessness in the face of parents' brutality against their own children. In the Grégoire case from 1897, a young boy died of pneumonia after being burned, tortured, and deprived of food and care by his father. A few years earlier, another case of parental brutality– this time against a young girl named Adolphine Borlet – had similarly aroused considerable public commentary. In 1891, nine-year-old Adolphine was subjected to appalling acts of cruelty and violence by her parents to which the penal code was impotent to respond sufficiently harshly. Both the Borlet and Grégoire cases exposed the impotence of France's criminal justice system to punish negligent or abusive parents.[80]

Although the 1898 law would be rarely applied, it nonetheless represented a significant shift in power dynamics between the family and the state, enabling the latter to intervene to protect children from physical abuse suffered at the hands of their own parents.[81] When it came to the physical disciplining of children, until the very end of the nineteenth century France's legal system upheld the idea of the family as the legal property of fathers to correct as they saw fit.[82] On the eve of the twentieth century, jurist Adolphe Berlet observed that legislators had only recently found it necessary to act to protect children's very existence through criminalizing acts of cruelty and brutality committed against them at the hands of their fathers.[83]

The original and primary motivation for the 1898 legislation was to plug this gap in existing law to provide protection for children who were physically mistreated by their parents. The 1889 Roussel law had not targeted such incidents, concentrated as it was on neglect and "moral abandonment" rather than active brutality and cruelty. But in the end the 1898 law went much further, recognizing the enfant en danger and the enfant dangereux as two sides of the same coin. The idea that juvenile offenders were similar to neglected children in the sense that the root cause of their condition was parental neglect was "dormant in [the law of] 1889," but became explicit in the 1898 legislation, as Dominique Messineo has written.[84]

When first presented to and approved by the Chamber of Deputies, the bill only extended the proposed provisions to juvenile victims of parental physical abuse: enfants en danger. On the bill's arrival at the Senate, however, René Bérenger intervened. Driven by a belief that all juveniles – whether agents or victims of crime – were deserving of the possibility of protection, Bérenger took it upon himself to modify articles 4 and 5, insisting on a particular wording of the legislation that effectively collapsed delinquent and physically brutalized children into a single category. As a result of this conflation, legal authorities would be empowered to remove from their parents' custody juveniles who were victims of physical abuse at the hands of their parents and juveniles who had themselves committed an offence and place them in the care of a relative, a charitable person or institution, or, as a last resort, an institution of the Assistance publique. Instead of being made to appear before a court and, if not returned to their parents, detained in a reformatory ("maison de correction"), a juvenile offender could now be entrusted directly to a patronage society. The dangerous mixing of convicted juveniles with ones acquitted under Article 66 could thereby be avoided, the problems of the Corne law transcended.

Addressing the longstanding shortcomings of the 1850 law was precisely Bérenger's intention in modifying the bill to include juvenile offenders. As a result of his interventions, juvenile delinquents could be seen as equivalent to victims of familial mistreatment and therefore deserving of welfarist measures rather than punishment or correction. To punish such a child for what were, effectively, the faults of the parents would be a betrayal of the basic legal principle of personal responsibility. The 1898 law concretized the notion – which had been developing within the discourse of prevention that had started to solidify from the late 1870s – that focusing on a juvenile offender's moral judgment was a distraction from the most pressing consideration:

family and social influence. "Discernement" was effectively marginalized as a criterion for determining the appropriate response to juveniles. This was important, as it paved the way for the law of 1912 that decriminalized all offences committed under the age of thirteen. As Éric Pierre has observed, "while [the 1898 law] did not directly decriminalize juvenile delinquency, it offered the judge the possibility of placing young perpetrators of crime and offences in institutions entirely free of penal character."[85]

The effort to protect juveniles as much as possible from criminal prosecution and incarceration made possible by the 1898 law, thanks to Bérenger's interventions, was reinforced the following month by the justice minister, Victor Milliard. On 31 May, Milliard distributed a circular to public prosecutors warning against engaging in the harmful practice of sentencing juveniles found to have acted "avec discernement" to short periods in prison and urging them to wherever possible spare the young person the taint of a first conviction. Warnings should be issued and only after a repeated or serious offence should the wheels of prosecution be made to turn. This was not to say that arrested juveniles should be disregarded. On the contrary, Milliard cautioned against authorities simply dismissing cases they deemed to be insufficiently serious without investigating them. When it came to juveniles, the minister insisted, prosecutors needed to carefully probe each and every case in order to best understand the circumstances and conditions that had led to the young person coming into conflict with the law.[86] Only after all other avenues had been exhausted should a prosecution take place, and in the case of a conviction, incarceration in a maison de correction was always to be preferred over prison.

Official statistics from the years that followed suggest that these recommendations were respected by the courts. Between 1891 and 1900 an average of 6,339 juveniles under sixteen were brought before the courts each year. Between 1901 and 1904 this dropped to 4,615. In 1905 the figure declined further to 4,375, of whom 747 were convicted as having acted "avec discernement."[87] Opening up alternative measures to detention in a juvenile colony or return to parents, the 1898 law addressed major shortcomings in the administration of juvenile justice in place since 1850.

But in attending to one problem, the 1898 law would itself give rise to new ones. One week after the law was passed, *Le Temps* newspaper printed on its front page a letter from Henri Rollet expressing admiration for the good intentions of the legislators but raising questions about the practical implications of the legislation, particularly the costs that were likely to be incurred by private charities, which, as under the 1850 law, were privileged over public institutions. Under articles 4 and 5, only if a patronage society was non-existent or unwilling to receive a juvenile was the young person to be entrusted to public welfare. Whereas the Corne law had specified that the state would subsidize private colonies and the 1889 Roussel law had laid down that the Assistance publique would bear the costs of raising a child whose parents were found to be unfit, the 1898 law was entirely silent on the question of finances. Rollet expressed the hope that the state would invest in private protective initiatives to enable them to provide these necessary services.[88]

Within just a few years of the law's application, evidence demonstrated that the removal of acquitted juveniles from colonies – while admirable – had simply transposed problems onto a welfare sector inadequately resourced to deal with them. With no new investment offered, associations of private philanthropy and institutions of public welfare were unable to meet the new demand imposed on them. Although the law through its wording privileged the placement of juveniles in private hands, non-state organizations were afforded the right of refusal. Public welfare, by contrast, had no such right – at least in theory. In fact, it was found that public administrators were refusing to accept juvenile offenders transferred to their care under the terms of the 1898 legislation, prompting the Cour de cassation to issue a decree reminding the Assistance publique of its non-negotiable obligation to provide support.[89] Inadequately resourced, these publicly run welfare institutions struggled to provide for and manage the young people entrusted to them. In a series of reports published in the SGP journal in the early 1900s, lawyer and devout Catholic Paul Drillon described how welfare institutions had been overwhelmed by the transfer of juvenile delinquents into their care. In the area around Lille, Drillon reported, these youngsters were running wild, breaking windows, and threatening to set fire to the buildings in which they were held.[90]

Not only did the 1898 legislation put pressure on public welfare institutions; it also produced challenges for juvenile colonies, which found it difficult to adapt to the new conditions to which the law had given rise. Within a couple of years, the composition and atmosphere of correctional institutions were seen have been profoundly transformed. In 1900, Henri Joly reported that directors of private and public colonies were complaining that magistrates were choosing to send them only the worst cases – recidivists and the most morally corrupted. There was also a noted tendency to entrust older youths to juvenile colonies. Joly quoted one director who told him that "the children who come to us are … generally worse, because they come to us at a later age." Having been raised without the influence of religious instruction, the director remarked, they lacked a moral framework and their encounters with the world had given them a taste for "independence, laziness and even insubordination."[91]

In the years that followed, the 1898 law was generally viewed by reformers and administrators as well intentioned but poorly conceived. In March 1903, Paul Jolly described to the Parisian Comité de défense des enfants traduits en justice how the 1898 law was fundamentally flawed in bringing together two categories – the enfant en danger and the enfant dangereux – that, he said, required distinct treatment. It was René Bérenger, Jolly commented, "with his big heart and tireless devotion to the cause of children," who had taken it upon himself to add three simple but significant words – "par des enfants" – to the 1898 legislation, thereby opening the way to non-correctional institutions being overrun.[92] From its original incarnation as a law for mistreated children, the text of the bill, Jolly said, was extended to juvenile delinquents for whom it "was not made … and not suited," and while "the text … perhaps meets the needs of one of these situations, it does not meet the needs of the other."[93] In an article published in the SGP's journal in 1906 Paul Cuche and Dr Louis-Victor Mouret, a medical doctor and inspector attached to the Assistance publique, wrote that legislators' decision to extend the provisions of the 1898 bill to juvenile perpetrators as well as victims represented a dangerous, spur-of-the-moment action reflective not of well-considered opinion but rather of the high degree of influence Bérenger enjoyed within the parliament over matters of criminal justice and child welfare.[94]

At a meeting of the Comité de défense des enfants traduits en justice in Paris in July 1904, jurist Manuel Fourcade commented on the serious complications produced by the 1898 legislation. Fourcade applauded legislators for having recognized that despite the best efforts of philanthropists to make maisons de correction into educational institutions, they were, at least in the case of state-run colonies, ultimately and resolutely penal in character.[95] In the eyes of young people and in the view of many in wider society too, these institutions were simply prisons without high walls. While removing juveniles considered particularly receptive to reform from colonies made sense, it also caused problems. And while the Corne law of 1850 had mingled acquitted and convicted offenders within the same institutions, it was not clear how the 1898 law offered considerable improvements on this score. Fourcade told of how the conflation of juvenile perpetrators and victims of crime and their placement in maisons de correction had in effect transposed onto the welfare sector the confusion that had long reigned in juvenile colonies.

Eventually, in response to these problems, the parliament passed a new law authorizing institutions of public welfare to arrange the transfer of troublesome juveniles into correctional institutions. The law of 28 June 1904 vested authorities in the Assistance publique with the right to apply for the removal of troublesome youths from their care and their placement in a juvenile colony.[96] Significantly, this process of transfer was administered entirely outside of the correctional sphere, which effectively meant that civil authorities were empowered to revise the decision of criminal justice authorities who had earlier refused to impose a correctional sentence.[97] Although this law provided state welfare with some means of controlling the composition of its institutions, it also reopened the way for children in need to be relegated to correctional establishments – precisely what the 1898 law had been formulated to avoid.

## Segregating Children from Adolescents

In 1879 SGP members, including Théophile Roussel, formed a special committee to examine possible reforms to the processing and treatment of juvenile offenders. The Corne law, Roussel told fellow SGP members, was rightly criticized for allowing to mix "prisoners aged over twelve, already adolescents, with children aged under twelve."[98] Foreign experiments, Roussel went on, were already demonstrating that children under the age of twelve should always be spared any punishment because their "moral development does not yet include responsibility."[99] The SGP committee's recommendations brought forward what had been recommended by the Haussonville Commission and in many respects anticipated measures that would eventually be set down in the legislation of 1912.

In his report to the Haussonville Commission a few years earlier, Félix Voisin had suggested that rather than being detained in colonies, all juveniles found to have committed an offence "sans discernement" and acquitted under Article 66 but who could not be returned to their parents' custody be sent to a new type of institution – an *école de réforme* – and that they be held there until they reached the age of twenty-one, so as to align their release with the attainment of their full civic rights.[100] The fact that the 1850 law had not brought the age of release into line with the age of civil majority needs to be understood, as Dominique Messineo has pointed out, as a deferential nod to patriarchal power; the assumption was that the released minor would return to the family's care, at least until they came of age.[101]

Voisin's suggestion that the family be bypassed was an assertion of the superior rights, if not yet of the child, then certainly of institutions over the rights of the family, especially of fathers. Both recommendations from the Haussonville Commission were supported by the SGP committee. For juveniles presumed to have acted "sans discernement," the committee recommended that their cases be heard in closed court.[102] In a significant shift, the committee also proposed that institutional detention be different depending on the age of the juvenile acquitted under Article 66. Those under twelve would be held in an école de réforme, while older ones who gave no sign of a "precocious perversity" would be detained in new institutions (*écoles industrielles*) equivalent to the industrial schools already in existence in England and the United States.[103]

In a discussion of these proposals, SGP member Dr Jules Lunier, general inspector of the psychiatric service with more than thirty years' experience in prison administration, went a step further, proposing that all children under the age of twelve be uniformly presumed to have acted "sans discernement" and that they be placed not in an école de réforme but in an *école de préservation*.[104] The physician also advocated for the introduction of new powers for magistrates to assess juveniles convicted under articles 67 and 69 to determine whether they might be placed in a correctional education section on completion of their sentence and held until they turned twenty-one, rather than being immediately returned to their parents.

Fernand Desportes agreed that an automatic assumption of irresponsibility be applied to juveniles under the age of twelve, arguing that "there are children precocious for bad as there are some precocious for good ... [but] no matter their precocity, in their early childhood [that is, before the age of twelve], they cannot be considered to have a moral freedom sufficient to make them responsible for their actions."[105]

In his 1909 book *La Criminalité dans l'adolescence*, sociologist Guillaume Duprat drew attention to fundamental qualities that distinguished children from adolescents. In sharp contrast to other areas of life by this time, particularly labour and education, France's criminal law made no systematic distinction between children and adolescents. Noting this, Duprat urged legislators and policymakers to recognize what he saw as essential differences that marked young people off from each other depending on which side of puberty they stood.[106] In the treatment of juvenile offenders, Duprat called for the creation of special institutions or at least special quarters to enable the regular separation of adolescent offenders from their younger, more docile counterparts. Reflecting a growing sensitivity in French society to the stricter segregation of age groups, Duprat insisted that in order to effectively prevent moral corruption, juveniles needed to be detained separately according to their chronological age.[107]

The suggestion that child and adolescent offenders be held separately, as historian Henri Gaillac has commented, represented the advent of "an idea which would find its legislative concretization in the law of 22 July 1912."[108] Chronological age was starting to be more fully recognized as meaningful in the appropriate treatment of young offenders. Legislators and reformers continued to debate the most appropriate and effective methods for treating juvenile offenders for years. Among the issues they pondered was the extent to which, when it came to young offenders, chronological age should override all other considerations. Gradually the idea solidified that in addition to distinguishing between juveniles and adults, it was also important to distinguish between children and adolescents. The main rationale for subdividing juvenile detainees into different age categories was the need to stem moral contamination; this was the same logic that underpinned detaining juveniles under the age of sixteen separately from adult prisoners. As we saw in chapter 3, while the legislators of the 1791 and 1810 codes had recognized the incomplete growth of young people up to the age of sixteen and their need for separate incarceration from older offenders (although without actually carrying through with creating any such institutions), they had not found it necessary to stipulate any age below which prosecution was inconceivable.

By the final decades of the nineteenth century, there was a growing sense that further age-based discriminations were needed. "It is certain," Haussonville wrote in 1875, "that the experience of evil increases in children over time, and that the influence of the older on the younger can rightly be feared."[109] There was also a general perception that the age at which a juvenile offender entered a correctional institution had a bearing on their likely reform – the younger they were, the easier it was thought to be to prepare them for re-entry into society. Age-based classification of prisoners was, Haussonville observed, "the most rational and the easiest to accomplish."[110] But at the same time, he and other reformers were aware that chronological age was not always a reliable indicator of maturity or moral development. "In some children," Haussonville commented, "the progress of intelligence is not related to the development of the body," and sometimes an older child had the capacities of a younger one. For Haussonville, this demonstrated "all that was illusory about systems of classification," and for this reason a certain flexibility was warranted, with the older youth better detained with the younger ones.[111]

In systematically decriminalizing offences committed by children under the age of thirteen, the law of 1912 on juvenile courts would cement a core, age-based distinction between child and adolescent offenders. But well before the passage of that legislation, penal administrators and reformers were already recognizing that chronological age was a criterion worthy of more substantial consideration beyond simply separating juveniles under sixteen from older offenders. Although the Corne law did not require it, some institutions had developed the practice of distributing detainees into separate sections on the basis of their age, particularly those below and above the age of twelve. Well before the first écoles de réforme were created, children under twelve were routinely housed in distinct quarters in colonies, in what was referred to as the "little section" (*petit quartier*), generally placed under the charge of nuns (*sœurs des prisons*). Juvenile colonies regularly sorted detainees into *petits*, *moyens*, and *grands*, but significantly this separation was not spatially absolute, with the younger detainees often mixing with the older ones.[112]

Despite recommendations from the Haussonville Commission and, later, the SGP, the state made no change to existing legislation, leaving it instead to private institutions, which still dominated the sector, to take the first steps towards implementing a treatment of young offenders distinguished on the basis of age. The first école de réforme, for young offenders under the age of twelve who had been acquitted under Article 66, was established at Saint-Éloi near Limoges in 1876. It was followed the next year by another, Saint-Joseph at Frasnes-le-Château in the Haute Saône. At that time, offenders under twelve made up around a third of the population of colonies pénitentiaires,[113] and a fifth of all juvenile detainees.[114] Both Saint-Éloi and Saint-Joseph were Catholic institutions run by nuns. A consensus held by reformers was that women, like mothers, were the most appropriate figures for raising the youngest category of offenders.[115] In 1895, Louis Puibaraud described to the International Prison Congress the central role played by women in managing young offenders up to the age of twelve.[116] By 1900 it was observed that écoles de réforme had taken on a distinctly feminine character.[117] Following the creation of Saint-Éloi and Saint-Joseph, the first Protestant institution was created for detainees under the age of twelve: Sainte-Foy-la-Grande in the Dordogne region in southwestern France. Initially, Saint-Eloi took in both boys and girls. Classes for the two sexes were held in separate classrooms, about 500 metres apart. The girls were instructed by nuns, the boys by lay teachers, but they all performed farming tasks together. By 1890, however, this approach had been abandoned and girls were no longer admitted.[118] At the start, Sainte-Foy also admitted both boys and girls up to the age of twelve, but this was soon abandoned.[119]

It was not until 1891 that public institutions began to adopt a system of segregated detention of child and adolescent detainees, starting first with the Colonie agricole of Chanteloup in western France. Part of the Colonie pénitentiaire of Saint-Hilaire in the Nouvelle-Aquitaine region around Bordeaux, Chanteloup was solely for juvenile delinquent boys aged under twelve. On reaching twelve they progressed to a different, entirely separate farm within the juvenile colony (Bellevue), and later, once they turned fifteen, to a third (Boulard).[120] In a short report written for the SGP in 1894, Paul Cuche offered a positive assessment of Chanteloup, describing it as "mak[ing] a place for itself in the middle of our penal institutions and … tak[ing] an honourable rank among them."[121] So encouraged was Cuche by what he observed at Chanteloup that he expressed the hope that it might prompt magistrates, when confronted by children in their courtrooms, to take appropriate action: "when magistrates know that by sending young children for correction, they are taking real measures to protect and save them from a corrupt environment in order to place them in a moral and religious environment, they will no longer hesitate in declaring acquittals and renounce the disastrous jurisprudence of short prison sentences."[122] Léon Pissard, a functionary from the interior ministry, told the 1895 International Prison Congress in Paris of the positive achievements being witnessed at Saint-Hilaire. Boys detained at the juvenile colony for at least three years, he said, were taller, heavier, and stronger than new arrivals: all evidence of the utility of sustained detention in a juvenile colony over short-term incarceration in prison or return to harmful familial environments.[123]

In 1894, Louis Puibaraud presented a report to the Comité de défense des enfants traduits en justice in which he recommended creating "écoles de préservation" that would be dedicated institutions for vagrant juveniles, with separate detention for those below and above the age of twelve. Puibaraud's reasoning for selecting that age as the threshold point was that since the usual minimum age for prosecution of juveniles was eight and the upper limit was sixteen, twelve represented the "average age between two limits."[124] As a sorting mechanism of classification, Puibaraud observed, chronological age was "the most natural, the most exact, the easiest to follow, and, in reality, the one that holds the fewest surprises."[125]

It was not until 1902 that the first of these institutions – the École de préservation Théophile Roussel – appeared, emerging in response to the complications produced by the 1898 law. Carved out of the Colonie pénitentiaire Le Peletier de Saint-Fargeau at Montesson, the École de préservation Théophile Roussel was positioned somewhere between the semi-repressive juvenile colony and a foundling hospital. From its inception, these écoles de préservation were conceived of as entirely distinct from correctional establishments. As Renée de la Bussière (pseudonym of Renée Rollet, spouse of Henri Rollet) commented in 1906, while écoles de préservation and maisons de correction bore "a certain resemblance" in that each received difficult children in need of "a reformative upbringing" who were raised there with firm discipline and who received practical training that would prepare them for their future, they were nonetheless also significantly different – "mainly in the mode of recruitment of the population."[126] Operating entirely independently of the prison administration, the École de préservation Théophile Roussel was authorized to receive children transferred under articles 4 and 5 of the 1898 law, along with undisciplined primary school children from the Paris region (admitted with the permission of their parents), wards of the state from public welfare, and children detained under correction paternelle. Despite the longstanding and widespread preference for capping the age of entrants at twelve, the institution admitted boys from the age of seven up to fourteen,[127] who could only be held until the age of sixteen (unlike juvenile colonies, which could detain juveniles up to the age of twenty).

Efforts such as these to prevent the spread of moral corruption by segregating younger juveniles acquitted under Article 66 from their older, convicted counterparts inevitably had flow-on effects for the composition of established institutions for reforming wayward youths, especially privately run colonies such as Mettray. Until the 1880s private initiative dominated the sector of juvenile corrections; in the 1850s, largely as a result of the Corne law that preferred them, at least initially, France had twice as many privately run colonies pénitentiaires (the majority of them Catholic) as state-run ones. In 1889, there were 2,616 boys in public colonies versus 2,072 in private ones.[128] Into the new century, there was an intensifying shift away from private colonies to public ones, and by 1910 the proportion of boys in state-run colonies far exceeded those in private colonies.[129]

Back in the 1870s, following revelations of alleged systemic abuse in private colonies, the Haussonville Commission had recommended the expansion of the state-run sector so that responsibility for juvenile correctional facilities was better balanced between private and public initiative. Sharing this belief in the need for co-existence of private and public institutions, in 1878 Charles Lucas sold his Val d'Yèvre juvenile colony near Bourges in central France to the state.[130] Lucas was a constant advocate for shared responsibility for juvenile correctional institutions, and for the state to provide subsidies for private initiative – something that was entirely lacking in Britain at the time, and which Lucas considered a major shortcoming of what he viewed as an otherwise impressive system across the English Channel.[131]

As time went on, the reputation of privately run juvenile institutions suffered considerable damage. Through the 1880s, as school policy became republicanized and a secularizing wave swept over French society, former detainees' allegations of brutality and mistreatment at privately run colonies circulated in the republican press, leading in some cases to the institutions' closure. Among the most shocking revelations came from former detainees from the Colonie pénitentiaire of Cîteaux near Dijon, who claimed that they had been raped by the Brothers of Saint Joseph.[132] The critique of colonies was also taken up by novelists; in 1896 François Coppée published *Le Coupable*, in which he portrayed these institutions as cruel, ineffective, and worse still, counterproductive.[133] In a review of the novel for the SGP, Senator Ferdinand Dreyfus praised Coppée for generally championing the cause of the downtrodden, but criticized him for misrepresenting the conditions within these institutions.[134] They were, he insisted, institutions of correction, discipline, and improvement, not of gratuitous punishment.

## Conclusion

In April 1897, the political daily newspaper *Le Petit marseillais* printed on its front page an opinion piece denouncing the detention of juvenile offenders in colonies. Written by Pierre Baudin, a left-leaning barrister who would soon enter the French parliament aligning with the radical-socialists, the article drew particular attention to the rising levels of delinquency among youths aged between sixteen and twenty-one, who were committing offences at a rate four times higher than they had fifty years earlier.[135] Baudin attributed these rocketing increases to colonies, which, he claimed, were nothing more than "odious prisons" and "hothouses of recidivists." Three days later, the same newspaper published a response by Aristide Vidal-Naquet, president of the Marseilles chapter of the Comité de défense des enfants traduits en justice, which rejected Baudin's characterization. While conceding that institutions for juvenile offenders were far from perfect, with state-run colonies overcrowded and privately run colonies struggling to provide for their charges in the face of inadequate state subsidies, Vidal-Nacquet pointed to the low rate of reoffending among boys released from colonies: just 40 per cent, dropping to 28 per cent among those boys who on release were taken under the wing of the Société de protection des engagés volontaires.

Rather than colonies, the real enemy when it came to treating juvenile delinquents, Vidal-Naquet declared, was short periods of detention in prison. This accusation, as we have seen, was a familiar one; Georges Kaps served as a particularly prominent example. "A few weeks, a few months in prison," Vidal-Nacquet wrote, "are not enough to correct a child, to reform his character, to bring his bad penchants under control."[136] Noting the alarming increase in the rate of offending among "children aged between sixteen and twenty," Vidal-Naquet argued that the real cause of criminality among these older youths was not juvenile colonies but rather that the boys in question had not spent time in them. In response, he called for measures to be extended to allow older youths to be treated as juveniles. "The [civil] juvenile aged between sixteen and eighteen," Vidal-Naquet wrote, "should no longer be thought of as a man and be hit only with that punishment of prison, incapable of correcting him, capable only of tainting him with a criminal record and making of him, fatally, a recidivist." Instead, he insisted, these older youths should be allowed to be placed in a house of correction for extended educative treatment. Such measures, he asserted, would reduce the number of criminals considerably as "opening a house of correctional education is to later close a prison."[137] Vidal-Naquet's suggestion would finally be taken up in 1906, when the age of criminal majority was raised to eighteen. This measure, which enabled more young people (most especially boys) to avoid a criminal conviction by being found to have acted "sans discernement," would also facilitate the entry of greater numbers of young men into the ranks of the regular army. In the years preceding the outbreak of the First World War, procedures of criminal justice, childrearing, and military defence became increasingly entangled. In the process, the matter of chronological age became ever more salient, as the next chapter will explore.

# CHAPTER 5

# The Republican Army as a School of Moralization?

When it came to the criminality of young people, Parisian lawyer Jules Jolly observed in a lengthy report delivered to the SGP in April 1904, "jeunesse" could be divided into two periods: "enfance," a legally prescribed category encompassing juveniles up to the age of sixteen, and "adolescence," a more fluid stage in legal terms, stretching from the age at which a person was considered criminally responsible through to twenty-one, when they acquired their full civil rights as an adult. Although the legal system suggested neatly compartmentalized, age-defined stages, Jolly pointed out that it was "almost impossible to study the criminality of children while absolutely isolating the criminality of adolescents."[1] What was laid bare when jeunesse was taken in its fullest sense, Jolly pointed out, was the dramatic impact that age had on criminal prosecution patterns. Indeed, while official statistics revealed a drop in the rate of prosecutions of young people under the age of sixteen, they indicated a striking increase for older youths – individuals whom the criminal law treated as adults, but who were still considered minors in the eyes of the civil law.

In the case of juveniles, Jolly argued, these patterns were the result of the application of new techniques and laws that saw criminal proceedings more rarely taken against offenders under the age of sixteen and were part of a broader attitude of clemency or even indulgence towards young offenders that had been developing for decades.[2] This same culture of indulgence was said to be encouraging criminal behaviours in older youths (as we saw in response to the case of Georges Kaps in the previous chapter). It was the age bracket between sixteen and twenty-one that was of greatest concern. In the space of half a century, between 1831 and 1881, Jolly declared, there had been a "frightening increase [in criminal prosecutions] both absolute and proportional" among this age cohort, "and this increase continues."[3] In 1831, 10 per cent of all defendants were aged between sixteen and twenty-one, the vast majority of them boys. Fifty years later, the number had increased by well over a factor of four, accounting for 15 per cent of the whole. In 1901, boys and girls between sixteen and twenty-one accounted for 17 per cent of all prosecutions.[4]

For French reformers and legislators in the early twentieth century, the implications of these figures extended far beyond matters of criminal justice, tapping into central, even existential questions concerning the moral health and defence and, indeed, very survival of the nation. While legislators, policymakers, and reformers were grappling with what could be done to better address criminality in juveniles under sixteen, around the turn of the twentieth century they were also increasingly concerned with what could and should be done about offenders who straddled the stages between childhood and adulthood – the stage of life that Jules Jolly termed adolescence.

On 12 April 1906, the French parliament resolved this question of ever-increasing prosecution rates among older youths by raising the age of criminal majority from sixteen to eighteen. Rather than simply absorbing these older offenders into the established category of juvenile, however, the 1906 law carved out an additional category of criminal majority: offenders aged over sixteen and under eighteen. This was not the first time young people aged between sixteen and eighteen had been recognized as a distinct legal category. The labour law of 2 November 1892, which prohibited the employment of children, similarly split adolescence into two phases: from thirteen to sixteen, and from sixteen to eighteen. Workers (whether boys or girls) between thirteen and sixteen were permitted to work up to ten hours per day, while those aged between sixteen and eighteen were allowed to work up to eleven hours per day and a sixty-hour week overall. All workers under eighteen were banned from night work.[5]

According to the 1906 law, the presence of "discernement" in older delinquent youths could not be automatically presumed, as for an adult, but instead needed to be established in each and every case, as for their younger counterparts. If determined to have acted "sans discernement," these youths would be acquitted and detained just like their younger equivalents. If found to have acted "avec discernement," however, they were not protected from the harshest penalties but rather subject to the same punishments as adults. Adolescence, in other words, was not recognized as a fixed legal category of its own. Rather, it was a fluid status on a sliding scale. Depending on the legal authorities' assessment of "discernement," a young person between the ages of sixteen and eighteen was to be treated as either a juvenile or an adult. Jean Grosmolard, director of the Colonie correctionnelle d'Eysses, offered a succinct explanation of the distinction: "the *acquitted* juvenile between sixteen and eighteen years is a child; *convicted*, he becomes a man."[6] The idea of punishing as adults youths aged between sixteen and eighteen who knowingly broke the law aligned with the views of members of the Union des sociétés de patronage, a group with close connections to the SGP and formed with the aim of fostering greater cooperation and communication between the mosaic of patronage societies that proliferated across France.[7] As ever, the responsibility for determining the presence or absence of the nebulous yet significant quality of "discernement" rested in the hands of magistrates.

Although, as we saw in chapter 3, the suggestion that all children under a certain age threshold might be automatically assumed criminally irresponsible was not entirely without controversy, it nonetheless proved considerably less contentious than the suggestion that offenders over sixteen might be treated as juveniles. In the popular imagination, while the figure of the young delinquent child conjured up images of cheeky but ultimately needy and deserving street urchins, like the fictional character of Gavroche in Victor Hugo's *Les Misérables*, older youths were generally viewed with less sympathy. From the 1890s onwards, the most prominent youth type in French popular culture was the so-called "apache," members of urban gangs whose disruptive exploits regularly stained the *faits-divers* section of daily newspapers. Politician Pierre Baudin wrote of eighteen-year-old gang leaders, their bodies tattooed with chevrons, at permanent war with society.[8]

The passage of the 1906 law raising the age of criminal majority to eighteen came at a time of intense debate about the most effective strategies of reducing criminality. It was a time of an alleged "crisis of repression," which, as Dominique Kalifa has argued, was a manifestation of an always latent opposition in juridical circles to the republican-propelled humanization and secularization of the law at the end of the nineteenth century.[9] Just two months before the passage of the 1906 law, Armand Fallières – a fervent abolitionist who, as we saw in chapter 1, would regularly commute sentences (including for the two Jully killers) – had assumed office as France's president. Before the year was out, various bills were introduced to parliament by the radical-socialist prime minister, Georges Clemenceau, who had taken over the position from an ailing Ferdinand Sarrien. Among them was one bill proposing the abolition of the death penalty. In early 1907 the SGP tackled the question of abolishing capital punishment, with Joseph Reinach, a radical deputy, arguing in favour, and Henri Joly presenting the case for the retentionists.[10] In the end, the bill failed, but the debate it aroused, highly visible in the popular press, on the purpose of criminal justice and the most effective means of controlling crime, persisted for a long time afterwards.[11]

The proposal to raise the age of criminal majority was motivated by at least three considerations. One was the concern among governing authorities about reducing the rate of repeat offending, as historian Rachel Fuchs has pointed out.[12] In addition, it was also a reflection of the growing "sensitivity to adolescence" in turn-of-the-century France.[13] And finally, and most saliently for the Third Republic, enabling older youths to be found to have acted "sans discernement" made them eligible for a more lengthy detention, after which, it was hoped, they would get married (in the case of girls) or they would enter the military (in the case of boys).[14]

When reformers discussed the problem of youth criminality, they were primarily concerned about boys. Throughout the nineteenth century, the overwhelming majority of juveniles prosecuted by the courts in France were boys,[15] and four out of five young prisoners were male, most of them indicted for theft.[16] Although girls constituted a smaller contingent held in correctional institutions, interestingly they made up a higher proportion of youngsters incarcerated under the provisions of correction paternelle. For the period between 1851 and 1896, Bernard Schnapper estimates that each year no more than a thousand boys were imprisoned or threatened with imprisonment by their fathers.[17] Parents' more frequent recourse to correction paternelle for their daughters is likely explained, as Françoise Tétard and Claire Dumas have argued, by the heightened concern about protecting girls from moral (that is, sexual) corruption.[18] Once "fallen," it was believed, a girl could only with great difficulty be redeemed. This thinking contributed to the passage of legislation on juvenile prostitution in 1908, spearheaded by the indefatigable moral crusader René Bérenger.[19]

In general, delinquent girls were understood to be afflicted with a particular kind of moral disorder over which they could exercise less control than boys. The presumed greater vulnerability of girls and the danger they posed to society if their misconduct was not addressed served to intensify reformers' protective attitudes towards them. Writing in 1892, Henri Joly argued that "an unsupervised girl is in more danger than a boy."[20] And although the number of incarcerated girls was a shadow of the number of boys held – in 1892, 1,000 girls as opposed to 4,800 boys – it was reasonable to "assume that these 1,000 girls, in freedom, would provoke, facilitate, perhaps spread as much harm as several thousand little boys."[21] For girls, the imperative was to protect their morality and prepare them for "marriage and motherhood."[22] For boys of the Third Republic, on the other hand, the desired fate upon their release from detention was entry into the military. For both girls and boys, the aim was the same: to preserve their purity. As one SGP member put it in 1888, French society had an interest in protecting the "judicial virginity" – that is, the criminal record – of delinquent boys in order to facilitate their entry into the regular ranks of the military.[23]

Debates on raising the age of criminal majority were tied up in disputes over the role of military service in the formation of the republican citizen. According to republicans, self-sacrifice for the defence and glory of the French nation was a vehicle through which a young offender could demonstrate his regenerated moral character and worthiness for citizenship. The notion that the military was an appropriate and effective destination for the nation's troubled young men rested on a transformed idea about France's army itself as a "school of moralization," an idea actively pursued by republicans in the final decades of the nineteenth century. At the same time, this notion was inseparable from a growing scepticism about the capacity of the existing prison system to effectively reform lawbreakers, running alongside a doubt in other quarters about the capacity for lawbreakers to effectively reform themselves. As we will see, at the turn of the twentieth century, the matter of age and criminal majority was tightly implicated in core debates preoccupying French reformers and legislators over the most effective means to respond to criminality, over the character and composition of the armed forces, and over the relationship between institutions of criminal justice, the military, and broader society.

## Regenerating the Criminal through Military Service

In 1891, the director of France's prison administration, Louis Herbette, gathered together various textual materials from a display at the world's fair held in Paris two years earlier and published them in a book entitled *L'Œuvre pénitentiaire.*[24] The book, which traced the current state of France's prison administration and was deliberately published in 1891 to coincide with the centenary of France's first penal code, opened with a striking frontispiece by artist Hippolyte Berteaux, a student of the celebrated neo-classical painter Hippolyte Flandrin, and a figure now best remembered as the artist responsible for painting the ceiling mural in the opera house in Nantes.[25] Berteaux's frontispiece offered an allegorical rendering of France's criminal justice system (see figure 5.1). Shaped in the form of a pyramid, the system is represented as centred on the objective of rehabilitation and improvement.

At the pyramid's apex sits a female statue dressed in classical garb atop a stone plinth inscribed with the word "law" – the secular deity of the French republic. Beneath the statue extends a world divided vertically into two halves: a light-filled, fertile space of the virtuous and law-abiding above, and a murky, cavernous area of the immoral and criminal below. In the upper plane, a St Jerome figure (identifiable by the lion seated behind him) pores over a book, while the tools of healthy and productive industry (a hammer and scythe) lie momentarily set aside at his feet. Adjacent to him on the same plane, a young girl demonstrates her virtue, genuflecting before the statue. In the lower plane, by contrast, is a world of hardship: a man engages in the gruelling and unedifying work of breaking rocks, while a woman nearby grasps desperately to a rocky ledge, a helpless young child at her feet. Still further down, the head and shoulders of a man emerge from the rocks. Marking the boundary between the two planes – the moral and the immoral, the law-abiding and the law-breaking, the productive and the futile – stands an infant. This disconcertingly muscular figure, a sort of Christ child, holds aloft a flaming torch, presumably symbolizing hope and enlightenment.

Particularly noteworthy in Berteaux's allegorical depiction is the fact that only one figure is represented as successfully negotiating their way from the lower plane of immorality and crime and into the upper one of virtue. That figure is a boy soldier. Dressed in military uniform and bearing a rifle, the youngster – in a movement eerily prescient of soldiers in the First World War going over the top of the trenches – hoists himself up and into the upper

Figure 5.1
Allegory of the regenerative power of republican justice – frontispiece illustration by Hippolyte Berteaux

plane to take his place alongside St Jerome and the genuflecting girl. In a brief analysis of Berteaux's image, Mireille Gueissaz has pointed to the apparent idealism in the artist's depiction of the young girl. "The judicial institution," Gueissaz writes, "seems to devote itself body and soul to the redemption, to the salvation of the young girl."[26] This claim, however, underestimates the central importance of the artist's depiction of the young boy. Berteaux's frontispiece to Herbette's book, which neatly encapsulates core ideas about law, criminality, and moralization in the Third Republic, is particularly important for what it tells us about the gendered nature of regeneration. Indeed, his depiction of the boy soldier offers a compelling portrayal of the perceived power of service in the military that dominated republican thinking and policy in the decades preceding the First World War.

While Herbette's book celebrated the penal system and especially the modern penitentiary as both a humanitarian and an effective tool of rehabilitation, what he neglected to acknowledge was the increasing questioning of the efficacy of the prison as a tool of rehabilitation in this period. The final decade of the nineteenth century was marked by a widespread pessimism about the potential for prisons (at least in their current state) to positively affect detainees' morality. This pessimism contributed to the development of legislation that enshrined various alternatives to imprisonment. At one extreme was the relegation law of 1885, while at the other was the 1891 law on suspended sentences (*sursis*) sponsored by René Bérenger, which enabled first-time offenders to provisionally avoid a custodial sentence and conviction on the condition that they demonstrate sustained good conduct over the ensuing five years. If after that time they had not re-offended, their criminal record would be expunged. If, on the other hand, they committed another offence they would serve the original sentence on top of the sentence handed down for the subsequent offence. As a further deterrent, the suspended sentence was made harsher than it would have been if the punishment had been applied immediately.

For Bérenger and like-minded reformers, one of the clearest benefits of suspended sentences was that they enabled young men to avoid incurring a criminal conviction that might complicate their capacity to serve in the military, thus compromising the nation's capacity to defend itself. But where advocates of the suspended sentence saw it as a means to enhance national defence, opponents saw the mechanism as a major point of weakness, which when applied to young men risked imperilling the discipline of the troops and therefore would endanger the nation.

The issue essentially boiled down to the following: was society strengthened or weakened by deploying disciplinary alternatives to imprisonment in the penitentiary? Responses to that question were shaped not only by beliefs of corrigibility and the right (and need) to punish offenders, but also by ideas about the most effective means of defending the nation from military attack. Did optimal military defence rest on a select body of highly trained, professional soldiers – the model that had prevailed in France since the Napoleonic era – or did it depend, as republicans contended, on the mobilization of a larger number of ordinary men – even convicted criminals – conscripted into the armed forces for a shorter period of active service?

## Protecting the Purity of the Military: Logics of Exclusion

Throughout the nineteenth century and up until the fin de siècle, military recruitment policy in France was overwhelmingly defined by its appeal to exclusiveness. From the period of the Bourbon Restoration until the introduction of universal military service in 1889, although some degree of nonvoluntary service existed through the drawing of lots, France's military prided itself on being a largely professional body of troops distinguished by tight discipline and the unblemished backgrounds of its soldiers. After the fall of the Napoleonic Empire and until the end of the nineteenth century, rather than impose service on unwilling recruits or open the ranks to all comers, France's successive regimes pursued a military ideal centred on elitism. In contrast to the military culture of both the revolutionary and Napoleonic regimes, which emphasized the entanglement of military and civilian worlds, the Restoration championed a model focused on the segregation of the military.[27] Faced with the perennial problem of insufficient military manpower, legislators repeatedly weighed up the relative merits of two basic options: on the one hand, improve conditions for soldiers in order to encourage more men into their ranks, or, on the other, facilitate lengthier terms of enlistment and re-enlistment to ensure the continuity of a professionalized military in which conscripts would need to be called on as rarely as possible. Between the Restoration and the Third Republic, it was the second of these two options that predominated.[28]

Until the passage in 1889 of a law "sur le recrutement de l'armée" (on army recruitment) introducing universal military service (known as the

Freycinet law, named after its sponsor, Charles de Freycinet),[29] France maintained a recruitment practice centred on the idea of professionalism and exclusiveness. Beginning with the Bourbon Restoration, successive regimes had sought to minimize conscription and asserted the honour of the troops by preventing convicted offenders from entering.[30] The Restoration government, which came to power with the fall of Napoleon in 1814, chose to abolish conscription as a political tactic, in order to curry favour both with an ordinary population wearied by decades of war and with nobles who desired a return to the military structure of the Old Regime with a smaller body of professional officers and long-service troops.

Although conscription was commonly associated with the revolutionary and Napoleonic periods, especially the *levée en masse* of 1792–95 and the Jourdan-Delbrel conscription law of 1798, it was, in truth, an Old Regime practice. Introduced at the end of the seventeenth century, conscription served to make up for the lack of enthusiasm for voluntary enlistment. In centuries past, conscription had been a deeply unpopular measure, not so much because people feared dying on the battlefield but because service wrenched them away from their communities. This intensified in the eighteenth century as terms of service were lengthened and soldiers were housed in barracks. Service in the military was commonly associated with society's outcasts, whose sacrificial death on the battlefield would make them more socially useful than being left to live in ordinary society. Enlightened philosophes did little to dispel negative perceptions of the army, portraying war as pointless and destructive cruelty running counter to the values of a civilized society.[31] Military service introduced during the revolutionary and Napoleonic periods was glorified by authorities but was far from universally embraced.[32]

In pursuing its agenda to re-professionalize the military, the Restoration engaged in "a reaction against the excessive freedom with which the recruitment of troops had operated in the past," as one jurist observed in 1905.[33] Held at a remove from civilian society, the military in the post-Napoleonic era through to 1889 consisted mostly of an army of voluntarily enlisted soldiers within a structure that effectively operated as "a State within the State," with a culture, values, and even a legal system of its own over which the civilian world had next to no authority.[34] By re-professionalizing the military and removing conscription, the Restoration government saw itself as restoring honour to France's military. Significantly, this process was seen to require greater discrimination in the sorts of men permitted to enlist; exclusion was upheld as a key means of ensuring the health and discipline of the troops. For this reason, it became a particular priority to prevent all lawbreakers, including vagrants, from entering the armed forces.

The Restoration's exclusion of vagrants from the military marked a break not only with revolutionary and Napoleonic practice, but with the Old Regime as well. Since the seventeenth century, the French state had put those with no fixed address ("sans aveu") into the army.[35] Under Article 2 of the Gouvion-Saint-Cyr law of 1818, however, vagrants and convicted offenders ("repris de justice") were explicitly prevented from enlisting. Prospective soldiers were required to produce documentation attesting to their good character and full possession of their civic rights. But in the absence of a networked system of record keeping, restricting enlistment was difficult.[36] Although the term "repris de justice" had a particular legal meaning, referring only to convicts sentenced to physical punishment as opposed to a fine or deprivation of liberty, the terms of reference in the 1818 law were more vague and were regularly interpreted by military recruitment officers as signifying the exclusion of *all* convicted offenders.[37] Within a few short years, faced with insufficient numbers of voluntary recruits, the Restoration government quietly reinstated (limited) conscription.[38] The bar on convicted offenders, however, remained in place.

Under the Third Republic, with the introduction of universal military service and the removal of longstanding exclusions and exemptions, this central idea of the exclusivity of the military was overhauled.[39] Instead of the honour of the military being contingent on the pre-existing honour of its soldiers, the army itself became imbued with a transformative power capable of making soldiers honourable. The military, in other words, became an active agent of moralization capable of transforming imperfect men into upstanding soldiers and republican citizens. Although the idea that the army could serve as an instrument of social and cultural regeneration was not unique to the Third Republic, it was in this period that the program of harnessing the military for national regeneration took centre stage.[40] The fate of the nation was placed in the hands of a reformed army, appointed with a double mission of carrying out revenge on Prussia and instilling moral virtues capable of regenerating the nation.

From the earliest years of the Third Republic, conservatives like Adolphe Thiers continued to hold onto the established idea that the strength and integrity of the military rested on a strong sense of esprit de corps, effective leadership from the officer class, a strict respect for hierarchy, and a grounding in traditional Judeo-Christian values. While their idea of morality was centred on Catholicism, Judeo-Christian religion more broadly was recognized as similarly useful. Attributing the French army's defeat by Prussia to the absence of formal religion in French military life, conservatives pushed for the appointment of a permanent and official military chaplaincy, a standard feature of the Prussian army. In May 1874 conservatives succeeded in securing legislation that provided for Catholic, Protestant, and Jewish chaplains in military barracks (their distribution determined by the religious affiliations of the troops). This marked the first time that Judaism could be legally represented within the French army.[41]

Republicans, by contrast, argued that the strength of an army derived from a deep patriotism within every soldier and an unwavering commitment to voluntarily leap to the nation's defence. According to this republican thinking, citizenship was synonymous with military engagement, to the extent that, as Léon Gambetta famously declared to the French parliament in June 1871, "when in France a citizen is born, he is born a soldier."[42] For Gambetta and his fellow republicans, a Frenchman with basic military training, raised in republican values, always primed to fight out of righteous belief in the nation, made a finer, more loyal soldier than a professional who fought out of blind obedience. In addition, the army was identified as serving a similar purpose to the primary school in instilling core republican values. To conservatives, however, the republican idea of the military as a school-like institution through which all eligible (male) citizens would pass was unacceptable, primarily because they believed a citizens' army made up of short-term recruits risked replicating the National Guard, which, as the 1848 Revolution and even more recently the Paris Commune had shown, laid down conditions for popular insurrection.

According to republican thinking, military men were no longer to be considered part of a separate, protected caste subject to their own rules and rituals, but rather a reflection and extension of civil society. The passage of the Freycinet recruitment law in 1889, in the wake of the Boulanger Affair, in which Georges Boulanger, an army general turned politician, was accused of planning to overthrow the republic, helped to significantly narrow the longstanding distinctions between military and civilian society. The Bou langer Affair confirmed in republicans' minds that an unreformed army was a dangerous incubator of reaction and helped fuel the determination to bring the army into closer alignment with civil society and to revise how officers and troops related to one another. Through the Freycinet law, the army and nation effectively became synonymous, the respectability of each dependent on the other. The significance of this transformation cannot be underestimated. Whereas in the years immediately following (and even preceding) the Franco-Prussian War the military had been accused of contributing to the degeneration of the French nation,[43] by century's end it was upheld as the key means for regeneration – both individual and collective. Military service, long viewed with resentment by the general population,[44] was promoted as the most perfect expression of citizenship (even though, in keeping with a principle first introduced during the French Revolution, the active exercise of one's citizenship through military service entailed the soldier surrendering his political voice).[45]

During the Third Republic the army came to be promoted as an institution that should be an extension of general society.[46] The barracks – previously a space cut off from civilian society – was brought into much closer alignment with the wider community. This process also entailed a winding back of the autonomy of military justice, which since the revolutionary period had essentially functioned – like the military itself – as a closed shop in order to optimize discipline among troops.[47] Aided by the opening up of new networks of roads and railways, which disrupted centuries-old regional ties and fostered a new sense of nation-based identity, republican legislation made military service into a common experience for all Frenchmen.[48] The army was called on to serve as a sort of republican finishing school, a school of moralization.

Perhaps the most controversial part of the military recruitment law of 1889 was its provisions regarding entry for former convicted offenders. As well as removing certain exemptions (including for university students and seminarians), the Freycinet law not only enabled but indeed *obliged* service from men previously excluded on account of their criminal backgrounds. However, in order to prevent these recruits from potentially demoralizing their law-abiding counterparts, the legislation stipulated the placement of these soldiers on a probationary basis in special battalions in North Africa known as the Bataillons d'infanterie légère d'Afrique, routinely abbreviated to "Bataillons d'Afrique" and commonly known as the "Bat' d'Af." Set up in 1832 as part of the Armée d'Afrique, until 1889 these served exclusively as disciplinary camps for unruly trained soldiers. The Freycinet law, as John Cerullo has pointed out, transformed these North African camps into "military halfway houses" by stationing men without military training within them.[49] On satisfactory completion of a specified period of probation, these former convicts would be eligible for transfer to the metropole where they would take their place alongside the regular troops.[50]

Required to serve, yet kept separate from other recruits, these "exclus de l'armée," as they were officially termed, were treated as provisional citizens – at once part of the army and separate from it, their isolation intended as a safety measure to protect the purity of the social body. Their liminal status was marked not only geographically but also physically through their distinct uniforms.[51] Isolated in what Dominique Kalifa has labelled a "decontamination chamber [*sas de décontamination*]" in North Africa, these soldiers were effectively a military underclass,[52] "at once within and outside of the army."[53] After a specified period of distinguished service or impressive display during combat, soldiers stationed in the Bataillons d'Afrique could be reintegrated into the regular army corps.[54]

The simultaneous inclusion and segregation of convicted offenders in the French armed forces reflected the general ambivalence of French legislators and military administrators towards the participation of former prisoners. By including convicted offenders, the French state could maximize available manpower, while still going some way to protecting the security of the nation and the honour of the army by isolating them. For prison reformers, the question of convicted offenders serving in the military was related to their general concern about facilitating reintegration. For René Bérenger, the Freycinet law did not go far enough in its inclusion of former prisoners. During the parliamentary debates on Freycinet's bill, Bérenger expressed concern about its discriminatory treatment of convicted offenders. Segregating convicted offenders in distinct bodies of troops, Bérenger observed, even only temporarily, would effectively make military service into a second punishment.[55] If the purpose of requiring military service from convicted offenders was to transform them into good soldiers and citizens, he argued, it would be more effective to distribute them throughout ordinary regiments where they would be subjected to discipline and exposed to the positive influence of good role models. In later years other prominent statesmen, including Félix Voisin and Jean Jaurès, expressed similar concerns about the legislation causing former prisoners to be perpetually stigmatized.[56]

While military men like General Récamier (who had direct experience of the Bataillons d'Afrique, having led troops from this section during France's Mexican campaign) saw the army's strength and efficacy as resting on the composition of its forces, penal reformers like René Bérenger saw potential for the armed forces to serve as a vehicle for both individual redemption and national regeneration. Given that many offenders were prosecuted for minor offences, issuing a blanket prohibition barring all convicted offenders from entering the armed services made no practical sense to Bérenger. As for ongoing segregation of former convicts in distant battalions, this effectively compromised their reintegration into society, undermining any rehabilitative outcomes achieved while in detention and endangering the very society these measures were supposed to protect. Perceived as a second punishment, service in the disciplinary camps of the Bat' d'Af would cause a resentment that would ultimately serve to perpetuate these soldiers' anti-social tendencies. As Félix Voisin told a meeting of the SGP in 1897, whereas a regular military uniform was worn with pride, bestowing honour on the young soldier, for the exclus de l'armée the distinct uniform of the Bat' d'Af signalled the double taint of prison and disciplinary military service. All of this significantly compromised the moralizing purpose of service in the military.[57]

Those opposed to the inclusion of convicted offenders in the military, on the other hand, tended to reach for two basic arguments: first, that it compromised the strength of the military (thus endangering the nation), and second, that it undermined the prestige of the military as an institution, thereby diminishing the sense of honour for others serving within its ranks. Prior to the Third Republic, the only unit of the French military open to convicted offenders was the Foreign Legion. According to Bérenger, this made the Foreign Legion a "useful refuge for unfortunates who, determined to make sincere efforts to make amends for a guilty youth, turned to military discipline for the support that they could no longer hope to find from society."[58] Others, however, continued to hold the view that the integrity of the army was contingent on denying entry to certain categories of people, especially convicted offenders. Among the subscribers to this position was Loys Brueyre, who told the SGP that keeping such men out of the military was paramount because protecting the army's honour by refusing service was equivalent to protecting the honour of France itself.[59]

In 1902, French General Jules Bourelly, who had received his training at the elite military academy of Saint Cyr and had had a long and distinguished career, penned a long article published in *Le Correspondant de Paris* critiquing the republican view of the army as constituting a mirror for civilian society. Asserting that "the army is not the nation," Bourelly argued that "France's civilian and military worlds were not only separate but almost ontologically distinct realms," as John Cerullo has put it.[60] For Bourelly, a fundamental flaw in the republican military program was that by attempting to fuse the army and the nation it had politicized the military, thereby compromising the purity and strength of the armed forces and endangering the nation. The egalitarianism and social solidarity that were inflecting modern French society, Bourelly maintained, had no place in the army, which, in the interests of effective defence, needed to be a space of hierarchy and the voluntary submission of the weak to the strong. The central problem, according to Bourelly, was that "the Third Republic [was putting] an increasingly feeble and decadent citizenry in uniform, then [asking] the army to adapt itself to that citizenry's limitations rather than requiring citizens to assume a military bearing."[61] Civilian society, with its "egoism, immoderate love of well-being, contempt for authority, and class hatred," he insisted, was compromising the integrity of an institution that had previously distinguished itself as a "school of order, of morality, of discipline, of respect for authority."[62]

In 1905, much to the consternation of military men like Bourelly and other conservatives, the French parliament, by then dominated by radical republicans determined to disrupt what they saw as a dangerous intimacy between the military and the Catholic Church, passed additional legislation on military recruitment that further chipped away at the professionalism of the army. The fact that during the Dreyfus Affair the most influential military officers were defiantly and very publicly anti-Dreyfusard cast a pall over the officer class generally and strengthened republican denunciations of the army as clerical, reactionary, and, despite what figures like Bourelly claimed, overtly political. The so-called "alliance of the sword and the cross," republicans argued, breached the requisite neutrality of the army and endangered the republic itself.[63]

On 21 March 1905, the parliament approved the Berteaux law, which initiated the most radical overhaul of military recruitment policy to date. The most inclusive recruitment legislation of its kind passed before the First World War, the Berteaux law was upheld by republicans as embodying the intimate link between military service and citizenship that they prized so dearly. As the prime minister, Georges Clemenceau, put it in 1906, the Berteaux law "consecrated the identification of the army with the nation." This, Clemenceau continued, imbued the military with a moral, educative purpose: "The regiment must be an extension of the school. We would like it that generations, after having drawn from it habits of good hygiene and principles of civic education, depart from it better and more fit for social life."[64] Accordingly, military officers were called on to relate to their troops in a similar way to how teachers in republican primary schools related to their pupils: with an affectionate firmness, instead of authoritarian discipline.

This drive to nurture a less hierarchical culture within the military had been growing for some time. Many years earlier, on 15 March 1891, an article published anonymously in the *Revue des deux mondes* made the case for the importance of fostering a sense of common identity between military officers and ordinary troops.[65] (The article's author was later revealed to be Hubert Lyautey, an officer who would rise to the highest ranks of the French army.) The Berteaux law facilitated the formation of this more overtly egalitarian culture within the military. As one French captain, Pierre Lebaud, wrote in his 1908 book *L'Éducation dans l'armée d'une démocratie*: "the coercive discipline of yesteryear has … given way to a larger, more humane discipline of feelings … Today, in the regiment there are only *educative officers*, tasked with a patriotic high mission, and free and conscious *citizens* of a great Republic, who come to fulfill a sacred duty."[66]

While republicans like Clemenceau celebrated the Berteaux law, conservatives pushed back, presenting it as a major threat to the security and moral integrity of the nation. Their opposition centred on two key points: the shortened duration of obligatory military service (which, they maintained, impeded the professionalism and discipline of the corps) and the removal of probationary stationing of convicted offenders in North Africa. The 1905 legislation reduced the period of compulsory military service from three down to two years and lifted the existing cordon sanitaire separating former prisoners from other troops by enabling direct entry for convicted offenders into the ordinary troops on metropolitan soil rather than first having to pass through the Bat' d'Af. These changes, particularly the second, provoked a furore among conservatives, who saw former convicts as a sure source of contamination.

In the years following, newspapers regularly ran stories about marauding "apaches" in uniform corrupting well-behaved boys in metropolitan barracks and terrorizing French society while on leave.[67] Criticisms were repeatedly levelled at magistrates for allegedly being too lenient on offenders who, it was argued, deserved and needed to be treated with a firm hand. A colour supplement to the Sunday edition of the Parisian newspaper *Le Petit journal* for 17 November 1907 provided a particularly striking image of the problem (see figure 5.2). Above the caption "Too many lazy youths … Too many young criminals! Juvenile criminality has almost tripled in fifty years," a split image revealed the day and night exploits of a group of young boys in the city: lounging on a park bench during the day, while an oblivious policeman strolls by; at night they come alive, lurking on a dark street corner, waiting to pounce on an unsuspecting gentleman in a top hat.

In a similar vein, in 1912, just a few months before the law on juvenile courts was passed, the popular fortnightly magazine *Lectures pour tous* published an article titled "The reign of the apache," outlining the practices of this troublingly subversive subculture of youth. Part of the article contrasted the alleged culture of indulgence and leniency of contemporary justice with what, it was claimed, had been the more sensible, moderate approach employed in the past. The *Lectures pour tous* journalist argued that new techniques such as suspended sentences and the raising of the age of criminal majority to eighteen had fuelled rather than fixed the problem of criminal youths. A figurative illustration, juxtaposing two magistrates – one from 1892, the other from 1910 – captured succinctly the journalist's argument (see figure 5.3). The two magistrates, dressed in identical robes but with a notably different bearing, each hold a sieve filled with a similar number of miniature-sized young men. The rather forbidding-looking 1892 magistrate is depicted handling the young criminals in a sober and disinterested manner, only allowing a few of them to avoid prison. By contrast, the magistrate of 1910, a rosy-cheeked and affable-looking fellow, gazes indulgently at the young men collected in his sieve, tilting it in such a way as to enable most of them to escape detention. The effect of this indulgence is immediately apparent: dropping to the ground, their arms raised, these are not, the illustration suggests, reformed, orderly young men.

A similar portrait was put forward at more or less the same time by Guillaume Loubat, a public prosecutor from Lyon, in the more learned forum of the *Revue politique et parlementaire*. In two articles published in 1911, Loubat declared that France was experiencing a "crisis of repression."[68] Pulling no punches in his critique of contemporary judicial culture, Loubat emerged as one of the most outspoken critics of a new "subjective" culture of criminal justice that, it was argued, was responsible for fostering a less rigorous application of the law and weakening the deterrent function of the whole system. In a sense, the crisis that Loubat and others described was as much one of representation as repression. Loubat argued that over the course of the previous twenty years France had been overcome by "a wave

# Le Petit Journal

Le Petit Journal
CHAQUE JOUR – 6 PAGES – 5 CENTIMES
Administration : 61, rue Lafayette
Le Supplément illustré
CHAQUE SEMAINE 5 CENTIMES

5 CENTIMES SUPPLÉMENT ILLUSTRÉ 5 CENTIMES

Le Petit Journal Militaire, Maritime, Colonial.... 10 cent.
Le Petit Journal agricole, 5 cent. ~ La Mode du Petit Journal, 10 cent.
Le Petit Journal illustré de la Jeunesse, 10 cent.
On s'abonne sans frais dans tous les bureaux de poste

ABONNEMENTS

| | SIX MOIS | UN AN |
|---|---|---|
| SEINE et SEINE-ET-OISE.. | 2 fr. | 3 fr. 50 |
| DÉPARTEMENTS.......... | 2 fr. | 4 fr. » |
| ÉTRANGER.............. | 2 50 | 5 fr. » |

Les manuscrits ne sont pas rendus

Dix-huitième Année — DIMANCHE 17 NOVEMBRE 1907 — Numéro 887

TROP DE JEUNES PARESSEUX... TROP DE JEUNES CRIMINELS !
La criminalité juvénile a presque triplé en cinquante ans

Figure 5.2
The dangers of unemployed youth, from the front page of *Le Petit journal*, 17 November 1907

Figure 5.3
The dangers of excessive indulgence by French magistrates, from *Lectures pour tous*, January 1912

of indulgence and pity" about the welfare of criminals, while victims and their families were sidelined, apparently quickly forgotten.[69] The criminal justice system, Loubat lamented, was suffering from an "incurable benevolence" that was producing "a veritable warping [*déformation*]" of its true purpose of deterring, and therefore reducing, crime.[70] Loubat drew particular attention to the wisdom of the law of 12 April 1906, which, as we will see in the next section, raised the age of criminal majority from sixteen to eighteen. He questioned the timeliness of introducing a measure that increased the chances for older youths to be absolved of responsibility precisely at the time, he claimed, that they were maturing earlier. Was it really the right moment, he asked, "to open this new gap [*brèche*] in our penal system, when the precocity of criminals is greater and more worrying than ever?"[71] In Loubat's view, the overly indulgent attitude of magistrates (and juries) towards criminals was running the risk of further cultivating a hazardous perception among society's youth that they were invincible and above the law.

The stationing of convicted offenders among metropolitan troops similarly aroused controversy. In 1909, Georges Berry, deputy in the National Assembly representing the Seine department, confronted the minister of war on the issue, telling the parliament that "the ranks of our army are infested by the presence of 13,621 apaches."[72] In September that same year, an article printed in *Le Temps* newspaper reiterated the harms posed by convicted offenders serving in the military. Under the headline "Common law convicts in the barracks," the journalist remarked on the misguided approach of "a handful of humanitarians, of philanthropists, always ready to throw themselves into this false sentimentalism that has caused us so much harm." This culture, the journalist contended, had seen the 1905 recruitment law passed and convicted offenders allowed to serve alongside ordinary troops without at least being required to serve a probationary period in a North African battalion. "The barracks," wrote the journalist, "is not a penal institution or a reformatory [*maison de correction*]. The government does not have the right to inflict on honest boys whom it has taken from their families the incessant company of, the forced close contact [*coudoiement*] with apaches and thieves. It is not the role of non-commissioned officers and officers to keep watch over these apaches, in order to prevent them from committing some new offence [*méfait*]." To claim, the journalist continued, that mixing these convicted offenders in with ordinary troops diluted their potential or actual harm and helped raise the bad up to the level of the good was simply unfounded. In fact, the reverse was true: if vinegar is poured into wine, the journalist observed, the vinegar is not improved; rather it ruins the wine.[73]

In 1904, an officer (later revealed to be George Albert Bazaine-Hayter, an army general who had spent a long time commanding French troops in Africa) presented a similar argument in a note submitted anonymously to the SGP. The logic behind the Bataillons d'Afrique, he wrote, was to "preserve the bulk of the army from dubious elements which might corrupt it." However, the officer pointed out, protecting the "good" from the "bad" by concentrating the latter together could also produce undesirable consequences. "By bringing them together," he claimed, "it did not take long to create veritable hotbeds of infection in which badness outbids itself, out of which only badness can emerge; from a moral point of view, the coming together of elements of the same nature always results in inflaming them."[74]

Within the SGP, concerns were repeatedly expressed about the effects of the 1905 law on military discipline within the metropolitan troops. According to Paul Kahn, speaking to the group in late 1908, "there is one point on which we are all agreed, [which is] that it is important to rid the metropolitan army of bad elements who have been introduced into it in too great number."[75] Early the following year, General Récamier extolled the advantages of stationing men with criminal records in the Bat' d'Af, writing to the SGP that the cultivation of essential soldierly qualities of "courage, abnegation, devotion, cult of honour and duty" required "absolutely avoid[ing] keeping in the corps of the regular army, any man known to be corrupt [*taré*]."[76]

In the end, these conservative voices would win out. In 1910, the parliament revoked the generous conditions introduced by the 1905 and reinstated the exclusion of so-called "incorrigibles" from immediate service in regular units stationed in the metropole.[77] As previously, the exclus de l'armée would provisionally serve in the Bat' d'Af before potentially being integrated into the metropolitan troops, thus assuaging conservatives, who viewed convicted criminals with ongoing suspicion. Although reformers like Bérenger, keen to see the military deployed as a school of moralization for former prisoners, must surely have been frustrated by the overturning of this aspect of the Berteaux law, they could comfort themselves with other mechanisms in place that were achieving similar ends – chief among them the 1906 legislation raising the age of criminal majority to eighteen.

## Strengthening the Pipeline from Reformatory to Barracks

In *Surveiller et punir*, Michel Foucault traces the emergence of modern penal and disciplinary practices. A core argument presented in the book is that a basic continuum exists between the judicial discipline of the modern penitentiary and the cultures of conformity instilled in ostensibly non-punitive institutions, including the primary school, the factory, and the military barracks. While many people might see the prison as the antithesis of society, to Foucault, the modern penitentiary is in fact characterized by everyday practices and logics simply pushed to their extremes. Indeed, according to Foucault, the essential likeness between these institutions helps to explain public tolerance for prisons. "How could the prison not be immediately accepted," Foucault asks, "when, by imprisoning, correcting and rendering docile, it merely reproduces, with a little more emphasis, all the mechanisms that are to be found in the social body? The prison: a rather rigorous barracks, a strict school, a gloomy workshop, but ultimately [*à la limite*] not qualitatively different."[78] To substantiate his argument, Foucault takes as emblematic the Mettray juvenile reformatory. There, Foucault insists, was manifested "the disciplinary form at its most extreme, the model in which are concentrated all the coercive technologies of behaviour. In it were to be found 'cloister, prison, school, regiment.'"[79] With its military drilling, punctilious management of time, and absence of high walls, which dissolved the overt distinction between inside and outside, Mettray was, as we saw in the previous chapter, the perfect embodiment of what Foucault termed the "carceral archipelago."[80]

During the Third Republic, a period that lies outside the frame considered by Foucault in *Surveiller et punir*, the nexus between military training and juvenile corrections became considerably tighter. In the final decades of the nineteenth century, juvenile institutions like Mettray took on a more overtly militaristic culture. From its inception, Mettray had always included a significant component of military-style discipline. In these early years, this discipline was intended to serve a more general purpose beyond necessarily preparing a youth for actual service in the military. The skills developed through this disciplinary training, Mettray's founders thought, would stand the youth in good stead for whatever future occupation the boy would enter into upon release. This was reflected in the opening statement of an early promotional brochure for Mettray: "The duties of the *colon* are honourable, they are the same as those of the French soldier, who obeys his chiefs and who is subjected to discipline. Without discipline, no army, no [juvenile] colony: no association of men is possible. With a good discipline, well observed, an army covers itself in glory, a [juvenile] colony does great things, a people becomes invincible."[81] The idea that military drills served a general purpose in the reforming of delinquent boys was not unique to Mettray. For instance, in the 1850s a Trappist monk – in words that anticipated Foucault by over a century – observed that "there is continuity between military discipline of the juvenile colony [*colonie*] and that of the army."[82]

Throughout the nineteenth century juvenile colonies regularly laid emphasis on personal qualities like valour and bravery, and maintained a general culture that prepared the young detainees for entry into the military,[83] if that were to be their preferred path. But until the Third Republic, there was no widespread expectation that these boys would actually enlist. Although from the very outset of their creation during the July Monarchy juvenile reformatories did employ military-style drills as a useful tool for instilling good discipline and self-regulation, until the Freycinet recruitment law passed in 1889 it was not presumed that boys, even ones detained under Article 66, would *necessarily* go on to actually serve in the military itself. Before the 1870s, any military culture employed in juvenile colonies was conscientiously tempered by an appeal to an affectionate, familial culture.

From the 1870s, juvenile colonies gradually took on a more overtly militarized character. So, too, did primary schools. In the final decades of the nineteenth century, primary schools and the military came to be identified as critical in the formation of the responsible republican citizen. In 1879, a senator presented a bill calling for compulsory physical education in primary schools, arguing that this would lead to the formation of better recruits and enable shorter terms of military service.[84] The following year, both chambers of France's parliament unanimously passed a bill requiring primary schools to teach gymnastics and military exercises.[85] Perhaps most illustrative of the militarization of primary schools was the signing of a decree in July 1882 by the ministries of public education, war, and the interior establishing so-called *bataillons scolaires*. This system of bataillons scolaires was formed in state-run primary schools, *collèges*, and *lycées* for children aged over twelve and saw volunteer non-commissioned officers from the reserves and territorial army brought in to conduct twice-weekly physical education classes and military training for boys, including rifle marksmanship.[86] Conservatives were hostile to the bataillons scolaires from the start, seeing them as vehicles for republican dominance or even as part of a masonic conspiracy. In the end, the program did not enjoy great success. By 1886 many bataillons scolaires existed only in name, and in 1892 the ministry of public instruction issued a circular announcing their abolition.[87] But the disappearance of the bataillons scolaires did not reflect a waning of enthusiasm among republicans for the cultivation of military skills among the general population. The Freycinet law of 1889 cemented the connection between republican citizenship and military skills.

Over this period juvenile colonies similarly took on a more militarized character. In the mid-1880s, one disgruntled former staff member at Mettray claimed that "old military men" were being hired who had "no understanding of what it was to reform children," contributing to what he considered a poisonous, militarized culture that betrayed the familial ethos previously pursued by the colony's founder, Frédéric-Auguste Demetz. This shift, the former employee claimed, had come about following Demetz's death.[88] By the late 1870s, the maxim "everything for the land," which had defined colonies like Mettray decades earlier, was increasingly replaced by "everything for the army,"[89] as delinquent boys, acquitted but detained in these institutions, were encouraged to voluntarily enlist in the armed forces.

Beyond Mettray, these changes were similarly observable, as the pathway from juvenile colony to the military became more overtly defined. In 1878, the Société de protection des engagés volontaires élevés sous la tutelle administrative was established expressly in order to facilitate delinquent boys' transition from reformatory to barracks. Co-founded by Félix Voisin, SGP member and senior jurist, and Gabriel Fournier, general inspector of prisons within the interior ministry, the group aimed to assist juvenile offenders acquitted but detained under Article 66 with voluntary enlistment.[90] The assistance provided to young recruits was material, but even more particularly moral, and extended through the full length of their enlistment. As Voisin wrote in his president's report for 1882, "it is not by distributing money that our unfortunate young people can be moralized, it is … by communicating with him, heart and soul."[91]

State functionaries pointed to the notion of a natural and desirable continuity between juvenile reformatories and the military. In 1878, a senior administrator from the interior ministry issued a circular declaring that for juveniles acquitted under Article 66, military enlistment was the "natural outcome of correctional education" and that placement in the army after release from a juvenile colony helped prevent possible relapses into immoral or unlawful conduct.[92] The pipeline linking reformatory and barracks took stronger shape, but until the passage of the Freycinet recruitment law, the flow of youngsters between these institutions was still just a trickle. Before 1889, the Société de protection des engagés volontaires contributed an average of a couple of hundred voluntary enlistments each year,[93] and between 1874 to 1885, only about 10 per cent of all boys released from reformatories enlisted in the army.[94]

In *Surveiller et punir* Foucault drew attention to the disciplinary logics that linked otherwise distinct institutions like schools, prisons, and barracks. But what is very striking about the final decades of the nineteenth century is that these institutions became more overtly connected, each of them being made to serve the priorities of the republican state. As a result of the republicanization of primary schools, juvenile colonies (which, as we saw in the previous chapter, were increasingly turned over to state control from the 1880s onwards), and the military, there was greater continuity between them not only in terms of their ideological underpinnings, but also in the make-up of their very populations. The movement of populations between reformatory and barracks would be particularly transformed through the introduction in 1889 of universal military service and the creation of that new category of conscript – the exclus de l'armée – which opened up the possibility of convicted offenders (not just those acquitted under Article 66) serving in the nation's forces. Considerations of age and criminal responsibility were of critical importance here. Indeed, as Voisin told a meeting of the Comité de défense des enfants traduits en justice in 1903, for all young men, especially those released from a reformatory, "enlistment in the army or navy was the surest means of safeguarding their future." And as a result, Voisin continued, legislators needed to take every measure possible to prevent young men from receiving a conviction up to the age of eighteen (at which point they would be free to voluntarily enlist without requiring their parents' permission).[95]

## Raising the Age of Criminal Majority

At the turn of the twentieth century, as we saw at the start of this chapter, rates of offending among young men over the age of sixteen were increasing at an alarming rate, carrying with them serious implications for national defence. If, jurists and reformers wondered, these youths could not be stopped from breaking the law, what if they could, through the raising of the age of criminal majority, be prevented from incurring a conviction? Being acquitted under Article 66 would enable them to maintain a clean criminal record while at the same time allowing the state to direct them into a juvenile colony where, like their younger counterparts, they might be prepared for entry into the military either as conscripts or as voluntary recruits.

The law on suspended sentences, sponsored by Bérenger and introduced in 1891, had already, at least in theory, promised to facilitate the entry of greater numbers of young men into the regular ranks of the French military. In practice, however, much to the frustration of Bérenger and like-minded reformers, military administrators regularly treated suspended sentences as though they were convictions, dispatching young recruits off to perform probationary service in the Bat' d'Af.[96] SGP president Émile Cheysson observed that stationing in the Bat' d'Af caused these young men to experience their military service as a humiliation rather than as an honour.[97] A subsequent law, passed on 4 May 1897, aimed to correct this anomaly, but inconsistency and confusion persisted.[98] Félix Voisin observed that a similar misapprehension pertained to the processing of juveniles acquitted under Article 66 and raised in colonies who chose to enlist in the army. In those cases, too, military recruitment officers frequently treated the prospective recruits as equivalent to convicted offenders and funnelled them into the Bataillons Afrique.[99]

In the early years of the new century, reformers hoped that raising the age of majority might have more certain results. On 12 April 1906, eighteen was approved as the age of criminal majority. By the time the legislation was passed in France, many European countries, including Germany and Spain, had already adopted eighteen as the age of criminal majority. Austria had gone even further, setting it at twenty. The United Kingdom, on the other hand, chose to maintain a lower bar of fourteen.[100] Since at least the 1890s, the question of what to do with older youths and the appropriate age for criminal majority had been subjected to extended debate internationally. At meetings of the International Prison Congress (IPC), delegates sparred politely over what they considered to be the acceptable and effective limits of "preventive" and "non-punitive" responses to crime.

Among the most progressive voices internationally on raising the age of criminal majority was Russian jurist Dimitri Drill. At the 1890 IPC in Saint Petersburg, Drill argued before his fellow delegates that the impairment of free will so readily observed in children did not simply decrease with age, but that it was actually exacerbated in the teenage years because of physiological changes. "All those conditions, on which criminal responsibility relies," Drill insisted, "are absent not only at the age of twelve, but [also] at the more advanced age of sixteen."[101] Drill went further than most in calling for an automatic presumption of irresponsibility for all juveniles up to the age of eighteen and the uniform application of educative, non-punitive measures.[102] Although Drill failed to convince his IPC colleagues to support decriminalizing offences committed by offenders up to the age eighteen, the Russian delegate did manage to gain some ground on a related proposal that offenders aged between sixteen and twenty be eligible for alleviated sentences in recognition of their incomplete physical development.[103]

In the ensuing years, the idea of introducing more lenient treatment for older youths would gain further traction internationally, promoted most notably by the English prison reformer Evelyn Ruggles-Brise, best known as the architect of the Borstal system of juvenile reformatories.[104] At the 1900 IPC in Brussels, Ruggles-Brise proposed that the age of criminal majority be set at twenty-one, in recognition, he said, of the fact that this was the age at which the human body, including the brain – the organ he considered responsible for decisions of moral conduct – reached its full development. While conceding that no scientific data existed to prove it, Ruggles-Brise argued that it was plausible that the brain followed a similar path and rate of growth to maturity to that of the body.[105]

In 1895, IPC delegates in Paris were invited to submit reports addressing the following question: "With regard to boys, should the limit of criminal majority be pushed back to the age of [voluntary] military engagement?" Among the respondents was Henri Lefuel, a Parisian lawyer, SGP member, and recent recipient of the award of the legion of honour, who expressed his approval of the suggestion. Observing that the barracks were "the best school of devotion, honour and patriotism," Lefuel argued that putting military discipline to work on young offenders achieved two key results: it allowed them to achieve their moral regeneration while at the same time providing the nation with "a few more good citizens."[106] Henri Joly, however, took an opposing view, arguing that to treat youths over the age of sixteen as lacking in responsibility and allow them to be absorbed into existing institutions for juveniles would do more bad than good by exposing the younger, impressionable detainees to the corrupting influence of older boys.[107]

The most ardent advocate among French reformers for raising the age of criminal majority was Félix Voisin. In a presentation to the 1895 IPC, Voisin recounted how his fellow Frenchmen frequently responded with incredulity and hostility to the idea on the grounds that sparing older youths the harshest punishments, including the death penalty, would "undermine punishment."[108] But, Voisin asked, how effective a threat was capital punishment really for such offenders? After all, he claimed, it had done little to dissuade "certain sixteen- and eighteen-year-old monsters" from committing murder.[109] Rather than calculated bravado, Voisin declared, this insensibility derived from the fact that these youths were not yet sufficiently developed to be able to fully understand the consequences of their actions. Young people under the age of eighteen, he insisted, were "still at the age when one must not despair [of them], when the question of *discernement* must be posed" – for the sake both of the youth in question and of society.[110]

In the minds of many French reformers in the fin de siècle, the limits set down in the revolutionary and Napoleonic penal codes failed to meet the demands of a society that had been profoundly transformed by such factors as the growth of industry and mass urbanization. In addition, they were concerned about the flow-on effects from a criminal justice system that they considered to stigmatize offenders and thereby worsen the very criminality that the system was ostensibly supposed to address. This was certainly the position of René Bérenger. Opponents, however, insisted that sixteen represented a judicious age for criminal majority. Henri Joly, for instance, argued that the years between the ages of sixteen and twenty-one were characterized "by habits of independence, precocious cunning, cynical vice." To exonerate such youths, especially in France, he asserted, would arouse "the protests of public conscience."[111] If anything, Joly argued, present-day conditions required that the age of criminal majority be *lowered* not raised. "We live at a time," he told the IPC in 1895, "when a twelve-year-old child knows and does what an eighteen-year-old did not know and did not do twenty years ago."[112] Interestingly, precisely the same arguments would be put forward in the United Kingdom a century later; in 1994 a judge in the High Court adjudicating over a case involving a twelve-year-old boy caught with a companion playing around with a motorbike ruled that the principle of doli incapax was "no longer part of the law of England" and that "whatever may have been the position in an earlier age, when there was no system of universal compulsory education and when perhaps children did not grow up as quickly as they do nowadays, this presumption at the present time is a serious disservice to our law."[113] For Joly, there was "nothing more natural" than posing the question of "discernement" to children "who are neither mad, nor *idiots*, nor even simpleminded, but who after all are children." However, to pose this question to offenders over the age of sixteen would be "something shocking."[114] In 1906, despite qualms like these, the French parliament would raise the age of criminal majority to eighteen – one of the most significant legislative changes in juvenile justice procedure prior to the establishment of juvenile courts in 1912.

The creation in 1906 of this new category of offender, which floated between the status of juvenile and adult, was bound up in two core priorities for reformers and legislators in this period: to reduce recourse to the penitentiary – which, as we saw in the previous chapter, was considered as much a source of criminality as a cure for it – and to maximize military manpower at a time of increasing international tension and competition for territory and global resources. In deciding to approve raising the age of criminal majority to eighteen, no doubt legislators were motivated at least to some extent by humanitarian and perhaps even physiological considerations. What was most salient, however, was the certain impact the change would have on military recruitment: by enabling the acquittal and detention of older youths, this would, in turn, facilitate their entry into the armed forces, either as conscripts or through voluntary enlistment.

As Jules Leveillé, a professor of criminal law and criminal justice at the Sorbonne and a Parisian deputy in the French parliament, observed to his SGP colleagues during a discussion of the issue in 1896: "Deep down the reason for this campaign" to raise the age of criminal majority beyond sixteen is that "you want a young man of seventeen who is sentenced to prison for an offence not to pass through prison; [instead] you want him to go into a reformatory [*maison de correction*], into a juvenile colony [*colonie pénitentiaire*]."[115] With their "judicial virginity" left intact, these youths would be able to move directly into the military, where they would receive a salutary discipline and be put to more constructive use.[116] For after all, as one Toulouse lawyer observed in 1905, it was far better for offenders to improve themselves through service in the military and actively contribute to the nation's defence than to simply languish in prison.[117]

## Conclusion

Following the passage of the 1906 law raising the age of criminal majority, members of the Union des sociétés de patronage emphasized the urgent need to avoid confusing those aged between sixteen and eighteen who had been deemed to have committed offences "sans discernement" with their counterparts who broke the law in full knowledge of the consequences; the former were juveniles; the latter were adults. Young people aged between sixteen and eighteen found to have committed an offence "avec discernement," the union insisted, had to be treated as adults, receiving the full penalty that any older offender would rather than potentially being handed a reduced sentence out of observance of their youth.[118] In an article published in *Le Petit parisien* newspaper a week after the legislation was enacted, Senator Paul Strauss asked rhetorically whether the law would mean that "the little rascals, burglars or precocious assassins" were going "to benefit from an excess of indulgence." No, Strauss responded, because, he said, "the legislator has taken care not to weaken repression."[119]

Such an argument was met with considerable resistance from conservatives who regularly presented the raising of the age of criminal majority as part of a widespread culture of excessive indulgence when it came to responding to crime. While the legislation raising the age of criminal majority attracted less coverage than the (ultimately unsuccessful) proposal in 1908 to abolish capital punishment, it was taken by those on the political right to represent at best a legislative sleight of hand and at worst a wanton act of social endangerment.[120] In August 1907, Émile Faguet, a literary critic and member of the Académie française, contributed an article on the subject to the conservative newspaper *Le Gaulois*. The government, Faguet remarked, had become enamoured with legislating, presenting bills with such frequency that they were as numerous and nebulous as clouds in the sky, overlapping and dissolving into one another so that tracking their progress through the parliament became extremely challenging.[121] Several years later, jurist Émile Garçon made a similar observation about the frequency with which legislation was introduced, comparing it to the frivolous world of women's fashion.[122] The 1906 legislation on the age of criminal majority, Faguet declared, was a political stunt employed by the radical-socialist government to enable them to claim to be curbing adolescent crime, while simply manipulating the figures. By declaring that adolescents lacked "discernement," Faguet said, "there will be no more criminal adolescents and there will be no more adolescent criminality. Oh! My God, it's quite simple!"[123]

In the decades of mounting international tension that finally exploded into the First World War, views diverged within French society on how civil, penal, and military institutions and their respective populations should relate to one another. Opinions also varied on the capacity of the army to act as a moralizing force, especially when faced with recruits whose criminal backgrounds were less than pristine. Within the SGP, members were split on how best to respond to criminality and what role, if any, the military should play in its treatment. In one camp were those who supported the standard republican view, including Bérenger and Voisin, believing that the military offered a productive means of instilling general moral virtue in the nation's citizens. In the opposing camp, meanwhile, were conservative figures like Henri Joly, who considered such measures to not only do dishonour to the military but also to constitute a social danger by rewarding anti-social behaviours and even helping to propagate them further.

Whereas previous regimes had asserted the distinction of the military from civilian life and culture, during the Third Republic the army was upheld as the very embodiment of the French nation. With the introduction of compulsory military service from 1889, republicans transformed the army, as they had the primary school before it, turning it into a tool of moralization and asserting its importance for national defence and renewal. The effect of this was to narrow the gulf that had since the early nineteenth century separated the armed forces from ordinary society. For republicans, the military was a "school of moralization." This transformation in the relationship between the armed forces and broader society dovetailed with major changes in the treatment of criminality and ideas about the role of the state in forming virtuous citizens. The republicanization of primary schooling and, even more particularly, the republicanization of France's military unleashed huge debate and opposition from those who considered the armed forces to be an elite caste whose autonomy and segregation from government and broader society were intrinsic to its strength, integrity, and disciplinary ethos. Within these debates questions of age and criminal majority were integral. As the twentieth century dawned, republican legislators manoeuvred to craft a criminal justice system that better accommodated the defensive needs of the republic, including raising the age of criminal majority to eighteen in order to facilitate the entry of greater numbers of boys into the military.

# Conclusion

French reformers at the turn of the twentieth century were intensely preoccupied by issues of criminality, especially recidivism: a question that was bound up with wider social problems, both domestic and international. As we have seen, in the decades preceding the establishment of a distinct branch of justice for juveniles in 1912, reformers were significantly exercised by the question of how to protect the young from damaging exposure to bad influences (including within institutions intended to improve them) in the interests of best preparing them for adult life and citizenship. For boys, an essential part of that citizenship-building process was service in the military. Anxieties about national defence and social stability lay at the heart of policies and laws affecting young offenders in this period. Both the law of 1912 decriminalizing offences committed by children under the age of thirteen and the law of 1906 raising the age of criminal majority were largely motivated by the concern to make the fullest use possible of all available manpower.

Passed on 22 July 1912, the law on courts for children and adolescents came into effect on 5 March 1914. Just a few months later, France was at war. With the outbreak of hostilities in August, the French people were called on to put into action what they had effectively devoted over four decades to readying themselves for, ever since the devastating loss to Prussia that had marked the birth of the Third Republic in 1870. On the national level, the First World War was presented from its earliest days as a test of France's regenerative capacities.[1] For juvenile boy delinquents, the conflict was made to operate as a testing ground for proving they were worthy of bearing the status of citizen. By the start of the war, Félix Voisin's Société de protection des engagés volontaires had 4,500 young men under its sponsorship, and by the end of 1918, the number had expanded to 6,900.[2] The war would eventually claim the lives of over a million French soldiers, more than half of them killed within the first year and a half of the conflict.[3] How many of those had passed through juvenile correctional institutions is yet to be established.

As a result of the legislative changes introduced in 1912, French criminal law – for the first time since codification – stipulated that offenders under the age of thirteen, by nature of their youth, could never be held accountable for their actions and therefore could not be prosecuted by a criminal court or punished. While some jurists expressed a preference for different threshold points, thirteen was settled on because of its institutional correlation – it was the upper limit for compulsory attendance at primary school. The selection of eighteen as the upper limit for a decision of a lack of "discernement," introduced in 1906 and confirmed in 1912, was similarly determined by the benefits it offered for young men's service in the military.

By the start of the twentieth century, the idea that children should not be treated as adults at any stage of the criminal justice system had won such total acceptance that in 1907 Louis Delzons, a jurist and writer, could feel confident in declaring that "it goes without saying that the criminal child does not compel adult society to defend itself against them as it does against the criminal adult: it is not a question of making them atone [*expier*], but of preserving them, correcting them, healing them [*guérir*]."[4] In that same year, the prominent Parisian jurist Louis Albanel opened a presentation to the SGP on the subject of juvenile courts with the remark that "Childhood, gentlemen, has long had its schools, its hospitals, even its [own] prisons, could it not also be judged by special courts?"[5]

Amid a climate of concern about child protection, on the one hand, and youth gangs, on the other, the 1912 law on juvenile courts successfully placated both concerns for children's welfare and demands for a punitive response to older youths. While no child under thirteen could be placed in a punitive or correctional facility, this option remained available for offenders aged between thirteen and eighteen. In deciding to decriminalize offences committed by children under the age of thirteen, French politicians took decisions affecting the detention and punishment of young offenders out of the hands of magistrates. By absolving all lawbreakers under the age of thirteen of any criminal responsibility, the new law reconfigured the landscape of juvenile justice in its stipulation that chronological age, not the individual case, determined the presence or absence of criminal intent and responsibility in the youngest offenders. Not everyone agreed, however, that age constituted the most reliable index of maturity. Indeed, a particularly noteworthy skeptic was the psychologist Alfred Binet, co-inventor of the intelligence test. For him, chronological age, which "results from the date recorded on the birth certificate," was not the best gauge of a person's state of maturity. Instead, Binet advocated using a person's height, weight, muscular strength, dentition, the appearance of pubic hair, changes in voice pitch, "and all other signs of maturity."[6] For Binet, such physiological and anatomical data were better indicators of a person's "real, actually lived age" than chronological age, which, he said, "was nothing but a fiction."[7]

In the end, though, it would be the abstract, depersonalized criterion of chronological age that triumphed with the passage of the 1912 law. The significance of this decision should not be underestimated. Although legislators never once explicitly invoked the term "responsibility," by setting down the provisions that removed offenders under thirteen from the jurisdiction of criminal courts, they effectively put in place a minimum age of criminal responsibility – something that had not previously existed in modern French criminal law. The legislators' neglect of any reference to "responsibility" in that legislation was anything but an oversight. Rather than risk provoking a philosophical dispute over a child's capacity to distinguish right from wrong, their priority was to ensure that no child under the nominated age threshold would be subjected to a conviction or punishment. The primary intent behind removing children from a criminal jurisdiction, then, was not to enshrine an irrefutable presumption of children's absolute criminal irresponsibility (though this was a central effect). Rather, it was to ensure that no child could be given a criminal conviction and punished for their actions from the time they were born until the age at which they were no longer required to attend primary school.

The provisions introduced in 1912 would remain in place through the interwar years, a period that has often been incorrectly presented as a fallow stage in the evolution of ideas and practices towards juvenile offenders.[8] But by the 1920s, many experts considered existing laws regarding juvenile offenders to be out of kilter with innovations in sociology, psychology, and psychiatry, including neuropsychiatry. At the same time, the categories of the juvenile at risk (enfant en danger) and the juvenile delinquent (enfant dangereux) continued to be further conflated, coalescing into the concept of the "pre-delinquent," with suggestions put forward that all primary school pupils be medically screened in order to pinpoint "problem children" early.[9] With the opening up of the field of pediatric neuropsychiatry in France, largely through the work of Dr Georges Heuyer,[10] the juvenile delinquent evolved into the *enfant inadapté* (child with behavioural problems).[11] In 1927, colonies pénitentiaires were officially renamed *maisons d'éducation surveillée*. This measure, an attempt to show that something was being done to bring juvenile institutions into line with developments in education and medicine, was but a superficial "reform on paper."[12] Then, in 1935, juvenile vagrancy was decriminalized.[13] Independently of these reforms, the interwar period as a whole witnessed considerable tumult in institutions for juvenile offenders, including a major revolt by young detainees held at the juvenile colony on the island of Belle-Île-en-Mer, off the northwest coast of France near Quiberon,[14] dovetailing with a growing movement of opposition to France's bagne for transported convicts in French Guiana (the New Caledonian penal colony having already been closed). Juvenile colonies were denounced by the press as "bagnes d'enfants," and a substantial wave of public sympathy gathered in support of young detainees.[15] It was within this climate that in 1937, Mettray – once the crown jewel in France's criminal justice system – closed for good.[16]

With the outbreak of the Second World War and the fall of the Third Republic, the management of juvenile justice entered a new phase. The Vichy regime introduced new legislation significantly modifying various protective aspects of the provisions that had been set down thirty years earlier. The law of 27 July 1942 represented a hard-line response to juvenile offending; it removed the 1912 legislation's (implicit) presumption of absolute criminal irresponsibility in children under thirteen (although, in practice, courts continued to respect the provisions of the 1912 law) and lowered the age of criminal majority from eighteen to sixteen. Perhaps most significantly, the 1942 law abolished the mitigating excuse of minority for juveniles who committed an offence for which the sentence was life imprisonment – a reversion to the Roman law principle of malitia supplet aetatem.[17] In response to criticisms that the juvenile justice system was not keeping step with new research in medicine and educational theory, the 1942 law created medical-educational triage centres for individualized treatment based on educational and psychological principles. But at the same time, harsh measures were maintained for dealing with juveniles, including young children, said to have been made "savage" by the circumstances of war. In 1943, the main architect of the 1942 legislation, jurist Henri Donnedieu de Vabres (an important figure in international criminal law, who after the war would serve as the primary French judge in the Nuremberg trials),[18] made the revealing observation that "even with regard to offences committed by children, we must be careful not to exclude from the regime of sanctions the radiating and, if necessary, severe figure of justice."[19]

In the end, the Vichy legislation, never enacted, would be overtaken by an *ordonnance* issued less than three years later, on 2 February 1945. Some of the main points articulated in the *exposé des motifs* (explanatory statement) accompanying this ordonnance echoed the ones regularly uttered by reformers half a century earlier. The emphasis then as before was on the urgent need to protect France's children, whose value was only increased by the nation's non-competitive birth rate. "There are few problems as serious as those concerning the protection of children," the ordonnance's statement began. "France is not sufficiently well endowed with children to be entitled to neglect everything that can make them into healthy beings. The war and the material and moral upheavals caused by it have increased juvenile delinquency to worrying proportions. The issue of juvenile delinquency is among the most urgent of our times." The explanatory statement positioned the new legal provisions as an updating of and improvement on the 1912 law, which was said to have been "the most important step" in the evolution of a distinct system of law for juveniles. But that earlier legislation, the ordonnance read, was no longer in step with developments in criminal science and new medico-pedagogical knowledge.[20]

For jurists, it is not the 1912 legislation on courts for children and adolescents but rather this ordonnance of 1945 that is generally seen as the watershed moment in the formation of a distinct juvenile justice system in France. This is understandable, for in many ways the 1912 law did not go as far as it might have in enshrining a specialized system for juveniles. Indeed, having initially extolled the virtues of the American model, French reformers in the early twentieth century ultimately shied away from implementing its most ambitious modifications, such as the introduction of a specialized court and single courtroom judge. Without these provisions, as David Niget has noted, "the reform of 1912 remain[ed] largely unfinished."[21] Ultimately it would be a later generation of reformers who, through the

1945 ordonnance, would put in place many of the core ambitions of turn-of-the-century reformers. With the ordonnance of 1945 a distinct branch of justice for juveniles with a truly specialized staff centred around a *juge des enfants* was finally brought into being.

Yet in other ways, the 1912 legislation, despite leaving much unachieved at the time, represents a watershed moment in its own right, not least in its recognition of chronological age as a crucial aspect of personal identity and as an important criterion for the application of punishment. Indeed, the law of 1912 marks a highly important turning point in the imposition of age as a standard unit of measurement in the treatment of child offenders. In the end, the legacy of the reformers who helped shape the 1912 law lies less in what they managed to achieve through that legislation and more in the shift in thinking about age and criminality that they fostered. This shift would continue in the years to come. Indeed, as Dominique Dessertine has argued, the legislators of 1912 helped usher in a sea change that paved the way for further change, including the 1945 ordonnance[22] whereby "the indulgence that was obligatory for juveniles under thirteen [under the 1912 law was] ... applied to older children."[23]

The 1945 ordonnance's explanatory statement laid overwhelming emphasis on its educative and therapeutic objectives. "From now on," it stated, "all juveniles up to the age of eighteen who are accused of an offence under criminal law ... may only be subject to measures of protection, education or reform, under a regime of criminal irresponsibility which is only subject to exception in exceptional circumstances and by reasoned decision." In addition, the statement explained, "the distinction between juveniles under thirteen and juveniles under eighteen years of age disappears, as does the notion of *discernement*, which no longer corresponds to a true reality."[24] All references to "discernement," that cornerstone of criminal justice procedure for juveniles for over a century and a half, were entirely removed.

Whereas in 1912 the question of "discernement" had only been retained for assessing juveniles aged between thirteen and eighteen, its removal from the 1945 ordonnance suggested that the consideration of moral judgment was no longer relevant to any courtroom decision relating to juveniles. Considerable confusion hovered around this absence. In removing the distinction that legislators in 1912 had put in place between juvenile offenders below and above the age of thirteen, the ordonnance effectively abolished the irrefutable presumption of a lack of "discernement" for child offenders, thereby reopening the way for even very young children to be prosecuted for their actions, albeit within a juvenile court. As Maurice Patin observed in the *Recueil Dalloz* legal journal in 1957, if "discernement" were never to be taken into account even for very young children, this made it possible for a child of four found without a train ticket to be considered guilty of a railway offence and subjected to measures of re-education and monitoring.[25]

The issue of the 1945 ordonnance's silence on the criterion of "discernement" would eventually be clarified in French jurisprudence by a landmark ruling in 1956 by France's highest court. Known as the Laboube decision, the judgment by the Cour de cassation related to the case of Jean Laboube, a six-year-old boy tried in a Strasbourg court for causing *blessures involontaires* (unintentional injuries). The essence of the case was that as a result of a careless gesture, young Laboube had inflicted serious injury to a playmate's eye. Criminal authorities were alerted, but the public prosecutor had decided not to initiate proceedings. The father of the injured child, however, who was determined to press charges, brought a civil complaint against young Jean. An investigation was accordingly opened, and Jean was brought before the children's court in Colmar. In court, Jean's lawyer pleaded for the boy's acquittal, arguing that even though the material facts of the case were clear, Jean had been so young at the time of the events that he could not be held to have possessed sufficient intelligence to be able to understand the recklessness or consequences of his act. Without mens rea, Laboube's defence maintained, no offence could be deemed committed and therefore no responsibility (whether criminal or civil) could be imputed to Jean. The children's court, however, rejected this argument, declaring that the issue of "discernement" was irrelevant and that the only issue to be addressed was the actus reus. Given that the boy was acknowledged to be the material agent of the act in question, his culpability had to be acknowledged. As a result, Jean Laboube was declared guilty in fact and law, returned to his family as a measure of reform, and sentenced to pay damages, for which his father was declared civilly responsible.[26]

The Colmar court's decision to focus only on the actus reus in the case of Jean Laboube was ultimately rejected by the Cour de cassation, which stated that "while articles 1 and 2 of the ordonnance of 2 February 1945 laid down the principle of the criminal irresponsibility of juveniles, disregarding the *discernement* of the interested party, and determine the court's competence … to take the appropriate measures of reform with respect to juveniles … it is still necessary, in conformity with the general principles of law, that the juvenile whose participation in the actus reus has been established, should have understood and willed this act; every offence, even non-intentional ones, suppose[s] in effect that its author has acted with intelligence and will."[27] Deemed to have been too young to have possessed sufficient awareness of the effects of his careless actions, Jean Laboube was exonerated by the Cour de cassation of any offence. This was a decision of crucial importance for juvenile jurisprudence; while the 1945 ordonnance had declared obsolete the concept of "discernement," the Laboube decision reinstated it as a central consideration for juvenile justice procedure.

The term "discernement," removed in 1912 in reference to offenders under the age of thirteen and not mentioned at all in the 1945 ordonnance, would resurface many decades later in France's revised penal code put in place in 1994, replacing the Napoleonic code. Article 122-8 of the new code referred to "les mineurs capables de discernement," with the implication that not all juveniles can be understood to exercise this capacity, as the prominent legal scholar and magistrate Jean Pradel observed.[28]

In the immediate wake of the issuing of the 1945 ordonnance, its provisions were understood by jurists to signal that when it came to juveniles, not only were rehabilitative and therapeutic responses to be preferred, but they entirely overrode any punishment. In this way, in the years following the passage of the ordonnance, juvenile courts proceeded according to the false understanding that no juvenile was ever to be punished for their offence, and that only measures of re-education were to be applied.[29] Judges who applied the law in a uniquely welfare-oriented fashion were adhering to the section of Article 2 of the ordonnance that stated that the juvenile court "will, depending on the case, pronounce measures of protection, assistance, supervision, education or reform that seem appropriate." But they were ignoring the next sentence, which stated that "it may … when the circumstances and the personality of the offender appear to require it, impose a criminal sentence on a juvenile over thirteen years of age by application of articles 67 and 69 of the penal code." This same article also empowered a court, "by a specially reasoned provision," to waive the mitigating excuse of minority for juveniles aged over sixteen, thereby making them eligible to receive the harshest punishments, including the death penalty. This had similarly been a component of the 1942 Vichy legislation.[30] Henri Donnedieu de Vabres expressed his approval for punishing as adults juveniles aged over sixteen convicted of serious crimes, arguing that the ability for the justice system to treat older juveniles as adults "is a safety valve whose usefulness, in the current state of morals, and in view of the singular precocity of young criminals, will not be disputed by anyone."[31]

The 1945 ordonnance branded itself as a major rupture with established practice. But even to the casual observer, there was much that essentially carried on as before. Although juvenile colonies were reformed, updated, and professionalized, they did not disappear.[32] At the same time, the so-called *milieu ouvert* approach was developed (wherein juvenile offenders were monitored by welfare authorities while remaining in their own homes). This was a further extension of *éducation surveillée* (correctional education) that had been in place for decades.[33] Perhaps most importantly, although a rhetoric of protection prevailed in the post-war decades, juveniles continued nevertheless to be incarcerated. Despite the efforts of reformers more than a century earlier, and in the face of years of opposition and campaigning, juveniles were still institutionalized and imprisoned, some even placed within adult prisons.[34] Remarkably, it was only from the 1970s that the wishes of the legislators of 1791 were finally realized and these patterns started to shift, as young prisoners were systematically detained separately from adults. A law of 17 July 1970 outlawed the detention of all juveniles under the age of thirteen, while another dated 30 December 1987 abolished the remand of juveniles under sixteen accused of délits (as opposed to crimes). This latter change led to a significant drop in the number of incarcerated juveniles. A law of 6 July 1989 limited the length of time a juvenile accused of a crime could be held on remand.[35]

In more recent decades, the question of how most appropriately and effectively to respond to young offenders has continued to provoke much debate in France. A considerable component of the discourse has come to be centred around responsibility. At the start of this century, under President Jacques Chirac, France's politicians set the country down a punitive path in its approach to juvenile justice. This hard-line approach grew out of a tendency from the 1990s to issue punishments to juvenile offenders.[36] On 9 September 2002 the French parliament passed a law enabling children as young as ten to be subject to "educative sanctions," while from thirteen they were liable to punishment.[37] This legislation, which became known as the Perben law, modified Article 122-8 of the 1994 penal code to the effect that juveniles as young as ten who were deemed to have acted "avec discernement" were considered criminally responsible, and a tougher range of sanctions was introduced.[38] This measure earned the approval of legal scholar

Jean Pradel, who considered it an appropriate rebalancing of a justice system that, he claimed, had become overly indulgent, with juveniles too often seen simply as victims of their environment.[39] Under Nicolas Sarkozy's presidency, the functioning of juvenile justice in France underwent particularly significant change. Getting tough on juvenile offenders was one of Sarkozy's pre-election promises, and among his proposals was that it should be possible to treat juveniles who broke the law the same as adults. In 2007, a few months after Sarkozy was elected president, the National Assembly approved bills presented by the justice minister, Rachida Dati, setting down very severe provisions for repeat offenders and introducing minimum sentences for juveniles, not just adults.

France's punitive trajectory around the turn of the twenty-first century, as sociologist Francis Bailleau has pointed out, put the country dramatically at odds with general trends in Europe,[40] which were then tending towards approaches more influenced by the emerging global framework focused on "children's rights" and centred around the United Nations Convention on the Rights of the Child (UNCRC), which had emerged out of post-war UN human rights treaties.[41] The "rights" implied by this global framework are quite different to the paternalistic and ultimately disempowering ones upheld by reformers of the late nineteenth century. The UNCRC framework asserts children's human rights and their distinct rights as developing beings. The UNCRC, as legal scholar Michael Freeman has written, shifted the view on children and childhood such that "no longer is the child's remedy to grow up ... No longer are children to be seen as becomings only. Now they are beings."[42] Furthermore, according to the children's rights framework, as psychologist Philip E. Veerman has put it, "the perception of the child changed from the *object* of rights in need of protection to the *subject* of rights whose opinion is voiced and asked for."[43] The children's rights movement shifted perceptions of the status of children "from passive objects subsumed within the family requiring protection to full human beings with a distinct set of rights ... [that are] civil, political, economic, social, and cultural" and which were "previously recognized in the context of adults." At the same time, the movement "also recognizes rights unique to children, such as the right to know and be cared for by one's parents."[44]

The children's rights framework, which aims to recognize the dignity of children, provides a means of dealing with a criminal justice approach centred on justice. Whereas the welfarist model of the late nineteenth and early twentieth centuries tended to adopt a rights-centred discourse (thereby reducing juveniles to the status of objects in need of adult guidance and protection), the justice model instead emphasizes responsibility. The children's rights approach sees juveniles as situated along a continuum, with children's evolving capacities acting as the stabilizing force for the competing interests of rights at one end and responsibilities at the other.[45] In contrast to the older welfare response traced in this book, which saw the state impose itself on and between a child and their family, the children's rights approach sees the family and guardian as an active part of the response.[46] Indeed, one of the most striking differences between our contemporary notion of children's rights and that of a century ago is that today the defence of children's rights includes activating parents as a check on state powers. Whereas the reformers traced in this book saw child removal as the key to reforming delinquent juveniles, the children's rights approach encourages the maintenance and fostering of connections between child, family, and community.[47]

Since the Second World War, juvenile justice measures in France have undergone numerous modifications. Legal provisions have been refashioned as circumstances have arisen and as the balance of forces in politics has shifted. The ordonnance of 1945 was subjected to around forty legislative modifications, which became especially significant after 2002.[48] Critics claimed that this accretion was producing a lack of coherence that compromised the whole system's legibility. This prompted a proposal for the introduction of a juvenile criminal justice code, which would bring together all measures relating to the administration of justice for juveniles into a single code. This, advocates argued, would help to speed up criminal justice procedures and enable juvenile justice professionals to take better care of the needs of young people.

On 11 December 2020, the French parliament voted to approve the creation of a Code de la justice pénale des mineurs, with overwhelming bipartisan support. Coming into effect on 30 September 2021, this new code grouped together nearly 280 articles into a single legal text[49] and reaffirmed the founding principles of 1945: education was to take precedence over repression, criminal responsibility was attenuated according to age, and courts and procedures were specialized. The code also added a fourth principle, a gesture to children's rights: that the best interests of juveniles were taken into account in the conditions for the implementation of their criminal liability.[50] Like the law of 1912, the new code established a presumption of a lack of "discernement" for minors under the age of thirteen, thereby bringing France into compliance with Article 40 of the UNCRC. Unlike the law of 1912, however, this presumption was not made absolute and could be overturned on evidence. This meant that a child could be declared criminally responsible and subjected to sanctions if the circumstances made it necessary. Here we can see the priorities of justice colouring the provision of children's rights. The same article of the code also states that "the juvenile [under thirteen] is capable of *discernement* who has understood and wilfully committed their act and who is able to understand the meaning of the criminal procedure to which they are subject." Juveniles between thirteen and eighteen, meanwhile, are presumed to be capable of "discernement."[51]

**

The period from the start of the Third Republic through to the First World War witnessed an intense questioning of and experimentation with longstanding principles of criminal justice. Debates reached a particular intensity around the turn of the century, fuelled by anxieties over a perceived increase in the number and precocity of juvenile criminals. These questions, of course, remain salient through to the present, as France, like many other nations, continues to wrestle with questions about the purpose and efficacy of incarceration and age thresholds for imposing punishments. Reformers at the turn of the twentieth century effectively opened up a conversation about the significance of chronological age for moral development and criminal responsibility, and set down a distinct treatment for children and adolescents on the basis of age. To this day, chronological age remains a fundamental sorting mechanism for the legal definition of different rights and duties. Indeed, when compared to other aspects of identity, chronological age has proved tenacious. As Jean-Jacques Yvorel has pointed out, whereas certain distinctions on the basis of social hierarchy, religion, or race were formally abolished by law following the French Revolution, with gender distinctions in civil law and labour law undergoing considerable reform at the end of the 1960s, age continues to exercise a meaningful presence throughout private and public law in France.[52]

Through to the present, when it comes to criminal justice issues, young people continue to find themselves in the crosshairs of ideologically driven agendas. Many of the issues that preoccupied reformers at the turn of the twentieth century – prison overcrowding, recidivism, social cohesion – remain alive in France today. These concerns continue to intersect with anxieties about the conduct of young people, especially in urban areas.

Fears of the "apache" more than a century ago have today been replaced by fears of unruly youth from the *banlieues*, and a moral panic over disorderly behaviour among young people from migrant backgrounds, especially those of France's former colonies.[53] Respect for medical expertise has further expanded over the course of the past century. While in 1912 the medical expert was just beginning to exercise an influence in the juvenile justice system, in more recent decades theories of neuroscience have come to play a more important part in determining decisions on juvenile justice. For instance, a 2012 ruling in the United States, which outlawed states from mandating life without parole for crimes committed by juveniles, drew on scientific studies of the adolescent brain to conclude that teenagers, on account of their psychological and neurobiological immaturity, are not as responsible for their actions as adults.[54] Today's scholarship emphasizes children's incomplete cognitive development, susceptibility to peer influence, and inclination to risk-taking, and their reduced capabilities for self-control and self-regulation.[55] While reformers more than a century ago expressed concern about magistrates' capacity to exercise an impartial and learned judgment on juveniles' "discernement," methods used in the present day remain fraught. Chronological age constitutes one measure for ascertaining development and maturity, and it remains imperfect; in 2016, Laurence Bellon, vice-president of Lyon children's court, explained that the first thing she does when questioning a juvenile is ask them their weight and height. But physical measurements, she specifies, are not sufficient for determining "discernement."[56]

The treatment and conceptualization of juvenile offenders function as something of a bellwether for broader trends and attitudes concerning criminality and social relations. In a modern state like France, debates on questions of age and criminal justice serve to illuminate essential conditions of individuals' rights and responsibilities, while also helping to expose ideas about the purpose and efficacy of methods of punishment and welfare. Reformers at the turn of the twentieth century grappled with issues that continue to provoke discussion. For example, at what age is it acceptable to deprive a young person of their liberty? What age constitutes an appropriate threshold for prosecuting and imposing a punishment on a young person? More generally, too, what is the relationship between rights and responsibilities, between the ages of civil and criminal majority?

Today, the rights of young people represents the final frontier in the expansion of political enfranchisement. In recent years there have been growing calls for children to receive the right to vote.[57] Altering arrangements for the expression of children's political preferences raises questions about the functioning of the criminal justice system. Since young people are legally disempowered and denied political agency by being considered too young to cast a vote, does it follow that they should not be subject to its penalties to the same degree as an adult? If so, the corollary of this is, as philosopher Gideon Yaffe has reasoned, that if children were given the right to vote, then they should be treated the same as an adult in terms of punishment.[58]

Chronological age and age-defined categories, so often taken for granted as "natural" today, have their roots in the debates and concerns of the turn of the twentieth century. Many of the foundations laid at that time still inform the parameters for age, rights, and responsibilities in contemporary France. Despite the passage of time and significant shifts in the conceptualization of child and adolescent development, including in relation to the rise of the children's rights movement, reformers, legislators, policymakers, and other professionals continue to confront challenges not so different from the ones tackled over a century ago.

# Notes

INTRODUCTION

1 Coffignon, *L'Enfant à Paris*, 1.

2 Schafer, *Children in Moral Danger*; Quincy-Lefebvre, *Familles, institutions et déviances*; Gaillac, *Les Maisons de correction*; and Messineo, *Jeunesse irrégulière*.

3 Stora-Lamarre, *La République des faibles*.

4 See Fuchs, *Poor and Pregnant in Paris*; and Accampo, Fuchs, and Stewart, *Gender and the Politics of Social Reform*.

5 "Loi du 22 juillet 1912 sur les tribunaux pour enfants et adolescents," 498.

6 Ibid., 498–504.

7 Perrot, "Dans le Paris de la Belle Époque," 364.

8 Badinter, *La Prison républicaine*, 366.

9 For general discussion of the provisions of these codes as they related to juveniles, see Lascoumes, "Les Mineurs et l'ordre pénal," 37–44.

10 Treas, "Age in Standards and Standards for Age," 75.

11 See, for example, Lassonde, "Age, Schooling, and Development"; and Chudacoff, *How Old Are You?*

12 Heywood, *Growing Up in France*; and Sachs, *An Age to Work*.

13 Loriga, "The Military Experience," 26.

14 Heywood, "The Market for Child Labour"; Weissbach, "Child Labor Legislation"; and Weissbach, *Child Labor Reform*.

15 Niget, *La Naissance du tribunal pour enfants*, 24.

16 Fuchs, *Abandoned Children*, 51.

17 Bonzon, *Le Crime et l'école*, 6.

18 "Loi du 28 mars 1882 sur l'enseignement primaire obligatoire," 87.

19 Ariès, *L'Enfant et la vie familiale*, 49.

20 Norris, "Reinventing Childhood."
21 Thiercé, *Histoire de l'adolescence*, 217–46.
22 Ibid., 7.
23 See Gillis, *Youth and History*.
24 "Article 3, Titre V: De l'influence de l'âge des condamnés sur la nature et la durée des peines," in *Code pénal du 25 septembre 1791*, 6.
25 "Articles 5 and 6, Titre V: De l'influence de l'âge des condamnés sur la nature et la durée des peines," in *Code pénal du 25 septembre 1791*, 6.
26 Lascoumes, Poncela, and Lenoël, *Au nom de l'ordre*, 88–151.
27 Guignard, *Juger la folie*, 36–66.
28 O'Brien, *Promise of Punishment*, 121.
29 Tétard and Dumas, *Filles de justice*, 119–20.
30 Petit, *Ces peines obscures*.
31 O'Brien, *Promise of Punishment*, 4.
32 Garland, *Punishment and Welfare*.
33 Radzinowicz, *History of English Criminal Law*.
34 Foucault, *Surveiller et punir*.
35 Ignatieff, *A Just Measure of Pain*; and Garland, *Punishment and Welfare*.
36 Donzelot, *Policing of Families*; and Meyer, *L'Enfant et la raison d'État*.
37 Platt, *Child Savers*, xv and xvii.
38 Articles 4 and 17, "22 juillet 1912: Loi sur les tribunaux pour enfants et adolescents et sur la liberté surveillée."
39 Donzelot, *Policing of Families*, 150.
40 See, for instance, Cage, *The Science of Proof*; Chauvaud, *Les Experts du crime*; Chappuis et al., *Faire parler les corps*; Foucault, *Les Anormaux*; Goldstein, *Console and Classify*; Guignard, *Juger la folie*; Harris, *Murders and Madness*; Nye, *Crime, Madness, and Politics*; and Renneville, *Crime et folie*.
41 Donzelot, *Policing of Families*, 133.
42 Tomlinson, "The 'Disappearance' of France."
43 Nye, *Crime, Madness, and Politics*, 132–70. See also Barrows, *Distorting Mirrors*; Ellis, *The Physician-Legislators of France*; and Hildreth, *Doctors, Bureaucrats, and Public Health*.
44 Stora-Lamarre, *La République des faibles*, 17–18.
45 Schafer, *Children in Moral Danger*, 10–11. For a general overview of the function of justice during the Third Republic, see Martin, *Crime and Criminal Justice under the Third Republic*.
46 See, for instance, John E.B. Myers, *Child Protection in America*; Covey, *The Smallest Victims*; Behlmer, *Child Abuse and Moral Reform in England*;

Hendrick, *Child Welfare*; McK. Norrie, *A History of Scottish Child Protection Law*; and Swain and Hillel, *Child, Nation, Race and Empire.*

47 Ariès, *L'Enfant et la vie familiale.*

48 Davis, "The Reasons of Misrule"; and Darnton, *The Great Cat Massacre*, chapter 2.

49 Wilson, "The Infancy of the History of Childhood."

50 Heywood, "Centuries of Childhood," 347.

51 Heywood, *A History of Childhood*, 11; and King, "Concepts of Childhood," 372.

52 See, for instance, Lovett, "Age: A Useful Category of Historical Analysis"; Mintz, "Reflections on Age as Category of Historical Analysis"; Lassonde, "Age and Authority"; Paris, "Through the Looking Glass"; and Maynes "Age as a Category of Analysis." See also Field and Syrett, "Introduction."

53 Maza, "The Kids Aren't All Right."

54 Mintz, "AHA Exchange: Children's History Matters."

55 Pande, *Sex, Law, and the Politics of Age*, 19.

56 Hendrick, "The Child as a Social Actor," 38.

57 Toth, *Mettray*, chapter 3; and Gossard, *Young Subjects.*

58 Kaluszynski, "Enfance coupable et criminologie," 116. See also Kaluszynski, "De l'apache au sauvageon."

59 See, for example, Dr Marjolin, "Séance de la Société générale des prisons [henceforth SGP] du 5 décembre 1877: Rapport sur l'établissement des jeunes filles libérées et détenus de M. l'abbé Podevin, à Rouen," *Bulletin de la SGP* 1, no. 2 (1877): 128–45; and [Élie] Robin, "Séance générale du 5 janvier 1878: Rapport sur les écoles industrielles et la protection des enfants insoumis et abandonnés," *Bulletin de la SGP* 2, no. 1 (1878): 6–24.

60 Perrot, "Dans le Paris de la Belle Époque"; Kalifa, *L'Encre et le sang*, 152–61; and Nye, *Crime, Madness and Politics*, 196–223.

61 Pearson, *Hooligan*; and Hendrick, *Images of Youth.*

## CHAPTER ONE

1 For a more detailed account and analysis of the Jully case, see Neilson, "Youth, Literacy and Social Emancipation."

2 Signorel, "Le Crime et la défense sociale," 28. On the Soleilland case, see Berlière, *Le Crime de Soleilland.*

3 Kalifa, "Magistrature et 'crise de la répression.'"

4 *Le Matin*, 19 December 1909.

5 On these themes, see, for instance, Schafer, *Children in Moral Danger*;

Berenson, *The Trial of Madame Caillaux*; Berlière, *La Police des mœurs*; Corbin, *Les Filles de noces*; Harsin, *Policing Prostitution*; Bernheimer, *Figures of Ill Repute*; Prestwich, *Drink and the Politics of Social Reform*; Nourrisson, *Le Buveur du XIXe siècle*; Barrows, "After the Commune"; Wagniart, *Le Vagabond*; and Roberts, *Disruptive Acts*.

6 Chevalier, *Classes laborieuses*.

7 Weber, *France*, 40.

8 Kalifa, *L'Encre et le sang*, 152–61; Nye, *Crime, Madness and Politics*; 196–223; and Perrot, "Dans le Paris de la Belle Époque," 351–64.

9 *L'Écho de Paris*, 18 November 1908.

10 Kahn, "Rapport sur le traitement des jeunes criminels," 83.

11 Kalifa, *L'Encre et le sang*, 244.

12 *Le Petit parisien*, 14 December 1909.

13 *Le Petit journal*, 13 December 1909.

14 *L'Illustration*, 18 December 1909.

15 *L'Yonne*, 13 December 1909.

16 Archives départementales de l'Yonne, 2FI Jully 5–14, cartes postales.

17 *Le Petit journal*, 14 December 1909.

18 *La Gazette de Lausanne*, 14 December 1909.

19 Archives départementales de l'Yonne, 2Y 38 Registre d'écrou des accusés et condamnés en matière criminelle de la prison d'Auxerre, 17 mars 1892–21 juillet 1924, détenus 369 et 370.

20 *L'Yonne*, 11 December 1909.

21 Claretie, *Drames et comédies judiciaires*, 218.

22 Pick, *Faces of Degeneration*, chapter 3.

23 On Lamarck, see Otis, *Organic Memory*, chapters 1–3. On Lombroso, see Renneville, "La Réception de Lombroso"; and Verplaetse, *Localizing the Moral Sense*, 145–89.

24 Lacassagne, "Section de biologie criminelle," 167.

25 Tarde, "Sur quelques criminalistes italiens"; and Barrows, *Distorting Mirrors*, chapter 6.

26 Tarde, "La Jeunesse criminelle," 200.

27 Ibid., 198. On these themes more generally, see Toth, "Desire and the Delinquent."

28 Barrès, *Les Déracinés*.

29 Quoted by Taine, *Les Origines de la France contemporaine*, 112 n1.

30 Tarde, "La Jeunesse criminelle," 197.

31 Morache, *La Responsabilité*, 80.

32 McMillan, *France and Women*, 141.

33 See, for instance, Hunter, "The Problem of the French Birth Rate"; Cole, *The Power of Large Numbers*; and Offen, "Depopulation, Nationalism and Feminism."

34 Sussman, *Selling Mothers' Milk*; Cole, "'A Sudden and Terrible Revelation'"; Fuchs, *Poor and Pregnant*, chapter 3; and Rollet-Echalier, *La Politique à l'égard de la petite enfance.*

35 Fuchs, *Abandoned Children*, 50.

36 Prévost, "Rôle des institutions charitables," 405.

37 Lasserre, *L'Enfant devant la justice répressive*, 22.

38 Heywood, *Childhood in Nineteenth-Century France*; Weissbach, *Child Labor Reform in Nineteenth-Century France*; Schafer, *Children in Moral Danger*; and Schafer, "Law, Labor, and the Spectacle of the Body."

39 Zelizer, *Pricing the Priceless Child.*

40 Donzelot, *Policing of Families*, 128.

41 Binet and Simon, *Les Enfants anormaux.*

42 Perrot, "Sur la segrégation de l'enfance," 204.

43 Rosanvallon, *Le Sacre du citoyen*, 449–515.

44 Pécaut, *L'Éducation publique*, 126.

45 Singer, "From Patriots to Pacifists," 414.

46 Azéma and Winock, *Naissance et mort*, 131.

47 Weber, *La Fin des terroirs*, 691.

48 Durkheim, *L'Éducation morale*, 15.

49 Durkheim, "Pédagogie et sociologie," 52.

50 Durkheim, *L'Éducation morale*, 194–5, 207–9.

51 Bruno, *Instruction morale et civique*, i.

52 Norris, "Reinventing Childhood," 153–223; and Stock-Morton, *Moral Education.*

53 Stedman Jones, "Charles Renouvier and Émile Durkheim."

54 Renouvier, "L'Éducation et la morale," 276. For more on Renouvier's philosophical thinking in relation to moral education, see Stock-Morton, *Moral Education*, 47–60.

55 Durkheim, "Éducation"; and Guyau *Éducation et hérédité.*

56 Hayward, "Solidarity," 262–3. See also Hayward, "The Official Social Philosophy"; and Blais, *La Solidarité.*

57 Bourgeois, *La Politique de la prévoyance sociale*, 57.

58 Déloye, *École et citoyenneté*, 92.

59 Nora, "Le 'Dictionnaire de pédagogie.'"

60 Durkheim, "Éducation."
61 Chaumeil, *Manuel de pédagogie psychologique*, 433.
62 Rousseau, *Émile*, 11.
63 Kloppenberg, *Uncertain Victory*.
64 Fouillée, *La France au point de vue moral*, 29.
65 Liard, *Morale et enseignement civique*, vi.
66 Ibid., 3.
67 Ibid., 7.
68 Durkheim, "Pédagogie et sociologie," 46.
69 LePlay, *L'Organisation de la famille*, 106.
70 Pitt, "Frédéric LePlay and the Family."
71 Buisson "Leçon de clôture," 331.
72 Ibid. For further discussion, see Surkis, *Sexing the Citizen*, 43–68.
73 Gaillard, "Discipline scolaire," 717.
74 Ibid.
75 Caron, *À l'école de la violence*; and Curtis, *Educating the Faithful*, 99–101.
76 Ferry, "Lettre du 17 novembre 1883," 146.
77 Buisson, "Intuition et méthode intuitive."
78 Cousinet, "Intelligence."
79 Adam, "Sensibilité, sentiments."
80 Durkheim, "Pédagogie et sociologie," 46.
81 Lasserre, *L'Enfant devant la justice répressive*, 22.
82 Félix Voisin, "Séance solennelle de la SGP du 21 mars 1903: Discours de M. Voisin," *Revue pénitentiaire: Bulletin de la SGP* 27, no. 4 (1903): 513.
83 Louis Puibaraud, "La Responsabilité des enfants," *Revue pénitentiaire: Bulletin de la SGP* 17, no. 4 (1893): 447.
84 Jules Jolly, "Séance de la SGP du 20 avril 1904: Rapport sur les causes de la criminalité de l'enfance," *Revue pénitentiaire: Bulletin de la SGP* 28, no. 5 (1904): 662–98.
85 Jolly, "Séance de la SGP du 20 avril 1904," 676.
86 Ibid., 677.
87 Ibid., 678.
88 Ibid., 675.
89 Ibid., 676.
90 Ibid., 673.
91 Ibid., 681.
92 Ibid., 678.
93 Ibid.

94 Guillot, *Observations pratiques*, 4. For more on Guillot, see Quincy-Lefebvre, "À la recherche d'un nouveau paradigme."
95 Guillot, *Observations pratique*, 6.
96 Ibid., 4.
97 Guillot, "L'Enfant vagabond," 450.
98 Guillot, "L'Enfance," 310.
99 Ibid., 313.
100 Ibid., 314–15.
101 Bonjean, *Enfants révoltés*, 21.
102 Drillon, *La Jeunesse criminelle*, 35.
103 Wright, *Between the Guillotine and Liberty*, 112.
104 Buisson, "La Jeunesse criminelle et l'éducation," 295.
105 Tarde, "La Jeunesse criminelle," 207.
106 Jolly, "Séance de la SGP du 20 avril 1904," 685.
107 Ibid.
108 Gillis, "Institutional Dynamics," 1304.
109 Allen, *In the Public Eye*, 42.
110 See Lyons, *Readers and Society*, 156–61; and Shapiro, *Breaking the Codes.*
111 Le Bon, *La Psychologie des foules.* On Le Bon's theories of collective psychology, see Nye, *The Origins of Crowd Psychology.*
112 Fouillée, "Les Jeunes criminels," 434.
113 Joly, "Les Lectures," 310; and Tomel and Rollet, *Les Enfants en prison*, 8.
114 Guillot, "L'Enfant vagabond," 462.
115 Guillot, *Paris qui souffre*, 257.
116 Lombroso, "Traitement moral du jeune criminel," 216.
117 Baldet, *La Criminalité juvenile*, 13–14.
118 Schwartz, *Spectacular Realities*, 37.
119 Talmeyr, "Le Roman-feuilleton et l'esprit populaire," 203.
120 Drillon, *La Jeunesse criminelle*, 20.
121 Tarde, "La Jeunesse criminelle," 207.
122 Charles Lucas, "Séance de la SGP du 7 juin 1877," *Bulletin de la SGP* 1, no. 1 (1877): 33.
123 Aubry, *La Contagion du meurtre*, 85. See also Aubry, "De l'influence contagieuse de la publicité."
124 Fouillée, "Les Jeunes criminels," 426.
125 *Le Temps*, 18 December 1896.
126 Fouillée, *France au point de vue moral*, 161.
127 Ibid.

128 Tarde, "La Jeunesse criminelle: Lettre à Ferdinand Buisson," 203–4.

129 Fouillée, *France au point de vue moral*, 162.

130 Ibid., 153–4.

131 Rey, *Assistance aux enfants*, 7.

132 Compayré, "Facultés de l'âme," 985.

133 Zeldin, *France, 1848–1945*, vol. 1, 315.

134 Robert, "La Criminalité juvénile," 103.

135 See Surkis, *Sexing the Citizen*, 125–83; Lamanna, *Émile Durkheim on the Family*; and Lenoir, "La Famille conjugale."

136 Durkheim, "La Famille conjugale," 4. Note: the words in brackets are additions by editor Marcel Mauss.

137 Durkheim, "Compte rendu du lire de C.V. Starcke," 370.

138 Farge and Foucault, *Le Désordre des familles.*

139 Toth, "The Contard Affair." See also Toth, *Mettray*, 137–63.

140 Balzac, *Mémoires de deux jeunes mariés*, 65.

141 Hunt, *The Family Romance*, 53. See also Poumarède, "Les Tribulations de l'autorité paternelle."

142 Quoted by Guillot, "L'Enfance," 301–2.

143 Faron, "Father-Child Relations in France," 366.

144 Schnapper, "La Correction paternelle," 338.

145 Guillot, "L'Enfance," 302.

146 Rosanvallon, *Le Sacre du citoyen*, 147–8.

147 Gaufrès, "Mère."

148 Surkis, *Sexing the Citizen*, 35–8.

149 Kimble, "No Right to Judge," 617.

150 Jolly, *Des moyens de préservation*, 9.

151 Bonzon, *La Législation de l'enfance*, 182; and Berlanstein, *The Working People of Paris*, 18. See also Lequin, "Apprenticeship in Nineteenth-Century France"; and Haine, "The Development of Leisure."

152 Joly, *La France criminelle*, 218.

153 Duprat, *La Criminalité dans l'adolescence*, 19.

154 Ibid., 53.

155 Ibid., 23.

156 Giuliani, *L'Adolescence criminelle*, 13.

157 Ibid., 11.

158 O'Brien, *The Novel of Adolescence in France*; and Neubauer, *The Fin-de-Siècle Culture of Adolescence*, 75–84.

159 Perrot, "Worker Youth," 104.

160 Surkis, *Sexing the Citizen*, 29.

161 Quoted in *Le Matin*, 1 November 1908.

162 Guillot, *Paris qui souffre*, 257.

163 Jules Jolly, "Séance de la SGP du 20 avril 1904: Rapport sur les causes de la criminalité de l'enfance," *Revue pénitentiaire: Bulletin de la SGP* 28, no. 5 (1904): 676.

164 Henri Robert, "Séance de la Société du 29 juin 1904: Fin de la discussion du rapport de Jules Jolly sur les causes de la criminalité de l'enfance," *Revue pénitentiaire: Bulletin de la SGP* 28, nos 7–10 (1904): 854.

165 François-Charles Merveilleux du Vignaux, "Séance de la SGP du 29 juin 1904: Fin de la discussion du rapport de Jules Jolly sur les causes de la criminalité de l'enfance," *Revue pénitentiaire: Bulletin de la SGP* 28, nos 7–10 (1904): 856–8.

166 Georges Bonjean, "Séance de la SGP du 18 mai 1904: Suite de la discussion du rapport de Jules Jolly sur les causes de la criminalité de l'enfance," *Revue pénitentiaire: Bulletin de la SGP* 28, no. 6 (1904): 769.

167 Robert, "Séance de la Société du 29 juin 1904," 853.

168 Ibid., 854.

169 Henri Lévy-Alvarès, "Séance de la SGP du 18 mai 1904: Suite de la discussion du rapport de Jules Jolly sur les causes de la criminalité de l'enfance," *Revue pénitentiaire: Bulletin de la SGP* 28, no. 6 (1904): 757.

170 Beurdeley, "Après l'école," 204.

171 Crubellier, *L'Enfance et la jeunesse*, 297–335; Alaimo, "Adolescence in the Popular Milieu"; Alaimo, "Shaping Adolescence in the Popular Milieu"; Downs, *Childhood in the Promised Land*; Faure, "Enfance ouvrière, enfance coupable"; Pomfret, "'A Muse for the Masses'"; Thiercé, *Histoire de l'adolescence*, 180–3; and Weber, "Gymnastics and Sport."

172 Alaimo, "Shaping Adolescence in the Popular Milieu," 423. See also Alaimo, "Adolescence, Gender and Class in Education Reform in France."

173 Quoted in Bérenger, "De l'école au régiment: Lettre de M. Léon Bourgeois," 297.

174 Grosmolard, "La Criminalité juvenile (suite et fin)," 258.

175 Bérenger, "De l'école au régiment: Enquête sur l'éducation des adultes," 227.

176 Ibid.

177 Ibid.

178 Robert, "La Criminalité juvénile," 109.

179 Albanel, *Le Crime dans la famille*, 115.

180 Kaluszynski, *La République à l'épreuve du crime*, 174. See also Kaluszynski, "Le Retour de l'homme dangereux."

181 Foucault, "La Vérité et les formes juridiques," 1461.

182 On responses to juvenile vagrants, see Berlanstein, "Vagrants, Beggars, and Thieves"; and Sachs, "'A Sad and … Odious Industry.'"

183 Casabianca, "Rapport sur la première question," 41–2.

184 Donzelot, *The Policing of Families*, 130.

CHAPTER TWO

1 Nye, *Crime, Madness and Politics*, 93.

2 Lyon-Caen, "Notice sur la vie et les travaux de René Bérenger."

3 Charles Lucas, "Séance de la SGP du 7 juin 1877: Allocation du doyen d'âge," *Bulletin de la SGP* 1, no. 1 (1877): 12.

4 "Arrêté du préfet de police en date du 22 mai 1877," *Bulletin de la SGP* (1877): 99.

5 Picot, *Théophile Roussel.*

6 Stora-Lamarre, "Morale religieuse," 165n44.

7 Kaluszynski, "Réformer la société," 76.

8 Henri Joly, "Séance de la SGP du 20 décembre 1893: Rapport sur l'internement par voie de correction paternelle," *Revue pénitentiaire: Bulletin de la SGP* 1, no. 1 (1894): 25.

9 René Bérenger, "Séance de la SGP du 27 février 1907: Projet relatif à la suppression de la peine du mort," *Revue pénitentiaire: Bulletin de la SGP* 31, no. 3 (1907): 320. See also Schnapper, "Le Sénateur René Bérenger."

10 Henri Joly, "Séance de la SGP du 20 mars 1907," *Revue pénitentiaire: Bulletin de la SGP* 31, no. 4 (1907): 310–12. For a broader sense of Joly's position at this time, see Joly, "Le Problème criminel au moment présent."

11 Ozouf, *La Fête révolutionnaire*; and Ozouf, *L'Homme régénéré.*

12 Berstein, "Les Institutions républicaines," 151.

13 Badinter, *La Prison républicaine*, 20–2.

14 Schnapper, "De la magistrature domestique," 19.

15 Victor Bournat, "Procès-verbal du cinquième séance, 17 mai [1872]." In Assemblée nationale, *Enquête parlementaire sur le régime des établissements pénitentiaires*, vol. 1. Versailles: Cerf, 1873, 37.

16 Bérenger, "Rapport sur le régime des établissements pénitentiaires," 63–4.

17 Ibid., 70.

18 Voisin, "Rapport sur le projet de loi relatif à l'éducation et au patronage des jeunes détenus," 8.

19 Pierre, "Débats parlementaires, politiques correctionnelles"; and Messineo, *Jeunesse irrégulière*, 81–126.

20 Haussonville, "Rapport sur le régime des établissements pénitentiaires," 236.

21 Ibid., 258.

22 Assemblée Nationale, *Enquête parlementaire sur les établissements pénitentiaires*, vol. 1, v–vi; and "Appendice: Documents relatifs à la SGP, IV, Liste des membres," *Bulletin de la SGP* 1, no. 1 (1877): 106–24.

23 Joly, "René Bérenger," 51.

24 Quoted by Stora-Lamarre, *La République des faibles*, 58.

25 René Bérenger, "Séance du Sénat du 27 février 1899," *Journal officiel, Débats parlementaires, Sénat* (28 February 1899): 194.

26 Zeldin, *France, 1848–1945*, vol. 2, 994.

27 Gibson, "Why Republicans and Catholics."

28 Quincy-Lefebvre, "La Prostitution des mineurs"; Felter-Kerley, "The Art of Posing Nude"; and Mansker, *Sex, Honor and Citizenship*, 193–233. See also Stora-Lamarre, *L'Enfer de la IIIe République*.

29 Joly, "René Bérenger," 48.

30 Ibid., 53.

31 Ibid., 55.

32 René Bérenger, "Séance solennelle de la SGP du 21 mars 1903," *Revue pénitentiaire: Bulletin de la SGP* 27, no. 4 (1903): 500.

33 Lucas, "Séance de la SGP du 7 juin 1877: Allocation du doyen d'âge," 20.

34 O'Brien, *Promise of Punishment*, 191–204.

35 Nattan, *Essais sur la réforme pénitentiaire*, 44.

36 Badinter, *La Prison républicaine*, 61–75.

37 Wright, *Between the Guillotine and Liberty*, 137.

38 Pierre Deyon, *Le Temps des prisons*, 130.

39 Gabriel Paul Othenin d'Haussonville, "Séance solennelle de la SGP du 21 mars 1903," *Revue pénitentiaire: Bulletin de la SGP* 27, no. 4 (1903): 494.

40 Badinter, *La Prison républicaine*, 19.

41 O'Brien, *Promise of Punishment*, 20.

42 *L'Univers*, 20 May 1875.

43 Badinter, *La Prison républicaine*, 83–4.

44 Nye, *Crime, Madness and Politics*, 37–8.

45 Lucas, "Séance de la SGP du 7 juin 1877," 18–19.

46 Sanchez, "La Relégation des récidivistes"; Sanchez, *À perpétuité*; Sanchez, "La Relégation des femmes récidivistes"; and Nye, *Crime, Madness and Politics*, 82–95.

47 René Bérenger, "Proposition de loi sur les moyens préventifs de combattre la récidive," *Bulletin de la* SGP 7, no. 1 (1883): 34.

48 "Loi du 5 février 1893 relative à la réforme des prisons pour courtes peines."

49 Kaluszynski, "La Prison (et sa réforme)."

50 Fernand Desportes, "Projets de loi relatifs aux jeunes détenus," *Bulletin de la* SGP 3, no. 1 (1879): 73.

51 Lucas, "Séance de la SGP du 7 juin 1877," 13.

52 Resnick, *Femmes et associations.*

53 Kaluszynski, "Réformer la société," 82; "Liste des membres de la SGP au 1er janvier 1914," *Revue pénitentiaire et de droit pénal, Bulletin de la* SGP 38, nos 1–2 (1914): 13–42; and Kaluszynski, "Un paternalisme juridique," 180.

54 Coffignon, *L'Enfant à Paris*, 371.

55 "Appendice: Documents relatifs à la SGP: IV Liste des membres," *Bulletin de la* SGP 1, no. 1 (1877): 111 and 123.

56 René Bérenger, "Nécrologie: M. L'Amiral Fourichon," *Bulletin de la* SGP 8, no. 7 (1884): 843–4.

57 See Du Camp, "La Place de la Roquette"; and Turgenev, "The Execution of Tropmann."

58 Le Béguec, *La République des avocats.*

59 Nord, *The Republican Moment*, 115.

60 Gaudemet, *Les Juristes*, 22, 23, and 25.

61 Ibid., 15–16 and 20–1.

62 Nord, *The Republican Moment*, 127.

63 Fernand Desportes, "La SGP," *Bulletin de la* SGP 1, no. 1 (1877): 9.

64 Spach, "Histoire de la SGP," 462.

65 Desportes, "La SGP," 10.

66 Joly, "René Bérenger," 73.

67 Bérenger, *Manuel pratique pour la lutte contre la pornographie.*

68 Quoted by Fernand Desportes, "La SGP," *Bulletin de la* SGP 1, no. 1 (1877): 6.

69 "Statuts de la SGP," *Bulletin de la* SGP 1, no. 1 (1877): 100–5.

70 Kaluszynski, "Un paternalisme juridique," 181.

71 Lucas, "Séance de la SGP du 7 juin 1877," 14.

72 Ibid.

73 Jules Leveillé, "Rapport sur l'engagement militaire des condamnés correc-

tionnels dans les corps spéciaux destinés à être employé hors du térritoire continental," *Revue pénitentiaire: Bulletin de la* SGP 20, no. 7 (1896): 1008.

74 Dr Frederick Wines, "État actuel de la réforme pénitentiaire dans les pays civilisés," *Bulletin de la* SGP 2, no. 8 (1878): 821.

75 Gabriel Paul Othenin d'Haussonville, "Séance solennelle de la SGP du 21 mars 1903," *Revue pénitentiaire: Bulletin de la* SGP 27, no. 4 (April 1903): 498.

76 Albert Rivière, "Séance solennelle de la SGP du 21 mars 1903," *Revue pénitentiaire: Bulletin de la* SGP 27, no. 4 (April 1903): 492.

77 Albert Rivière, "Séance de la SGP du 21 janvier 1914: Discours du président," *Revue pénitentiaire et de droit pénal, Bulletin de la* SGP 38, nos 1–2 (1914): 92.

78 Albert Gigot, "Séance de la SGP du 29 juin 1904: Fin de la discussion du rapport de Jules Jolly sur les causes de la criminalité de l'enfance," *Revue pénitentiaire: Bulletin de la* SGP 28, nos 7–10 (1904): 873.

79 Bérenger, "Allocution à messieurs les membres de la Société," ix.

80 Léon Lefébure quoted by Fernand Desportes, "La SGP," *Bulletin de la* SGP 1, no. 1 (1877): 5.

81 Charles Lucas, "Séance de la SGP du 7 juin 1877," *Bulletin de la* SGP 1, no. 1 (1877): 13.

82 Kaluszynski, "Réformer la société," 83n29.

83 Ibid., 80 and 90.

84 Lombroso, *Les Applications de l'anthropologie criminelle*, 34.

85 Haussonville, "Rapport sur le régime des établissements pénitentiaires," 112–13.

86 Horne, *A Social Laboratory*, 130–1.

87 See Kalaora and Savoye, *Les Inventeurs oubliés*.

88 Stora-Lamarre, *L'Enfer de la IIIe République*, 123.

89 Le Play, *La Réforme sociale*, iii, 319.

90 For a snapshot of the veteran reformer's views, see Lucas, *Conclusion générale*, liv–lv; and O'Brien, *Promise of Punishment*, 30–3.

91 Lucas, "Séance de la SGP du 7 juin 1877," 17.

92 Gaillac, *Les Maisons de correction*, 71.

93 Félix Voisin invoked Lucas' phrase in his "Rapport sur le project de loi relatif à l'éducation et au patronage des jeunes détenus," 8.

94 Lucas, "Séance de la SGP du 7 juin 1877," 20.

95 Duprat, *Le Temps des philanthropes*; and Duprat, "Punir et guérir."

96 Lucas, "Séance de la SGP du 7 juin 1877," 12.

97 Fernand Desportes, "La SGP," *Bulletin de la* SGP 1, no. 1 (1877): 4.

98 Baron Charles Daru and Victor Bournat, "La Société royale des prisons, 1819–1830," *Bulletin de la SGP* 2, no. 1 (1878): 57.
99 Daru and Bournat, "La Société royale des prisons," 70.
100 Quoted by Jules Dufaure, "Séance générale du 27 juin 1877: Discours du président," *Bulletin de la SGP* 1, no. 1 (1877): 38–9.
101 Gaillac, *Les Maisons de correction*, 40.
102 Duprat, "Punir et guérir."
103 Voisin, "Rapport sur le project de loi relatif à l'éducation et au patronage des jeunes détenus," 15.
104 Gaillac, *Les Maisons de correction*, 62–3.
105 Tétard and Dumas, *Filles de justice*, 120.
106 Luaire, *Le Rôle d'initiative privée*, 12.
107 Gaillac, *Les Maisons de correction*, 181–2.
108 Joly, *L'Enfance coupable*, 204.
109 Weissbach, "Oeuvre Industrielle"; and Heywood, "The Catholic Church."
110 Triqueti, *Exposé des œuvres*, 209; and Bucquet, *Tableau de la situation morale*, 41–2.
111 Weissbach, "Oeuvre Industrielle," 106.
112 Robert, "La Criminalité juvénile," 110–11.
113 Lacousse, "L'Engagement dans l'armée."
114 Dufaure, "Séance générale du 27 juin 1877: Discours du président," 41.
115 Ibid., 41–2.
116 Wright, *Between the Guillotine and Liberty*, 56.
117 Charles Lucas, "Communication à l'Académie des sciences morales et politiques," *Bulletin de la SGP* 2, no. 3 (1878): 302.
118 Lucas, "Communication à l'Académie des sciences morales et politiques," 303.
119 Ibid., 304.
120 Dufaure, "Séance générale du 27 juin 1877: Discourse du président," 42.
121 René Bérenger, "Allocution à messieurs les membres de la Société," *Bulletin de la SGP* 11 (1887), vii–ix.
122 Bérenger, "Proposition de loi sur les moyens préventifs de combattre la récidive," 53.
123 Schnapper, "De la magistrature domestique," 20.
124 Michaux, "Procès-verbal de la troisième séance, 22 août 1878," in Louis Guillaume (ed.), *Actes du Congrès pénitentiaire international de Stockholm 1878*, vol. 1 (Stockholm: Bureau de la Commission pénitentiaire internationale, 1879), 176.

125 Harris, *Murders and Madness*, 95.

126 Neilson, "The Paradox of Penal Colonization."

127 Nye, *Crime, Madness and Politics*, 95.

128 Kaluszyński, *La République à l'épreuve du crime*, 179.

129 Garraud, "Rapport sur la première question de la quatrième section," 6.

130 Dupont-Bouchat, Éric Pierre, et al., *Enfance et justice*, 250.

131 See, for instance, René Bérenger, "Moyens préventifs de combattre la récidive," *Bulletin de la SGP* 7, no. 1 (1883): 35 and 55–63.

132 For a discussion of the *casier judiciaire* and Bérenger's concerns, see C. de Vence, "Séance de la SGP du 13 mai 1891: Rapport sur le casier judiciaire," *Bulletin de la SGP* 15, no. 6 (1891): 730–9.

133 Quoted in Koeppel, "Prophylaxie sociale," 145.

134 Albanel, *Le Crime dans la famille*, viii.

135 Schafer, *Children in Moral Danger*, 7.

136 Louis Puibaraud, "La Responsabilité des enfants," *Revue pénitentiaire: Bulletin de la SGP* 17, no. 4 (April 1893): 447.

137 Dreyfus, *Misères sociales*, 2.

138 Ibid.

139 Ibid., 2–3.

140 Bonjean, *Enfants révoltés*, 13.

141 Lacassagne and Martin, "Les Données de la statistique criminelle," 850.

## CHAPTER THREE

1 Ortolan, *Éléments de droit penal*, 110.

2 Haussonville, *L'Enfance à Paris*, 358.

3 Ibid.

4 Nilan, "Hapless Innocence," 255.

5 Marc, *De la folie*, 97–121.

6 Maison, *Honoré Daumier*, nos 643, 644, and 645. The three works are also described and reproduced in Maison, "Daumier Studies."

7 Haussonville, *L'Enfance à Paris*, 358–9.

8 Ibid., 359.

9 On the history of juvenile criminality in England in this period, see Shore, *Artful Dodgers*.

10 Rey, *Dictionnaire historique*, 1095, 1096–7.

11 See Foucault, "26 March 1980."

12 Lemaître, "Avant la Communion solennelle," 22.

13 Aquinas, "Question LXII: Du sacrement de confirmation."

14 Fonsegrive, *Essai sur le libre arbitre.*

15 Proal, *Le Crime*, 346–7.

16 Cousin, *Du vrai*, 352. See also Goldstein, *The Post-Revolutionary Self*, esp. chapters 4–6.

17 Brocher, *Étude sur l'influence légitime de la conscience morale*, 2.

18 Carrau, *De l'éducation*, 46.

19 Desportes, "Rapport sur le Congrès pénitentiaire tenu à Cincinnati les 12 et 18 octobre 1870," 455.

20 Brocher, *Étude sur l'influence légitime de la conscience morale*, 3.

21 Tourdes, "Considérations médico-légales sur les âges," 178.

22 Gervais, "De la liberté surveillée: Rôle du tribunal pour enfants, après la sentence," 550.

23 Norris, "Mentir à l'âge de l'innocence."

24 Messineo, *Jeunesse irrégulière*, 30–1.

25 Félix Drelon, "Discussion de la proposition de loi adoptée par le Sénat, sur les tribunaux pour enfants et adolescents et sur la liberté surveillée," *Journal officiel de la République française*, Chambre des députés, 2e séance du 12 juillet 1911 (13 July 1911): 2827.

26 Perrot, "Sur la notion d'intérêt de l'enfant," 41.

27 Esmein, *Histoire de la procédure criminelle*; and Emsley, *Crime, Police, and Penal Policy*, 77–95.

28 Silverman, *Tortured Subjects.*

29 Donovan, *Juries and the Transformation of Criminal Justice*; Savitt, "Villainous Verdicts?"; Donovan, "Magistrates and Juries"; and Donovan, "Justice Unblind."

30 Grassi, *Discours prononcé*, 28–9.

31 Garat, "Assemblée nationale: Séance du lundi 6 juin 1791."

32 Bongert, "Délinquance juvénile," 76.

33 Tourdes, "Considérations médico-légales sur les âges," 178–9.

34 Chauveau and Hélie, *Théorie du Code pénal*, vol. 1, 187.

35 Nye, *Crime, Madness and Politics*, 24.

36 Schafer, *Children in Moral Danger.*

37 Le Poittevin, *Dictionnaire-formulaire des parquets et de la police judiciaire*, vol. 1, 304.

38 O'Brien, *Promise of Punishment*, 120.

39 Yvorel, "L'Enfermement des mineurs," 80.

40 Ibid., 102.

41 Messineo, *Jeunesse irrégulière*, 119.

42 Kaluszynski, *La République à l'épreuve du crime*, 174; Foucault, "La Vérité et les formes juridiques," 1461.

43 Haussonville, "Rapport sur le régime des établissements pénitentiaires," 237.

44 Raux, *Nos jeunes détenus*, 225.

45 Foucault, *Surveiller et punir*, 300.

46 Carlier, *La Prison aux champs*.

47 Gaillac, *Les Maisons de correction*, 19–186.

48 *Code pénal du 25 septembre 1791*, 5–6; and *Code pénal*, 168–9.

49 Chauveau and Hélie, *Théorie du Code pénal*, vol. 1, 194.

50 Yvorel, "L'Enfermement des mineurs," 80.

51 Lefuel, "Rapport sur la première question de la quatrième section," 38.

52 Beaumont and Tocqueville, *Du système pénitentiaire aux États-Unis*, 226.

53 Puibaraud, "Rapport sur la quatrième question de la quatrième section," 502.

54 Ibid., 501–2.

55 Ibid., 503.

56 Ibid., 502.

57 Houyvet, "Suite de la discussion sur les écoles industrielles et la législation relative à l'éducation correctionnelle: Séance générale du mercredi 7 mai 1879," *Bulletin de la* SGP 3, no. 5 (1879): 479.

58 See, for instance, Vigneron d'Heucqueville, *Étude sur la condition des mineurs*, 56.

59 Mabille, *De la question de discernement*, 66.

60 Nye, *Crime, Madness and Politics*, 30–1.

61 Mabille, *De la question de discernement*, 67.

62 Ibid., 68–9.

63 Rossi, *Œuvres completes*, 22.

64 Chauveau and Hélie, *Théorie du Code pénal*, vol. 1, 188.

65 Donovan, *Juries and the Transformation of Criminal Justice*.

66 Blanche, *Études pratiques sur le Code pénal*, 402–3.

67 *Code d'instruction criminelle*, 60.

68 Jules Jolly, "Séance de la SGP du 20 avril 1904: Rapport sur les causes de la criminalité de l'enfance," *Revue pénitentiaire: Bulletin de la* SGP 28, no. 5 (1904): 664.

69 Yvorel, "L'Enfermement des mineurs," 100.

70 Messineo, *Jeunesse irrégulière*, 44.

71 Ibid.

72 Nilan, "Incarcerating Children," 44.

73 Ibid., 45.
74 Yvorel, "L'Enfermement des mineurs de justice," 77, 78, and 84–5.
75 Nilan, "Incarcerating Children," 29n43.
76 Harris, *Murders and Madness*, 137.
77 Martin, "The Courts, the Magistrature, and Promotions," 984–5.
78 Ibid., 985.
79 Meyer, *L'Enfant et la raison d'État*, 39.
80 Dreyfus, "L'Enfance devant la justice repressive," 350.
81 Article 1 of the statutes of the Comité in *L'Enfant*, no. 6 (15 April 1891): 4.
82 Dreyfus, "L'Enfance devant la justice repressive," 350.
83 Cruppi, *La Cour d'assises*, 5.
84 Albanel, *Étude statistique*, 11.
85 Ibid., 12.
86 Badinter, *La Prison républicaine*, 288.
87 Guillot, *Observations pratiques*, 22.
88 Quincy-Lefebvre, "À la recherche d'un nouveau paradigme," 199.
89 *La Lanterne*, 20 September 1906.
90 Ibid., 23 September 1906.
91 Bulot, "Circulaire concernant les enfants traduits en justice," *Revue pénitentiaire: Bulletin de la SGP* 24, no. 2 (1900): 312n1.
92 Olson-Raymer, "The American History of Juvenile Justice."
93 Deschanel, "Séance solennelle d'ouverture," 47.
94 Kleine, "Les Tribunaux pour enfants en France," 157.
95 Horne, *A Social Laboratory for Modern France.*
96 Julhiet, "Les Tribunaux pour enfants aux États-Unis."
97 Georges Frèrejouan Du Saint, "Régime pénitentiaire et système pénal dans quelques états étrangers," *Revue pénitentiaire: Bulletin de la SGP* 30, no. 1 (1906): 107.
98 René Bérenger, cited by Henri Prudhomme, "La Question des tribunaux pour enfants devant le Sénat et la Chambre," *Revue pénitentiaire et de droit pénal: Bulletin de la SGP* 36, nos 7–10 (1911): 853–4.
99 Leonards, "Border Crossings"; and Leonards and Randeraad, "Transnational Experts."
100 Dekker, *The Will to Change the Child*; Driver, "Discipline without Frontiers?"; and Grant, "Model Colonies."
101 Cipriani, *Children's Rights*, 74.
102 Valensi, *Comité de défense des enfants traduits en justice*, 5.
103 Ibid.

104 Neilson, "The Paradox of Penal Colonization."
105 Nillus, "La Minorité pénale."
106 Robert, "La Législation française relative à l'enfance," 3.
107 Louis Puibaraud, "Rapport sur la quatrième question," 575. Italics in the original.
108 Brueyre, "Séance générale de la SGP du 16 décembre 1891," 11.
109 Morache, *La Responsabilité*, 76.
110 Hugo, "Le Crapaud," 176.
111 Schinz, "La Moralité de l'enfant," 266.
112 Rousseau, *Émile*, 58.
113 Schinz, "La Moralité de l'enfant," 267.
114 Quoted in "Informations diverses," *Revue pénitentiaire et de droit pénal: Bulletin de la SGP* 38, nos 1–2 (1914): 239.
115 Prudhomme, "Spécialisation d'une juridiction de mineurs," 265.
116 Kleine, "Les Tribunaux pour enfants en France," 161.
117 Robert, *Traité de droit des mineurs.*
118 Prudhomme, "La Question des tribunaux pour enfants devant le Sénat et la Chambre," 844; Leclec'h, *Les Tribunaux pour enfants*, 29.
119 Chauveau and Hélie, *Théorie du Code pénal*, vol. 3, 52.
120 Boitard, *Leçons de droit criminel*, 362.
121 Thiercé, *Histoire de l'adolescence*, 21.
122 Haussonville, "Rapport sur le régime des établissements pénitentiaires," 236–7.
123 Vigneron d'Heucqueville, *Étude sur la condition des mineurs*, 58.
124 Pécaut, "Vie humaine (Âges)," 2487.
125 Compayré, "La Psychologie de l'adolescence," 374.
126 Compayré, "La Pédagogie de l'adolescence," 591.
127 G. Leredu, "Le Ve Congrès pénitentiaire international: Rapport sur la quatrième section," *Revue pénitentiaire: Bulletin de la SGP* 19, no. 7 (1895): 1047.
128 Valensi, *Comité de défense des enfants traduits en justice*, 13.
129 Bonzon, *Le Crime et l'école*, 81.
130 Ibid., 80.
131 Demangeot, *De quelques innovations récentes*, 81.
132 Grimanelli, "L'Enfance coupable," 470–1.
133 Foinitsky, "Rapport présenté par la Société juridique de Saint-Pétersbourg," 637–8.
134 Conti, "Rapport sur la troisième question de la quatrième section," 367.
135 Drill, "Rapport sur la cinquième question de la première section," 659.

136 Lasserre, *L'Enfant devant la justice repressive*, 27.

137 Garraud, *Précis de droit criminel*, 186.

138 Pierre Teulon, quoted by Chauveau, *Code pénal progressif*, 190.

139 Chauveau, *Code pénal progressif*, 194.

140 Ortolan, *Éléments de droit pénal*, 124.

141 Ibid., 111.

142 Billault, "Circulaire du 4 juin 1855."

143 Théophile Roussel, "Rapport sur l'éducation correctionnel, Séance générale du 6 février 1879," *Bulletin de la SGP* 3, no. 2 (1879): 142.

144 Charles Lucas, "Discussion sur les écoles industrielles et la législation relative à l'éducation correctionnelle: Séance générale du 5 mars 1879," *Bulletin de la SGP* 3, no. 3 (1879): 233.

145 Houyvet, "Suite de la discussion sur les écoles industrielles et la législation relative à l'éducation correctionnelle," 478.

146 Fernand Desportes, "Suite de la discussion sur les écoles industrielles et la législation relative à l'éducation correctionnelle: Séance générale du mercredi 7 mai 1879," *Bulletin de la SGP* 3, no. 5 (1879): 501.

147 Théophile Roussel, "Suite de la discussion sur les écoles industrielles: Séance générale du 12 juin 1879," *Bulletin de la SGP* 3, no. 6 (1879): 600–1.

148 Dreyfus, "L'Enfance devant la justice répressive," 349. For the bills presented by Roussel, Bérenger, Dufaure, and Fourichon, see Paul Flandin, "Éducation correctionnelle (application des articles 66 et 67 du Code pénal," *Bulletin de la SGP* 12, no. 3 (1888): 344.

149 Loys Brueyre, "Séance générale de la SGP du 16 décembre 1891: Rapport sur l'âge de l'irresponsabilité pénale," *Revue pénitentiaire: Bulletin de la SGP* 16, no. 1 (1892): 19.

150 Brueyre, "Séance générale de la SGP du 16 décembre 1891," 11.

151 Ibid., 6.

152 Ibid., 12.

153 Ibid.

154 Ibid., 12–13.

155 Adolphe Guillot, "Séance générale de la SGP du 16 décembre 1891: Rapport de Loys Brueyre sur l'âge de l'irresponsabilité pénale," *Revue pénitentiaire: Bulletin de la SGP* 16, no. 1 (1892): 20.

156 Guillot, "Séance générale de la SGP du 16 décembre 1891," 20.

157 Adolphe Guillot, "Séance de la SGP du 20 janvier 1892: Suite de la discussion sur l'âge de l'irresponsabilité," *Revue pénitentiaire: Bulletin de la SGP* 16, no. 2 ( 1892): 143.

158 Dr Ballet quoted by Guillot, "Séance de la SGP du 20 janvier 1892," 143. Italics in the original.

159 Guillot, "Séance de la SGP du 20 janvier 1892," 145.

160 Ibid.

161 Guillot, "Séance générale de la SGP du 16 décembre 1891," 21.

162 Guillot, "Séance de la SGP du 20 janvier 1892," 145.

163 Pasteur Arboux, "Séance générale de la SGP du 16 décembre 1891: Rapport de Loys Brueyre sur l'âge de l'irresponsabilité pénale," *Revue pénitentiaire: Bulletin de la SGP* 16, no. 1 (1892): 25.

164 Duverger, "Séance générale de la SGP du 16 décembre 1891: Rapport de Loys Brueyre sur l'âge de l'irresponsabilité pénale," *Revue pénitentiaire: Bulletin de la SGP* 16, no. 1 (1892): 16.

165 Petit, "Séance de la SGP du 20 janvier 1892: Suite de la discussion sur l'âge de l'irresponsabilité," *Revue pénitentiaire: Bulletin de la SGP* 16, no. 2 (1892): 157.

166 Albert Rivière, "Séance de la SGP du 20 janvier 1892: Suite de la discussion sur l'âge de l'irresponsabilité," *Revue pénitentiaire: Bulletin de la SGP* 16, no. 2 (1892): 159–60.

167 Georges Bonjean, "Séance du jeudi 4 juillet, quatrième séance de la quatrième section." In Congrès pénal et pénitentiaire international, *Ve Congrès pénitentiaire international de Paris 1895*, vol. 2. Melun: Imprimerie administrative, 1897, 662–3.

168 Georges Bonjean, "Assemblée générale, vendredi 5 juillet (soir)." In Congrès pénal et pénitentiaire international, *Ve Congrès pénitentiaire international de Paris 1895*, vol. 1. Melun: Imprimerie administrative, 1897, 108.

169 Arboux, "Séance générale de la SGP du 16 décembre 1891," 25–6.

170 Ibid.

171 Hatzfeld, *Du discernement chez les enfants coupables*, 9.

172 Ibid., 8.

173 As noted by Charles Lambert, "Comité de défense, Séance du 7 avril 1897," *Revue pénitentiaire: Bulletin de la SGP* 21, no. 5 (1897): 826.

174 Prudhomme, "Rapport sur la quatrième question de la quatrième section," 461.

175 Quoted by Leclec'h, *Les Tribunaux pour enfants*, 29.

176 *Gazette des tribunaux*, 26 February 1906.

177 Grimanelli, "Rapport sur la première question de la quatrième section," 163.

178 Mialane, *La Criminalité juvénile*, 186–7; Campinchi, "Le Statut de l'enfance délinquante"; and Chassot, *Les Conséquences pénales*.

179 Alfred Le Poittevin, "Minorité pénale: Proposition de loi Cruppi," *Revue pénitentiaire: Bulletin de la SGP* 29, nos 7–10 (1905): 1068.

180 Loys Brueyre, quoted in Rollet, "De l'application à Paris et dans les départements de la loi du 12 avril 1906," 24.

181 Note: in French sources, Drill's first name is regularly transliterated as "Dmitri."

182 Richter, "Rehabilitating Juvenile Criminals in Russia," 74.

183 Drill, "Rapport sur la cinquième question de la première section," 661.

184 Paul Drillon, "Les Mineurs délinquants en province," *Revue pénitentiaire: Bulletin de la SGP* 27, no. 7 (1903): 1100–9.

185 Haussonville, "Rapport sur le régime des établissements pénitentiaires," 262 and 237–8.

186 Bruschi, *Parquet et politique pénale*, 210.

187 Charles Petit, "Séance de la SGP du 16 mars 1892: Suite de la discussion sur l'âge de l'irresponsabilité," *Revue pénitentiaire: Bulletin de la SGP* 16, no. 4 (1892): 443.

188 Loys Bruyere, "Séance générale de la SGP du 16 décembre 1891: Rapport sur l'âge de l'irresponsabilité pénale," *Revue pénitentiaire: Bulletin de la SGP* 16, no. 1 (1892): 5.

189 Puibaraud, "Rapport sur la quatrième question de la quatrième section," 489.

190 Mialane, *La Criminalité juvénile*, 182; and Georges Leloir, "Séance de la SGP du 19 janvier 1910: La contrebande par les mineurs de 18 ans," *Revue pénitentiaire et de droit pénal: Bulletin de la SGP* 34, no. 2 (1910): 238.

191 Louis Albanel, "Comité de défense, Séance du 7 mars 1906: Âge minimum de la responsabilité pénale et de l'imputabilité pénale chez l'enfant," *Revue pénitentiaire: Bulletin de la SGP* 30, no. 4 (1906): 580.

192 Ernest Passez, "Séance de la SGP du 16 mars 1892: Suite de la discussion sur l'âge de l'irresponsabilité," *Revue pénitentiaire: Bulletin de la SGP* 16, no. 4 (1892): 416.

193 Henri Joly, "Séance générale de la SGP du 16 décembre 1891: Rapport de Loys Brueyre sur l'âge de l'irresponsabilité pénale," *Revue pénitentiaire: Bulletin de la SGP* 16, no. 1 (1892): 24.

194 Joly, "Séance générale de la SGP du 16 décembre 1891," 24.

195 Puibaraud, "Rapport sur la quatrième question," 574.

## CHAPTER FOUR

1 Ferdinand Dreyfus, "Séance du mardi 5 septembre 1905: Quatrième section." In *Actes du Congrès pénitentiaire international de Budapest 1905*, vol. 1,

edited by Jules Rickl de Bellye and Louis Guillaume (Budapest: Bureau de la Commission pénitentiaire internationale, 1907), 298.

2 Taïeb, *Hiding the Guillotine*, 10.

3 Brumfield, "Invitation to a Beheading."

4 *Le Petit journal*, 21 December 1889.

5 Faure, *Souvenirs de la Roquette*, 233–46.

6 Quoted by Joly, "Jeunes criminels parisiens," 170.

7 Taïeb, *Hiding the Guillotine*, 235.

8 Joly, "Jeunes criminels parisiens," 169.

9 *Le Petit parisien*, 31 October 1889; Laurent, *L'Anthropologie criminelle*, 168; and Bataille, *Causes criminelles et mondaines*, 394.

10 Beliard, "M[E] Henri Robert."

11 Quoted in *Le Petit parisien*, 31 October 1889.

12 Faure, *Souvenirs de la Roquette*, 239.

13 Joly, "Jeunes criminels parisiens," 173.

14 Georges Kaps quoted by Joly, "Jeunes criminels parisiens," 173.

15 Ibid.

16 Joly, "Jeunes criminels parisiens," 161; and Joly, *Le Combat contre le crime*, 279.

17 "Circulaire du Garde des sceaux sur les courtes peines d'emprisonnement et les courts renvois appliqués aux mineurs," *Bulletin de la* SGP 13, no. 2 (1889): 228.

18 Albert Rivière, "Séance de la SGP du 18 décembre 1889: Discussion de la question des dangers des courtes peines, surtout pour les mineurs de seize ans," *Bulletin de la* SGP 14, no. 1 (1890): 12.

19 Rivière, "Séance de la SGP du 18 décembre 1889," 8.

20 Ibid.

21 Ibid., 9.

22 Victor Bournat, "Séance de la SGP du 18 décembre 1889: Discussion de la question des dangers des courtes peines, surtout pour les mineurs de seize ans," *Bulletin de la* SGP 14, no. 1 (1890): 14, italics in the original.

23 Tomel and Rollet, *Les Enfants en prison*, 279.

24 Haussonville, "Rapport sur le régime des établissements pénitentiaires," 381. See also Tétard and Dumas, *Filles de justice*.

25 Bourquin, "La Rochefoucauld-Liancourt."

26 Charles Daru and Victor Bournat, "La Société royale des prisons, 1819–1830," *Bulletin de la* SGP 2, no. 1 (1878): 71.

27 Gaillac, *Les Maisons de correction*, 40.

28 Ibid., 55.

29 Argout, "Circulaire du 3 décembre 1832," 158.

30 Villeneuve, *Jurisprudence du XIXe siècle*, 325.

31 Pierre Van Meenen, quoted in Congrès pénitentiaire, *Débats du congrès pénitentiaire international de Bruxelles*, 94.

32 Gaillac, *Les Maisons de correction*, 49.

33 Prade, "Les Colonies pénitentiaires."

34 Demetz, *Fondation d'une colonie agricole*, 20.

35 Messineo, *Jeunesse irrégulière*, 60–1.

36 Gaillac, *Les Maisons de correction*, 64.

37 Sencourt, *The Life of the Empress Eugenie*, 214–15; and Perrot, "Les Enfants de la Petite-Roquette."

38 Ministère de l'intérieur, *Statistique des prisons pour l'année 1865*, lx.

39 Dr Marjolin, "Séance de la SGP du 7 mai 1879," *Bulletin de la SGP* 3, no. 5 (1879): 490.

40 "Loi du 5 août 1850 sur l'éducation et le patronage des jeunes détenus."

41 O'Brien, *Promise of Punishment*, 139–40.

42 Persigny, "Circulaire du 5 juillet 1853," 282.

43 Messineo, *Jeunesse irrégulière*, 92–3.

44 Corne, *Étude sur l'éducation correctionnelle*, 21.

45 Charles Lucas, "Séance de la SGP du 5 mars 1879: Suite de la discussion sur les écoles industrielles et la législation rélative à l'éducation correctionnelle," *Bulletin de la SGP* 3, no. 3 (1879): 225.

46 Théophile Roussel, "Séance générale du 6 février 1879: Rapport sur l'éducation correctionnelle," *Bulletin de la SGP* 3, no. 2 (1879): 141–2.

47 Messineo, *Jeunesse irrégulière*, 87.

48 Smith, "The Ideology of Charity."

49 Corne, *Rapport et projet de loi sur le patronage des jeunes détenus*, 23.

50 Messineo, *Jeunesse irrégulière*, 74 and 100.

51 Goffman, *Asylums*, 11.

52 Cited by Ducpétiaux, *De la condition physique et morale des jeunes ouvriers*, 365.

53 Foucault, *Surveiller et punir*, 303–4.

54 Ibid., 304. See also Chassat, "Le Cercle carré du carcéral."

55 Toth, *Mettray*, 137–63. See also Chauvaud, "Le Scandale de Mettray"; and Toth, "The Contard Affair."

56 Toth, *Mettray*, 137.

57 Loys Brueyre, "Séance de la SGP du 20 décembre 1893: Rapport de Henri

Joly sur l'internement par voie de correction paternelle," *Revue pénitentiaire: Bulletin de la SGP* 18, no. 1 (1894): 36.

58 Bucquet, *Situation morale et matérielle*, 12.

59 Persigny, "Circulaire du 5 juillet 1853," 282.

60 Billault, "Circulaire du 4 juin 1855."

61 Théophile Roussel, "Séance de la SGP du 6 février 1879: Discussion du rapport de M. le pasteur Robin sur les écoles industrielles," *Bulletin de la SGP* 3, no. 2 (1879): 140.

62 Schnapper, "La Correction paternelle," 336.

63 Henri Joly, "Séance de la SGP du 19 décembre 1894: Le Service de la correction paternelle au tribunal de la Seine," *Revue pénitentiaire: Bulletin de la SGP* 19, no. 1 (1895): 30.

64 Messineo, *Jeunesse irrégulière*, 127–8.

65 Vingtrinier, *Des enfants dans les prisons*, 208.

66 Ibid., 55.

67 Haussonville, *L'Enfance à Paris*, 189.

68 Schafer, *Children in Moral Danger*, 44.

69 Ibid.

70 Fuchs, *Abandoned Children*, 260.

71 [Élie] Robin, "Séance générale du 5 janvier 1878: Rapport sur les écoles industrielles et la protection des enfants insoumis et abandonnés," *Bulletin de la SGP* 2, no. 1 (1878): 19.

72 "Assistance aux enfants moralement abandonnés: Rapport présenté par M. le Directeur de l'administration générale de l'Assistance publique à M. le Préfet de la Seine," *Bulletin de la SGP* 4, no. 7 (1880): 730.

73 Quoted in Office central des œuvres de bienfaisance et services sociaux, *Paris charitable et prévoyant*, 86. See also Quincy-Lefèbvre, *Familles, institutions et deviances*, 185.

74 Schafer, *Children in Moral Danger*, 167–84.

75 Ibid., 148.

76 "Loi du 24 juillet 1889 sur la protection des enfants maltraités ou moralement abandonnés."

77 Meyer, *L'Enfant et la raison d'État*, 59.

78 "Loi du 24 juillet 1889 sur la protection des enfants maltraités ou moralement abandonnés."

79 Schafer, *Children in Moral Danger*, 67.

80 Messineo, *Jeunesse irrégulière*, 266–9; and Badinter, *La Prison républicaine*, 354.

81 Dessertine, "Les Tribunaux face aux violences."
82 Lascoumes et al., *Au nom de l'ordre*, 190–1.
83 Berlet, *Commentaire théorique et pratique*, 9.
84 Messineo, *Jeunesse irrégulière*, 288.
85 Pierre, "La loi du 19 avril 1898."
86 Milliard, "Circulaire relative aux mesures à prendre par le magistrat instructeur," 35.
87 Badinter, *La Prison républicaine*, 357n2.
88 *Le Temps*, 27 April 1898.
89 Loys Brueyre, "Revue du patronage des institutions préventives: Comité de défense – Loi de 1898," *Revue pénitentiaire: Bulletin de la SGP* 27, no. 4 (1903): 583.
90 Paul Drillon, "Les Mineurs délinquants en province (fin)," *Revue pénitentiaire: Bulletin de la SGP* 28, no. 1 (1904): 108.
91 Quoted by Joly, "De l'enfance coupable et de nos maisons de correction à l'heure actuelle," 66–7.
92 Paul Jolly, "Examen critique de la loi du 19 avril 1898 (art. 4 à 5)," *Revue pénitentiaire: Bulletin de la SGP* 27, no. 3 (1903): 339–40.
93 Jolly, "Examen critique de la loi du 19 avril 1898," 350–1.
94 Dr L.-V. Mouret and Paul Cuche, "Les Lacunes de la législation de l'enfance moralement abandonnée," *Revue pénitentiaire: Bulletin de la SGP* 30, no. 6 (1906): 876.
95 Manuel Fourcade, "Les Écoles de préservation," *Revue pénitentiaire: Bulletin de la SGP* 28, nos 7–10 (1904): 889.
96 Quincy-Lefebvre, "Assistance publique et enfants difficiles vers 1900."
97 Messineo, *Jeunesse irrégulière*, 294.
98 Théophile Roussel, "Séance générale du 6 février 1879: Discussion du rapport de M. le pasteur Robin sur les écoles industrielles," *Bulletin de la SGP* 3, no. 2 (1879): 142.
99 Roussel, "Séance générale du 6 février 1879," 142.
100 Félix Voisin, "Rapport sur le projet de loi relative a l'education et au patronage des jeunes détenus," 60. See also [Élie] Robin, "Séance générale du 3 juillet 1878: Rapport sur les écoles industrielles et la protection des enfants insoumis et abandonnés," *Bulletin de la SGP* 2, no. 7 (1878): 672–3; and Dupont-Bouchat et al., *Enfance et justice*, 268–72.
101 Messineo, *Jeunesse irrégulière*, 92–3.
102 Théophile Roussel, "Séance générale du 12 juin 1879: Suite de la discussion sur les écoles industrielles," *Bulletin de la SGP* 3, no. 6 (1879): 599–600.

103 Roussel, "Séance générale du 12 juin 1879," 599–600. On the perceived purpose and advantages of écoles industrielles, see [Élie] Robin, "Séance générale du 5 janvier 1878: Rapport sur les écoles industrielles et la protection des enfants insoumis et abandonnés," *Bulletin de la SGP* 2, no. 1 (1878): 6–24; "Séance générale du 6 mars 1878: Rapport sur les écoles industrielles et la protection des enfants insoumis et abandonnés (deuxième partie)," *Bulletin de la SGP* 2, no. 3 (1878): 211–44; "Séance générale du 3 juillet 1878: Rapport sur les écoles industrielles et la protection des enfants insoumis et abandonnés (3e et dernière partie)," *Bulletin de la SGP* 2, no. 7 (1878): 643–83. See also Robin, *Des écoles industrielles.*

104 Dr Jules Lunier, "Séance générale du 7 mai 1879: Suite de la discussion sur les écoles industrielles et la législation relative à l'éducation correctionnelle," *Bulletin de la SGP* 3, no. 5 (1879): 486.

105 Fernand Desportes, "Séance générale du 7 mai 1879: Suite de la discussion sur les écoles industrielles et la législation relative à l'éducation correctionnelle," *Bulletin de la SGP* 3, no. 5 (1879): 501.

106 Duprat, *La Criminalité dans l'adolescence*, 20.

107 Ibid., 166–7 and 186–7.

108 Gaillac, *Les Maisons de correction*, 166.

109 Haussonville, *Les Établissements pénitentiaires*, 418.

110 Ibid.

111 Ibid.

112 Gaillac, *Les Maisons de correction*, 166.

113 E. Pagès "Les Établissements pénitentiaires français: Statistique du ministère de l'intérieur pour 1876," *Bulletin de la SGP* 4, no. 7 (1880): 766.

114 Théophile Roussel, "Séance générale du 6 février 1879: Rapport sur l'éducation correctionnelle," *Bulletin de la SGP* 3, no. 2 (1879): 142.

115 Le Courbe, "Deux écoles de réforme pour les enfants: École de Saint-Eloi à Chaptelat, près de Limoges, et École de Saint-Joseph, à Frasne-le-Château (Haute-Saône)," *Bulletin de la SGP* 14, no. 4, (1890): 446.

116 Puibaraud, "Rapport sur la quatrième question de la quatrième section," 491.

117 Paul Flandin, "Séance de la Société du 17 janvier 1900: Rapport sur la réforme des maisons de correction," *Revue pénitentiaire: Bulletin de la SGP* 24, no. 2 (1900): 225.

118 E. Pagès, "École de réforme de Saint-Éloi," *Bulletin de la SGP* 7, no. 4 (1883): 437–43.

119 Beaussire, "Un apôtre," 466.

120 Gaillac, *Les Maisons de correction*, 166 and 169; Dupont-Bouchat et al., *Enfance et justice*, 297.

121 Paul Cuche, "École de réforme de Chanteloup (Saint-Hilaire)," *Revue pénitentiaire: Bulletin de la SGP* 18, no. 6 (1894): 893.

122 Cuche, "École de réforme de Chanteloup (Saint-Hilaire)," 896–7.

123 Pissard, "Rapport sur la cinquième question de la quatrième section," 611.

124 Louis Puibaraud, "Essai d'un plan de réforme de la loi de 1850," *Revue pénitentiaire: Bulletin de la SGP* 18, no. 2 (1894): 216.

125 Puibaraud, "Essai d'un plan de réforme de la loi de 1850," 216.

126 R. de la Bussière, "Assistance publique et bienfaisance privée: les écoles de preservation et la loi du 28 juin 1904," *L'Enfant*, 15 January 1906, 29.

127 Quincy-Lefebvre, *Familles, institutions et deviances*, 189–92.

128 Puibaraud, *Les Maisons d'éducation préventive et correctionnelle*, 22–3.

129 Juste, *Statistique pénitentiaire pour l'année 1910*, 67.

130 Dupont-Bouchat et al., *Enfance et justice*, 294.

131 Charles Lucas, "Les Institutions répressives et pénitentiaires et les institutions préventives à l'égard de l'enfance en Angleterre et en France," *Bulletin de la SGP* 2, no. 3 (1879): 287.

132 Baratay, "Affaire de mœurs."

133 Coppée, *Le Coupable.*

134 Ferdinand Dreyfus, "Le Roman pénitentiaire – 'Le Coupable,' par François Coppée," *Revue pénitentiaire: Bulletin de la SGP* 20, no. 8 (1896): 1431–3.

135 Pierre Baudin, "L'Enfance criminelle," *Le Petit marseillais*, 10 April 1897.

136 A. Vidal-Naquet, "La Défense des enfants," *Le Petit marseillais*, 13 April 1897.

137 Vidal-Naquet, "La Défense des enfants."

## CHAPTER FIVE

1 Jules Jolly, "Séance de la SGP du 20 avril 1904: Rapport sur les causes de la criminalité de l'enfance," *Revue pénitentiaire: Bulletin de la SGP* 28, no. 5 (1904): 663–4.

2 Jolly, "Séance de la SGP du 20 avril 1904," 665.

3 Ibid., 666.

4 Ibid.

5 Alaimo, "Adolescence in the Popular Milieu," 204–66.

6 Grosmolard, "La Lutte contre la criminalité juvenile (fin)," 163, italics in the original.

7 See Henri Rollet, "Rapport: De l'application à Paris et dans les départements de la loi du 12 avril 1906, fixant à 18 ans l'âge de la majorité pénale, à

l'assemblée générale du 18 décembre 1906," *Bulletin de l'Union des sociétés de patronage de France* 13, no. 1 (1907): 18.

8 "Enfance criminelle," *Le Petit marseillais*, 10 April 1897.

9 Kalifa, "Magistrature et 'crise de la répression,'" 43.

10 See "Séance de la SGP du 27 février 1907: Discussion de la communication de Joseph Reinach sur le projet relatif à la suppression de la peine de mort et à son remplacement par un internement perpétuel," *Revue pénitentiaire: Bulletin de la SGP* 31, no. 3 (1907): 297–341; and "Séance de la SGP du 20 mars 1907: Suite de la discussion de la communication de Joseph Reinach sur le projet de loi relatif à la suppression de la peine de mort et à son remplacement par un internement perpétuel," *Revue pénitentiaire: Bulletin de la SGP* 31, no. 4 (1907): 721–63.

11 Nye, *Crime, Madness and Politics*, chapter 8.

12 Fuchs, "Juvenile Delinquency in Nineteenth-Century France," 268.

13 Alaimo, "Shaping Adolescence in the Popular Milieu," 432.

14 Quincy-Lefebvre, "Âge et justice," 265. See also Quincy-Lefebvre, "Droit, régulation et jeunesse."

15 Levade, *La Délinquance des jeunes*, vol. 2, table 1(a). See also Levade, *La Délinquance des jeunes en France*, vol. 1; Costa-Lascoux, *La Délinquance des jeunes en France*, vol. 3; and Costa-Lascoux, *La Délinquance des jeunes en France*, vol. 4.

16 O'Brien, *Promise of Punishment*, 112.

17 Schnapper, "La Correction paternelle," 332.

18 Tétard and Dumas, *Filles de Justice*, 136–7.

19 Quincy-Lefebvre, "La Prostitution des mineurs"; Yvorel, "Légiférer sur la sexualité de la jeunesse"; and Kœppel, "Prophylaxie sociale."

20 Joly, "L'Éducation correctionnelle des jeunes filles en France," 130.

21 Ibid., 131.

22 Ibid., 348.

23 Albert Rivière, "Séance de la SGP du 21 décembre 1887," *Bulletin de la SGP* 12, no. 1 (1888): 11.

24 Herbette, *Œuvre pénitentiaire*.

25 [n.a.], *La Gazette des Beaux-arts*, 8.

26 Gueissaz, "Image sublime, image prosaïque," 123.

27 For a general overview, see Girardet, *La Société militaire*.

28 Roynette, *Bon pour le service*, 45.

29 "Loi du 15 juillet 1889 sur le recrutement de l'armée."

30 Ibid., 28–30.

31 On Old Regime and revolutionary military structures, see Forrest, "La Patrie en Danger."
32 Forrest, *Conscripts and Deserters*; and Woloch, "Napoleonic Conscription."
33 Cournet, *Les Voleurs, les vagabonds, et l'armée*, 52.
34 Marabail, *De l'influence de l'esprit militaire*, 226.
35 Meyer, *L'Enfant et la raison d'État*, 31–2.
36 Pasquier, "Circulaire du 7 octobre 1818."
37 Favard de Langlade, *Nouvelle législation civile*, 745.
38 Porch, "The French Army Law of 1832," 752.
39 On Third Republic military culture, see Ralston, *The Army of the Republic*; and Lambelet, "Manifestly Inferior?"
40 Roynette, "L'Armée, une institution républicaine?," 101.
41 Boniface, *L'Armée, l'église et la République*, 27.
42 Gambetta, *Discours de M. Gambetta*, 12–13.
43 Roynette, *Bon pour le service*, 62.
44 Trochu, *L'Armée française en 1867*, 47; and Roynette, *Bon pour le service*, 27.
45 On voting rights for military men, see Serman, *Les Officiers français dans la nation*, chapter 2; and Edelstein, "Le Militaire-citoyen."
46 Weber, *Peasants into Frenchmen*, 298.
47 Cerullo, *Minotaur*, 23–45.
48 Weber, *Peasants into Frenchmen*, 302.
49 Cerullo, *Minotaur*, 55. On the broader context of the Armée d'Afrique and the conquest of Algeria, see Sessions, *By Sword and Plow*.
50 Ben Mahmoud, *Les Bat' d'Af*, 24.
51 Kalifa, *Biribi*, 119.
52 Ibid., 103.
53 Ibid., 119.
54 Clayton, *France, Soldiers, and Africa*, 212–16.
55 René Bérenger, "Les Condamnés dans l'armée: Discussion au Sénat, séance du 26 avril 1888," *Bulletin de la SGP* 12, no. 6 (1888): 760.
56 Félix Voisin, "Séance de la Société du 20 janvier 1897," *Revue pénitentiaire: Bulletin de la SGP* 21, no. 2 (1897): 258; and Kalifa, *Biribi*, 115.
57 Voisin, "Séance de la Société du 20 janvier 1897," 258.
58 René Bérenger, "Engagement militaire des libérés: Lettre à M. le Président de l'armée coloniale," *Bulletin de la SGP* 15, no. 7 (1891): 969.
59 Raymond Saleilles, "L'Engagement militaire des condamnés (Rapport de la 1re Section)," *Revue pénitentiaire: Bulletin de la SGP* 21, no. 3 (1897): 492–3.
60 Cerullo, *Minotaur*, 11.

61 Ibid., 17.

62 Bourelly quoted by Cerullo, *Minotaur*, 12.

63 Serman, *Les Officiers français*, 105–9. On the military and the Dreyfus Affair, see Boniface, *L'Armée, l'église et la république*, chapter 5.

64 Georges Clemenceau, cited in Capitaine Lebaud, *L'Éducation dans l'armée*, 38.

65 [Lyautey], "Du rôle social de l'officier."

66 Lebaud, *L'Éducation dans l'armée*, 15.

67 Roynette, "Les Apaches à la caserne."

68 Loubat, "La Crise de la répression"; and Loubat, "La Crise de la répression: Les rémèdes."

69 Loubat, "La Crise de la répression," 437.

70 Ibid., 464.

71 Loubat, "La Crise de la répression," 451.

72 "La Suppression des conseils de guerre: Proposition de loi de M. Gouzy," *Revue pénitentiaire et de droit pénal: Bulletin de la SGP* 33, nos 11–12 (1909): 1301.

73 "Les Condamnés de droit commun à la caserne," *Le Temps*, 9 September 1909.

74 "Transformation éventuelle des Bataillons d'Afrique," *Revue pénitentiaire: Bulletin de la SGP* 28, nos 7–10 (1904): 920.

75 Paul Kahn, "Séance de la SGP du 16 décembre 1908," *Revue pénitentiaire et de droit pénal: Bulletin de la SGP* 33, no. 1 (1909): 69.

76 Général Récamier, "Séance de la SGP du 20 janvier 1909: Suite de la discussion du rapport de M. Raiberti sur les inconvénients de l'incorporation des condamnés de droit commun dans les régiments," *Revue pénitentiaire et de droit pénal: Bulletin de la SGP* 33, no. 1 (1909): 198.

77 Cerullo, *Minotaur*, 162. See also Roynette, "Les Apaches à la caserne."

78 Foucault, *Surveiller et punir*, 235.

79 Ibid., 300.

80 Ibid., 304.

81 Giraud, *Colonie de Mettray*, 3–4.

82 Debreyne, *Colonie agricole monastique*, 46n1.

83 Jablonka, "Un discours philanthropique," 136.

84 Spivak, "La Préparation militaire en France," 86.

85 Marchand, "Les Petits soldats de demain," 771.

86 See Spivak, "La Préparation militaire en France"; Marchand, "Les Petits soldats de demain"; Merlier, "Les Bataillons scolaires en France 1882–1892"; and Arnaud, *Le Militaire, l'écolier, le gymnaste*, 173–206.

87 Lambelet, "A Reluctant Reconciliation," 64–5.

88 Guimas, *Colonie agricole de Mettray*, 9.

89 Grosmolard, "La Lutte contre la criminalité juvénile," 151.

90 Louis Rivière, "M. le conseiller Félix Voisin," *Revue pénitentiaire et de droit pénal: Bulletin de la SGP* 39, no. 5 (1915): 583–99. For more on Voisin, see Lacousse, "L'Engagement dans l'armée comme 'remède suprême et nécessaire.'"

91 Félix Voisin, "Rapport du président de la Société de protection des engagés volontaires élevés sous la tutelle administrative," 1882, 29, Archives nationales de France, 25 AS 7.

92 "Circulaire relative aux propositions pour la mise en liberté de jeunes détenus, 20 mars 1878," *Bulletin de la SGP* 2, no. 4 (1878): 411.

93 Bérenger, "Les Condamnés dans l'armée," 761.

94 O'Brien, *Promise of Punishment*, 246.

95 Félix Voisin, "Comité de défense: Rapport sur les modifications à l'article 66 du Code pénal," *Revue pénitentiaire: Bulletin de la SGP* 27, no. 3 (1903): 401.

96 M. Crémieux, "Séance de la SGP du 17 juin 1896: Rapport de M. Leveillé sur l'engagement militaire des condamnés correctionnels dans des corps spéciaux destinés à être employé hors du territoire continental," *Revue pénitentiaire: Bulletin de la SGP* 20, no. 7 (1896): 1017, 1018.

97 Émile Cheysson, "Séance de la SGP du 17 juin 1896: Rapport de M. Leveillé sur l'engagement militaire des condamnés correctionnels dans des corps spéciaux destinés à être employé hors du territoire continental," *Revue pénitentiaire: Bulletin de la SGP* 20, no. 7 (1896): 1017.

98 Roux, "De l'engagement militaire des condamnés correctionnels," 89.

99 Félix Voisin, "Comité de défense, séance du 7 février: Casier des mineurs," *Revue pénitentiaire: Bulletin de la SGP* 24, no. 2 (1900): 307.

100 Badinter, *La Prison républicaine*, 358.

101 Drill, "Rapport sur la cinquième question de la première section," 659.

102 Dmitri Drill, "Procès-verbal de la sixième séance." In *Actes du Congrès pénitentiaire international de Saint-Pétersbourg 1890*, vol. 1, edited by Louis Guillaume. Saint Petersburg: Bureau de la Commission d'organisation du Congrès, 1892, 210.

103 Dmitri Drill, "Annexe: Rapport sur la cinquième question de la première section," 663.

104 For a discussion of the origins and functioning of the Borstal system, see Ruggles-Brise, *The English Prison System*, 85–100.

105 Ruggles-Brise, "Rapport sur la deuxième question à la deuxième section," 255.
106 Lefuel "Rapport sur la première question de la quatrième section," 38.
107 Joly, "Rapport sur la première question de la quatrième section," 31.
108 Félix Voisin, "Assemblée générale de vendredi 5 juillet (soir): Troisième séance." In Congrès pénal et pénitentiaire international, *Ve Congrès pénitentiaire international de Paris 1895*, vol. 1. Melun: Imprimerie administrative, 1897, 103.
109 Voisin, "Assemblée générale de vendredi 5 juillet (soir)," 103.
110 Ibid., 102.
111 Henri Joly, "Procès-verbal de la quatrième section." In *Actes du Congrès pénitentiaire international de Saint-Pétersbourg 1890*, vol. 1, edited by Louis Guillaume. Saint Petersburg: Bureau de la Commission d'organisation du Congrès, 1892, 143.
112 Henri Joly, "Séance du jeudi 4 juillet (matin), quatrième séance de la quatrième section." In Congrès pénal et pénitentiaire international, *Congrès pénitentiaire international de Paris 1895*, vol. 2. Melun: Imprimerie administrative, 1897, 657.
113 Quoted in Arthur, *Young Offenders and the Law*, 46–7.
114 Henri Joly, "Rapport sur la première question de la quatrième section," 29.
115 Jules Leveillé, "Séance de la SGP du 17 juin 1896: Rapport de M. Leveillé sur l'engagement militaire des condamnés correctionnels dans des corps spéciaux destinés à être employé hors du territoire continental," *Revue pénitentiaire: Bulletin de la SGP* 20, no. 7 (1896): 1016.
116 Albert Rivière, "Séance de la SGP du 21 décembre 1887," *Bulletin de la SGP* 12, no. 1 (1888): 11.
117 Cournet, *Les Voleurs, les vagabonds, et l'armée*, 13.
118 Henri Rollet, "Rapport: De l'application à Paris et dans les départements de la loi du 12 avril 1906," 18.
119 *Le Petit parisien*, 17 April 1906.
120 The debates over the abolition of the death penalty are treated in detail in Nye, *Crime, Madness and Politics*, chapter 8.
121 *Le Gaulois*, 18 July 1907.
122 Émile Garçon, "Séance de la SGP du 22 avril 1914: Les tribunaux pour enfants et adolescents," *Revue pénitentiaire et de droit pénal: Bulletin de la SGP* 38, no. 5 (1914): 549.
123 *Le Gaulois*, 18 July 1907.

CONCLUSION

1 See, for instance, Audoin-Rouzeau, "Morale et anomie de guerre en 1914–1918"; Becker, *La Guerre et la foi*, 11–47; Le Naour, *Misères et tourments de la chair*; Boniface, *Histoire religieuse de la Grande Guerre*, 217–51; and Rasmussen, "Mobilising Minds."

2 Morisse, "La Fin des 'apaches?,'" 160. See also Morisse, "Régénérer les 'apaches' par la boue, le feu et le sang."

3 Goya, *Flesh and Steel during the Great War*, 169.

4 Delzons, "L'Enfant et la famille," 169.

5 Louis Albanel, "Séance de la SGP du 17 avril 1907: Les Tribunaux pour enfants et la mise en liberté surveillée," *Revue pénitentiaire: Bulletin de la SGP* 31, no. 5 (1907): 573.

6 Binet, *Les Idées modernes sur les enfants*, 48.

7 Ibid., 49.

8 Niget, *La Naissance du tribunal pour enfants.*

9 Fishman, *The Battle for Children*, 13, 28–30, and 152–4.

10 See Heuyer, *Enfants anormaux et délinquants juvéniles.*

11 Renouard, *De l'enfant coupable à l'enfant inadapté.*

12 Yvorel "L'Influence des réformes de l'administration pénitentiaire."

13 Fishman, *The Battle for Children*, 38.

14 Quincy-Lefebvre, "Émotion et opinion dans la justice des mineurs."

15 Fishman, *The Battle for Children*, 35–7.

16 Toth, *Mettray*, 164–94.

17 Robert, *Traité de droit des mineurs*, 94.

18 Mégret, "Henri Donnedieu de Vabres."

19 Quoted by Niget, "La Jeunesse déviante," 586–7.

20 "Ordonnance 45-174 du 2 février 1945," 530.

21 Niget, *La Naissance du tribunal pour enfants*, 46.

22 Dessertine, "Aux origines de l'assistance éducative," 140.

23 Ibid.

24 Ibid.

25 Patin, "Cour de cassation chambre criminelle: 13 décembre 1956," 350.

26 Ibid.

27 Quoted by Rassat, *Droit pénal général*, 472–3.

28 Pradel, "Quelques observations sur le statut pénal du mineur en France," 190.

29 Rassat, *Droit pénal général*, 472.

30 Robert, *Traité de droit des mineurs*, 94.

31 Donnedieu de Vabres, *Traité de droit criminel*, 187.
32 Gardet and Vilbrod, *L'Éducation spécialisée en Bretagne.*
33 Jurmand, "Une histoire de milieu ouvert."
34 See Yvorel, *Les Enfants de l'ombre.*
35 Bruyn, "Regard statistique sur la détention des mineurs," 23–4.
36 Pradel, "Quelques observations sur le statut pénal du mineur en France," 187.
37 Loi 2002-1138 du 9 septembre 2002 d'orientation et de programmation pour la justice (1).
38 Durand, "La loi Perben et la majorité pénale à 10 ans."
39 Pradel, "Quelques observations sur le statut pénal du mineur en France," 188.
40 Bailleau, "France: Breaking with the European Line of Juvenile Justice?," 162–3.
41 Cipriani, *Children's Rights*, chapter 2; Hammarberg, "The UN Convention on the Rights of the Child"; and Melton, "Building Humane Communities."
42 Freeman, *Children's Rights*, 3.
43 Veerman, *The Rights of the Child*, 396.
44 Todres and King, "Introduction," 1.
45 Cipriani, *Children's Rights*, 31.
46 Ibid., 22.
47 Ibid., 36–7.
48 Lazerges, "Chronique de politique criminelle," 175.
49 Jacquin, "Les Députés votent la création d'un code de la justice pénale des mineurs."
50 Ibid.
51 Article L11-1, Chapitre Ier: Des principes généraux du droit pénal applicable aux mineurs, "Code de la justice pénale des mineurs," version in effect as of 30 September 2021, www.legifrance.gouv.fr/codes/article_lc/LEGIARTI000043203791, accessed 10 May 2024.
52 Yvorel, "Comment le droit pénal construit les catégories d'âge," 30.
53 See Courtin, "France: La Responsabilité pénale des mineurs."
54 Steinberg, "The Influence of Neuroscience."
55 Monahan, Steinberg and Piquero, "Juvenile Justice Policy."
56 Bellon, "Discours et pratiques sur le discernement de l'enfant," 77–8.
57 Wall, *Give Children the Vote.*
58 Yaffe, *The Age of Culpability.*

# Bibliography


ARCHIVES

Archives départementales de l'Yonne
Archives nationales de France

NEWSPAPERS AND JOURNALS CONSULTED

*Bulletin de la Société générale des prisons*
*Bulletin des lois de la République française*
*L'Écho de Paris*
*L'Enfant*
*Le Gaulois*
*La Gazette de Lausanne*
*La Gazette des tribunaux*
*L'Illustration*
*Journal officiel de la République française*
*La Lanterne*
*Le Matin*
*Le Petit journal*
*Le Petit marseillais*
*Le Petit parisien*
*Revue pénitentiaire et de droit pénal*
*Le Temps*
*L'Univers*
*L'Yonne*

## LEGISLATION

"Code de la justice pénale des mineurs," version in effect as of 30 September 2021, available at www.legifrance.gouv.fr/codes/texte_lc/LEGITEXT000039086952/2021-09-30, accessed 10 May 2024.

*Code d'instruction criminelle*. Paris: Le Prieur, 1811.

*Code pénal du 25 septembre 1791*. Bruxelles: F. Hayez, 1796.

*Code pénal*. Paris: A. Belin, 1812.

"Loi du 5 août 1850 sur l'éducation et le patronage des jeunes détenus." In *Collection complète des lois, décrets, ordonnances, réglemens, et avis du Conseil-d'État*, edited by J.B. Duvergier, 380–2. Paris: A. Guyot et Scribe, 1850.

"Loi du 5 février 1893 relative à la réforme des prisons pour courtes peines." In *Collection complète des lois, décrets, ordonnances, réglemens, et avis du Conseil-d'État*, edited by J. Duvergier and E. Goujon, 188–9. Paris: L. Larose, 1893.

"Loi du 15 juillet 1889 sur le recrutement de l'armée." In *Collection complète des lois, décrets, ordonnances, réglemens, et avis du Conseil-d'État*, edited by J. Duvergier and E. Goujon, 440–516. Paris: Charles Noblet, 1889.

"Loi du 22 juillet 1912 sur les tribunaux pour enfants et adolescents et sur la liberté surveillée." In *Collection complète des lois, décrets, ordonnances et réglemens*, edited by Gustave Lange, 493–506. Paris: Recueil Sirey, 1912.

"Loi du 24 juillet 1889 sur la protection des enfants maltraités ou moralement abandonnés." In *Collection complète des lois, décrets, ordonnances, réglemens, et avis du Conseil-d'État*, edited by J. Duvergier and E. Goujon, 428–34. Paris: Charles Noblet, 1889.

"Loi du 28 mars 1882 sur l'enseignement primaire obligatoire." In *Collection complète des lois, décrets, ordonnances, réglemens, et avis du Conseil-d'État*, edited by J.B. Duvergier, 74–95. Paris: Larose et Forcel, 1882.

Loi 2002-1138 du 9 septembre 2002 d'orientation et de programmation pour la justice (1), *Journal officiel de la République française, lois et décrets*, 10 September 2002, 14934–53.

Ordonnance 45-174 du 2 février 1945 relative à l'enfance délinquante, *Journal officiel de la République française, Ordonnances et décrets* (4 February 1945): 530–4.

## BOOKS AND ARTICLES

[n.a.] *La Gazette des Beaux Arts: Annuaire*. Paris: J. Claye, 1870.

Accampo, Elinor, Rachel Fuchs, and Mary Lynn Stewart. *Gender and the Politics of Social Reform in France, 1870–1914*. Baltimore: Johns Hopkins University Press, 1995.

Adam, Adolphe. "Sensibilité, sentiments." In *Nouveau dictionnaire de pédagogie et d'instruction*, edited by Ferdinand Buisson. Paris: Hachette, 1911, available at www.inrp.fr/edition-electronique/lodel/dictionnaire-ferdinand-buisson/document.php?id=3622, accessed 10 May 2024.

Alaimo, Kathleen. "Adolescence, Gender and Class in Education Reform in France: The Development of *Enseignement Primaire Supérieur*, 1880–1910." *French Historical Studies* 18, no. 4 (1994): 1025–55.

– "Adolescence in the Popular Milieu in France during the Early Third Republic: Efforts to Define and Shape a Stage of Life." PhD diss., University of Wisconsin-Madison, 1988.

– "Shaping Adolescence in the Popular Milieu: Social Policy, Reformers and French Youth, 1870–1920." *Journal of Family History* 17, no. 4 (1992): 419–38.

Albanel, Louis. *Le Crime dans la famille*. Paris: Rueff, 1900.

– *Étude statistique sur les enfants traduits en justice*. Paris: Marchal et Billard, 1897.

Allen, James S. *In the Public Eye: A History of Reading in Modern France, 1800–1940*. Princeton: Princeton University Press, 1991.

Aquinas, Saint Thomas. "Question LXII: Du sacrement de confirmation." In *La Somme théologique de Saint Thomas*, vol. 7, 1–19. Translated by Abbé Drioux. Paris: Belin, 1854.

Argout, Comte d'. "Circulaire du 3 décembre 1832 sur le placement en apprentissage des enfants jugés en vertu de l'article 66 du Code pénal." In *Code des prisons. 1670 à 1845*, vol. 1, edited by Louis-Mathurin Moreau-Christophe, 157–61. Paris: Paul Dupont, 1845.

Ariès, Philippe. *L'Enfant et la vie familiale sous l'ancien régime*. Paris: Seuil, 1975.

Arnaud, Pierre. *Le Militaire, l'écolier, le gymnaste: Naissance de l'éducation physique en France (1869–1889)*. Lyon: Presses universitaires de Lyon, 1991.

Arthur, Raymond. *Young Offenders and the Law: How the Law Responds to Youth Offending*. London: Routledge, 2010.

Assemblée nationale. *Enquête parlementaire sur le régime des établissements pénitentiaires*, vol. 1. Versailles: Cerf, 1873.

– *Enquête parlementaire sur le régime des établissements pénitentiaires*, vol. 3. Paris: Imprimerie nationale, 1875.

– *Enquête parlementaire sur le régime des établissements pénitentiaires*, vol. 6. Versailles: Cerf, 1874.

– *Enquête parlementaire sur le régime des établissements pénitentiaires*, vol. 7. Paris: Imprimerie nationale, 1874.

– *Enquête parlementaire sur le régime des établissements parlementaires*, vol. 8. Paris: Imprimerie nationale, 1875.

Aubry, Paul. *La Contagion du meurtre: Étude d'anthropologie criminelle*, 2nd ed. Paris: F. Alcan, 1894.

– "De l'influence contagieuse de la publicité des faits criminels." *Archives de l'anthropologie criminelle* 8, no. 48 (1893): 565–80.

Audoin-Rouzeau, Stéphane. "Morale et anomie de guerre en 1914–1918." In *Incontournable morale*, Actes du colloque de Besançon, 1997, edited by Annie Stora-Lamarre, 233–43. Besançon: PUFC, 1998.

Azéma, Jean-Pierre, and Michel Winock. *Naissance et mort: La Troisième République 1870–1914*. Paris: Calmann-Lévy, 1970.

Badinter, Robert. *La Prison républicaine (1871–1914)*. Paris: Fayard, 1992.

Bailleau, Francis. "France: Breaking with the European Line of Juvenile Justice? The Successive Reforms of the Ordinance of 2 February 1945." In *The Criminalisation of Youth Juvenile Justice in Europe, Turkey and Canada*, edited by Yves Cartuyvels et al., 155–86. Brussels: VUB Press, 2010.

Baldet, N. *La Criminalité juvénile: La conscience et la volonté*. Paris: Chagniat, 1912.

Balzac, Honoré de. *Mémoires de deux jeunes mariés*. Paris: Calman Lévy, 1891.

Baratay, Eric. "Affaire de mœurs, conflits de pouvoir et anticléricalisme: La fin de la congrégation des frères de Saint-Joseph en 1888." *Revue d'histoire de l'Église de France* 84, no. 213 (1998): 299–322.

Barrès, Maurice. *Les Déracinés*. Paris: Bibliothèque-Charpentier, 1897.

Barrows, Susanna. "After the Commune: Alcoholism, Temperance, and Literature in the Early Third Republic." *Consciousness and Class Experience in Nineteenth-Century Europe*, edited by John M. Merriman, 205–18. New York: Holmes & Meier, 1979.

– *Distorting Mirrors: Visions of the Crowd in Late Nineteenth-Century France*. New Haven: Yale University Press, 1981.

Bataille, Albert. *Causes criminelles et mondaines de 1889*. Paris: E. Dentu, 1890.

Beaumont, Gustave de, and Alexis de Tocqueville. *Du système pénitentiaire aux États-Unis et de son application en France*, 3rd ed. Paris: Gosselin, 1845.

Beaussire, Émile. "Un apôtre: La colonie pénitentiaire de Sainte-Foy (Dordogne)." *Revue des deux mondes* 30 (Nov. 1878): 460–8.

Becker, Annette. *La Guerre et la foi: De la mort à la mémoire 1914–années 1930*, 2nd ed. Paris: Armand Colin, 2015.

Behlmer, George Kinkel. *Child Abuse and Moral Reform in England, 1870–1908*. Stanford: Stanford University Press, 1982.

Beliard, Octave. "Me Henri Robert." *Les Hommes du jour*, 9 July 1910, 1–2.

Bellon, Laurence. "Discours et pratiques sur le discernement de l'enfant." In *Ré-*

*former le droit des mineurs délinquants: D'une évolution de la jeunesse à l'adaptation de la justice*, edited by Franck Ludwiczak, 68–91. Paris: Harmattan, 2016.

Ben Mahmoud, Feriel. *Les Bat' d'Af: La légende des mauvais garçons*. Paris: Mengès, 2005.

Bérenger, Henry. "De l'école au régiment: Enquête sur l'éducation des adultes." *Revue bleue* 4 (July–Dec. 1895): 227–30.

– "De l'école au régiment: Lettre de M. Léon Bourgeois." *Revue bleue* 4 (July–Dec. 1895): 297–8.

Bérenger, René, et al. *Les Institutions pénitentiaires de la France en 1895*. Paris: La Société générale des prisons, 1895.

Bérenger, René. "Rapport sur le régime des établissements pénitentiaires." In Assemblée nationale, *Enquête parlementaire sur le régime des établissements pénitentiaires*, vol. 7. Paris: Imprimerie nationale, 1874.

Berenson, Edward. *The Trial of Madame Caillaux*. Berkeley: University of California Press, 1992.

Berlanstein, Lenard R. *The Working People of Paris, 1871–1914*. Baltimore: Johns Hopkins University Press, 1984.

Berlet, Adolphe. *Commentaire théorique et pratique de la loi sur la répression des violences*. Paris: Chevalier-Marescq, 1899.

Berlière, Jean-Marc. *Le Crime de Soleilland (1907): Les journalistes et l'assassin*. Paris: Tallandier, 2003.

– *La Police des mœurs sous la IIIe République*. Paris: Seuil, 1992.

Bernheimer, Charles. *Figures of Ill Repute: Representing Prostitution in Nineteenth-Century France*. Cambridge: Harvard University Press, 1989.

Berstein, Serge. "Les Institutions républicaines." In *Le Modèle républicain*, edited by Serge Berstein and Odile Rudelle, 147–57. Paris: PUF-Hachette, 1992.

Beurdeley, Paul. "Après l'école: Le placement des enfants." *Revue pédagogique* 26, no. 3 (March 1895): 204–10.

Billault, Adolphe. "Circulaire du 4 juin 1855, contenant communication des instructions adressées aux procureurs généraux par M. le Ministre de la justice au sujet de l'accroissement de nombre des jeunes détenus." In *Code des prisons*, vol. 2, edited by Louis-Mathurin Moreau-Christophe, 422. Paris: Dupont, 1856.

Binet, Alfred. *Les Idées modernes sur les enfants*. Paris: Flammarion, 1910.

Binet, Alfred, and Théodore Simon. *Les Enfants anormaux: Guide pour l'admission des enfants anormaux dans les classes de perfectionnement*. Paris: Armand Colin, 1907.

Blais, Marie-Claude. *La Solidarité: histoire d'une idée*. Paris: Gallimard, 2007.

Blanche, Antoine. *Études pratiques sur le Code pénal*, 2nd ed. Paris: Cosse et Marchal, 1864.

Boitard, Joseph-Edouard. *Leçons de droit criminel contenant l'explication complète des codes pénal et d'instruction criminelle*. Paris: Cotillon, 1867.

Bongert, Yvonne. "Délinquance juvénile et responsabilité pénale du mineur au XVIIIe siècle." In *Crimes et criminalités en France sous l'Ancien Régime*, edited by André Abbiatecci, François Billacois et al., 49–90. Paris: A. Colin, 1971.

Boniface, Xavier. *L'Armée, l'église et la République, 1879–1914*. Paris: Nouveau Monde, 2012.

– *Histoire religieuse de la Grande Guerre*. Paris: Fayard, 2014.

Bonjean, Georges. *Enfants révoltés et parents coupables: Étude sur la désorganisation de la famille et ses conséquences sociales*. Paris: A. Colin, 1895.

Bonzon, Jacques. *Le Crime et l'école*. Paris: Guillaumin, 1896.

– *La Législation de l'enfance, 1789–1894: Cent ans de lutte sociale*. Paris: Guillaumin, 1894.

Bourgeois, Léon. *La Politique de la prévoyance sociale: La doctrine et la méthode*, vol. 1. Paris: E. Fasquelle, 1914.

Bourquin, Jacques. "La Rochefoucauld-Liancourt et le projet de prison d'essai pour jeunes détenus." In *Protéger l'enfant: Raison juridique et pratiques socio-judiciaires XIXe–XXe siècles*, edited by Michel Chauvière, Pierre Lenoël, and Éric Pierre, 59–69. Rennes: Presses universitaires de Rennes, 1996.

Brocher, Charles. *Étude sur l'influence légitime de la conscience morale en droit pénal*. Paris: E. Thorin, 1878.

Brumfield, William C. "Invitation to a Beheading: Turgenev and Troppmann." *Canadian-American Slavic Studies* 17, no. 1 (1983): 79–88.

Bruno, G. *Instruction morale et civique pour les petits enfants*. Paris: E. Belin, 1883.

Bruschi, Christian. *Parquet et politique pénale depuis le XIXe siècle*. Paris: Presses universitaires de Paris, 2002.

Bruyn, Florence de. "Regard statistique sur la détention des mineurs et sur la récidive après la Libération." In *Mineurs: L'éducation à l'épreuve de la détention*, 23–32. Paris: Travaux et documents, 2012, available at www.justice.gouv.fr/sites/default/files/migrations/portail/art_pix/Travaux_et_Doc_82_Mineurs.pdf, accessed 10 May 2024.

Bucquet, Paul. *Situation morale et matérielle en France des jeunes détenus et des jeunes libérés*. Paris: Charles Gosselin, 1853.

– *Tableau de la situation morale et matérielle en France des jeunes détenus et des jeunes libérés et recherches statistiques sur les colonies agricoles, les établissements correctionnels et les sociétés de patronage de jeunes détenus*. Paris: P. Dupont, 1853.

Buisson, Ferdinand. "Intuition et méthode intuitive." In *Nouveau dictionnaire de pédagogie et d'instruction*, edited by Ferdinand Buisson. Paris: Hachette, 1911, available at www.inrp.fr/edition-electronique/lodel/dictionnaire-ferdinand-buisson/document.php?id=2943, accessed 10 May 2024.

– "La Jeunesse criminelle et l'éducation: Réponse à Gabriel Tarde." *Revue pédagogique* 41 (5 April 1897): 295–308.

– "Leçon de clôture du cours de pédagogie: Éducation de la volonté." *Revue pédagogique* 35 (July–Dec. 1899): 310–45.

Buisson, Ferdinand, ed. *Dictionnaire de pédagogie et d'instruction primaire*, vol 1. Paris, Hachette, 1887.

– *Nouveau dictionnaire de pédagogie et d'instruction*. Paris: Hachette, 1911, available at www.inrp.fr/edition-electronique/lodel/dictionnaire-ferdinand-buisson/, accessed 10 May 2024.

Bussière, R. de la. "Assistance publique et bienfaisance privée: Les écoles de préservation et la loi du 28 juin 1904." *L'Enfant*, 15 January 1906, 29–34.

Cage, E. Claire. *The Science of Proof: Forensic Medicine in Modern France*. Cambridge: Cambridge University Press, 2022.

Campinchi, Hélène. "Le Statut de l'enfance délinquante et la loi du 27 juillet 1942." In *Études de science criminelle et de droit pénal comparé*, edited by Donnedieu de Vabres Hugueney, 161–214. Paris: Recueil Sirey, 1945.

Carlier, Christian. *La Prison aux champs: Les colonies d'enfants délinquants du nord de la France au XIXe siècle*. Paris: L'atelier, 1994.

Caron, Jean-Claude. *À l'école de la violence: Chatiments et sévices dans l'institution scolaire au XIXe siècle*. Paris: Aubier, 1999.

Carrau, Ludovic. *De l'éducation: Précis de morale pratique*. Paris: A. Picard & Kaan, 1888.

Casabianca, Pierre de. "Rapport sur la première question." In *Actes du Congrès pénitentiaire international de Washington 1910*, vol. 4, edited by Louis Guillaume and Eugène Borel, 41–88. Groningen: Bureau de la Commission pénitentiaire internationale, 1912.

Cerullo, John J. *Minotaur: French Military Justice and the Aernoult-Rousset Affair*. DeKalb: Northern Illinois University Press, 2011.

Chappuis, Loraine, et al. *Faire parler les corps: François-Emmanuel Fodéré à la genèse de la médecine légale moderne*. Rennes: Presses universitaires de Rennes, 2021.

Chassat, Sophie. "Le Cercle carré du carcéral: Mettray par Foucault." In *Éduquer et punir: La colonie agricole et pénitentiaire de Mettray (1839–1937)*, edited by Luc Forlivesi, Georges-François Pottier, and Sophie Chassat, 211–21. Rennes: Presses universitaires de Rennes, 2005.

Chassot, Maurice. *Les Conséquences pénales et civiles de l'infraction commise par un mineur à la suite de la loi du 27 juillet 1942 sur l'enfance délinquante.* Law thesis. Dijon: Imprimerie de Darantière, 1943.

Chaumeil, Jean. *Manuel de pedagogie psychologique*, 2nd ed. Paris: E. Belin, 1886.

Chauvaud, Frédéric. "Le Scandale de Mettray (1909): Le trait enténébré et la campagne de presse." In *Éduquer et punir: La colonie agricole et pénitentiaire de Mettray (1839–1937)*, edited by Luc Forlivesi, Georges-François Pottier, and Sophie Chassat, 175–93. Rennes: Presses universitaires de Rennes, 2005.

– *Les Experts du crime: La médecine légale en France au XIXe siècle.* Paris: Aubier, 2000.

Chauveau, Adolphe. *Code pénal progressif: Commentaire sur la loi modificative du Code pénal.* Paris: L'éditeur, 1832.

Chauveau, Adolphe, and Faustin Hélie. *Théorie du Code pénal*, vol. 1. Bruxelles: A. Wahlen, 1837.

– *Théorie du Code pénal*, vol. 3. Bruxelles: A. Wahlen, 1840.

Chevalier, Louis. *Classes laborieuses et classes dangereuses à Paris pendant la première moitié du XIX siècle.* Paris: Plon, 1958.

Chudacoff, Howard F. *How Old Are You? Age Consciousness in American Culture.* Princeton: Princeton University Press, 1989.

Cipriani, Don. *Children's Rights and the Minimum Age of Criminal Responsibility: A Global Perspective.* Abingdon: Routledge, 2016.

Claretie, Georges. *Drames et comédies judiciaires, deuxième année, 1910.* Paris: Berger-Levrault, 1911.

Clayton, Anthony. *France, Soldiers, and Africa.* London: Brassey's Defence Publishers, 1988.

Coffignon, Ali. *L'Enfant à Paris.* Paris: Ernest Kolb, 1889.

Compayré, Gabriel. "Facultés de l'âme." In *Dictionnaire de pédagogie et d'instruction primaire*, part 1, vol. 1, edited by Ferdinand Buisson, 983–6. Paris: Hachette, 1887.

– "La Pédagogie de l'adolescence." *Revue philosophique de la France et de l'étranger* 61 (June 1906): 569–98.

– "La Psychologie de l'adolescence." *Revue philosophique de la France et de l'étranger* 61 (April 1906): 345–77.

Congrès international d'anthropologie criminelle. *Comptes-rendus du VIe Congrès international d'anthropologie criminelle, Turin 1906.* Turin: Bocca, 1908.

Congrès pénal et pénitentiaire international. *Actes du Congrès pénitentiaire international de Bruxelles 1900*, vol. 3. Bruxelles: Bureau de la Commission pénitentiaire internationale, 1901.

– *Actes du Congrès pénitentiaire international de Bruxelles 1900*, vol. 5. Bruxelles: Bureau de la Commission pénitentiaire internationale, 1901.

– *Ve Congrès pénitentiaire international de Paris 1895*, vol. 1. Melun: Imprimerie administrative, 1897.

– *Ve Congrès pénitentiaire international de Paris 1895*, vol. 2. Melun: Imprimerie administrative, 1897.

– *Ve Congrès pénitentiaire international de Paris 1895*, vol. 6. Melun: Imprimerie administrative, 1896.

Congrès pénitentiaire. *Débats du congrès pénitentiaire international de Bruxelles.* Bruxelles: Deltombe, 1847.

Conti, Ugo. "Rapport sur la troisième question de la quatrième section." In Congrès pénal et pénitentiaire international, *Ve Congrès pénitentiaire international de Paris 1895*, vol. 6, 363–84. Melun: Imprimerie administrative, 1896.

Coppée, François. *Le Coupable.* Paris: Alphonse Lemerre, 1896.

Corbin, Alain. *Les Filles de noces: Misère sexuelle et prostitution, 19e et 20e siècles.* Paris: Aubier Montaigne, 1978.

Corne, Anatole. *Étude sur l'éducation correctionnelle des jeunes détenus du département de la Seine.* Paris: Auguste Durand, 1864.

Corne, Hyacinthe. *Rapport et projet de loi sur le patronage des jeunes détenus présentés au nom de la Commission de l'assistance publique.* Paris: Imprimerie nationale, 1849.

Costa-Lascoux, Jacqueline. *La Délinquance des jeunes en France*, vol. 3, la bibliographie. Paris: CUJAS, 1975.

– *La Délinquance des jeunes en France*, vol. 4, textes législatifs et règlementaires. Paris: CUJAS, 1978.

Cournet, Jean-Gabriel. *Les Voleurs, les vagabonds, et l'armée.* Toulouse: Marqués, 1905.

Courtin, Christine. "France: La responsabilité pénale des mineurs dans l'ordre interne et international." *Revue internationale de droit pénal* 75, no. 1–2 (2004): 337–53.

Cousin, Victor. *Du vrai, du beau et du bien*, 12th ed. Paris: Didier, 1867.

Cousinet, Roger. "Intelligence." In *Nouveau dictionnaire de pédagogie et d'instruction*, edited by Ferdinand Buisson. Paris: Hachette, 1911, available at www.inrp.fr/edition-electronique/lodel/dictionnaire-ferdinand-buisson/document.php?id=2937, accessed 10 May 2024.

Covey, Herbert C. *The Smallest Victims: A History of Child Maltreatment and Child Protection in America.* New York: Bloomsbury Publishing, 2018.

Crubellier, Maurice. *L'Enfance et la jeunesse dans la société française, 1800–1950.* Paris: A. Colin, 1979.

Cruppi, Jean. *La Cour d'assises.* Paris: C. Lévy, 1898.

Curtis, Sarah. *Educating the Faithful: Religion, Schooling, and Society in Nineteenth-Century France.* Carbondale: Northern Illinois University Press, 2000.

Darnton, Robert. *The Great Cat Massacre and Other Episodes in French Cultural History.* New York: Basic Books, 1984.

Davis, Natalie Zemon. "The Reasons of Misrule: Youth Groups and Charivaris in Sixteenth-Century France." *Past and Present* 50, no. 1 (1971): 41–75.

Debreyne, Pierre Jean Corneille. *Colonie agricole monastique, fondée à la Grande-Trappe, près Mortagne (Orne) pour les jeunes détenus.* Paris: Poussielgue-Rusand, 1856.

Dekker, Jeroen. *The Will to Change the Child: Re-Education Homes for Children at Risk in Nineteenth-Century Western Europe.* Bern: Peter Lang, 2001.

Déloye, Yves. *École et citoyenneté: L'individualisme républicain de Jules Ferry à Vichy – controverses.* Paris: Presses de Sciences Po, 1994.

Delzons, Louis. "L'Enfant et la famille." *Revue des deux mondes* 41 (1 Sept. 1907): 166–97.

Demangeot, Jules. *De quelques innovations récentes au sujet de enfants délinquants: Étude de droit comparé – tribunaux spéciaux, mise en liberté surveillée.* Doctoral thesis. Paris: Imprimerie Bonvalot-Jouve, 1907.

Demetz, Frédéric-Auguste. *Fondation d'une colonie agricole pour jeunes détenus à Mettray.* Paris: Duprat, 1839.

Deschanel, Paul. "Séance solennelle d'ouverture." In *Actes du premier Congrès international des tribunaux pour enfants, Paris 1911*, edited by Marcel Kleine, 45–9. Paris: A. Davy, 1912.

Desportes, Fernand. "Rapport sur le Congrès pénitentiaire tenu à Cincinnati les 12 et 18 octobre 1870, lu à la séance du 20 février 1874." In Assemblée nationale, *Enquête parlementaire sur le régime des établissements pénitentiaires*, vol. 3, 349–497. Paris: Imprimerie nationale, 1875.

Dessertine, Dominique. "Aux origines de l'assistance éducative: Les tribunaux pour enfants et la liberté surveillée (1912–1941)." In *Protéger l'enfant: Raison juridique et pratiques socio-judiciaires (XIXe et XXe siècles)*, edited by Michel Chauvière, Pierre Lenoël, and Éric Pierre, 137–47. Rennes: Presses universitaires de Rennes, 1996.

– "Les Tribunaux face aux violences sur les enfants sous la Troisième République." *Revue d'histoire de l'enfance 'irrégulière'* 2 (1999): 129–41.

Deyon, Pierre. *Le Temps des prisons: Essai sur l'histoire de la délinquance et les origines du système pénitentiaire*. Lille: Université de Lille III, 1977.

Donnedieu de Vabres, Henri. *Traité de droit criminel et de législation pénale comparée*. Paris: Librairie du recueil Sirey, 1947.

Donovan, James M. *Juries and the Transformation of Criminal Justice in France in the Nineteenth and Twentieth Centuries*. Chapel Hill: The University of North Carolina Press, 2010.

– "Justice Unblind: The Juries and the Criminal Classes in France, 1825–1914." *Journal of Social History* 15, no. 1 (1981): 89–107.

– "Magistrates and Juries in France, 1791–1952." *French Historical Studies* 22, no. 3 (1999): 379–420.

Donzelot, Jacques. *The Policing of Families*. Translated by Robert Hurley. New York: Pantheon Books, 1979.

Downs, Laura Lee. *Childhood in the Promised Land: Working-Class Movements and the Colonies de Vacances in France, 1880–1960*. Durham: Duke University Press, 2002.

Dreyfus, Ferdinand. "L'Enfance devant la justice repressive." *Revue politique et parlementaire* 11, no. 32 (1897): 347–60.

– *Misères sociales et études historiques*. Paris: P. Ollendorff, 1901.

Drill, Dmitri. "Rapport sur la cinquième question de la première section." In *Actes du Congrès pénitentiaire international de Saint-Pétersbourg 1890*, vol. 1, edited by Louis Guillaume, 658–63. Saint Petersburg: Bureau de la Commission d'organisation du Congrès, 1892.

Drillon, Paul. *La Jeunesse criminelle*. Paris: Bloud, 1905.

Driver, Felix. "Discipline without Frontiers? Representations of the Mettray Reformatory Colony in Britain." *Journal of Historical Sociology* 3, no. 3 (1990): 273–93.

Du Camp, Maxime. "La Place de la Roquette: Le quartier des condamnés à mort et l'échafaud." *Revue des deux mondes* 85 (Jan. 1870): 182–213.

Ducpétiaux, Édouard. *De la condition physique et morale des jeunes ouvriers et des moyens de l'améliorer*, vol. 2. Bruxelles: Méline, Cans & Cie, 1843.

Dupont-Bouchat, Marie-Sylvie, Éric Pierre, et al. *Enfance et justice au dix-neuvième siècle: Essais d'histoire comparée de la protection de l'enfance, 1820–1914 – France, Belgique, Pays-Bas, Canada*. Paris: Presses universitaires de France, 2001.

Duprat, Catherine. "Punir et guérir: En 1819, la prison des philanthropes." *Annales historiques de la Révolution française* 228 (1977): 204–46.

– *Le Temps des philanthropes: La philanthropie parisienne des Lumières à la Monarchie de Juillet*, vol. 1. Paris: Éditions du CTHS, 1993.

Durand, Damien. "La loi Perben et la majorité pénale à 10 ans: Quelles conséquences pour les jeunes et les éducateurs?" *Éduquer* 15 (2007), https://doi.org/10.4000/rechercheseducations.250, accessed 10 May 2024.

Durkheim, Émile. "Compte rendu du livre de C.V. Starcke, '*La Famille dans les différentes sociétés*,' Paris, Giard et Brière, 1899." *L'Année sociologique* 3 (1898–99): 365–70.

– "Éducation." In *Nouveau dictionnaire de pédagogie et d'instruction*, edited by Ferdinand Buisson. Paris: Hachette, 1911, available at www.inrp.fr/edition-electronique/lodel/dictionnaire-ferdinand-buisson/document.php?id=2630, accessed 10 May 2024.

– *L'Éducation morale*. Paris: Presses universitaires de France, 1974.

– "La Famille conjugale." *Revue philosophique* 90 (1921): 2–14.

– "Pédagogie et sociologie." *Revue de métaphysique et de morale* 11, no. 1 (Jan. 1903): 37–54.

Duvergier, J.B. *Collection complète des lois, décrets, ordonnances, réglemens et avis du Conseil d'État*, vol 21. Paris: A. Guyot et Scribe, 1827.

Edelstein, Melvin. "Le Militaire-citoyen, ou le droit de vote des militaires pendant la Révolution française." *Annales historiques de la Révolution française* 310 (1997): 585–600.

Ellis, Jack D. *The Physician-Legislators of France: Medicine and Politics in the Early Third Republic, 1870–1914*. Cambridge and New York: Cambridge University Press, 1990.

Emsley, Clive. *Crime, Police, and Penal Policy: European Experiences 1750–1940*. Oxford: Oxford University Press, 2007.

Esmein, Adhémar. *Histoire de la procédure criminelle en France et spécialement de la procédure inquisitoire, depuis le XIIe siècle jusqu'à nos jours*. Paris: L. Larose et Forcel, 1882.

Farge, Arlette, and Michel Foucault. *Le Désordre des familles. Lettres de cachet des Archives de la Bastille au XVIIIe siècle*. Paris: Gallimard, 2014.

Faron, Olivier. "Father-Child Relations in France: Changes in Paternal Authority in the Nineteenth and Twentieth Centuries." *History of the Family* 6, no. 3 (2001): 363–75.

Faure, Alain. "Enfance ouvrière, enfance coupable: Essai sur la délinquance des enfants à Paris au début du XXe siècle." *Les Révoltes logiques* 13 (1980–81): 13–35.

Faure, Jean-Baptiste. *Souvenirs de la Roquette: Au pied de l'échafaud*. Paris: Dreyfous & Dalsace, 1896.

Favard de Langlade, Guillaume-Jean. *Nouvelle législation civile, commerciale et administrative*, vol. 4. Paris: Firmin Didot, 1824.

Felter-Kerley, Lela. "The Art of Posing Nude: Models, Moralists, and the 1893 Bal des Quat'z-Arts." *French Historical Studies* 33, no. 1 (2010): 69–97.

Ferry, Jules. "Lettre du 17 novembre 1883." In *Documents d'histoire contemporaine*, vol. 1, edited by Jean-Paul Jourdan, 145–7. Pessac: Presses universitaires de Bordeaux, 2002.

Field, Corinne T., and Nicholas L. Syrett. "Introduction." *American Historical Review* 125, no. 2 (2020): 371–84.

Fishman, Sarah. *The Battle for Children: World War II, Youth Crime and Juvenile Justice in Twentieth-Century France*. Cambridge: Harvard University Press, 2002.

Foinitsky, Ivan. "Rapport présenté par la Société juridique de Saint-Pétersbourg." In *Actes du Congrès pénitentiaire international de Saint-Pétersbourg 1890*, vol. 2, edited by Louis Guillaume, 637–53. Saint Petersburg: Bureau de la Commission d'organisation du Congrès, 1890.

Fonsegrive, George. *Essai sur le libre arbitre: Sa théorie et son histoire*. Paris: F. Alcan, 1887.

Forlivesi, Luc, Georges-François Pottier, and Sophie Chassat, eds. *Éduquer et punir: La colonie agricole et pénitentiaire de Mettray (1839–1937)*. Rennes: Presses universitaires de Rennes, 2007.

Forrest, Alan. "La Patrie en Danger: The French Revolution and the First Levée en Masse." *The People in Arms: Military Myth and National Mobilization since the French Revolution*, edited by Daniel Moran and Arthur Waldron, 8–32. Cambridge: Cambridge University Press, 2003.

– *Conscripts and Deserters: The Army and French Society during the Revolution and Empire*. New York: Oxford University Press, 1989.

Foucault, Michel. "La Vérité et les formes juridiques." In Michel Foucault, *Dits et Écrits*, vol. 1, 1406–514. Paris: Gallimard, 2001.

– *Les Anormaux: Cours au Collège de France (1974–1975)*. Paris: Seuil/Gallimard: 1999.

– "26 March 1980." In *On the Government of the Living: Lectures at the Collège de France 1979–1980*, edited by Michel Senellart, translated by Graham Burchell, 288–320. Houndmills: Palgrave Macmillan, 2014.

– *Surveiller et punir: Naissance de la prison*. Paris: Gallimard, 1975.

Fouillée, Alfred. *La France au point de vue moral*, 5th ed. Paris: F. Alcan, 1911.

– "Les Jeunes criminels, l'école et la presse." *Revue des deux mondes* 67 (Jan. 1897): 417–49.

Freeman, Michael, ed. *Children's Rights: New Issues, New Themes, New Perspectives*. Leiden: Brill, 2018.

Fuchs, Rachel G. *Abandoned Children: Foundlings and Child Welfare in Nineteenth-Century France.* Albany: State University of New York Press, 1984.

– "Juvenile Delinquency in Nineteenth-Century France." In *History of Juvenile Delinquency: A Collection of Essays on Crime Committed by Young Offenders, in History and in Selected Countries*, edited by Albert G. Hess and Priscilla Ferguson Clement, 265–87. Aalen: Scientia, 1990.

– *Poor and Pregnant in Paris: Strategies for Survival in the Nineteenth Century.* New Brunswick: Rutgers University Press, 1992.

Gaillac, Henri. *Les Maisons de correction, 1830–1945.* Paris: Éditions CUJAS, 1991.

Gaillard, J. "Discipline scolaire." In *Dictionnaire de pédagogie et d'instruction primaire*, Part 1, vol. 1, edited by Ferdinand Buisson, 716–21. Paris: Hachette, 1887.

Gambetta, Léon. *Discours de M. Gambetta prononcé à Bordeaux le 26 juin 1871.* Paris: Lachaud, 1871.

Garat, Dominique. "Assemblée nationale: Séance du lundi 6 juin 1791." In *Archives parlementaires de 1787 à 1860*, vol. 27, edited by M.J. Lavidal and M.E. Laurent, 6. Paris: Paul Dupont, 1887.

Gardet, Mathias, and Alain Vilbrod. *L'Éducation spécialisée en Bretagne, 1944–1984: Les coordinations bretonnes pour l'enfance et l'adolescence inadaptées.* Rennes: Presses universitaires de Rennes, 2008.

Garland, David. *Punishment and Welfare: A History of Penal Strategies.* Aldershot: Gower, 1985.

Garraud, René. *Précis de droit criminel comprenant l'explication élémentaire de la partie générale du Code pénal, du Code d'instruction criminelle en entier et des lois qui ont modifié ces deux codes.* Paris: L. Larose & Forcel, 1885.

– "Rapport sur la première question de la quatrième section." In *Actes du Congrès pénitentiaire international de Bruxelles 1900*, vol. 5, 5–12. Bruxelles: Bureau de la Commission pénitentiaire internationale, 1901.

Gaudemet, Yves. *Les Juristes et la vie politique de la Troisième République.* Paris: Presses universitaires de France, 1970.

Gaufrès, Mathieu-Jules. "Mère." In *Nouveau dictionnaire de pédagogie et d'instruction*, edited by Ferdinand Buisson. Paris: Hachette, 1911, available at www.inrp.fr/edition-electronique/lodel/dictionnaire-ferdinand-buisson/document.php?id=3168, accessed 10 May 2024.

Gervais, Fernand. "De la liberté surveillée: Rôle du tribunal pour enfants, après la sentence." In *Actes du premier Congrès international des tribunaux pour enfants, Paris 1911*, edited by Marcel Kleine, 547–60. Paris: A. Davy, 1912.

Gibson, Ralph. "Why Republicans and Catholics Couldn't Stand Each Other in the Nineteenth Century." In *Religion, Society and Politics in France since 1789*, edited by Frank Tallett and Nicholas Atkin, 107–20. London: Hambledon Press, 1991.

Gillis, A.R. "Institutional Dynamics and Dangerous Classes: Reading, Writing and Arrest in Nineteenth-Century France." *Social Forces* 82, no. 4 (2004): 1303–32.

Gillis, John R. *Youth and History: Tradition and Change in European Age Relations, 1770–Present*. New York: Academic Press, 1974.

Girardet, Raoul. *La Société militaire de 1815 à nos jours*. Paris: Perrin, 1998.

Giraud, Auguste-Ambroise. *Colonie de Mettray: Devoirs du colon*. N.p.: n.p., 1843.

Giuliani, Albert. *L'Adolescence criminelle: Contribution à l'étude des causes de la criminalité toujours croissante de l'adolescence et des remèdes à y apporter*. Villefranche: Imprimerie du Réveil du Beaujolais et du Sud-Est, 1908.

Goffman, Erving. *Asylums: Essays on the Social Situation of Mental Patients and Other Inmates*. Harmondsworth: Penguin, 1968.

Goldstein, Jan E. *Console and Classify: The French Psychiatric Profession in the Nineteenth Century*. Chicago: University of Chicago Press, 2001.

– *The Post-Revolutionary Self: Politics and Psyche in France, 1750–1850*. Cambridge, MA: Harvard University Press, 2005.

Gossard, Julia M. *Young Subjects: Children, State-Building and Social Reform in the Eighteenth-Century French World*. Montreal: McGill-Queen's University Press, 2021.

Goya, Michel. *Flesh and Steel during the Great War: The Transformation of the French Army and the Invention of Modern Warfare*. Translated by Andrew Uffindell. Barnsley: Pen & Sword Military, 2018.

Grant, Christine. "Model Colonies: A Transnational Study of Penitentiary Agricultural Colonies for Young Detainees in France, Russia, and the Soviet Union, 1839–1937." PhD diss., Carnegie Mellon University, 2019.

Grassi, Philippe. *Discours prononcé à l'audience solennelle de rentrée de la Cour d'appel d'Aix: Des mineurs, au point de vue pénal*. Aix: Impr. de Vve Remondet-Aubin, 1882.

Grimanelli, Périclès. "L'Enfance coupable: Conférence publique faite le 5 septembre 1905." In *Actes du Congrès pénitentiaire international de Budapest 1905*, vol. 1, edited by Jules Rickl de Bellye and Louis Guillaume, 461–85. Budapest: Bureau de la Commission pénitentiaire internationale, 1907.

– "Rapport sur la première question de la quatrième section." In *Actes du Congrès pénitentiaire international de Washington 1910*, vol. 4, edited by Louis Guillaume and Eugène Borel, 147–75. Groningen: Bureau de la Commission pénitentiaire internationale, 1912.

Grosmolard, Jean. "La Criminalité juvenile (suite et fin)." *Archives de l'anthropologie criminelle* 18 (1903): 257–75.

– "La Lutte contre la criminalité juvenile au XIXe siècle." *Archives de l'anthropologie criminelle* 22 (1907): 94–119.

– "La lutte contre la criminalité juvénile au XIXe siècle (fin)." *Archives de l'anthropologie criminelle* 22 (1907): 145–67.

Gueissaz, Mireille. "Image sublime, image prosaïque de la jeune fille dans l'imagerie de la justice." *Ancres, Revue trimestrielle de l'Éducation surveillée* 2 (1986): 121–39.

Guignard, Laurence. *Juger la folie: La folie criminelle devant les Assises au XIXe siècle*. Paris: Presses universitaires de France, 2010.

Guillaume, Louis, ed. *Actes du Congrès pénitentiaire international de Saint-Pétersbourg 1890*, vols 1 & 2. Saint Petersburg: Bureau de la Commission d'organisation du Congrès, 1892.

– *Actes du Congrès pénitentiaire international de Stockholm 1878*, vol. 1. Stockholm: Bureau de la Commission pénitentiaire internationale, 1879.

Guillaume, Louis, and Eugène Borel, eds. *Actes du Congrès pénitentiaire international de Washington Octobre 1910*, vols 3–4. Groningen: Bureau de la Commission pénitentiaire internationale, 1912.

Guillot, Adolphe. "L'Enfance." In *Les Institutions pénitentiaires de la France en 1895*, 301–77. Paris: La Société générale des prisons, 1895.

– "L'Enfant vagabond et l'école de préservation." *La Nouvelle revue* 82 (1 June 1893): 449–68.

– *Observations pratiques au sujet des enfants traduits en justice*. Paris: Alcan-Lévy, 1890.

– *Paris qui souffre: La basse geôle du Grand-Châtelet et les morgues modernes*. Paris: Rouquette, 1888.

Guimas, Prudent. *Colonie agricole de Mettray: Souvenirs d'un fonctionnaire*. Tours: Rouillé-Ladevèze, 1885.

Guyau, Jean-Marie. *Éducation et hérédité*. Paris: Félix Alcan, 1889.

Haine, W. Scott. "The Development of Leisure and the Transformation of Working-Class Adolescence, Paris 1830–1940." *Journal of Family History* 17, no. 4 (1992): 451–76.

Hammarberg, Thomas. "The UN Convention on the Rights of the Child – And How to Make It Work." *Human Rights Quarterly* 12, no. 1 (1990): 97–105.

Harris, Ruth. *Murders and Madness: Medicine, Law and Society in the Fin de Siècle*. Oxford: Clarendon Press, 1989.

Harsin, Jill. *Policing Prostitution in Nineteenth-Century Paris.* Princeton: Princeton University Press, 1985.

Hatzfeld, Adolphe. *Du discernement chez les enfants coupables.* Melun: Imprimerie administrative, 1897.

Haussonville, Gabriel Paul Othenin d'. *L'Enfance à Paris.* Paris: Calmann Lévy, 1879.

– *Les Établissements pénitentiaires en France et aux colonies.* Paris: Michel Lévy, 1875.

– "Rapport sur le régime des établissements pénitentiaires." In Assemblée nationale, *Enquête parlementaire sur le régime des établissements pénitentiaires*, vol. 6, 7–235. Paris: Imprimerie nationale, 1874.

Hayward, J.E.S. "Solidarity: The Social History of an Idea in Nineteenth-Century France." *International Review of Social History* 4, no. 2 (1959): 261–84.

– "The Official Social Philosophy of the French Third Republic: Léon Bourgeois and Solidarism." *International Review of Social History* 6, no. 1 (1961): 19–48.

Hendrick, Harry D. *Child Welfare: England 1872–1989.* Abingdon: Routledge, 1994.

– "The Child as a Social Actor in Historical Sources: Problems of Identification and Interpretation." In *Research with Children: Perspectives and Practices*, edited by Pia Christensen and Allison James, 36–62. London: Falmer Press, 2000.

– *Images of Youth: Age, Class, and the Male Youth Problem, 1880–1920.* Oxford: Clarendon Press, 1990.

Herbette, Louis. *Œuvre pénitentiaire.* Melun: Imprimerie administrative, 1891.

Heuyer, Georges. *Enfants anormaux et délinquants juvéniles.* Paris: Steinheil, 1914.

Heywood, Colin. "The Catholic Church and the Formation of the Industrial Labour Force in Nineteenth-Century France: An Interpretative Essay." *European History Quarterly* 19 (1989): 509–33.

– "Centuries of Childhood: An Anniversary and an Epitaph?" *Journal of the History of Childhood and Youth* 3, no. 3 (2010): 341–65.

– *Childhood in Nineteenth-Century France: Work, Health, and Education among the "Classes Populaires."* Cambridge: Cambridge University Press, 1988.

– *Growing up in France: From the Ancien Régime to the Third Republic.* Cambridge: Cambridge University Press, 2007.

– *A History of Childhood: Children and Childhood in the West from Medieval to Modern Times.* Cambridge: Polity Press, 2001.

– "The Market for Child Labour in Nineteenth-Century France." *History* 66, no. 216 (1981): 34–49.

Hildreth, Martha L. *Doctors, Bureaucrats, and Public Health in France, 1888–1902.* New York: Garland, 1987.

Horne, Janet R. *A Social Laboratory for Modern France: The Musée Social and the Rise of the Welfare State*. Durham: Duke University Press, 2002.

Hugo, Victor. "Le Crapaud." In *La Légende des siècles*, vol. 2, 175–81. Paris: Hetzel, 1859.

Hunt, Lynn. *The Family Romance of the French Revolution*. Berkeley: University of California Press, 1992.

Ignatieff, Michael. *A Just Measure of Pain: The Penitentiary in the Industrial Revolution, 1750–1850*. London: Macmillan, 1978.

Jablonka, Ivan. "Un discours philanthropique dans la France du XIXe siècle: La rééducation des jeunes délinquants dans les colonies agricoles pénitentiaires." *Revue d'histoire moderne et contemporaine* 47, no. 1 (2000): 131–47.

Jacquin, Jean-Baptiste. "Les Députés votent la création d'un code de la justice pénale des mineurs." *Le Monde*, 12 December 2020, www.lemonde.fr/societe/article/2020/12/12/les-deputes-votent-la-creation-d-un-code-de-la-justice-penale-des-mineurs_6063116_3224.html, accessed 10 May 2024.

Jolly, Jules. *Des moyens de préservation à employer vis-à-vis des enfants rendus à leur famille après ordonnance de non-lieu ou acquittement*. Paris: Aux bureaux du journal "La Loi," 1901.

Joly, Henri. *Le Combat contre le crime*. Paris: L. Cerf, 1892.

– "L'Éducation correctionnelle des jeunes filles en France et à l'étranger." *Le Correspondant* 169 (10 October 1892): 129–49.

– "L'Éducation correctionnelle des jeunes filles en France et à l'étranger." *Le Correspondant* 169 (25 October 1892): 343–63.

– "L'Éducation correctionnelle des jeunes filles en France et à l'étranger." *Le Correspondant* 169 (10 November 1892): 532–63.

– *L'Enfance coupable: Économie sociale*. Paris: V. Lecoffre, 1904.

– *La France criminelle*. Paris: L. Cerf, 1889.

– "Jeunes criminels parisiens." *Archives de l'anthropologie criminelle* 5 (1890): 117–74 and 393–406.

– "Les Lectures dans les prisons de la Seine." *Archives de l'anthropologie criminelle* 3 (1888): 305–17.

– "Le Problème criminel au moment présent." *Revue des deux mondes* (Dec. 1907): 674–708.

– "Rapport sur la première question de la quatrième section." In Congrès pénal et pénitentiaire international, *Ve Congrès pénitentiaire international de Paris 1895*, vol. 6, 27–32. Melun: Imprimerie administrative, 1896.

– "René Bérenger." *Revue des deux mondes* 30 (Nov. 1915): 43–74.

Julhiet, Édouard. "Les Tribunaux pour enfants aux États-Unis." In *Les Tribunaux spéciaux pour enfants*, edited by Henri Rollet et al., 1–71. Paris: Administration de la revue "L'enfant," 1906.

Jurmand, Jean-Pierre. "Une histoire de milieu ouvert." *Les Cahiers dynamiques* 40, no. 1, (2007): 22–9.

Juste, C. *Statistique pénitentiaire pour l'année 1910: Exposé général de la situation des services et des divers établissements.* Melun: Imprimerie administrative, 1912.

Kalaora, Bernard, and Antoine Savoye. *Les Inventeurs oubliés: Le Play et ses continuateurs aux origines des sciences sociales.* Seyssel: Champ Vallon, 1989.

Kalifa, Dominique. *Biribi: Les bagnes coloniaux de l'armée française.* Paris: Perrin, 2016.

– *L'Encre et le sang: Récits de crimes et société à la Belle Époque.* Paris: Fayard, 1995.

– "Magistrature et 'crise de la répression' à la veille de la grande guerre, 1911–1912." *Vingtième siècle: revue d'histoire* 67 (2000): 43–59.

Kaluszynski, Martine. "De l'apache au sauvageon. L'enfance délinquante: un enjeu républicain." *Informations sociales* 84 (2000): 12–17.

– "Enfance coupable et criminologie. Histoire d'une construction réciproque (1880–1914)." In *Protéger l'enfant: Raison juridique, pratiques socio-judiciaires XIXe–XXe siècles*, edited by Michel Chauvière, Pierre Lenoël, and Éric Pierre, 107–21. Rennes: Presses universitaires de Rennes, 1996.

– "Un paternalisme juridique: Les hommes de la Société générale des prisons (1877–1900)." In *Laboratoires du nouveau siècle: La nébuleuse réformatrice et ses réseaux en France, 1880–1914*, edited by Christian Topalov, 161–85. Paris: EHESS, 2000.

– "La Prison (et sa réforme), un enjeu formateur pour l'État républicain en construction." *Criminocorpus*, Miscellanies, 24 February 2016, https://doi.org/10.4000/criminocorpus.3173, accessed 10 May 2024.

– "Réformer la société: Les hommes de la Société générale des prisons (1877–1900)." *Génèses* 28 (Sept. 1997): 76–94.

– *La République à l'épreuve du crime.* Paris: LGDJ, 2002.

– "Le Retour de l'homme dangereux: Réflexions sur la notion de dangerosité et ses usages." *Champ pénal/Penal field* V (2008), https://doi.org/10.4000/champpenal.6183, accessed 10 May 2024.

King, Margaret L. "Concepts of Childhood: What We Know and Where We Might Go." *Renaissance Quarterly* 60, no. 2 (2007): 371–407.

Kleine, Marcel, ed. *Actes du premier Congrès international des tribunaux pour enfants, Paris 1911.* Paris: A. Davy, 1912.

– "Les Tribunaux pour enfants en France: Une campagne d'action sociale." In *Actes du premier Congrès international des tribunaux pour enfants, Paris 1911*, edited by Marcel Kleine, 153–66. Paris: A. Davy, 1912.

Kloppenberg, James T. *Uncertain Victory: Social Democracy and Progressivism in European and American Thought, 1870–1920*. New York: Oxford University Press, 1986.

Koeppel, Béatrice. "Prophylaxie sociale, sécurité du citoyen ou la loi du 11 avril 1908." *Annales de Vaucresson* 24 (1986): 145–61.

Lacassagne, Alexandre, and Étienne Martin. "Les Données de la statistique criminelle." *Archives de l'anthropologie criminelle* 21 (1906): 836–50.

Lacousse, Magali. "L'Engagement dans l'armée comme 'remède suprême et nécessaire': La Société de protection des engagés volontaires élevés sous la tutelle administrative (1878–1965)." *Revue d'histoire de l'enfance "irrégulière"* 8 (2006): 153–64.

Lambelet, André José. "A Reluctant Reconciliation: Army Officers, Conscription, and Democratic Citizenship in the French Third Republic, 1870–1940." PhD diss., University of California, Berkeley, 2001.

– "Manifestly Inferior? French Reserves, 1871–1914." In *Scraping the Barrel: The Military Use of Sub-Standard Manpower*, edited by Sanders Marble, 54–78. New York: Fordham University Press, 2012.

Lascoumes, Pierre. "Les Mineurs et l'ordre pénal dans les codes de 1791 et 1810." In *Protéger l'enfant: Raison juridique et pratiques socio-judiciaires (XIXème-XXème siècles)*, edited by Michel Chauvière, Pierre Lenoël, and Éric Pierre, 37–44. Rennes: Presses universitaires de Rennes, 1996.

Lascoumes, Pierre, Pierrette Poncela, and Pierre Lenoël. *Au nom de l'ordre: Une histoire politique du code pénal*. Paris: Hachette, 1989.

Lasserre, Emmanuel. *L'Enfant devant la justice repressive*. Bordeaux: Gounouilhou, 1891.

Lassonde, Stephen. "Age, Schooling, and Development." In *The Routledge History of Childhood in the Western World*, edited by Paula S. Fass, 211–28. Abingdon: Routledge, 2013.

– "Age and Authority: Adult-Child Relations during the Twentieth Century in the United States." *Journal of the History of Childhood and Youth* 1, no. 1 (2008): 95–105.

Laurent, Émile. *L'Anthropologie criminelle et les nouvelles théories du crime*. Paris: Société d'éditions scientifiques, 1891.

Lavidal, M.J., and M.E. Laurent, eds. *Archives parlementaires de 1787 à 1860*, vol. 27. Paris: Paul Dupont, 1887.

Lazerges, Christine. "Chronique de politique criminelle." *Revue de science criminelle et de droit pénal comparé* 1, no. 1 (2020): 175–90.

Le Béguec, Gilles. *La République des avocats*. Paris: Armand Colin, 2003.

Le Bon, Gustave. *La Psychologie des foules*. Paris: F. Alcan, 1895.

Le Naour, Jean-Yves. *Misères et tourments de la chair durant la Grande Guerre: Les mœurs sexuelles des Français 1914–1918*. Paris: Aubier, 2002.

Le Play, Frédéric. *L'Organisation de la famille*, 2nd ed. Tours: Alfred Mame, 1875.

– *La Réforme sociale en France déduite de l'observation comparée des peuples européens*. Tours: Alfred Mame, 1878.

Le Poittevin, Gustave. *Dictionnaire-formulaire des parquets et de la police judiciaire*, vol. 1. Paris: Arthur Rousseau, 1884.

Lebaud, Pierre-Charles-Émile. *L'Éducation dans l'armée d'une démocratie*. Paris: Berger-Levrault, 1908.

Leclec'h, Jules. *Les Tribunaux pour enfants et adolescents et la liberté surveillée: D'après la loi du 22 juillet 1912 et le décret du 31 août 1913*. Paris: Guyomard, 1913.

Lefuel, Henri. "Rapport sur la première question de la quatrième section." In Congrès pénal et pénitentiaire international, *Ve Congrès pénitentiaire international de Paris 1895*, vol. 6, 33–8. Melun: Imprimerie administrative, 1896.

Lemaître, Nicole. "Avant la Communion solennelle." In *La Première Communion: Quatre siècles d'histoire*, edited by Alain Cabantous and Jean Delumeau, 15–32. Paris: Desclée de Brouwer, 1987.

Lenoir, Rémi. "La Famille conjugale: une catégorie d'État selon Durkheim." *Revue internationale de philosophie* 280, no. 2 (2017): 141–55.

Leonards, Chris. "Border Crossings: Care and the 'Criminal Child' in Nineteenth-Century European Penal Congresses." In *Becoming Delinquent: British and European Youth, 1650–1850*, edited by Pamela Cox and Heather Shore, 105–21. Aldershot: Ashgate, 2002.

Leonards, Chris, and Nico Randeraad. "Transnational Experts in Social Reform, 1840–1880." *International Review of Social History* 55, no. 2 (2010): 215–39.

Lequin, Yves. "Apprenticeship in Nineteenth-Century France: A Continuing Tradition or a Break with the Past." In *Work in France: Representations, Meaning, Organization and Practice*, edited by Steven Kaplan and Cynthia Koepp, 457–74. Ithaca: Cornell University Press, 1984.

Levade, Maurice. *La Délinquance des jeunes en France, 1825–1968*, vol. 1: *Les graphiques*. Paris: CUJAS, 1972.

– *La Délinquance des jeunes en France, 1825–1968*, vol. 2. Paris: CUJAS, 1972.

Liard, Louis. *Morale et enseignement civique à l'usage des écoles primaires*. Paris: Librairie Léopold Cerf, 1883.

Lombroso, César. *Les Applications de l'anthropologie criminelle*. Paris: Félix Alcan, 1892.

– "Traitement moral du jeune criminel." In *Papers on Moral Education, Communicated to the First International Moral Education Congress, London 1908*, 2nd ed., edited by Gustav Spiller, 216–22. London: David Nutt, 1909.

Loriga, Sabina. "The Military Experience." In *A History of Young People in the West*, vol. 2, edited by Giovanni Levi and Jean-Claude Schmitt, 11–36. Translated by Carol Volk. Cambridge, MA: Belknap, 1997.

Loubat, Guillaume. "La Crise de la répression." *Revue politique et parlementaire*, June 1911, 434–68.

– "La Crise de la répression: Les rémèdes." *Revue politique et parlementaire*, July 1911, 5–27.

Lovett, Laura L. "Age: A Useful Category of Historical Analysis." *Journal of the History of Childhood and Youth* 1, no. 1 (2008): 89–90.

Luaire, René. *Le Rôle d'initiative privée dans la protection de l'enfance délinquante en France et en Belgique*. Lyon: Bosc Frères, 1936.

Lucas, Charles. *Conclusion générale de l'ouvrage sur le système pénitentiaire en Europe et aux États-Unis*. Paris: Timothée Dehay, 1830.

[Lyautey, Hubert]. "Du rôle social de l'officier. " *Revue des deux mondes* 104, no. 2 (1891): 443–59.

Lyon-Caen, Charles. "Notice sur la vie et les travaux de René Bérenger." In *Séances et travaux de l'Académie des sciences morales et politiques*, vol. 84, edited by Charles Lyon-Caen, 25–54. Paris: Félix Alcan, 1923.

Lyons, Martyn. *Readers and Society in Nineteenth-Century France: Workers, Women, Peasants*. London: Palgrave Macmillan, 2001.

Mabille, Gustave. *De la question de discernement relative aux mineurs de seize ans*. Doctoral thesis. Paris: A. Rousseau, 1898.

Maison, K.E. "Daumier Studies – 1: Preparatory Drawings." *Burlington Magazine* 96, no. 610 (1954): 13–17.

– *Honoré Daumier: Catalogue Raisonné of the Paintings, Watercolours and Drawings*, vol. 2. London: Thames & Hudson, 1968.

Mansker, Andrea. *Sex, Honor and Citizenship in Early Third Republic France*. London: Palgrave Macmillan, 2011.

Marabail, Paul. *De l'influence de l'esprit militaire sur l'œuvre d'Alfred de Vigny*. Paris: Librairie Croville-Morlant, 1905.

Marc, Charles. *De la folie, considérée dans ses rapports avec les questions médico-judiciaires*, vol. 1. Paris: Baillière, 1840.

Marchand, Philippe. "Les Petits soldats de demain: Les bataillons scolaires dans le département du Nord, 1882–1892." *Revue du Nord* 67, no. 266 (1985): 769–803.

Martin, Benjamin F. "The Courts, the Magistrature, and Promotions in Third Republic France, 1871–1914." *American Historical Review* 87, no. 4 (1982): 977–1009.

– *Crime and Criminal Justice under the Third Republic: The Shame of Marianne.* Baton Rouge: Louisiana State University Press, 1990.

Mavidal, Jérôme et al., eds. *Archives parlementaires de 1787 à 1860: Recueil complet des débats législatifs et politiques des chambres françaises*, vol. 27. Paris: Paul Dupont, 1887.

Maynes, Mary Jo. "Age as a Category of Historical Analysis: History, Agency, and Narratives of Childhood." *Journal of the History of Childhood and Youth* 1, no. 1 (2008): 114–24.

Maza, Sarah. "The Kids Aren't All Right: Historians and the Problem of Childhood." *American Historical Review* 125, no. 4 (2020): 1261–85.

Mégret, Frédéric. "Henri Donnedieu de Vabres: Penal Liberal, Moderate Internationalist and Nuremberg Judge." In *The Dawn of a Discipline: International Criminal Justice and Its Early Exponents*, edited by Frédéric Mégret and Immi Tallgren, 146–73. Cambridge: Cambridge University Press, 2020.

Melton, Gary B. "Building Humane Communities Respectful of Children: The Significance of the Convention on the Rights of the Child." *American Psychologist* 60, no. 8 (2005): 918–26.

Merlier, Georges. "Les Bataillons scolaires en France 1882–1892." *Bulletin de la Société d'histoire moderne* 15, no. 19 (1977): 19–27.

Messineo, Dominique. *Jeunesse irrégulière: Moralisation, correction et tutelle judiciaire au XIXe siècle.* Rennes: Presses universitaires de Rennes, 2015.

Meyer, Philippe. *L'Enfant et la raison d'État.* Paris: Seuil, 1977.

Mialane, Lucien. *La Criminalité juvénile: Ses causes, ses remèdes.* Doctoral law thesis. Paris: Presses modernes, 1926.

Milliard, Victor. "Circulaire du 31 mai 1898 relative aux mesures à prendre par le magistrat instructeur en vue de la moralisation et du relèvement des mineurs de 16 ans inculpés." *Bulletin officiel du ministère de la justice* 90 (April–June 1898): 35–9.

Mintz, Stephen. "AHA Exchange: Children's History Matters." *American Historical Review* 125, no. 4 (2020): 1286–92.

– "Reflections on Age as Category of Historical Analysis." *Journal of the History of Childhood and Youth* 1, no. 1 (2008): 91–4.

Monahan, Kathryn, Laurence Steinberg, and Alex R. Piquero. "Juvenile Justice

Policy and Practice: A Developmental Perspective." *Crime and Justice* 44 (2015): 577–619.

Morache, Georges. *La Responsabilité: Étude de socio-biologie et de médecine-légale.* Paris: F. Alcan, 1906.

Morisse, Shaïn. "La Fin des 'apaches'? Représentations sociales du crime et de la délinquance en France pendant la Première Guerre mondiale." Master 2 research thesis, Centre d'Histoire du XIXe siècle, University Paris 1-Panthéon Sorbonne, 2017.

– "Régénérer les 'apaches' par la boue, le feu et le sang." *Crime, Histoire & Sociétés / Crime, History & Societies* 27, no. 2 (2024): 75–99.

Myers, John E.B. *Child Protection in America: Past Present and Future.* Oxford: Oxford University Press, 2006.

Nattan, James. *Essais sur la réforme pénitentiaire: La transportation.* Paris: Chaix, 1886.

Neilson, Briony. "The Paradox of Penal Colonization: Debates on Convict Transportation at the International Prison Congresses 1872–1895." *French History and Civilization* 6 (2015): 198–210.

– "Youth, Literacy and Social Emancipation in Third Republic France: The 'Crime de Jully.'" *Crime, Histoire & Sociétés / Crime, History & Societies* 18, no. 1 (2014): 81–100.

Neubauer, John. *The Fin-de-Siècle Culture of Adolescence.* New Haven: Yale University Press, 1992.

Niget, David. "La Jeunesse déviante entre ordre moral et raison expertale: Production du droit et politiques publiques de protection de la jeunesse sous le régime de Vichy." *Droit et société* 79, no. 3 (2011): 573–90.

– *La Naissance du tribunal pour enfants: Une comparaison France-Québec (1912–1945).* Rennes: Presses universitaires de Rennes, 2009.

Nilan, Kathleen [Cat]. "Hapless Innocence and Precocious Perversity in the Courtroom Melodrama: Representations of the Child Criminal in a Paris Legal Journal, 1830–1848." *Journal of Family History* 22, no. 3 (July 1997): 251–85.

– "Incarcerating Children: Prison Reformers, Children's Prisons, and Child Prisoners in July Monarchy France." PhD diss., Yale University, 1992.

Nillus, Renée. "La Minorité pénale dans la législation et la doctrine du XIXe siècle." In *Le Problème de l'enfance délinquante*, edited by Marc Ancel and Henri Donnedieu de Vabres, 95–117. Paris: Sirey, 1947.

Nora, Pierre. "Le 'Dictionnaire de pédagogie' de Ferdinand Buisson: Cathédrale de l'école primaire." In *Les Lieux de mémoire*, vol. 1, edited by Pierre Nora, 327–47. Paris: Gallimard, 1997.

Nord Philip G. *The Republican Moment: Struggles for Democracy in Nineteenth-Century France.* Cambridge, MA: Harvard University Press, 1998.

Norrie, Kenneth McK, *A History of Scottish Child Protection Law.* Edinburgh: Edinburgh University Press, 2020.

Norris, Katharine H. "Mentir à l'âge de l'innocence: Enfance, science et anxiété culturelle dans la France fin-de-siècle." *Sociétés & Représentations* 38, no. 2 (2014): 171–202.

– "Reinventing Childhood in Fin-de-Siècle France: Child Psychology, Universal Education and the Cultural Anxieties of Modernity." PhD diss., University of California, Berkeley, 2000.

Nourrisson, Didier. *Le Buveur du XIXe siècle.* Paris: Albin Michel, 1990.

Nye, Robert A. *Crime, Madness and Politics in Modern France: The Medical Concept of National Decline.* Princeton, NJ: Princeton University Press, 1984.

– *The Origins of Crowd Psychology: Gustave Le Bon and the Crisis of Mass Democracy in the Third Republic.* London: Sage Publications, 1975.

O'Brien, Justin. *The Novel of Adolescence in France: The Study of a Literary Theme.* New York: Columbia University Press, 1937.

O'Brien, Patricia. *The Promise of Punishment: Prisons in Nineteenth-Century France.* Princeton, NJ: Princeton University Press, 1982.

Office central des œuvres de bienfaisance et services sociaux. *Paris charitable et prévoyant.* Paris: E. Plon, Nourrit et Cie, 1897.

Olson-Raymer, Gayle. "The American History of Juvenile Justice." In *History of Juvenile Delinquency*, vol. 2, edited by Albert G. Hess and Priscilla F. Clement, 491–531. Aalen: Scientia Verlag, 1993.

Ortolan, Joseph. *Éléments de droit pénal: Pénalité, juridictions, procedure.* Paris: Plon, 1855.

Otis, Laura. *Organic Memory: History and the Body in the Late Nineteenth and Early Twentieth Centuries.* Lincoln: University of Nebraska Press, 1994.

Ozouf, Mona. *L'Homme régénéré.* Paris: Gallimard, 1989.

Pande, Ishita. *Sex, Law, and the Politics of Age: Child Marriage in India, 1891–1937.* Cambridge: Cambridge University Press, 2020.

Paris, Leslie. "Through the Looking Glass: Age, Stages, and Historical Analysis." *Journal of the History of Childhood and Youth* 1, no. 1 (2008): 106–13.

Pasquier, Étienne-Denis. "Circulaire du 7 octobre 1818 du garde-des-sceaux à MM. les procureurs généraux près les cours royales." In *Collection complète des lois, décrets, ordonnances, réglemens et avis du Conseil d'État* 22, edited by J.B. Duvergier, 17–18. Paris: A. Guyot et Scribe, 1828.

Patin, Maurice. "Cour de cassation chambre criminelle: 13 décembre 1956." In *Recueil Dalloz de doctrine, de jurisprudence et de législation* (1957): 349–50.

Pearson, Geoffrey. *Hooligan: A History of Respectable Fears.* London: Macmillan, 1983.

Pécaut, Élie. "Vie humaine (âges)." In *Dictionnaire de pédagogie et d'instruction primaire*, vol. 2, part 2, edited by Ferdinand Buisson, 2487–91. Paris: Hachette, 1887.

Pécaut, Félix. *L'Éducation publique et la vie nationale*, 3rd ed. Paris: Hachette, 1907.

Perrot, Michelle. "Dans le Paris de la Belle Époque: Les 'apaches,' premières bandes des jeunes." In *Les Ombres de l'histoire: Crime et châtiment au XIXe siècle*, edited by Michelle Perrot, 351–64. Paris: Flammarion, 2001.

– "Les Enfants de la Petite-Roquette." *L'Histoire*, no. 100 (May 1987): 30–8.

– "Sur la notion d'intérêt de l'enfant et son émergence au XIXe siècle." *Actes: Cahier d'action juridique*, no. 37 (1982): 40–3.

– "Sur la segrégation de l'enfance au XIXe siècle." *La Psychiatrie de l'enfant* 25, no. 1 (1982): 179–207.

– "Worker Youth: From the Workshop to the Factory." In *A History of Young People in the West*, vol. 2, edited by Giovanni Levi and Jean-Claude Schmitt, 66–116. Translated by Carol Volk. Cambridge, MA: Belknap, 1997.

Persigny, Victor de. "Circulaire du 5 juillet 1853, contenant diverses instructions sur l'exécution de la loi du 5 août 1850, relative aux jeunes détenus." In *Code des prisons*, vol. 2, edited by Louis-Mathurin Moreau-Christophe, 279–83. Paris: Dupont, 1856.

Picot, Georges. *Théophile Roussel: notice historique.* Paris, Hachette, 1905.

Pierre, Éric. "Débats parlementaires, politiques correctionnelles et vote de la loi de 1850." In *Protéger l'enfant: Raison juridique et pratique socio-judiciaires XIXe–XXe siècle*, edited by Michel Chauvière, Pierre Lenoël, and Éric Pierre, 71–105. Rennes: Presses universitaires de Rennes, 1996.

– "La Loi du 19 avril 1898 et les institutions." *Le Temps de l'histoire* 2 (1999): 113–27.

Pissard, Léon. "Rapport sur la cinquième question de la quatrième section." In Congrès pénal et pénitentiaire international, *Ve Congrès pénitentiaire international de Paris 1895*, vol. 6, 604–14. Melun: Imprimerie administrative, 1896.

Pitt, Alan. "Frédéric LePlay and the Family: Paternalism and Freedom in the French Debates of 1870s." *French History* 12, no. 1 (1998): 67–89.

Platt, Anthony M. *Child Savers: The Invention of Delinquency*, 2nd ed. Chicago: University of Chicago Press, 1977.

Pomfret, David M. "'A Muse for the Masses': Gender, Age, and Nation in France, Fin de Siècle." *American Historical Review* 109, no. 5 (2004): 1439–74.

Porch, Douglas. "The French Army Law of 1832." *Historical Journal* 14, no. 4 (1971): 751–69.

Poumarède, Jacques. "Les Tribulations de l'autorité paternelle de l'ancien droit au Code Napoléon." In *Protéger l'enfant: Raison juridique et pratiques socio-judiciaires (XIXe–XXe siècles)*, edited by Michel Chauvière, Pierre Lenoël, and Éric Pierre, 23–35. Rennes: Presses universitaires de Rennes, 1996.

Prade, Catherine. "Les Colonies pénitentiaires au XIX[E] siècle: De la genèse au déclin." In *Éduquer et punir: La colonie agricole et pénitentiaire de Mettray (1839–1937)*, edited by Luc Forlivesi, Georges-François Pottier, and Sophie Chassat, 27–37. Rennes: Presses universitaires de Rennes, 2005.

Pradel, Jean. "Quelques observations sur le statut pénal du mineur en France depuis la loi du 9 septembre 2002." *Revue internationale de droit comparé* 56 no. 1 (2004): 187–91.

Prestwich, Patricia E. *Drink and the Politics of Social Reform: Antialcoholism in France since 1870*. Palo Alto: Society for the Promotion of Science and Scholarship, 1988.

Proal, Louis. *Le Crime et la peine*. Paris: F. Alcan, 1892.

Prudhomme, Henri. "Rapport sur la quatrième question de la quatrième section." In Congrès pénal et pénitentiaire international, *Ve Congrès pénitentiaire international de Paris 1895*, vol. 6, 454–74. Melun: Imprimerie administrative, 1896.

– "Spécialisation d'une juridiction de mineurs." In *Actes du premier Congrès international des tribunaux pour enfants*, edited by Marcel Kleine, 259–65. Paris: A. Davy, 1912.

Puibaraud, Louis. *Les Maisons d'éducation préventive et correctionnelle: Essai d'un plan de réforme de la loi du 5 août 1850 sur les jeunes détenus*. Paris: Gazette du Palais, 1894.

– "Rapport sur la quatrième question de la quatrième section." In Congrès pénal et pénitentiaire international, *Ve Congrès pénitentiaire international de Paris 1895*, vol. 6, 475–516. Melun: Imprimerie administrative, 1896.

Quincy-Lefebvre, Pascale. "Âge et justice: Rester enfant, devenir adulte dans le débat pénal au XXe siècle." In *Les Âmes mal nées: Jeunesse et délinquance urbaine en France et en Europe, XIXe–XXIe siècles*, edited by Jean-Claude Caron, Annie Stora-Lamarre, and Jean-Jacques Yvorel, 261–78. Besançon: Presses universitaires de Franche-Comté, 2008.

– "Assistance publique et enfants difficiles vers 1900." In *Les Exclus en Europe 1830–1930*, edited by André Gueslin and Dominique Kalifa, 202–14. Paris: L'Atelier, 1999.

– "Droit, régulation et jeunesse: Réforme de la majorité pénale et naissance des 16–18 ans à la Belle Époque." In *Jeunesse oblige: Histoire des jeunes en France, XIXe–XXI siècles*, edited by Ludivine Bantigny and Ivan Jablonka, 95–108. Paris: Presses universitaires de France, 2009.

– "Émotion et opinion dans la justice des mineurs en France durant l'entre-deux-guerres." *Revue d'histoire de l'enfance 'irrégulière'* 17 (2015): 149–67.

– *Familles, institutions et deviances: Une histoire de l'enfance difficile, 1880–fin des années trente*. Paris: Economica, 1997.

– "La Prostitution des mineurs dans le débat républicain à la Belle Époque: L'expertise juridique et l'échec d'une politique." *Histoire@Politique* 14 (May–Aug. 2011): 4–23.

– "À la recherche d'un nouveau paradigme de l'enquête judiciaire: Magistrats et jeunes délinquants – les formes de l'expérience à la Belle Époque." In *L'Enquête judiciaire en Europe au XIXe siècle: Acteurs, Imaginaires, Pratiques*, edited by Jean-Claude Farcy, Dominique Kalifa, and Jean-Noël Luc, 195–208. Paris: CREAPHIS, 2007.

Radzinowicz, Leon. *History of English Criminal Law and Its Administration*, vol. 1. London: Stevens and Sons, 1948.

Ralston, David B. *The Army of the Republic: The Place of the Military in the Political Evolution of France, 1871–1914*. Cambridge, MA; MIT Press, 1967.

Rasmussen, Anne. "Mobilising Minds." In *The Cambridge History of the First World War*, vol. 3, edited by Jay Winter, 390–417. Cambridge: Cambridge University Press, 2014.

Rassat, Michèle-Laure. *Droit pénal général*, 4th ed. Paris: Éditions Ellipses, 2017.

Raux, Chanoine. *Nos jeunes détenus: Étude sur l'enfance coupable avant, pendant et après son séjour au quartier correctionnel*. Lyon: A. Storck, 1890.

Renneville, Marc. *Crime et folie: Deux siècles d'enquêtes médicales et judiciaires*. Paris: Fayard, 2003.

– "La Réception de Lombroso en France, 1880–1900." In *Histoire de la criminologie française*, edited by Laurent Mucchielli, 107–35. Paris: L'Harmattan, 1995.

Renouard, Jean-Marie. *De l'enfant coupable à l'enfant inadapté: Le traitement social de la déviance juvénile*. Paris: Centurion, 1990.

Renouvier, Charles. "L'Éducation et la morale." *Critique philosophique* 1 (June 1872): 273–80.

Resnick, Evelyne. *Femmes et associations, 1830–1880: Vraies démocrates ou dames patronesses?* Paris: Publisud, 1991.

Rey, Alain, ed. *Dictionnaire historique de la langue française*. Paris: Dictionnaires Le Robert, 2004.

Rey, Émile. *Assistance aux enfants des familles indigentes.* Melun: Impr. administrative, 1900.

Richter, Jude C. "Rehabilitating Juvenile Criminals in Russia, 1864–1917." PhD diss., Indiana University, 2008.

Rickl de Bellye, Jules, and Louis Guillaume, eds. *Actes du Congrès pénitentiaire international de Budapest 1905*, vol. 1. Budapest: Bureau de la Commission pénitentiaire internationale, 1907.

Robert, Henri. "La Criminalité juvénile." *Revue de Paris* 6 (1 Nov. 1913): 100–11.

– "La Législation française relative à l'enfance." *Revue des tribunaux pour enfants* 1 (Dec. 1913): 1–10.

Robert, Philippe. *Traité de droit des mineurs; place et rôle dans l'évolution du droit français contemporain.* Paris: CUJAS, 1969.

Roberts, Mary Louise. *Disruptive Acts: The New Woman in Fin-de-Siècle France.* Chicago: University of Chicago Press, 2002.

Robin, Élie. *Des écoles industrielles et de la protection des enfants insoumis ou abandonnés.* Paris: Bonhoure et Cie, 1879.

Rollet, Henri, "Rapport à l'assemblée générale du 18 décembre 1906: De l'application à Paris et dans les départements de la loi du 12 avril 1906, fixant à 18 ans l'âge de la majorité pénale." *Bulletin de l'Union des sociétés de patronage de France* 13, no. 1 (1907): 16–39.

Rollet-Echalier, Catherine. *La Politique à l'égard de la petite enfance sous la IIIe République.* Paris: Presses universitaires de France, 1990.

Rosanvallon, Pierre. *Le Sacre du citoyen.* Paris: Gallimard, 2008.

Rossi, Pellegrino. *Œuvres complètes: Traité de droit pénal*, vol. 2, 3rd ed. Paris: Guillaumin, 1863.

Rousseau, Jean-Jacques. *Émile ou de l'éducation.* Paris: Charpentier, 1848.

Roux, J.-A. "De l'engagement militaire des condamnés correctionnels." *Bulletin de l'Union des societies de patronage de France* 1 (Jan.–March 1898): 88–97.

Roynette, Odile. "Les Apaches à la caserne." In *La Plume et le sabre*, edited by Michel Biard, Annie Crépin, and Bernard Gainot, 353–68. Paris: Publications de la Sorbonne, 2002.

– "L'Armée, une institution républicaine?" In *Une contre-histoire de la IIIe République*, edited by Marion Fontaine, Frédéric Monier, and Christophe Prochasson, 97–109. Paris: La Découverte, 2013.

– *Bon pour le service: L'expérience de la caserne en France à la fin du XIXe siècle.* Paris: Belin, 2000.

Ruggles-Brise, Evelyn. *The English Prison System.* London: Macmillan, 1921.

– "Rapport sur la deuxième question à la deuxième section." In *Actes du Congrès pénitentiaire international de Bruxelles 1900*, vol. 3, 247–73. Bruxelles: Bureau de la Commission pénitentiaire internationale, 1901.

Sachs, Miranda. *An Age to Work: Working-Class Childhood in Third Republic Paris*. New York: Oxford University Press, 2023.

Sanchez, Jean-Lucien. *À Perpétuité: Relégués au bagne de Guyane*. Paris: Vendémiaire, 2013.

– "La Relégation des femmes récidivistes en Guyane française (1887–1907)." *Crime, Histoire & Sociétés / Crime, History & Societies* 17, no. 1 (2013): 77–100.

– "La Relégation des récidivistes: Enjeux politique et pénal." In *Les Récidivistes: Représentations et traitements de la récidive, XIXe–XXIe siècle*, edited by Jean-Pierre Allinne and Mathieu Soula, 155–68. Rennes: Presses universitaires de Rennes, 2011.

Savitt, William. "Villainous Verdicts? Rethinking the Nineteenth-Century French Jury." *Columbia Law Review* 96, no. 4 (1996): 1019–61.

Schafer, Sylvia. *Children in Moral Danger and the Problem of Government in Third Republic France*. Princeton: Princeton University Press, 1997.

– "Law, Labor, and the Spectacle of the Body: Protecting Child Street Performers in 19th-century France." *International Journal of Children's Rights* 4, no. 1 (1996): 1–18.

Schinz, Albert. "La Moralité de l'enfant." *Revue philosophique de la France et de l'étranger* 45 (1898): 259–95.

Schnapper, Bernard. "La Correction paternelle et le mouvement des ideés au dix-neuvième siècle (1789–1935)." *Revue historique* 263, no. 2 (1980): 319–49.

– "De la magistrature domestique à la liberté surveillée: Les pères de famille du code civil à 1889." *Archives aquitaines de recherche sociale [Bordeaux]* (1989): 13–28.

– "Le Sénateur René Bérenger et les progrès de la répression pénale en France (1870–1914)." In *Voies nouvelles en histoire du droit: La justice, la famille, la répression pénale (XVIe–XXe siecles)*, 353–73. Paris: Presses universitaires de France, 1991.

Schwartz, Vanessa R. *Spectacular Realities: Early Mass Culture in Fin-de-Siècle Paris*. Berkeley: University of California Press, 1999.

Sencourt, Robert. *The Life of the Empress Eugenie*. London: Ernest Benn, 1931.

Serman, William. *Les Officiers français dans la nation 1848–1914*. Paris: Aubier Montaigne, 1982.

Sessions, Jennifer E. *By Sword and Plow: France and the Conquest of Algeria*. Ithaca: Cornell University Press, 2011.

Shapiro, Ann-Louise. *Breaking the Codes: Female Criminality in Fin-de-Siècle Paris.* Stanford: Stanford University Press, 1996.

Shore, Heather. *Artful Dodgers: Youth and Crime in Early Nineteenth-Century London.* Rochester: Boydell Press, 1999.

Signorel, Jean. "Le Crime et la défense sociale (suite)." *Revue générale d'administration* (Jan. 1912): 13–33.

Silverman, Lisa. *Tortured Subjects: Pain, Truth, and the Body in Early Modern France.* Chicago: University of Chicago Press, 2001.

Singer, Barnett. "From Patriots to Pacifists: The French Primary School Teachers, 1880–1940." *Journal of Contemporary History* 12, no. 3 (1977): 413–34.

Smith, Timothy B. "The Ideology of Charity, the Image of the English Poor Law and Debates over the Right to Assistance in France, 1830–1905." *Historical Journal* 40, no. 4 (1997): 997–1032.

Spach, J. "Histoire de la Société générale des prisons." In *Actes du Congrès pénitentiaire international de Washington Octobre 1910*, vol. 3, edited by Louis Guillaume and Eugène Borel, 450–63. Groningen: Bureau de la Commission pénitentiaire internationale, 1912.

Spivak, Marcel. "La Préparation militaire en France, cheminement d'un concept 1871–1914." *Revue historique des Armées* 159 (June 1985): 83–95.

Stedman Jones, S.G. "Charles Renouvier and Émile Durkheim: 'Les règles de la méthode sociologique.'" *Sociological Perspectives* 38, no. 1 (1995): 27–40.

Steinberg, Laurence. "The Influence of Neuroscience on US Supreme Court Decisions about Adolescents' Criminal Culpability." *Nature Reviews Neuroscience* 14 (2013): 513–18.

Stock-Morton, Phyllis. *Moral Education for a Secular Society: The Development of Morale Laïque in Nineteenth-Century France.* Albany: State University of New York Press, 1988.

Stora-Lamarre, Annie. *L'Enfer de la IIIe République: Censeurs et pornographes, 1881–1914.* Paris: Imago, 1990.

– "Morale religieuse – morale laïque: Fonder l'homo republicanus 1870–1914." *Tumultes* 1, no. 1 (1992): 143–67.

– *La République des faibles: Les origines intellectuelles du droit républicain.* Paris: A. Colin, 2005.

Surkis, Judith. *Sexing the Citizen: Morality and Masculinity in France, 1870–1920.* Ithaca: Cornell University Press, 2006.

Swain, Shurlee, and Margot Hillel. *Child, Nation, Race and Empire: Child Rescue Discourse, England, Canada and Australia, 1850–1915.* Manchester: Manchester University Press, 2010.

Taïeb, Emmanuel. *Hiding the Guillotine: Public Executions in France, 1870–1939*. Translated by Sarah-Louise Raillard. Ithaca: Cornell University Press, 2020.

Taine, Hippolyte. *Les Origines de la France contemporaine*, vol. 3. Paris: Hachette, 1885.

Talmeyr, Maurice. "Le Roman-feuilleton et l'esprit populaire." *Revue des deux mondes*, Sept. 1903, 203–27.

Tarde, Gabriel. "La Jeunesse criminelle: Lettre à Ferdinand Buisson." *Revue pédagogique* 30 (Jan.–June 1897): 193–215.

Tétard, Françoise, and Claire Dumas. *Filles de Justice: Du Bon Pasteur à l'éducation surveillée, XIXe–XXe siècle*. Paris: Beauchesne-ENPJ, 2009.

Thiercé, Agnès. *Histoire de l'adolescence, 1850–1914*. Paris: Belin, 1999.

Todres, Jonathan, and Shani M. King. "Introduction." In *The Oxford Handbook of Children's Rights Law*, edited by Jonathan Todres and Shani M. King, 1–8. Oxford: Oxford University Press, 2020.

Tomel, Guy, and Henri Rollet. *Les Enfants en prison: Études anecdotiques sur l'enfance criminelle*. Paris: E. Plon, Nourrit et Cie, 1892.

Toth, Stephen A. "The Contard Affair: Private Power, State Control, and Paternal Authority in Fin-de-Siècle France." *Journal of Historical Sociology* 23, no. 2 (2010): 185–215.

– "Desire and the Delinquent: Juvenile Crime and Deviance in Fin-de-Siècle French Criminology." *History of the Human Sciences* 10, no. 4 (1997): 48–54.

– *Mettray: A History of France's Most Venerated Carceral Institution*. Ithaca: Cornell University Press, 2019.

Tourdes, Gabriel. "Considérations médico-légales sur les âges." In *Dictionnaire encyclopédique des sciences médicales*, series 1, vol. 2, edited by Amédée Dechambre et al., 146–85. Paris: G. Masson 1864.

Treas, Judith. "Age in Standards and Standards for Age." In *Standards and Their Stories: How Quantifying, Classifying, and Formalizing Practices Shape Everyday Life*, edited by Martha Lampland and Susan Leigh Star, 65–87. Ithaca: Cornell University Press, 2009.

Triqueti, Henry de. *Exposé des œuvres de la charité protestante en France*. Paris: C. Meyrueis, 1863.

Trochu, Louis-Jules. *L'Armée française en 1867*. Paris: Amyot, 1867.

Turgenev, Ivan. "The Execution of Tropmann, 1870." In *Turgenev's Literary Reminiscences and Autobiographical Fragments*, 244–70. Translated by David Magarshack. New York: Farrar, Straus and Cudahy, 1958.

Valensi, Raoul. *Comité de défense des enfants traduits en justice: De l'âge de la res-*

*ponsabilité pénale chez les mineurs*. Report on the session of 19 February 1894. Marseille: Barlatier et Barthelet, 1894.

Veerman, Philip E. *The Rights of the Child and the Changing Image of Childhood*. Leiden: Brill, 2021.

Verplaetse, Jan. *Localizing the Moral Sense: Neuroscience and the Search for the Cerebral Seat of Morality, 1800–1930*. Dordrecht: Springer, 2009.

Vigneron d'Heucqueville, Charles. *Étude sur la condition des mineurs en droit pénal dans les diverses législations anciennes et modernes*. Doctoral thesis. Paris: E. Duchemin, 1899.

Villeneuve, L.-M. de, ed. *Jurisprudence du XIXe siècle ou table tricennale du recueil général des lois et des arrêts, en matière civile, criminelle, commerciale et de droit*. Paris: Sirey, 1842.

Vingtrinier, Arthus-Barthélemy. *Des enfants dans les prisons et devant la justice*. Rouen: A. Péron, 1855.

Voisin, Félix. "Rapport sur le projet de loi relatif à l'éducation et au patronage des jeunes détenus." In Assemblée nationale, *Enquête parlementaire sur le régime des établissements pénitentiaire*, vol. 8. Paris: Imprimerie nationale, 1875.

Wagniart, Jean-François. *Le Vagabond à la fin du XIXe siècle*. Paris: Belin, 1999.

Wall, John, ed. *Give Children the Vote: On Democratizing Democracy*. London: Zed Books, 2021.

Weber, Eugen. *La Fin des terroirs: La modernisation de la France rurale (1870–1914)*. Paris: Fayard, 1983.

– "Gymnastics and Sport in Fin-de-Siècle France: Opium of the Classes?" *American Historical Review* 76, no. 1 (1971): 70–98.

– *Peasants into Frenchmen: The Modernization of Rural France, 1870–1914*. Stanford: Stanford University Press, 1976.

Weissbach, Lee S. "Child Labor Legislation in Nineteenth-Century France." *Journal of Economic History* 37, no. 1 (1977): 268–71.

– *Child Labor Reform in Nineteenth-Century France: Assuring the Future Harvest*. Baton Rouge: Louisiana State University Press, 1989.

– "Oeuvre Industrielle, Oeuvre Morale: The Sociétés de Patronage of Nineteenth-Century France." *French Historical Studies* 15, no. 1 (1987): 99–120.

Wilson, Adrian. "The Infancy of the History of Childhood: An Appraisal of Philippe Ariès." *History and Theory* 19, no. 2 (1980): 132–53.

Woloch, Isser. "Napoleonic Conscription: State Power and Civil Society." *Past & Present* 111 (1986): 101–29.

Wright, Gordon. *Between the Guillotine and Liberty: Two Centuries of the Crime Problem in France*. New York: Oxford University Press, 1983.

Yaffe, Gideon. *The Age of Culpability: Children and the Nature of Criminal Responsibility*. Oxford: Oxford University Press, 2018.

Yvorel, Élise. *Les Enfants de l'ombre: La vie quotidienne des jeunes détenus au XXe siècle en France métropolitaine*. Rennes: Presses universitaires de Rennes, 2008.

– "L'influence des réformes de l'administration pénitentiaire sur la vie quotidienne des colons. L'exemple de Saint-Hilaire (1930–1960)." *Musée Criminocorpus* (23 Jan. 2009), https://criminocorpus.org/fr/ref/25/17375/, accessed 10 May 2024.

Yvorel, Jean-Jacques. "Comment le droit pénal construit les catégories d'âge." *Journal du droit des jeunes* 322, no. 2 (2013): 30–3.

– "L'Enfermement des mineurs de justice au XIXe siècle, d'après le compte général de la justice criminelle." *Revue d'histoire de l'enfance "irrégulière"* 7 (2005): 77–109.

Zeldin, Theodore. *France, 1848–1945*, vol. 1. Oxford: Clarendon Press, 1973.

– *France, 1848–1945*, vol. 2. Oxford: Oxford University Press, 1977.

Zelizer, Viviana. *Pricing the Priceless Child: The Changing Social Value of Children*. New York: Basic Books, 1985.

# Index